WALKIN' WITH THE GHOST WHISPERERS

WALKIN' WITH THE GHOST WHISPERERS

Lore and Legends of the Appalachian Trail

J. R. "Model-T" Tate

To order additional copies of this book, contact:
Xlibris Corporation
1-888-795-4274
www.Xlibris.com
Orders@Xlibris.com
29094

Also by J.R. "Model-T" Tate

Walkin' on the Happy Side of Misery: A Slice of Life on the Appalachian Trail

Published by Xlibris Corporation, Philadelphia, PA 19113; copyright 2001
(ISBN: Hard cover 1-4010-2042-9; Soft cover 1-4010-2041-0)

Front cover semi-transparences:
Civil War scene: "Mosby, returning from a raid" from *The Memoirs of Colonel John S. Mosby*; Boston: Little Brown, and Company; 1917.

Indian scene: "Chief Metacom" aka "King Phillip," son of Massasoit" by T. Sinclair; taken from *Events in Indian History*; 1842

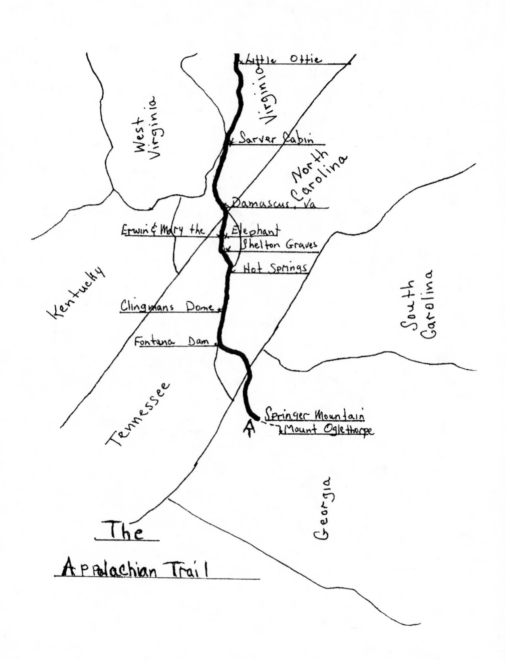

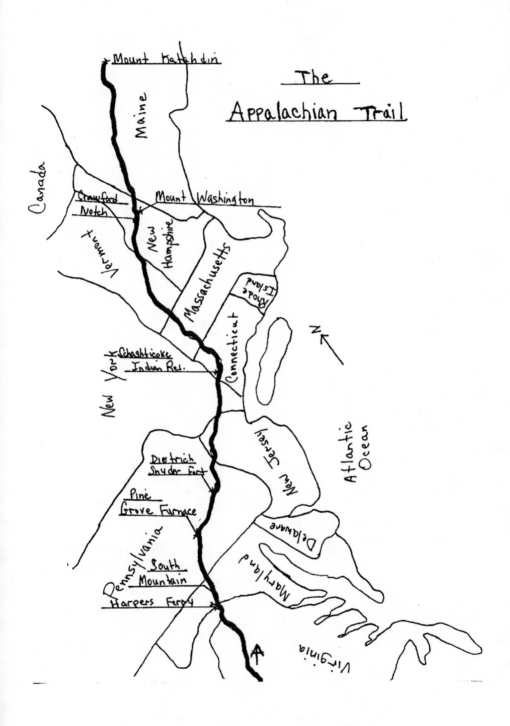

CONTENTS

Dedication

This book is lovingly dedicated to my children Kelly, Chris, Andrea, and Alyson, who have spiced up my life with much joy—and a few gray hairs. And as always, to my understanding wife, Judith, who somehow manages to hold things together and keeps the lawn mowed while I wander the mountains and beat out words at the keyboard.

Author's Note

Benton MacKaye was a remarkable man. His "beyond the horizon" vision of a footpath stretching along the high crests of America's Blue Ridge eventually became reality when the Appalachian Trail opened to "foot travel only" in 1937. He admonished those who wound their way over peaks and valleys heretofore accessible only to the most hardy and daring to "... *see, and to see what you have seen."* Well, when I first read these words, they made about as much sense as dribbling mustard on a jelly doughnut. If you saw something, you just *saw* it. Period.

What an idiot I was! On a fine summer day in 1998, on my third thru-hike, I stopped at a spring in a pretty little glade to air my aching hoofers—Pennsylvania rocks are murder, you know. While I sat there guzzling cold sweet water, my eyes strayed to a nearby aged stone marker. Its sparse wording let me know that my gratification came from Pilger Ruh Spring, where Count Zinzen-something-or-other and one Conrad Weiser had also quenched their thirst in 1742. Model-T, my pesky alter ego, whose sole mission in life is to make mine miserable, piped up, *Hey Diddlebrain, what's a Pilger Ruh?* Damned if I knew, but I wasn't about to let him—or "it" (I've never gotten a handle on our weird relationship)—have the satisfaction of calling me an ignoramus. *Well Mr. Stupid, if you knew anything at all, you'd know it's a German term meaning "place to cool your beer."*

And that's when the realization suddenly penetrated my Kentucky tow-headed cranium. Not only did I *not* know what a Pilger Ruh was; I didn't know diddly about most of what I'd seen—and yet had *not seen*, as strange as it sounds—between Georgia and Maine.

Hence, this book. An apology of sorts to Benton MacKaye, if you will. It's also an effort to bring closure to my hikes along the Trail, where I've stumbled in awkward ignorance. My Appalachian experiences could have been so much more! Hopefully, this book will help others to be better prepared, not only to enjoy the soul-gripping experience that comes from the power of the mountains, but also to *see what they've seen.*

Comes the disclaimer: *Walkin' with the Ghost Whiperers* is certainly not all-inclusive. Far from it, for if I had tried to research and write about each item of interest on the Trail, I'd be well on my way to breaking the record for drawing Social Security before I finished the book. Also, I freely acknowledge that factual information is only as good as the source. By necessity, a great deal of the research that went into this book was gleaned from the World Wide Web. I have tried to cull out erroneous or speculative information; to verify facts where possible when conflicts exist; and when unable to do so, to make known differing positions in the manuscript.

A note to the reader: Please don't look upon *Ghost Whisperers . . .* as a history book or boring travelogue. I've tried to make it entertaining and refreshing, bringing to light little known facts and some of the pertinent historical significance. This has taken me down some blue-blazed trails, and I've rambled on at times like an old, gray-bearded goob—which I happen to be.

All that said, now a few words about Model-T. Granted, we all are afflicted with alter egos. I suspect that mine happens to be stronger than most. (Gospel truth, I *don't* have a split personality.) Model-T basked in the limelight of authorship with *his* account of our first thru-hike in *Walkin' on the Happy Side of Misery: A Slice of Life on the Appalachian Trail*. He pulled the strings, spiced up the tale with words that I would never use (embarrassing), and gave me short shrift throughout.

Now it's my turn to grab some of the gravy. *Ghost Whisperers . . .* is *my* book, my words, no Model-T cluttering up the pages with inane hiker drivel—unless I choose to throw him a few crumbs. Okay, give the devil his due. Both books are tied together with literary duct tape, just like our contentious, conjoined, inseparable relationship. On occasion I've gritted my teeth and referred to *Walkin' on the Happy Side of Misery . . .* , in order to clarify or bring into perspective something that I've written about. But then, writing, like politics, sometimes creates strange bedfellows.

But the objective remains pure. For when you take to the Trail, may you . . . *see, and see what you see . . .*

J.R. "Model-T" Tate
Woodlawn, Tennessee
Summer, 2005

Prologue

April 4, 1948 began like most others. Around the globe, depending mostly on where the planet's perpetual spinning caused the ever-present sun to touch, people ate, slept, worked, procreated, became victims or predators, wept or laughed, or shoved against Fate to latch onto a better place in the pecking order. The most significant event to make the front page that day happened at a baseball spring training camp in Orlando, Florida, when the 84 year-old manager of the Phillies, Connie Mack, challenged the 78 year-old owner of the Senators, Clark Griffith, to a race from third base to home plate. Amazingly, the race ended in a tie. On that same morning, Andrew Lloyd Webber and Albert Arnold Gore, Jr., barely days out of their mothers' wombs, were just beginning to learn how to manipulate the business end of a bottle between their impatient lips. Up in Dayton, Ohio, Orville Wright's coffin had barely begun to settle into the spring-thawed sponge six feet under. And down in Georgia, another drama that would have far-reaching consequences on generations to come began to unfold.

A bone-chilling wind swept across Mount Oglethorpe and sent shivers rippling across the lone intruder's body. It had been a tough proposition, crawling out of the skimpy sleeping bag and into the damp predawn chill that permeated the rickety leanto, which he had called "home" the previous evening. He had planned to spend the night on Oglethorpe's summit, close to the diamond-shaped metal marker—the first of hundreds of metal and white-painted blazes that would be his guiding beacon over the next few months. But the brutally cold wind had quickly thwarted his plans and chased him off the summit, back down to the old leanto that he had passed the previous afternoon on his way to the top. Crumbling and sagging under years of neglect, it wasn't much to look at. But it had served its purpose.

A strong gust pushed him toward the battered sign that marked the southern terminus of the Appalachian Trail, as if to say, "get going . . . time's awastin'."

Restraining his eager legs, the hiker gathered his thoughts and tried to fix the moment firmly in his memory, a picture to bolster him through whatever lay between where he stood and a distant mountain in Maine. Impulsively, he reached out and touched the nearly invisible fog-shrouded statuary that adorned the summit—the tall monument that had been chiseled out of a massive block of "white gold" taken from Sam Tate's marble quarry. Georgians had erected the obelisk in 1930 to the memory of James Edward Oglethorpe, the state's founder.

A quiet moment of reflection. A picture of his childhood friend rose, unbidden, from somewhere far within, buried these past three years in a private place seldom visited. Walter Winemiller, his hiking companion in the carefree days before *the* war. Walter, forever gone, one of the 6821 Americans who never left the blood-soaked ashy soil of Iwo Jima. Walter, who had planned to be at his side on this dismal morning. The hiker swallowed his rising grief, then pushed the picture back into its private place and softly murmured, "This one's for you, Walter."

Time to go. Without further ado, twenty-nine year-old Earl Victor Shaffer from Shiloh, Pennsylvania, shifted his military issue rucksack into a more comfortable position, squared his shoulders, and set his jaw. Taking a deep breath, he pointed his moccasin-boots toward Maine—and walked into history.

No newspaper reporters came to Mount Oglethorpe that historic morning to pepper the young man with questions about why he was attempting to do "the impossible." At least that's what the hikers "in the know," those seasoned, venerable folks who had built the Appalachian Trail, called a continuous hike from Georgia all the way to Maine. Earl didn't even give it a thought. More pressing things bothered him—mainly, how to get his mind straightened out after nearly five years of combat duty on Jap-infested atolls in the South Pacific, where hordes of bandy-legged soldiers had tried to get him in their rifle sights. Down deep, Earl sensed that this journey of 2000 miles would act as a catharsis and purge the nightmares from his dreams.

Thus began the "Lone Expedition." Soon people he met began to question his good sense, and Earl began to refer to himself in his "Little Black Notebook" as the "Crazy One" (and the tradition of trail names was born). Came days spiced with meals of oatmeal or cornmeal mush cooked over a wood fire—no stove—and always liberally doused with brown sugar. Came endless nights spent at whatever place twilight found him, huddled beneath a Marine-issue poncho draped over a logged-out tree top, stoically enduring whatever Ma Nature had decided to serve up. And always came the twenty-mile plus days, constantly up and down, up and down, ever moving north.

On August 5, 124 days and 2050 miles after leaving Mount Oglethorpe, Earl Shaffer climbed mile-high Mt. Katahdin and proved the doomsayers wrong. A smattering of reporters latched onto his "impossible" achievement but gave it little space. No matter, for the nightmares had disappeared and Earl was ready to go on with his life. The demons had been laid to rest.

And for a generation of future hikers, infants even then sucking sweet milk from swollen breasts, the way had been made ready! An era had begun!

Chapter One

Springboard to Adventure

What a wonderful name—Springer Mountain! It immediately brings to mind images of dedicated hikers stepping out with strides full of purpose and determination. "Springer"—a springboard to adventure and glory! Yet, Springer's name predates the Appalachian Trail by at least a century and a half, and its birth is lost in the obscurity of time. Settlers with the name of Springer lived in the area in the 1800s, and a William Springer was appointed by the Georgia State Legislature about 1833 to improve the conditions of the north Georgia Cherokees. At one time, poor Springer was demeaned by being called Penitentiary Mountain. The sad fact is, Springer Mountain was once an understudy—a Johnny-come-lately.

When the Appalachian Trail was completed in 1937, hikers picked up the Trail's first metal marker or two-by-six inch painted white blaze (or last, depending on which way they were going) atop Mt. Oglethorpe. And this mountain was just perfect for the southern terminus of the Appalachian Trail! A lovely mountain with a stately monument on its summit and easily accessible by a paved road that led right to the Trail's beginning. Things were almost too good to be true! Lying nearly fifteen miles southeast of Springer Mountain as the crow flies, Mt. Oglethorpe was a respectable mountain, rising a bit over 3200 feet into the northeast Georgia sky. A regal obelisk crowned the summit, reaching toward the heavens—a fitting tribute from the citizens of Georgia to that intrepid statesman and adventurer, General James Edward Oglethorpe, who with his small band of colonists settled the state in the early 1700s. Mt. Oglethorpe was a grand site for the jump-off point of the Great Adventure— except for one fly in the soup. It was too accessible.

The mountain eventually fell prey to "progress." Chicken farms, clear-cut logging, hog farms, and trash heaps (the surest indicator of encroaching civilization) all impacted on and detracted from the natural beauty of the area. Mt. Oglethorpe had fallen on hard times. It had to go. The keepers of the "Holy Grail" cast their eyes to the north.

Springer Mountain didn't have a lot going for itself. To its disadvantage, Springer was just another hump—among many such humps—on the Appalachian Trail. The mountain had little to offer (except possibly its name), for it was only another mountain to be climbed and the experience stored away in some musty memory bank for future retrieval. On the plus side, however, at 3782 feet Springer Mountain was almost 500 feet higher than Mt. Oglethorpe. More importantly, the mountain served as the anchor for the two branches of the Blue Ridge chain, which extend northward for several hundred miles. (One giant arm sweeps eastward to grasp Mt. Mitchell, while the other stretches west to enfold the Great Smokies before rejoining its sister in southwest Virginia near the Peaks of Otter.) But the seller: The summit was inaccessible to wheeled vehicles!

By 1958, the lumber barons, chicken farmers, and trash heaps had won. The hikers threw in the towel, leaving Oglethorpe to the victors, and cast their lot with modest Springer.

In 1959, a bronze plaque, one of three which were sculpted in the early 1930s by Georgian hiker and amateur sculptor George Noble, was set into a broad rock on Springer's summit to commemorate its elevated status as the southern terminus of the Trail. The chicken farmers and log sharks could have Oglethorpe!

Chapter Two

Counting Coup

The Approach Trail! The beginning of the "Great Adventure" for a *few* hardy souls. (Only about twenty percent of the burdened hikers who plan to hoof it from Georgia to Maine on the Appalachian Trail take the Approach Trail.) Most opt to ride along the snaking curves of Forest Service Road 42 to Big Stamp Gap, which gets them to within .9 mile (albeit on the "wrong" or north side) of the first white blaze that marks the southern terminus of the Trail. But to honestly claim, "Yes, I started on Springer Mountain," they have to backtrack south to the summit and then retrace that mile. A distasteful bit of work for those champing at the bit to get started. Still, some hikers (like myself) accept the rigorous 8.8-mile Approach Trail as a must—an essential part of the whole experience. For in our minds if we choose the easier way, deep down we feel we have somehow cheated ourselves and have lost in the deal. So, puffed up with good intentions and quivering with anticipation, off we go—"purists" in every sense.

The Approach Trail, which begins at Amicalola Falls State Park near Dahlonega—the site of the Nation's first gold rush—was once part of the Appalachian Trail during the days when Mount Oglethorpe held its princely status as the Trail's southern terminus. Back then, the Trail brushed the Park's edge and climbed steeply to cross above the falls where the water starts its roller coaster ride, plunging 729 feet down a hazy abyss before crashing into a pool of churning thunder. The Cherokees gave the "tumbling waters" its lovely, lilting musical name of "Amicalola." Little did they realize that this majestic feature was the highest of its kind east of the Mississippi River; otherwise, the Falls might have been deified as a sacred shrine, with a celestial name to match.

The "locals" love the Approach Trail. For them, it can become a veritable gold mine of goodies—wonderful things grudgingly discarded from the crammed, grossly overweight packs of the uninitiated. During the prime thru-hiking season (March through May), the inhabitants of nearby hollows and gaps eagerly (and gleefully) take to the Approach Trail.

Why? Because lying there just for the taking are treasures galore! Full gallon cans of Coleman fuel . . . 16x20-foot vinyl tarps . . . gallon-size heavy metal pans . . . cast-iron Dutch ovens and skillets . . . enough extra clothing to outfit a fair-sized Goodwill Store . . . even fanny packs! And how about the six-person dome tents and tons of food (sometimes neatly contained in the original food bags)!

How can this happen? For some unfathomable reason, hikers have a tendency to toss rational thought right out the mental window when preparing for a thru-hike. (Yep, it happened to me, too!) We carefully research camping catalogs, talk with seasoned hikers, spend endless hours browsing outfitters' racks of high-tech, high dollar clothing and equipment. And then we max out the credit cards—but with minimum guilt pangs, for we *have been* prudent and discriminating, choosing the objects of our patient research with something approaching a religious rite. Home we go with our precious cargo, whistling and walking on air. *Dang! We're ready to rock-n-roll!* With appropriate ceremony, we carefully place our packages in a corner of the living room. Then comes the fondling, gently and affectionately as if we were caressing a beauty queen, while we pack—and repack—the gear over the course of the next several weeks.

Then it happens! The "what-if's" begin to creep in, slyly at first, little twinges of doubt that bespeak of dangers to come. After all, this is Big Time, Life On The Edge! The mental tweaks soon become a ground swell of sweaty armpits and Pepcid-laced meals as we begin to think about the endless miles that await and visualize every conceivable worse case scenario that can happen up in those mountainous wilds that will soon swallow us whole! Then we meekly brave the smirks of the wise and knowing clerks at the outfitters and buy *more and more*. Back in the same living room corner, we attempt to cram everything into what initially looked like a large enough pack. Failing miserably, we scratch our heads, eyeball the offending pile, and go buy a larger pack. After all, everything in the pile is *essential!*

When a hiker arrives at the Amicalola Falls Visitor Center, one of the first chores is to hoist the pack onto the hook of the large scale hanging there with one specific purpose—a reality check. Some aspiring thru-hikers nearly faint with shock as the large needle takes a clockwise flight up into the stratosphere of high double digits. Some try to cover their equipment bingeing with machismo. Bystanders are likely to hear forced comments disguised by falsetto strutting and feigned indifference, such as, "Seventy-eight pounds. Is that all? Heck, I shoulda brought that lawn chair after all."

The other side of the coin: Another hiker barely manages to lift a huge pack up to the scale and then turns sheet-white as the needle rockets toward triple digit territory. Groaning and rolling his eyes at the others awaiting their turn at the "Truth Teller" while covertly trying to flatten a bulging pre-hernia back into his abdomen, he blurts, "God A'mighty! Ninety-two pounds. This scale is *defective*. I'm not crazy enough to carry that much!" Right!

So the hike begins. Singly or in two's or three's, those who have decided to brave the rigors of the Approach Trail start the steep climb toward the top of the Falls. By the time that first small goal is achieved, a terrible realization strikes like a thunderbolt—*the scale didn't lie!* And when, a few miles up the trail, they stand and look in distaste at the offending monster of their own making, which benignly rests against a tree, the absurdity of their situation slowly dawns and they moan, "Oh my God! I'm not gonna make it." Weak-kneed, they sit in bewilderment beside the pack, oftentimes shedding tears while they pass through stages akin to severe trauma: shock, frustration, denial, and then resigned acceptance.

Tearfully, packs are emptied and the gear is sorted into two piles. One pile is returned to the pack, which now has *lots* of space. The other pile remains beside the trail—a short-lived monument to the school of hard knocks—until the jubilant "locals" arrive. God's truth! I've been there!

Okay, I've not been entirely honest. There *is* another way to get to Springer—that is, if a hiker can hitch a ride on a 4-wheeler or just happens to have a main battle tank to make the arduous trip up the badly-eroded and nigh-on impassable fourteen-mile USFS Road 28 to Nimblewill Gap. The Approach Trail crosses this road 2.2 miles on the "right" or south side of the terminus, which gives the hiker a straight shot to Maine. But there are much more interesting ways to experience misery on the Appalachian Trail than a side trip up USFS 28!

At the beginning of my second thru-hike in 1994 (four years older but a lot wiser in the ways of the Trail), I reached the top of Springer Mountain early on a cool, rainy morning. A man in his early thirties, clad in wet denim, was doing a "gotta get warm" dance around a vinyl tarp, which was spread over a pile of soaked gear on the soggy ground. He didn't look happy.

"You a thru-hiker?" I asked for openers. He didn't look like one.

"Hell, I thought I was," he muttered through shivering teeth. "I did that damn Approach Trail yesterday; lugged all this crap over eight miles. It damn near killed me." He kept on dancing while we talked, trying without much success to get warm. I could have told him he was wasting his time while he kept his wet cotton garments on. He glared at me, like I was the cause of all his misery, and growled, "This morning I almost walked away and left the whole damned mess here for whoever wanted it. But I guess I'll go ahead and pack it back out. I'm going back to Tampa. Shittin' place!"

Good move I thought as I wished him well and turned northward. The Approach Trail had counted another coup!

*   *   *

Any sketch of Springer Mountain would be incomplete without telling about how one thru-hiker reached the first white blaze, *albeit unusual*, on the long journey north.

When I read Larry Luxenberg's book, *Walking the Appalachian Trail*, I knew I had to meet Robie "Jumpstart" Hensley. Anyone with the daring to make such a grandiose entry onto Springer Mountain had to be either a fool or a man of steel. In my mind's eye, I imagined a tall, well-muscled replica of a cross between John Wayne and Sean Connery: Steely blue eyes, granite face, close cropped, iron-gray hair. Heck! He probably ate nails for breakfast and chased it down with rotgut Russian vodka! What I got was something entirely different.

I tracked "Jumpstart" down at his log house, not far from the post office where he had served as postmaster for several years before he finally retired and decided to hike the Trail. When I drove up, a short, hunched-over man with sprigs of gray landscaping his balding head was expertly maneuvering a riding lawnmower over a well-manicured lawn. The entire place was awash in color, even though it was early April. I thought, *Wow! Jumpstart has a gardener! I shoulda been a postmaster*. The "gardener" waved and parked the lawnmower. I walked over and said, "Hi. I'm J.R. Tate, also known as Model-T. Robie Hensley is expecting me. Is he around?"

The man wore a blue tee shirt with "Jumpstart" embossed in big letters on the front. On the back of the shirt, a thread-man dangled beneath an embroidered parachute. He smiled and extended his hand. "I'm Robie Hensley. Good to meet you."

I reset my brain as I shook his hand and tried to cover my confusion, still unable to visualize this mild man with smiling eyes that seemed as gentle as a soft spring drizzle riding a parachute toward tree-covered Springer Mountain. I took a closer look. Behind the smile and care lines that creased his face was a fount of energy that seemed to radiate outward, frolicking and sparkling his words and movements, belying his seventy-odd years and grandfatherly appearance. I felt myself drawn to him and thought *This is a man I would like to have hiked with*!

Jumpstart took me on a tour of the grounds. He walked slightly bent over, and I thought I detected a slight limp. A parachute accident? He noticed my puzzled look. "I had a little accident three years ago," he explained. "I was pruning a tree about twenty feet up on a ladder. When I cut off a limb, it snagged on my glove and yanked me off the ladder." He chuckled wryly, "I managed to get the glove off as I fell, like I was doing a free-fall (parachute) jump, and got myself lined up with the ground, but it was too late. The fall crushed three vertebrates and busted up my pelvis. The worst part though, it put a stop to my long distance hiking." Nearby, a pile of limbs, recently pruned and ready to be carted off, lay at the foot of a large tree.

I asked, "Did you do that?"

"Yep, just this morning." Noticing my incredulous look, he laughed and said, "I don't prune with gloves on anymore." His accident hadn't slowed him down. We looked at his vegetable garden, already cloaked in a mantle of several shades of green despite the early season. Like me, Robie enjoyed gardening, and his garden reflected a labor of love. Robie led me back to the house and I began to ask questions.

"Did you really parachute onto Springer?" A foolish question, one that he had undoubtedly been asked many times, but I had to start somewhere.

"Sure did," he answered proudly, like I was the first person to actually ask him about it. "It was on the ninth day of March in 1986. My son, Steve, flew the plane, a Cessna (182). My other son, Ted, and the plane's owner, David Shelton, went with me." Robie got a faraway gleam in his eyes, and that day seemed to resurface as though it had all happened yesterday. "We got down there and it was so foggy we couldn't even spot Springer. Steve took us over to Blairsville and we set down and waited for the clouds to lift. Steve and Ted were dead set against me jumping, but I was determined. I figured it was safe enough." Jumpstart smiled at the memory. "At one point, I thought they were going to tie me up. When the clouds finally lifted, we flew back to Springer and I could see the shelter and the small clearing I planned to land on." (Steve later wrote in the Preface to Robie's journal of his hike, which he published in 1992: "From eight thousand feet, the spot he (Robie) picked looked like a postage stamp on the side of the mountain.")

"Did you have any second thoughts?" I couldn't comprehend anyone jumping out of a perfectly good airplane. And as far as parachuting onto Springer went, well, to me that bordered on sheer lunacy!

"Not really." Another chuckle. "But my boys talked about holding me in the plane and not letting me jump. Anyway, they saw I'd made up my mind and was going to do it, so we floated a yellow weighted streamer down to see which way and how hard the wind was blowing. The wind took it right out of the county."

"How hard?" I asked, excited, for I was caught up in the tale and now sat right in the plane with them!

"At least forty miles per hour we figured, maybe more. Of course, that didn't set too well with Steve and Ted. We offset about two miles from the shelter, just about where Nimblewill Gap is. At eight thousand feet I jumped, and then pulled the ripcord at sixty-five hundred feet. Once the canopy popped, I turned into the wind to check my drift and estimated the wind was blowing me backward at about twenty-two miles an hour."

My hands were sweaty and my adrenaline pump went crazy! Oh yes! I was dangling from that chute right along with Jumpstart! "What'd you do?"

Robie said, "My daughter, Sherry, and her husband were waiting for me on Springer with my backpack. Sherry popped a red smoke grenade on the landing site and I just maneuvered the chute toward it, watching the smoke over my shoulder and backing in, holding against the wind." He said it nonchalantly, as if it were something he did every day. "Would've made it, too, if I hadn't hit a dead air space. My chute dumped me right into the trees, just a short stone throw from my target. My canopy got snagged between two trees and left me dangling about six feet off the ground." (In Robie's journal, he vividly described his predicament: " . . . like a grasshopper in a spider web.") "Sherry and her husband helped me down and radioed Steve that I was okay. I traded the parachute for my pack and went to Maine."

Robie's eyes refocused and his mind returned to the present. I gave a sigh of relief and felt the tenseness retreat . . . a wonderful feeling to be on firm ground!

Outside, I heard a car door slam shut. Robie said, "That's probably my wife, Lana, coming back from town." Lana turned out to be a kindly lady with sparkling eyes that reflected her friendly disposition and peaceful nature, which perfectly complemented the beautiful rainbow flower gardens in her yard.

Jumpstart and Ace Bandage, flanked by Model-T.
Short in stature but larger than life.

I quickly learned that she was also a hiker. Lana and Robie were wed in 1987. Shortly thereafter, Lana revealed she had harbored an urge to hike the Appalachian Trail for a long time. Her husband gladly volunteered to show her the way. Robie (now firmly entrenched in the annals of Trail lore as "Jumpstart"—what else) and Lana left Springer in March of 1988 and made the long trek to Katahdin. Lana quickly picked up the moniker "Ace Bandage"— so named because it became her constant companion on the Trail. Not yet ready to settle down, they left the next year to hike the Pacific Crest Trail.

I asked the obvious question. "Did the two of you start your thru-hike by parachuting onto Springer?"

Lana glanced at her hiking companion. "He wanted us to do it, but . . ." She left the sentence dangling, and her look said the rest. I knew exactly how she felt!

I asked Robie, "Was that your first jump?"

"Goodness no. I had at least four hundred, maybe five, before I jumped at Springer."

"How long have you been jumping?"

"I got my private pilot's license, and then went on to get my commercial license when I was in my forties. Before long I began flying 'jumpers' out of a local airfield. It looked like fun so I thought I might give it a go. Only trouble was, when I tried to get someone to teach me the basics, the first thing they asked was, 'How old are you?' When I told them fifty, they said 'Go home. You're too old.' One day I hit it lucky. I asked a fellow if he would teach me. He stared at me and asked, 'You got fifty dollars?' I've been jumping ever since; even parachuted into the ALDHA (Appalachian Long Distance Hikers Association) meeting at Pipestem (West Virginia) one year." A broad grin lit up his face. "Boy! Were they ever surprised!"

Then Jumpstart went silent, lost in his thoughts for a few seconds. Some of the shine seemed to fade from his face as if his soul were suddenly in the shadow of a drifting cloud. "My accident put a stop to my jumping days," he said, but there was no rancor in his words, just acceptance.

He shifted gears. "When I was on the Trail, Steve used to fly over and drop food to the other hikers and me. Fried chicken and all kinds of goodies! Then when I finished that first hike, the next year we dropped stuff to the hikers together. Steve really liked playing Santa." Then the cloud returned and his shoulders seemed to sag. "Steve died a few weeks ago." My heart ached for Robie and Lana at their loss, but words seemed inadequate.

A small bell sounded at the screen door. Robie brightened. "That's Sylvester, our cat. We have three. Lana, let him in and maybe he'll do his tricks for Model-T. Sylvester can shake hands and lay down."

After Sylvester had performed, it was time to go. When I said goodbye to this intrepid man who met life on his own terms, and hugged his warm, astute, caring wife, I felt humbled by their larger than life presence in my world. Their invitation to return, given from the heart, let me know I had made two new friends. My innards seemed to glow like a golden sunset.

When I turned out of their driveway, Jumpstart had already returned to his mowing.

*   *   *

The old shelter on top of Springer Mountain's summit, which gave me such wonderful refuge on my first night on the Trail in 1990, was disassembled in 1993 by the Georgia Appalachian Trail Club to make room for a new two-story shelter. The Club packed the old shelter down to the mountain's base at Black Gap. There, nestled in a small clearing just off the Approach Trail, Black Gap Shelter was given new life. Since then, it has become a welcome respite for those who have run out of steam (and curses) after a day of misery on the Approach Trail and just can't muster enough energy for that final push up the mountain.

When I hiked the Approach Trail on my second thru-hike in 1994, Black Gap Shelter was a pleasant surprise. Rain had just begun—it always seems to rain on the Approach Trail—and there it was, totally unexpected. At the trail junction, a weather-beaten arrow pointed down the mountainside toward the small spring where in 1990 Wahoola and I had filled our water bottles and readied ourselves to brave a vicious thunderstorm that was already beginning to assault Ol' Springer—where we were headed. (For a complete account, see *Walkin' on the Happy Side of Misery*, pp 26-34.)

Four excited faces stared at me from the dryness of the shelter. "How far you goin'?" I asked. "Maine!" came the exuberant reply, almost in unison as if directed by a hidden conductor. "A right far piece," I chuckled, dropping my pack in the space they quickly made for a fellow kinsman. I didn't know them from Adam but no matter, for we immediately became a happy, extended family, part of an exclusive brotherhood. As the storm pushed in and thunder echoed across the north Georgia mountains, we laughed and joked and spoke about things past and of things to come. It was good to be home again!

Chapter Three

Rangers!

In late March 2000, I had just finished a weeklong hike with some friends (the Approach Trail to Neels Gap) and planned to spend a few days in the area to do some research for this book. Soon after leaving the outskirts of Dahlonega early that Sunday morning, I noticed a small sign at roadside: "Camp Frank D. Merrill." On a whim, I pushed the steering wheel hard left and drove the ten twisting miles, made longer and lonelier by frigid, buffeting winds and sporadic intervals of spitting snow that squeezed out of the low, lead-gray clouds. I wanted to see the place that spawned the kind of "killing machines" that had surrounded me and yet had ignored me with such total indifference when I had braved a chilling north wind to eat a quick breakfast of gooey grits at Cooper Gap in 1990. (*Walkin'*... pp. 53-57.)

At the end of the desolate road, squatting at the base of the mighty Blue Ridge, a sprinkling of low-cut buildings huddled in obscure isolation. The complex—if it could be called that—was surrounded by the inevitable boundary fence that seems to sprout around all military installations much like uncut weeds along an unused path. A solitary sign by the entrance let me know I had reached Camp Frank D. Merrill, home of the 5th Ranger Battalion.

I didn't see any notice restricting my entry or requiring that I check in with anyone, but I had to start somewhere. An erect, poster-perfect specimen with close-cropped hair in civilian garb—obviously one of "those" I had come to see—walked up the steps of a small post exchange just inside the main entrance. I hailed him. "Is it okay if I drive in and look around some?" He looked me over like I was on a spy mission for the KGB, or whatever it's now called since the Soviet Union folded. Possibly my unkempt gray beard and neglected hair after a week on the Trail didn't help.

"Well, it's not a restricted area, but maybe you'd better check in with the 'staff duty' three buildings down." By his expression, I could tell he wasn't too sure about turning me loose now that he had me in his sights. I assured him I would do as he "suggested" and drove on down the street. In my review mirror, I watched him keep an eye on me until I pulled into the Headquarters Building parking lot.

Inside, the "staff duty," a clone of the "poster" soldier I had just met—tall, rugged, sense of purpose shining like orbs of steel from no nonsense eyes—warily gave me a visual pat down. His nametag said "Binion" and he wore the rank of staff sergeant on his collar.

I gave him my best smile. "Hi Staff Sergeant Binion. I'm J.R. Tate, here doing research for a book about the Appalachian Trail. I've seen you Ranger fellows up on the mountain near the Trail and wanted to write a little bit about you."

His look was noncommittal. "Yeah, we go up there a lot. See hikers every now and then." He eyeballed me like I was a spoonful of Castor Oil that he had to swallow. "Only, they don't see much of us."

I took out a note pad and pencil. "Where you from, Staff Sergeant Binion? I'll want to put you in my book." The pale steel eyes softened into gray marble. "Newnan, Georgia, a little southwest of Atlanta. You really mean to put me in your book?" Then he thawed and the granite face cracked into what might have passed for a smile. "My first name's Chris." We were off and running!

The camp, I soon learned, is named for Major General Frank Merrill, a daring officer who during WWII led a group of heroic men known affectionately as Merrill's Marauders. Their feats were later heralded in a movie of the same name (starring Jeff Chandler) in which the "Marauders" struggled through dense Burma jungle to rescue POWs from a Japanese camp. What Staff Sergeant Binion didn't mention—he didn't need to, for it was etched in the photographs that adorned the Headquarters Building walls—Camp Frank D. Merrill is also where elite young men who ache to "live on the edge" come to show what they're made of. And it's definitely not "sugar, spice, and everything nice." Staff Sergeant Binion gave me a quick, professional rundown on the purpose of Camp Frank D. Merrill:

The camp is a way station on the journey to becoming a U. S. Army Ranger. Here, the eager young men learn how to live and fight in the mountains. They make their debut at Camp Merrill by parachuting into camp. But to get here at all, they must first survive the rigors of advanced parachute training at Fort Benning, Georgia. Once the mountains are mastered, they then move on to the sandy beaches of Eglin Air Force Base in north Florida, where they delve into the finer points of amphibious operations. (Note: Too many broken legs from parachuting into the camp, the Army decided. Now the trainees are bussed in.)

Becoming a Ranger trainee at Camp Merrill is no small feat. Graduating from the camp is tantamount to walking on water! For one thing, the mountain phase continues to weed out all but "The Finest" from what is already considered to be "The Best." Indeed, in the twenty-odd days they will spend here (out of the total 65-day Ranger training cycle), seven days will be devoted to finding out who shouldn't be here at all. Fifty percent of a class of some three hundred trainees who come through the gates will pass back out again during this time, crestfallen because they couldn't measure up. Of the approximately remaining hundred and fifty, less than sixty will ultimately have the honor of wearing the patch that proudly tells the world that they are U.S. Army Rangers. (Some of the others might get a second chance—if they are lucky enough to get "recycled.")

Before the coveted patch is attained, these hopefuls will be subjected to stress and adversity beyond common sense and driven right to the brink of human endurance. Indeed, the School advocates that " . . . the constant pressures of operating within restrictive time limits all create this atmosphere of stress"; and, that there is " . . . necessity for sound decisions and the requirement for demonstrating calm forceful leadership under conditions of mental and emotional stress." Translation: The School is going to do everything it can to keep the ranks of "The Finest" pure.

To do this, the students are heaved out into the nearby mountains for eleven days running; usually fed one meal a day for the duration; and they might get three or four hours of sleep at night—if they're lucky. These harassed lads routinely lose twenty to thirty pounds during the time they romp around the mountains. By the end of all three phases, most lose over forty pounds, more than twice what male hikers usually lose in six months on the Appalachian Trail!

One of my neighbors, a Ranger, related to me that he and his buddy got so hungry while in the mountains above Camp Merrill that out of desperation they boiled a pine cone, still young and tender, and forced it down. The turpentine taste—and the "trots"—hung around through graduation day . . . a stark gastric reminder of HELL.

With my very own Ranger Mountain Training Orientation 101 finished, Staff Sergeant Binion said, "We have a good museum. It's closed, but if you'd like to see it, I'll open it for you." I assured him that would be super!

The Museum, a small, one-room building much like the others that surrounded it, turned out to be a treasure trove. Within its walls, the entire history of the U.S. Army Rangers was recorded in pictures, plaques, and artifacts. Major Robert Rogers formed the original Rangers in New Hampshire in 1756. The first of his "Standing Orders" was, "Don't Forget Nothing." (It probably still applies today!) In one corner stood the actual bunk and wall space, removed from another "hootch" (a slang term for living quarters) at some unstated time and reconstructed here—ultra-austere digs, a place to rest one's head, nothing more. The "hootch's" wall section was covered with the names of long gone students, scribed there for posterity in their own handwriting—a rite of passage during the years 1960 to 1989. A few had scribbled "macho-isms." One read, "Balls of steel, men of danger, mean M__F__'s." Nearby a small tilted handwritten message dangled from a bent nail: "Hang steel balls here when not in use."

Taped to the wall near the door was a copy of The Ranger's Creed. Certain phrases jumped out at me: "Never shall I fail my comrades . . . I will shoulder more than my share of the task, whatever it may be, one hundred percent and then some . . . Surrender is not a Ranger word . . . Under no circumstances will (I) ever embarrass my country . . ." Heady stuff, even for a Marine!

So where is all of this leading? When I sat in Cooper Gap in 1990, surrounded by aspiring Rangers and eating my grits, I had no idea how hungry and sleepy these young fellows were. My grits must have been a maddening temptation. And the urge to catch a quick snooze while lying out of sight of the instructor's ever-present eagle eye must have been overpowering. But, there was no indication of any discomfort. Such is the "stuff" these fine young men are made of.

Thinking back, I wish I could have slipped some (make that ALL) of my ramen to them. I thank my lucky stars that the lieutenant-instructor was present; else, I might have poured the contents of my food bag on the ground at their boots and said, "Take, eat; and go in peace."

Thanks, RANGERS!

Chapter Four

Woody Gap—An Escape Hatch

For the bullheaded who are unwilling to lighten their packs on the Approach Trail and contribute to the local economy, there *is* an "out." Just twenty miles—two days for most hikers—from Springer Mountain, the Trail crosses paved Georgia Highway 60 at Woody Gap. Hallelujah! Cross the highway; stick out the thumb; grin at the screech of brakes; and you and your monstrous pack are off to Suches, only two miles down the mountain. Yes, there is a post office with a sympathetic staff, who manage to hide the "you screwed up royally" looks. After all, the Suches Post Office has been the lifesaver for thru-hikers from the git-go. In 1957, Dorothy Laker, the second woman to continuously thru-hike the Appalachian Trail (Grandma Emma Gatewood did it first two years earlier), mailed nine of her thirteen tent stakes home, along with a set of deer antlers she had found and was unwilling to relinquish.

And contrary to what some of the citizenry would have you believe, the town didn't get its name because "'Suches' it is, it's all we've got." Nice story, but Suches was really named after a Cherokee chief.)

If things haven't gone well in those first twenty miles—as usually happens—Woody Gap becomes the perfect escape hatch for disgruntled and disillusioned thru-hikers. In just twenty miles, blisters can give birth to new blisters. Everything can get soggy wet from north Georgia downpours. Enthusiasm can leech out of the bottom of boot soles like cat pee on a thin carpet with each tired step. Shoulders can catch on fire from carrying way too many "essentials." Had enough?

The temptation to chuck it all and head for home becomes more than some can bear. Suches becomes like a dose of Valium to ease tortured bodies as "reality" sets in and "2148 more miles of this shit" sounds like the peel of doom. The "Dream" dissolves in watery tears of relief and recrimination.

But that's Suches. The thrust of this chapter lies with Woody Gap and the man whose name is memorialized on a plaque in this hauntingly beautiful place that overlooks the Yahoola Valley.

Arthur Woody had a conscience. In 1895 in nearby Fannin County, eleven year-old Arthur watched his father shoot the last white-tailed deer in North Georgia. He never got over the smirch that plagued his memory. In time, young Arthur joined the Forest Service as an axe-man and soon became a full-fledged FS Guard. Eventually he became a voice in the wilderness crying for the Federal Government to purchase vast tracts of land to save the forests. In 1918, when the government created the Georgia National Forest (later named the Chattahoochee National Forest), Arthur Woody became Georgia's first Forest Ranger.

Ranger Woody was larger than life. Described as a "giant hulk of a man; a cross between John Wayne, Jim Bowie, and Daniel Boone," he eschewed bureaucratic tomfoolery. His disdain for the official Forest Service uniform was legendary—he scoffed at the idea of a necktie and usually left his shirt unbuttoned at the neck and his trousers open at the waist, preserving his modesty by keeping them up with the help of a pair of broad suspenders.

When a Forest Service "big wig" from Washington, D.C. visited the area, he was told by some of the accompanying Atlanta dignitaries who knew the recalcitrant ranger that "Woody won't wear shoes." Remarked the executive, "Well, we've got to do something about that." As the story goes, the bigwig stopped by Woody's home while the others attended to other business elsewhere. When they returned to collect the bureaucrat, Woody and the man were both shoeless, feet propped up on a porch rail as they drank crisp apple brandy.

Another time, when another "higher up" had gone with Woody on a trip into the back woods, the man asked, "Where's the bathroom?" Woody snorted, "With 180,000 acres of woods around you, you don't need one."

Arthur Woody usually got what he wanted—albeit sometimes with a mountain man's finesse. When he asked the highway czars in Washington, D.C. to build a road from Suches to Stone Pile Gap so the mountain people could get to Dahlonega, he was told that they couldn't build any new roads; that they could only improve existing roads. Undeterred, Woody gathered every able-bodied man, along with horses and scrapers, and he dug out a trail through the mountains. That little chore done, he called the czars and told them, "I have my road. Now you can come and improve it." Today, the road leading north from Dahlonega is Woody's creation.

For thirty years, Ranger Woody, or "Kingfish" as he was often called, held sway over the Chattahoochee National Forest. He refereed feuds among the short-tempered mountain folks, but not always successfully, especially when "moonshining" was the issue and bullets flew faster than good sense. Always, he pushed for land acquisition to protect the forests for future generations. With what began as a purchase by the Federal Government in 1911 of 31,00 acres (at $7.00/acre) in the four contiguous counties of Fannin, Lumpkin, Gilmer, and Union, today the Chattahoochee National Forest encompasses a vast wilderness of 749,689 acres. And when Roy Ozmer finished laying out the proposed route of the Appalachian Trail from Virginia to Georgia in the late 1920s, it was Arthur Woody who put mattocks and shovels in the hands of his Forest Service personnel and exhorted them to "Dig." The Georgia section of the A.T. was finished in 1931.

What about the absence of deer that had so plagued Arthur from his childhood days? In 1927, he managed to scrape a few dollars together and made a trip to neighboring North Carolina, where he bought five fawns. He bottle-fed them, and when they were old enough he released them into the surrounding forest with a stern warning to the local populace, "Leave my deer alone." Arthur went back, time and again, bringing home more fawns to raise until the herd was re-established.

Like any other job he tackled, "Kingfish" did his job too well. The herd multiplied until it was obvious to everyone, including the herd's benefactor, that a hunting season was badly needed. The Ranger was at the Checkout Station on that first hunt in 1941. When hunters began to bring in the fine stags, tears began to stream down his cheeks. Folks said Woody was never the same after that day and that he suffered deep depression afterwards. Said some with a sideways shake of the head and a chuckle, "Mr. Woody was kinda funny about them deer."

Ranger Woody was laid to rest in June 1946. Over 1500 mourners came to the small mountain church to pay their respects. Many stayed well after dark, speaking in low respectful tones about the ways Arthur Woody had touched their lives.

And now, when the footsteps of hikers echo across the pavement of Highway 60, as they push toward the fulfillment of their "Dream," let them remember that the "touching" still goes on.

*   *   *

On the sun-splotched late afternoon when my hiking partner, Wahoola, and I emerged from the woods and stood at the edge of this island of asphalt among an endless ocean of trees called Woody Gap, I barely glanced at the plaque with the words, "Arthur Woody" inscribed thereon. But in my defense, my indifference was offset by the "mountain man" who sat at the pocked concrete picnic table in the small graveled area across the road. (Little did I know at the time that this was the picnic table which Gene Espy, the second person to thru-hike the A.T. [1951], used as a bed one evening.) Waving his arms to get our attention, he obviously had business of some kind on his mind. His unkempt, "red-neck" appearance immediately marked him as suspicious. We had heard horror tales about "locals" intimidating—even robbing—hikers, especially at road crossings. (*Walkin'*... pp. 60-63.)

With this in mind, we approached warily, like mice toward a baited trap. Turns out, all he wanted to do was to haul us down to Suches and back for five dollars. But Suches wasn't on our itinerary. When he realized he had a "no sale," the "mountain man" allowed as how he knew of a little flat spot on an old logging road just behind the picnic area with a good spring. He confessed with a sly grin, "I've been coolin' m'suds in it fer years." Still unconvinced of his good intentions, I insisted on taking his picture—just in case we got ripped off during the night. Of course nothing happened, except that my imagination got a good workout.

A strange sight, this "mountain man."

I've often regretted that missed opportunity to learn more about a unique person. I suspect he really was a "mountain man," a person who lived in oneness with these mountains much as Arthur Woody had. On my next two thru-hikes, I anxiously anticipated reaching Woody Gap, with the hope that across the highway, sitting at the picnic table, I'd see the "mountain man" waving. But, alas . . .

Chapter Five

Ta-lo-Ne-Ga

And what of this wild mountainous kingdom through which we trespass with our sweat-soaked garb and high hopes? Of places with names like Blood Mountain, Slaughter Mountain, and Slaughter Gap, where the slopes once glistened red with the blood of fallen warriors engaged in a mighty clash between two powerful nations—the Creek and Cherokee—long before the Spaniards first pulled their longboats ashore on Florida's pristine sands? An eerie place, this Slaughter Gap. One can almost sense the *Nunne'hi*—"the Immortals," those invisible spirit people of the Cherokee who befriend and help those in need. Never far away are their smaller cousins, the *Yunwi Tsundi'*, the "Little People," who try to ease the torment of ancient earthbound ghosts that seem to lurk in the shadowy depths along the Trail.

What about the enormous cache of gold—the wealth of the Cherokee Nation—supposedly hidden on nearby Slaughter Mountain by the Cherokees right before gold-hungry Georgians exiled them from their lands? Legend or Truth? If true, could the gold still be languishing in a dank cave just beyond the rat-a-tat echo of the ruff grouse's hollow drumming?

And what of the once powerful people who tamed this wild country? The story—and the guilt—lies trampled beneath the yellow-tarnished knees of those who bowed at the altar of "*Ta-lo-Ne-Ga.*"

The Cherokee referred to the yellowish metal as *Ta-lo-Ne-Ga*. The white man coveted it and called it "Gold."

The Cherokee have always been different from other southeastern tribes. Calling themselves the *Ani-Yun'wiya*—the "principal people" (although the name "Cherokee" derives from a Creek word "*Chelokee,*" which means "people of a different speech"), the Cherokee were the only "Iroquois-speaking" people of the five southern "civilized" tribes (although major differences do exist between the two languages). Indeed, there are significant cultural and societal ties that strongly support the belief that the Cherokee once lived in the northern lands occupied by the Iroquois and Delaware Nations and were forced south in the distant past. Even stranger, anthropologists now believe the Cherokee had distant roots in the islands off South America and in the Caribbean. Oddly, Cherokee basket and pottery styles closely resemble those of indigenous people in that area.

Regardless of the historical paths that led the Cherokee to the southern Appalachians, by the time Hernando DeSoto first made contact with the "*Chalaque*" on the banks of the Tennessee River in 1540, they enjoyed a thriving culture. Sweeping north chasing rumors of gold, DeSoto and his armor-coated Spaniards descended on the natives with guns, knives, chains, and vicious dogs. Finding little gold and showing no mercy, he took women, food, and slaves, and in his wake left a path of death and destruction. His parting "gift" to the scourged Indian villages: Small pox, which swept through whole communities like wildfire, time and again, until populations were decimated nearly in half. (A rusty plate of armor found in the 1880s at DeSoto Falls, a couple of miles down the south slope of Blood Mountain along Frogtown Creek, attests to the presence of Spaniards in the area.) But the Cherokee persevered and in time regained some semblance of their former prosperity.

And then came "*Ta-lo-Ne-Ga.*" The Cherokee had known about this strange metal with the dull yellow color for centuries. In fact, the Spanish had been mining gold near the Cherokee town of Sixes off and on since DeSoto's arrival, until they were driven out in the early 1800s. But the weird effect *Ta-lo-Ne-Ga* (also called "*dalanigei*") had on the encroaching settlers was a different tale. When Major Frank Logan's black servant found a nugget near Loudsville (White County) sometime around 1828, America's first gold rush was on. Benjamin Parks, who lived near present day Dahlonega, was another contender for the honor of first discovering gold in the area. He claimed for seventy years to anyone who would listen that it was *his* toe that kicked up the first gold—a yellowish egg yolk-like stone—as he headed toward a licklog on the west side of the Chestatee River to hunt deer. And moreover, the miraculous event happened on his birthday, October 27, 1828. (Most modern day historians and the State of Georgia discount Park's account and give credit to Major Logan's servant.)

Gold frenzy swept the Nation, and the sparse population swelled to epidemic proportions. Like a prolific mushroom, almost overnight the town of Auraria rose out of the red Georgia clay and became a lawless, boisterous community of one thousand miners. A few miles to the north, Licklog (later named Dahlonega—the Anglicized form of the Cherokee word for "yellow") erupted near the site of Park's discovery. The big dilemma though: All of this wonderful gold lay on Cherokee land.

As greed tossed rational behavior on the trash heap of wanton human behavior, the Georgia State Legislature soon declared the laws of the sovereign Cherokee Nation null and void. The Indians were forced to accept worthless treaty after treaty, each which diminished their holdings and pushed them further from the ore-rich valleys. Finally, in 1838 President Van Buren directed General Winfield Scott to remove the Cherokee people to lands beyond the Mississippi River, and the "Trail of Tears" became another blight on the sullied conscience of the American people. Cherokee property was awarded to Georgia residents by lottery.

The sadness is poignantly captured by the words of old Speckled Snake, believed to have been over one hundred years of age. He spoke to his peers in formal Council after President "Old Hickory" Jackson, an avowed Indian hater, sent the message that the only chance the Cherokee had to survive as a nation was to move to the west.

In a voice wise beyond words and rife with abject resignation, Speckled Snake said, "Brothers, I have listened to many talks from our great white father. When he first came over the waters, he was a little man, very little. His legs were cramped by sitting long in his big boat, and he begged for a little land to light his fire on. But when the white man had warmed himself before the Indians' fire and filled himself with their hominy, he became very large. With a step he bestrode the mountains, and his feet covered the plains and valleys. His hand grasped the Eastern and Western seas, and his head rested on the moon. Then he became our Great Father. He loved his red children, and he said, 'Get a little further, lest I tread on thee.' Brothers! I have listened to a great many talks from our Great Father. *But they always began and ended in this—'Get a little further; you are too near me'.*"

Dahlonega thrived. Gold dust flowed like magical amber potions, and in such quantities that the Federal Government built a U.S. Mint there in 1838. By 1848, over thirty-six million dollars in gold coinage had been minted. But all things eventually diminish, and by 1849, when word came that gold had been discovered in far off California, it was all over but the shouting. As miners packed their shovels and pans and began to head west, Dr. Stephenson, assayer for the U.S. Mint, stood on the Dahlonega Courthouse steps and chastised the departing miners, shouting, "Why go to California? In that ridge lies more gold than man ever dreamt of. There's millions in it!" (Mark Twain later expanded on Stephenson's exhortation and credited it to his enthusiastic character, Mulberry Sellers, as "Thar's gold in them thar hills.")

But the miners went anyway and Dahlonega's fame vanished. Slowly, the town resumed a semblance of normality, content to rest on its laurels. Yet even today, a handful of persistent miners still pan the creeks around Dahlonega, hoping with each pan of coarse gravel that fortune will strike again. And gold still glistens in the hills around Dahlonega! But modern-day mining costs make extraction of the ore impracticable. So *Ta-lo-Ne-Ga* remains an elusive siren.

Chapter Six

Much Ado About Hamburgers

How far would you walk (or hitch) for a really great hamburger? A mile? Two miles? Ten? Of course, just how high your calorie-starved hiker belly registers on the hunger scale can impair good judgment and send you ditty-bopping along scorching pavement for whatever kind of greasy burger is being dished up. But then, for a really great hamburger . . .

After three thru-hikes of the A.T., one gets to know all of the best (and least expensive) eating places within a reasonable distance of the Trail—not to mention becoming a connoisseur of greasy food. I fall into both categories.

The spaghetti dinners of the late 1980s and early 1990s at the Mountain Crossings hostel at Walaysi-Yi Center (right on the A.T. 30.7 miles north of Springer Mountain at Neels Gap) are legendary. Spurred on by visions of a huge plate overflowing with the saucy-red pasta, many a hiker undoubtedly risked limb and life as he or she rushed headlong down Blood Mountain toward Neels Gap—like moths fluttering wildly toward an irresistible date with destiny. Alas! When the hostel closed for repairs in the mid-90s, those fantastic spaghetti dinners were relegated to Trail history. (The hostel has since reopened, but the spaghetti dinners are still only a fond memory.)

So what does this have to do with hamburgers?

In 1998 on my third thru-hike, while I sat on the beautiful patio at Mountain Crossings sorting through the food box I had just picked up, I overheard a tourist talking with another man about this great hamburger he'd just eaten. My ears immediately tuned in when he said, "Not far at all. Just down at the bottom of the mountain." And when the other gentleman said, "We're headed that way. Maybe we'll stop and check it out," I really got interested. It didn't take much talking to "yogi" (more about this hiker thingy later) a ride with the Good Samaritan and his family of six (plus a "wiener" dog). Lucky he had a mini-van!

As soon as we pulled into the small parking lot, I immediately fell in love. The quaint pale yellow clapboard building with a sign that stretched across the frontage of the roof proclaimed in large red letters that we had arrived at Turner's Corner Café—est. 1928. *A great location*, I thought, for the place hogged the intersection of U.S. Highway 19 and GA Highway 129, both busily traveled highways.

Its shape reinforced my initial impression that the building had once been a gas station of sorts among the small cluster of buildings that make up Turner's Corner. A large covered deck attached to the rear of the café jutted over the edge of Chestatee River, a gushing mountain stream that once marked the boundary between the Cherokee Nation to the west and lands ceded to the whites to the east. Here and there, colorful fly fishermen parted the frothing current, arms outstretched as the sun momentarily grabbed the arcing lines that raced out toward waiting trout. A right-stirring sight, but what really massaged my senses was the tantalizing smell of food that wafted from the building.

I walked inside—into a time warp, circa 1940. Checkered oil cloths covered tables that sat on the original plank floor. An ancient wood stove gave off enough heat to temper the slight April chill. Across the room, on top of a century-old oak counter, stood a glass case stuffed with real homemade pies topped with meringue "icing" six inches deep. I nearly fainted!

Quickly, I disassociated myself from the family, who seemed bent on hurrying through lunch so they could head on down the road to the next tourist trap, and took a corner table. This was a place to be enjoyed like the last Snickers bar in the food bag, and I meant to take my time. And along with the great hamburger and fries, I got a memorable piece of north Georgia nostalgia . . .

U.S. Highway 19 was cut through Walasi-Yi Gap (Cherokee for "giant frog," so named because an Indian brave saw a monstrous frog there while hunting) in the mid 1920s. At the time the road was being built, the place was known as Frogtown Gap. But eventually it became Neels Gap to honor the surveyor who laid out the serpentine roadway over the mountain.

When the highway was finished in 1925, local resident Charlie Turner saw an opportunity. In 1928 he opened Turner's Store—a combination general store, café, and gas station, which sported the first gas in the area. Charlie, a first class wheeler-dealer, quickly realized that he needed a gimmick to attract customers, especially since he knew absolutely nothing about cars except that somehow gas made them go. Indeed, a carburetor was as foreign to Charlie as meatballs to a vegetarian. So he tamed a black bear he had acquired along the way, and soon "Smoky" was tolerating children's delightful screams as they rode around the premises on his broad black back.

Charlie Turner and his "gimmick," Smoky, entertain a young fan
by the banks of the Chestatee River.
(Photo courtesy of Rivers Edge Enterprises)

Charlie, who liked his bottle, was a contented man as he sat by the cash register, sipping a nip now and then while he watched Smoky entertain the children of the growing clientele. Life was good to Charlie, especially after he got rid of the gas pump and all the headaches of having to feign a mechanic's knowledge of moving auto parts.

Then fate threw Charlie a curve. Smoky died. Devastated, Charlie asked neighbor Oscar Cannon to come help him dig a grave for his deceased bruin. Oscar obliged, as good country folk are brought up to do. No sooner than the red clay dirt had started to fly that Charlie remembered he had to make a run over to Cleveland—an all day trip—to "pick up something." Charlie returned just as Oscar, aching and by now all cussed out, finished the job. They laid Smoky to rest, and Charlie went into mourning—for the loss of his main money "draw" as much as for the bear.

Finally, Charlie decided he needed a replacement for Smoky. He heard about a fellow over by Suches who had a bear cub and he went primed to buy. A rub: It was illegal to buy and sell wild animals, and the man refused to break the law. Charlie asked the man if he *could* sell, how much would the bear be worth? "A hunnert dollars," the man replied. Sly Charlie stuck a folded "Franklin" in the stump he was sitting on and said, "Lookee over thar. A cub just a-runnin' wild. Not your'n is it?" The other fellow grinned, shook his head "no," and reached for the money.

Charlie named his new acquisition "Herman," after then Georgia governor, Herman Talmadge. The governor had taken a liking to Charlie, who was a staunch political supporter. But Smoky's bear paws were too big for Herman to fill, and things were never the same.

By this time Charlie was hitting the bottle pretty heavy, and a neighbor lady took it upon herself to make him into a "teetotaler." So began a game of cat and mouse—with her ferreting out Charlie's many stashes, while he tried to stay one step ahead of the game. (Years later, one of Charlie's bottles was found in the water tank of the commode in the Men's Rest Room. Ingenious!)

Lady Luck wasn't finished with Charlie though. One evening he sat playing poker and he was hot. Charlie just knew he had a winning hand, but he couldn't meet the ante, which had ballooned into the stratosphere. So he put the store up as collateral for the pot and "called." Charlie lost the hand! Immediately regretting his rash act, he persuaded a couple of Atlanta friends, Johnny and Elizabeth Sparks, to put up the money to enable him to buy back the store.

When Charlie died at age 75 in the late 60s, Johnny and Elizabeth moved in and ran the café until Johnny's death in 1972. For several years the store was owned by a series of seasonal operators until 1991, at which time Joyce Gowder reopened the café. But the store retained most of the furniture and décor, including the old wood stove that had been there when Charlie Turner welcomed his first customers in 1928.

Back to the hamburger. The seven-mile trip back up the mountain was an easy hitch. After all, who could refuse a ride to one of Nature's sons—who held a chocolate pie topped with a mountain of meringue in his grubby hands?

So the question remains: *Just how far would you go for a hamburger . . .*

*   *   *

On that cold, cloudy Sunday in March 2000, after leaving Camp Frank Merrill, I came to the intersection of Highways 19 and 129 and there it was, just as I remembered it. Turner's Corner Café! Without giving it a second thought, I crunched the brakes and went inside. Joyce was gone, but new owner Kari Morris greeted me with a smile and a menu. The place hadn't changed much. The old stove still cranked out enough heat to cut the chill wind outside, and the pies inside the glass case still sported small mountains of meringue. I glanced at the menu. "I got a memorable hamburger here a couple of years ago. Still great?"

"Try our Jerry Burger," she said, her voice filled with confidence. "It's the best."

It was! Thank goodness "progress" doesn't change some things!

An update: In late June 2005, I took three of our nine grandchildren on a five-day hike from Amicalola Falls to Woody Gap. The old concrete picnic table in the pull-off on the north side of the highway was still there, but bare—no "mountain man." With a sudden rush of déjà vu, it was again 1990 and I could almost see the unkempt codger sitting there waving, hoping to make a couple of bucks by hauling Wahoola and me down to Suches.

I shrugged away my disappointment and told the kids about this great place to grab an awesome hamburger—since we were in the area. They had been constantly talking about thick juicy hamburgers since their second day into the hike.

Turner's Corner Café was still there, still open, and the food odors still made the saliva run. Kari Morris had moved on. New owners Rob and Fran Jones now manned the cash register. Thankfully, the burgers hadn't changed! Pies still graced the menu. But sadly, the glass display case filled with mile-high meringue-covered pies that made my day in 1998 has fallen to "progress." (Rob Jones promised that he would give serious consideration to putting it back in its regal position as soon as space could be made!)

Chapter Seven

The Fine Art of Yogi-ing

L ong distance hikers, especially thru-hikers, remain in a constant state of diminished starvation—to the point of doing almost anything for food. A mean trickster called "calorie deficit" causes this ravenous craving for anything remotely resembling food, which might be crammed down the gullet to appease the gnawing hunger. Thru-hikers can burn upwards to five, even seven thousand calories a day as they stomp up and down mountains lugging heavy backpacks. I've been told that this energy expenditure is the equivalent of running two marathons.

Early on, thru-hikers grabbed a lesson from Uncle Sam: Learn to live with a deficit. Like the Government, the deficit soon soars into a huge debt. Unlike the Government, though, thru-hikers cannot run an unlimited tab. They have to keep shoveling the food in or the fat reserves (which generate those little foot-tromping calories) will become depleted. Then, like bureaucracy running amok, the body starts to give up its protein (translate: muscle) to produce calories which, among other things, sustain life. The bottom line: Thru-hikers require food. Lots of food!

Obviously, thru-hikers cannot haul the prodigious quantities of food needed to overcome calorie deficit (although some have tried). Most can only carry enough to meet about half of what is required each day to offset calorie deficit. So the urge to open the food bag and slurp up all its contents in one glorious bingeing orgy is a constant threat and is only kept in check by the glaring reality of running out of food while still days from the next resupply point. (Yet, each hiker's food bag is his or her sacred domain. I know of no incident where a hiker has taken another's food without permission.)

On the other hand, food is where you find it!

Most thru-hikers have a little kid wandering around in their psyche (though few will admit to this). Just look at 'em gathered around a TV in a hostel. What do they watch? Cartoons! Who is their favorite? Yogi Bear! Why? Yogi is a master at separating vulnerable tourists from their food-laden picnic baskets. Admittedly, thru-hikers usually row their boats with strange looking paddles, but *dumb* they are not. Hikers have learned *much* from Yogi Bear and have put into practice the valuable lessons he has taught, with the end result manifesting itself as the fine art of "yogi-ing."

Yogi-ing is almost too simple: According to the unstated rule, thru-hikers never ask or beg for anything. They simply set up a situation where a likely "candidate" can give them something; e.g., food, a cold soda or beer, a meal at a restaurant, a night replete with shower and bed (with clean sheets), or possibly a ride. But to the uninitiated, yogi-ing can be as fruitless as a hen house full of roosters, and as frustrating. The hard cold fact is, most people resist being separated from their "picnic baskets." Technique is *everything*!

My delivery, developed and polished after nearly ten thousand miles of hiking, has evolved into something that an experienced con man would be jealous of. Not bragging—just fact. It wasn't always so. My first attempt at Clingmans Dome in 1990 (*Walkin'* . . . pp. 129-131) was a total bust. I've come a long way, baby!

It goes something like this. When I run into a likely looking "prospect," preferably a couple with young children who are more interested in playing than eating, or an older couple *with food*, I immediately do two things: Start a dialogue, and get out the tools of the trade. (Forget it if teenagers are present, for they will devour everything like hungry caterpillars.) "How ya doin'? I'm Model-T and I'm hiking the Appalachian Trail from Georgia to Maine. Okay if I sit a spell and eat a bite?" A raised eyebrow at the opening gambit, and a nod of permission—it would be rude not to.

I shrug off the pack, sling some sweat from my brow onto the ground and give a large sigh of relief at being free of the large burden.

The dialog continues as I zip open the side flap of the pack and whip out a water bottle, plastic spoon, a plastic bag containing a few dry crumbly ramen noodles, and the *"piece de resistance"*—a small, nearly empty jar of peanut butter held in reserve for just such an occasion. (I usually have a *large* jar of peanut butter tucked somewhere in the depths of my pack.) "Yeah, I left Georgia a couple of months ago and figure to reach Maine . . ." That's usually about as far as I get before the prospect, interest now whetted, begins to fire the questions.

"Wait a minute. What'da you mean, you left Georgia? Where's your car?"

I open the peanut butter jar, peer inside, frown slightly, and begin scraping the inside (loudly) until I collect some peanut butter on the spoon. Grimacing, I pop the gooey stuff in my mouth, follow with a few crumbs of ramen, and chew. Now comes the important part: Gag a couple of times and try to force it down, then help it along with a large slug of water. If I can manage a couple of tears, it's a bonus.

Phase One completed, I continue, "No car. I'm on foot." More loud scraping of the spoon as I enter Phase Two.

Really interested now, the man asks, "Where's this trail you say you're walking on?" I detect a note of skepticism. More peanut butter, more ramen, chew, gag, gag again, tears, wash it down. I point to a 2x6 inch white blaze on a tree at the edge of the clearing, while sneaking a quick glance at the sympathetic look that starts to build in the woman's eyes.

"We're sitting right on the Appalachian Trail." Pointing, I brag, "Maine is at the far end of this path, and that's where I'm going." I commence the third bout of scraping, mumbling, "Nasty stuff," and I toss in a small shudder for emphasis. "Food gets a little scarce out here."

I have *never* had to scrape the jar over three times. And it is always the lady—the mother instinct? "Would you like a sandwich? We have plenty."

"Gosh Ma'am, I don't want to impose." Then giving a big, grateful grin, I gush, "But sure! If you have plenty . . ."

Once the ice is broken, they will feed me until the last morsel has disappeared. But it is a *quid pro quo*, something for something, for all the time I'm cramming in their food, I'm telling the awed couple about my experiences on the Appalachian Trail. We both go our ways happy—they (foodless) with a new experience, and me with my belly pushing against my brain.

A wonderful thing, the fine art of yogi-ing!

*   *   *

On my third thru-hike in 1998, I reached Pine Grove Furnace State Park (Pennsylvania) early on the morning of July the Fourth. Delighted at my timing, my head swam with visions of picnic tables groaning under loads of food— despite a total bust in 1990 when I passed into the Park on another Fourth of July. ("Walkin . . ." pp. 357-361) I congratulated myself on my timing and the wonderful yogi-ing within my grasp, just waiting for some expert finesse. Then lengthening my stride in response to my stomach's insistent growling, I rushed toward my date with destiny.

Bummer! Empty picnic tables everywhere. Not a solitary person anywhere down the long stretch of trail as far as I could see. It was early, but the soft rosy glow of sun hanging a good foot above the mountain-humped horizon promised a perfect day. Baffled, my hopes deflated, I shuffled through the thin layer of dust that halfheartedly spread around my boots and as quickly settled back in the still air.

Hallelujah! At the far end of the Park, right by trailside, a rather large group, at least fifteen people, sat at two picnic tables that had been pulled together. Elbows bent back and forth as they went about the serious business of *eating*! Shades of déjà vu! The exact two tables where in desperation I had "scored" a cold greasy chicken "gizzert" and a "soder" from "Little Pot Belly" in 1990! (*Walkin'* . . . pp. 357-361)

You've got one shot at this. Don't blow it, warned my pesky alter ego, Model-T. I didn't plan to.

Jumpin' grasshoppers! I'd never seen so much food! Fresh fruit, bacon, ham, sausage, eggs, gravy, biscuits, cake, even grits! I went into mental shock and for the life of me couldn't think of an opening gambit. No one paid any attention as I neared the first table. Still struggling for words, I slowed down— and spotted a bowl of fresh apricots!

The delicate golden orange orbs shimmered in the soft sunlight as if King Midas himself had rubbed his fingers across the fruit. Without giving it any conscious thought I growled, "I'm a hungry thru-hiker and you'd better put a guard on those apricots."

A middle-aged lady with her back to me reached into the bowl. She held two apricots over her shoulder without turning around and said, "We're too busy eating to guard anything. Here's your payoff."

I stopped and carefully took the fruit. "My sincerest thanks. Can't remember the last time I had fresh fruit." (Well, it *was* the truth. Salivating like one of Pavlov's canine subjects, at that very moment I couldn't recall the fresh fruit binge I'd engaged in only two days before.)

She said, "Do you see anything else that looks good?" Did my ears deceive me?

I eyed a plate of sausage links. "A couple of those sausages would sure go good with these apricots."

Another lady across the table said, "Scoot over Myrtle and let this man sit down. Can't you see he's hungry?"

They started passing the food, even all the way from the other table. And I started cramming the assortment in as fast as I could swallow and talk, just in case it was all a dream. I wanted to get as much down as I could before I woke up. Of course the questions started. It is a right neat trick to be able to cram and talk at the same time without spewing food all over the place. Two opposing forces working against each other. I've never mastered that one, and when food began to fly out with my trail stories, I managed enough dignity to turn scarlet and mumble an apology without missing a bite.

Seems I had stumbled on the Lawrence Family's Annual Breakfast. Most were from Gettysburg, where a reenactment of the Civil War battle was taking place this very day. The town was jammed with tourists and grim-faced men sauntering around in Union blue and Confederate butternut, and the Lawrence clan decided it was time to get the heck out of Dodge. What luck!

I ate for thirty minutes while questions and stories flowed like good wine. Satiated at last, I went to the far end of the second table where the elders sat, to express my thanks for their generosity. A partially eaten "pinch cake" lay near the elbow of the senior Lawrence. Without thinking, I reached for a small piece that had broken off from the main mass. "This little orphan needs a home," I quipped as I popped it into my mouth.

Mr. Lawrence senior chuckled. "Seems like you might need to eat a mite more before you put that pack back on." A clean paper plate magically appeared, and I ate for another ten minutes.

Unable to hold another bite, I temporarily penned Mr. Lawrence's address on my hand so I could send a card letting the family know when I finished the Trail. My belly felt like a gigantic beanbag as I struggled to stand, and for a moment I thought it was all going to hurl as the pressure built. A couple of ladies walked over and handed me a large paper platter covered with foil. Gingerly, I lifted a corner and sneaked a peek. The platter was piled high with the rest of the fried goodies, along with some fruit and the remainder of the "pinch cake." Myrtle said, "You can do us a favor and take this with you if you can find the room. That way we won't have to haul it home."

Were they kidding? I got out a piece of cord and tied the platter on top of my pack, where it perched precariously like a big silver turtle. Giving my benefactors a grateful smile along with a big "Oooga," I inwardly groaned as I headed toward the Park's exit, wondering how in the world I was going to climb the mountain that reared upward right in my path.

Three hours later, I reached Tagg Run Shelter and ate the whole mess in one glorious blowout. Serendipity! And the fine art of yogi-ing!

Gospel truth!

Chapter Eight

Land of the Noonday Sun

The Nantahala Mountains! Rock-bound giants rooted in the bowels of Mother Earth herself, rising like monstrous waves as they ripple endlessly toward the far horizon. A land so precipitous that the sun only reaches into deep mysterious valleys and gorges for fleeting moments when at its zenith. The keepers of this rugged landscape, the native Cherokee, aptly named it "Nantahala"—"land of the noonday sun." And with the flourish and jiggling of a pen in 1920, much of the vast expanse became the Nantahala National Forest, a wooded gargantuan wonderland of over a half-million acres.

Hernando deSoto led his gold seekers through these mountains in 1539 when he traveled from Nikwasi (present day Franklin, North Carolina—the Cherokee called it "*Nucassee*") to the place we now know as Murphy, also in North Carolina. Two and a half centuries later, William Bartram, America's first native-born naturalist, made his way through the harsh country along Indian trails, hoofing it from Nikwasi to the Nantahala River and beyond on his memorable journey through the southeastern states. (Bartram would later record his adventures in *Travels*, which became a best seller in the United States and abroad.) Several years later, at the request of President Thomas Jefferson he accompanied Lewis and Clark on their history-making exploration of the Louisiana Territory.

One year later, in 1776, Revolutionary War General Griffith Rutherford led his regiment of 2400 Colonials into the "land of the noonday sun." His mission was to subdue the Cherokee, whose anger against the fledgling American nation that had brashly encroached on ancestral lands, had been fanned to violence. When the Indians began to lift a few scalps, the new Congress sent Rutherford to exact payment in kind. He took his assignment seriously and laid waste to thirty-six Cherokee towns, killing men, women, and children with unbridled enthusiasm.

One battle happened at Wayah Gap near where the Appalachian Trail begins its ascent to the summit of Wayah Bald. Here in September of 1776, Colonel Andrew Williamson's band of South Carolinians, which had been helping General Rutherford torch Cherokee villages, was ambushed by a large band of Indians. During the fierce battle, Williamson's forces were badly defeated and barely escaped. Williamson and his men managed to join up with Rutherford's army. The Cherokee were eventually forced to sue for peace, and in the Treaty of Long Island the following year, they ceded all lands east of the Blue Ridge, as well as their holdings along the Watauga, Nolichucky, Upper Holston, and New River.

The Cherokee Nation fought alongside "Old Hickory" at New Orleans, but he never forgave their perfidy for siding with the English during the Revolutionary War. So when he walked into the White House in 1828, Jackson pushed for their removal west of the Mississippi—his own form of "manifest destiny."

"Old Hickory" purged the Indians from the Nantahalas, but he failed to erase their legacy. Today, as one walks along the Trail, the moaning of long-dead warriors can almost be heard in the sighing wind as it stirs the branches overhead. And if one peers closely into the shadowy depths beside the Trail; well, who knows . . .

*   *   *

The Appalachian Trail meanders along the spine of Cherokee history like some kind of massive artery, now and then brushing ganglia that are pregnant with legends founded in misunderstood or unexplainable events that sprang from the mouths of the Ancients. For example:

At 5,498 feet, Standing Indian Mountain is the highest of the Nantahalas. But that's the white man's name. The Cherokee called it *Yun'wi-tsulenun'yi*, "where the man stood." And for good reason. Long ago, a winged monster carried a warrior's child to a cliff on top of the mountain. Helpless against the strong medicine of the monster, the Indians prayed to the Great Spirit to rescue the child. He answered their pleas by sending down a lightning bolt that destroyed the monster—and all the trees on the summit. A bolt also struck a lone Indian sentry there and turned him to stone.

The odd, human-shaped rock has since tumbled off the mountain, leaving only a tattered reminder—perhaps a last merciful release from earthly bondage by the Great Spirit. Or was it? Even today, sightings of a mysterious stranger standing on the summit continue to taint the solitude of the mountain.

Four miles or so north of Bly Gap, the A.T. passes the Chunky Gal Trail, which leads to nearby Chunky Gal Mountain. A rather unusual name for a mountain or a trail. The Cherokee tell of a well-endowed maiden who, lacking her father's approval, eloped with a Wayah brave. The angry father gave chase. Alas, when the couple stopped by a spring to pledge their troth and quaff their thirst, he caught them. No happy ending here, for the father made the daughter go back to the village and sent the young buck scurrying off into the woods.

The other village maidens were jealous of the bounteous gifts Nature had bestowed on the maiden and began to call her "Chunky Gal." And the mountain where the pair was caught? Ever after it became known as Chunky Gal Mountain—a lasting remembrance of failed love.

Long before the Cherokee ambushed Colonel Willianson's band at Wayah Gap, the place was already steeped in legend. *Wayah* is Cherokee for "wolf"— most probably named for the time when wolves freely roamed through the mountains. But the Cherokee also know the place as *A'tahi'ta*, "place where they shouted." It happened thus:

The villagers in nearby Briertown on the Nantahala River suffered greatly from a giant yellow jacket, *U'lagu'*, which swooped down without warning and carried their children and small animals away. Desperate, the people devised a plan: They hid the children and offered instead a deer with a long white string attached. The *U'lagu'* took the bait. However, the added weight made the giant yellow jacket fly slower, making the long string easily visible to the pursuers. When the warriors came to Wayah Gap, they could see *U'lagu's* lair inside a cave on the far side of the valley. They built fires around the cave's entrance, and the smoke killed the giant yellow jacket and all the smaller bees inside.

Unfortunately, not all the yellow jackets were inside the cave at the time. To this day, their descendants plague hikers traveling through the area.

*   *   *

The last shelter before reaching the Nantahala River and the delicious bit of *paradise* that sits athwart the nine-mile stretch of white water heaven, the Nantahala Gorge, is the Rufus Morgan Shelter. A neat shelter named after a remarkable man.

The Reverend A. Rufus Morgan was tailored from the same bolt of fabric as Arthur Woody. He inherited a hardy set of genes. Rufus was born in 1885 in a mountain valley not far from Franklin, North Carolina. From his first babble, he had the music of the mountains in his soul—a hand-me-down from his ancestors. Indeed, Albert Mountain (a nasty bit of business for hikers) was named for his grandfather, Albert Siler; and Siler's Bald in the Great Smoky Mountain National Park got its name from Rufus' great-great-uncle, Jesse Siler. Another Siler's Bald in the Nantahalas was named for his great-grandfather, William Siler. The mountains stirred Rufus' soul at an early age and stole his heart.

Reverend Morgan's ancestors were friends to the Cherokee. In 1838, when Winfield Scott's men cast their net across the land and gathered in the Cherokee for the disgraceful expulsion westward, Chief Chuttahsotee and his wife, Cunstagih, were captured. They managed to escape from the "Trail of Tears" somewhere in Tennessee, made their way back to Great-grandfather William Siler's home in Cartoogeechay Valley, and asked for protection. He bought a tract of land and deeded it to the Indians, for by law Indians owning property outside the Indian Territory were not subject to removal. In 1879, Chief Chuttahsotee was the first person buried in the churchyard at St. John's Church, built on land given by Rufus' grandfather, Albert. A day later, Cunstagih died and was interred by his side.

When he became an Episcopal clergy, "Moses of the Mountains," as Rufus Morgan was known to his flock, ministered to the Cherokee progeny, as well as the whites, in small churches throughout the Nantahalas. But his ministry didn't hinge on words alone. For to this Mountain Moses, deeds counted! Seeing a need, several times he took hammer in hand and worked alongside his brethren to build churches in the back woods where people lacked a place to worship, including the St. Francis of Assisi Church in Cherokee (North Carolina.) And always he championed the causes of the downtrodden and needy.

In the 1950s, Reverend Morgan was honored as the rural pastor of the year for North Carolina. A few years later he was awarded an honorary doctorate from General Theological Seminary, from which he had graduated.

But all this is not where I'm headed.

We hikers owe a debt to Reverend Morgan, a debt that will be hard to repay, if ever. He knew every nook and cranny of *his* mountains and had been tromping over hill and dale for twenty years before the Appalachian Trail became a reality. The beauty and magic of the Trail quickly seduced him. (Sound familiar?) For over 25 years he was the chief maintainer of the Appalachian Trail through the Nantahalas—often the only maintainer for the 55 miles. His tireless labors led to the founding of the Nantahala Hiking Club, which is now responsible for the Trail in this area. And arguably, he could have gone into *The Guinness Book of World Records*! Rufus Morgan made the six-mile trek to the summit of Mt. LeConte, his favorite place on the planet, at least 172 times—the final time to celebrate his ninety-second birthday!

So when you spread your sleeping pad in the shelter only a short mile from the tantalizing food aromas of the Nantahala Outdoor Center, a silent tribute to this man who gave his name to the shelter and so much of his life to the Trail would be in order.

And so it goes in *the land of the noonday sun.*

Chapter Nine

Snowbirds

Geographically speaking, when the Appalachian Trail crosses the Nantahala River it leaves the "land of the noonday sun" behind and enters the Snowbird Mountains. These granite giants wrinkle the earth's crust in dramatic upthrusts until they reach the Little Tennessee River, where *Dotsi*, a water monster, supposedly lurks in the depths of Fontana Lake. (A distant cousin to the Loch Ness monster, "Nessie"?)

The Cherokee call these mountains *Tuti'yi*, "Snowbird Place." The name also refers to Little Snowbird Creek, which empties into the Cheoah River not far from Robbinsville, North Carolina. This area was within the boundaries of the Cherokee Nation; thus, families were subject to removal during the great upheaval. However, many Cherokees managed to purchase tracts of ancestral land from the State of North Carolina and so were able to escape the move west. Today, many Cherokee families still live among the peaks and valleys of the Snowbird Mountains.

The Trail through the Snowbirds, which many refer to as "The Stecoahs," can be a nasty bit of business for hikers. (A case in point: The six-mile climb out of the Nantahala River Gorge to the top of Swim Bald.) At one time this thirty-mile exercise in perseverance and strenuous cussing enjoyed the dubious reputation of being even tougher than Maine. To further burden the psyche, a faded, crude, hand-painted sign on a guardrail where the Trail crosses Sweetwater Road at Stecoah Gap greeted sweat-blurred eyes and told hikers what they suspected all along: *Throo hikers beware—only 1 in 30 make it all the way. The test of staying power is here. The Smokies are vacation land.* "(Note: The painted sign has now been removed from the guardrail. A little piece of Trail history dissolved in paint remover. A shame!)

Thankfully, the Smoky Mountains Hiking Club decided to tame the Stecoahs in the late 1980s. Gentle switchbacks have replaced most of the knee-destroying straight ups and downs that once *tested the staying power*, and cuss words can now be saved for more serious matters.

*   *   *

Late in the afternoon on April 15, 1994, I climbed over the guardrail at Stecoah Gap, hardly giving the "Throo Hikers Beware" warning a second glance. The sky commanded my attention. Black, undulating, clouds fat with terror-portending, shrieking winds overwhelmed the heavens and threatened to send down a tornado and carry me to God only knows where. Jim, a fellow hiker I'd been leapfrogging with the past few days, was somewhere back down the Trail, hopefully not too far, for I wanted company this night. Tornado *warnings* were posted for the area.

Jim was having a rough time with the Trail. His endurance suffered from excessive pampering of his derriere and too many corn dogs. Jim was at least fifteen years my junior, but soft muscles and a budding paunch dragged him down. Simply put, Jim just couldn't match my pace. I kept pulling him along with encouragement; had even given him his trail name—"Little Engine That Could." I mentally gave Jim a fifty percent chance (or less) of getting to Maine.

I was tempted to pitch my tent beside the concrete table in the small pull-over at road's edge. Ordinarily, tenting where a mugger would have easy pickin's would be a "no-no," but a person would have to be bonkers (or desperate) to be driving this night. I let my tired brain massage the thought for about five seconds and decided to move on. Murphy's Law—if something could happen to throw a monkey wrench in the works, it probably would. *Waterless* Sweetwater Gap (*Walkin'. . .* pp 107-113) was only a mile on—thirty minutes or so, less if I put my legs into the task. Far enough away that would-be robbers wouldn't bother. I needed water, but another look skyward convinced me to forego the half-mile round trip to the spring that had poured forth wonderfully cold water on my previous thru-hike. Anyway, not to worry. Momma Nature was going to drop bucketsful of the stuff shortly.

By the time I reached Sweetwater Gap, the wind had eased a little and I decided to push on to Brown Fork Gap, where, according to the *Appalachian Trail Data Book,* there *was* water. Dusk had come early, but I could be there in another forty-five minutes and maybe get my tent up before the storm hit. I scribbled a quick note to Little Engine, letting him know where I was headed, and left it weighted down by a rock in the middle of the Trail.

Rushing through the heavy dusk, I almost missed the small hand-scrawled sign "Shelter," reinforced by a wobbly arrow pointing to the right down a faint blue-blazed path. *Shelter?* The *Data Book* didn't say anything about a shelter at Brown Fork Gap. The sky lit up in a fiery display as thunder rattled the earth and the sound of a freight train under a full head of steam rode the boiling sky. Fighting off rising panic, I took off down the path.

There was a shelter all right! To my astonishment, out in front a fire blazed chest high. Flames, gyrating wildly as they struggled to flee before the gusting wind, cast enough light into the shelter's dim interior to reveal two humps on the floor near the right side.

One of the mounds spoke in a low gravelly growl. "You a hiker?"

I thought that was obvious since I had a pack on my back. I moved closer. The mound, which was covered by a blanket of undetermined material, had a head. "Yeah, but I may be tornado meat before this lets up."

Another voice, high pitched, erupted from the dark shadows to my left. I hadn't seen him. "We's hikers, too. Goin' all the way to Maine." The words came quickly, pushed together, like he was trying to convince himself that it was the gospel truth. I caught a glimpse as the flames pushed his way. Two wild-looking eyes set in a round face covered with a black beard—*a Halloween mask of Bluebeard,* I thought. He was wrapped up in a dirty-white blanket that reminded me of pee on snow. *These characters don't look like hikers! Leave or stay?*

Another locomotive cannonballed through the racing clouds, pulling red embers from the fire into its wake until they disappeared as a gigantic flash of lightning split the overhead. The simultaneous convulsion made the decision easy. "I'm comin' in." Bluff my hand a little; let'em glimpse an ace. "My partner will be here in a few minutes." And I hoped he would! Fat raindrops began to splatter the roof as I climbed inside.

"Bluebeard" said, "Don't sleep in the middle. Gotta gap in the middle." His warning wasn't necessary because I'd already felt rain hitting my head. I looked up and sure enough, there was a two-inch gap where two tarps that had been stretched over the roof laths failed to meet. Bummer! No wonder the *Data Book* hadn't mentioned a shelter. It wasn't finished. And the floor was only a few loose boards with wide gaps haphazardly laid over joists. *Any port in a storm . . .*

I spread my Therm-a-Rest as close to "Bluebeard" as I dared, which barely got me out of splatter range, and set about making supper in the weak beam of my small flashlight. "First come; first served," I mumbled, more to ease my guilt than to make conversation. "Little Engine's gonna have to deal with the gap." The others sniggered loudly as if I'd made a joke and then snuggled in for the night as the downpour doused the flames.

A few minutes later, Little Engine pushed through the rain, nearly invisible in his blue rain suit, which was dimly silhouetted in the weak glow of his flashlight. "Any space left?" I barely heard the words above the howling wind and the rain drumming on the tarp-roof.

"Saved a place for you right on center stage." I massaged a mouthful of mac-n-cheese. "That's part of the good news. The other is, you've got your own personal shower," and shone my light upward to prove that I spoke with "straight tongue." Water swirled down through the narrow gap just like someone had turned on a shower.

Little Engine must have been too tired to cuss. He shrugged, resigned to a miserable night, and started supper. When he asked about our shelter-mates, I bent close to his ear. "The one on the other side of me is a maniac. The two on your side are only lunatics. How're you gonna keep dry?"

"Not a problem. I'll put my ground sheet on top of my sleeping bag." Sounded like a plan to me.

I finished eating and crawled into my sleeping bag. Little Engine quickly followed. And then the evening began to unravel. When he pulled the piece of plastic sheet over his bag, the water began to detour from its planned route to a gap between the planks. Instead, the drops hit the plastic . . . plunk . . . plunk . . . splattering my face. I tolerated it for a minute or so. Dang it all!

Annoyed, I flopped over to face "Bluebeard," who was snoring like a thirty-six inch chain saw chewing into a giant sequoia. Before long, I felt a wet spot along my thigh. And grabbed the flashlight. Fat silvery rivulets oozed down the plastic and made a puddle against the man-made cocoon I called a sleeping bag. "Dammit, Little Engine, I'm gettin' wet. This sucks."

"You know, Model-T, I'm a roofing contractor." (I didn't know. We'd never talked much about the *real world*.) "If you'll give me a hand, I think I can fix this."

He dug an 8x10 nylon tarp out of his pack. Tediously, we worked it between the polyvinyl roof-tarps and the supporting laths, slowly closing the gap. We finished the job by letting the end of the tarp drape down the outside of the back wall, which allowed the water to drain outside the shelter. Blessed dryness! Back to the sleeping bag.

I had just drifted off when the tragedy struck. The Engineer's project gave way with a loud swoosh and dumped a bathtub full of cold water down on Little Engine and myself. (An after-tragedy investigation by the Engineer concluded that water must have formed a small pocket in our jury-rigged "fix," and that the puddle quickly grew into a large pond.)

Talk about a rude awakening! Pissed—hell, call it for what it was, "fightin' mad"—I crawled out, seeking to vent my rage on the nearest victim. Like a crazed man, I shook the dripping sleeping bag right over "Bluebeard's" head. It didn't faze him.

I faced Little Engine with poison in my spittle-packed words. "Dammit all to hell! Did you say you *are* or *were* a roofing contractor? Now what're we gonna do?"

He ignored my outburst. "Do it again, only better this time."

So we did the job over. To Little Engine's credit, he went out into the rain and got several large rocks, which he put on the roof to keep the tarp taut so that it couldn't form pockets. I dozed fitfully the rest of the night, braced for another drenching. But it never came and the storm finally passed on, which exposed me to the full brunt of "Bluebeard's" raucous snoring and made me wish for another storm.

Our companions awoke while we were cooking breakfast. Even in the bleak gray of the morning's overcast, they looked well rested. Names went around. "Bluebeard" said with a touch of pride that his name was "Hurricane," while "gravelly voice" turned out to be Freight Train. Both wore frayed jeans. On the other hand, the other man wore a poly-pro sweatshirt and nylon shorts—thru-hiker apparel. He called himself Chicopee, after his hometown in Massachusetts, and he had no aspirations to climb Katahdin. "Just walkin' home," he said.

Chicopee's face looked as if it had argued with a pound of TNT—which in a way it had. He had worked in a tire shop. The previous year a truck tire had exploded while he was filling it with air and had ripped the top of his skull off. One eye was permanently froze several degrees off center, which made me wonder if he saw two of everything. He had come to the Trail to get his life back together.

The hikers, all in their early to mid-thirties, seemed nice enough. Their stories came out in bits and pieces while we packed. Chicopee and Hurricane were from the same town. Hurricane was on the short side and slightly frail and worked as a house painter. When he heard that his friend, Chicopee, planned to hike the Appalachian Trail, Hurricane decided he, too, needed an escape, mainly from his overbearing, dominating wife who had the build of a Marine Corps drill sergeant and ran their one-sided marriage like a boot camp. When Hurricane mentioned going off for six months, she boxed his ears, raised the roof with a few well chosen swear words, and stormed off to work. Undaunted, Hurricane called Chicopee and said, "Okay. How we goin' to get down to Georgia?"

Chicopee was two steps ahead. "My son has a friend in Florida he wants to visit. He can drive us if we can go in your car." (Neither Chicopee nor his 18 year-old son had a car.)

So Hurricane took the grocery money from the cookie jar and replaced it with a note to his wife, in which he told her the sad news—that someone had stolen their car and he and Chicopee were headed south, hot on the trail of the scoundrel. Hurricane promised to call her soon with a progress report. So off they went, and here they were.

Freight Train got his name because he had hopped freight trains and rode from Texas to Georgia. Somehow he got paired up with Hurricane and Chicopee before they got on the Trail and thought that it would be a great adventure. Freight Train bragged that everything he had was either stolen, had been given to him, or had been scrounged out of dumpsters.

Our ears were ringing from three life histories, so Little Engine and I took off, determined to put some *big* miles between them and us by nighttime!

The rest of the story: I met Freight Train again in the Smokies. He had made a giant leap up the Trail (by car). Chicopee, honest to his hike, had disassociated himself from his companions and was somewhere back down the Trail, as was Little Engine. Hurricane had gone back to Massachusetts to face the wrath of his wife. It seems the car had broken down after Chicopee's son had dropped him and Hurricane off, and it now sat in some south Georgia farmer's front yard. When Hurricane finally did call his wife, the "drill sergeant" told him to "get yer good-fer-nothin' ass home." He confessed, "Got no money." So she sent him enough to buy a bus ticket home.

Instead, Freight Train talked him into going to Bryson City (North Carolina) to celebrate his new windfall. The money was quickly gone, so poor Hurricane again had to make a call. This time, his wife sent him a bus ticket and he scurried home, tail between his legs, a beaten man who had chewed through his leash for one shining moment.

When Freight Train told me all this, we were taking a break in the Great Smoky Mountain National Park on Rocky Top, a high peak with grand views back to the south. Half in jest, I said, "You know that right now you are sitting in North Carolina and I'm sitting in Tennessee?"

He jumped up and hopped over to my state. "Damn, Model-T, I'm wanted for child support in North Carolina!" Then as quickly he scooted back over. "Damn, come to think of it, I'm also wanted for child support in Tennessee." He was serious.

I told him, "I'd really like to take your picture for my scrapbook, but are you wanted on *Unsolved Mysteries* or *America's Most Wanted*? I don't want to get hit in the head tonight while I'm sleeping."

He grinned. "Naw, you're okay, Model-T. I wouldn't do anything like that." But he never gave me a direct answer. And soon Freight Train faded into the wind—another statistic added to "those who couldn't" . . .

Little Engine surprised me. One sunny day in Virginia he passed me, and I ate his dust the rest of the way to Mount Katahdin.

Chapter Ten

Drillzibblers, Woggletobblers, and Slumgullionholes

Little did I know when I followed the white blazes across the intimidating heights of Fontana Dam that I was walking across the highest dam east of the Rockies. I say "intimidating," because I felt like an ant on a high wire. To my left, at a dizzying depth far below the floodgates that captured the dark frigid waters of Fontana Lake, employee vehicles shimmered in the bright midday sun. From my birds-eye perspective, they resembled Matchbox cars. Not surprising, since the parking lot lay nearly 480 feet below, near the dam's base where water churned and fought to escape the clutches of mighty turbines and flee on down the Little Tennessee River.

Vehicles at the dam's base looked like Matchbox toys,
and I felt like an ant on a high wire.

Strange, but an army of workers had shut down the roadway that went across the dam's top, barely leaving enough room for a hiker to get through. Think that's weird? They were drilling into the massive hunk of concrete, pushing twelve-inch holes down into the dam's interior.

The scene was like something out of a Dr. Seuss book. Strange gobbledygook words forced their way into my mind as I walked among the scurrying workers, and wham! I was seeing *drillzibblers* using *woggletobblers* to drill *slumgullionholes* to gosh knows where. Drilling holes into the dam—it just didn't make any sense!

The noise pounded into my head and corrupted my hearing, and soon a splitting headache warped the space between my ears. Worse, I had only gotten maybe a third of the way across the nearly half-mile length. No way to escape the bedlam—unless I wanted to jump or swim. I kept on walking.

A white pickup with a TVA logo pulled up alongside and stopped. A deeply tanned man wearing a dirty off-white hard hat climbed out. He looked like a supervisor. Perfect timing, for curiosity was roasting my cerebellum. I yelled into his ear, "Whatcha doin'? Drilling for water?"

He looked at me like I was the crazy one. Heck! I wasn't drilling holes in a perfectly good dam. "You mean that?" he shouted back, pointing at one of the *drillzibblers.* I nodded. He motioned for me to follow him, and we walked over to the side closest to the water where the noise was less. He chuckled. "Naw, we have plenty of water. Actually, the dam is shifting *upstream* a few inches each year. We're drilling holes down into the bedrock and anchoring steel cables in concrete to stabilize the dam."

Did he say *upstream*? Now *that* was crazier than *woggletobblers* and *slumgullionholes*. My face must have been a study in skepticism. He grinned and added, "The dam is so high that the force of the water is shifting the base and causing the top to move upstream."

"If you say so," I said and walked on.

*   *   *

About the dam:

It began as an idea that the Aluminum Company of America (ALCOA) had in the early 1920s to provide cheap electricity for making aluminum. The company completed the land survey in 1923, but rigorous government regulations caused ALCOA to shy away. The project lay dormant until Mitsubishi-made Zeros made a shambles of the United States Navy's Pacific

Fleet at Pearl Harbor in December 1941. Suddenly, the demand for aluminum spiraled and project plans were pulled from musty vaults and dusted off. The deal was, TVA would build the dam and ALCOA would operate it. Actual construction began in January 1942.

TVA pushed into the small hamlet of Fontana Village, carted away the nearby hills, and expanded the area until 5-7000 workers could be tented—although eventually small cottages ($5/month) were erected for supervisors and favored workers with families. Large wooden dormitories finally began to replace drafty humid tents, and common laborers could sleep in the dorms and eat for $2/week. Three shifts ran seven days a week, and every man or woman worked his or her shift—no excuses, no holidays—unless someone volunteered to fill in. Most did additional time at odd jobs in the Village.

Wages were good: Supervisors got a whopping $1.37/hour, while most laborers made 45 cents/hour—unless they volunteered for extra-hazardous work, like shooting concrete inside tunnels. Then they got another 25cents/hour. Do the math. Figuring a 60-hour week, most workers made about $25.00, less $2/week for room and board. Like I said, "Not bad money."

According to Joe Lee Patterson, one of the workers, about twenty-eight people were killed while working on the dam. One poor soul almost became a permanent addition to the dam's 2.8 million cubic yards of concrete. The man was part of a work gang that was putting the finishing touches on a large form. When the form was ready to receive concrete, the foreman sounded the signal for everyone to get out. For some reason, this fellow didn't hear the warning. Five yards of concrete filled the form, and then a large vibrator shook the form and settled the concrete so that no voids would be left. When the form was stripped away, there the man was, standing at attention against one wall with a hoe in his hand. The workers just slipped him out. The body left a perfect human facsimile in the hardened concrete.

In another instance, worker Bob Vickers barely cheated death, as did many others in the madcap rush to complete the project. Bob had signed on to pour concrete inside a tunnel—one of the more hazardous jobs, which earned him the extra twenty-five cents/hour. The concrete was being pumped 135 feet underground into a form where Bob manipulated a large hose to spread the mix evenly. He called the operator at the surface to hold the concrete, but somehow amid the racket the operator didn't get the word. By the time the valve was closed, concrete was up to Bob's nose and he was swearing (and praying) mightily. Some others pulled him out with a rope. Bob never went back into a tunnel again.

Claude Kelly, a supervisor, bragged that he poured the first bucket of concrete when construction started and the last bucket at the end, which completed the steps that go up to the spillway overlook. To finish off the job, Claude placed commemorative coins in the wet concrete. The coins have long since disappeared, but supposedly the impressions remain.

The drilling is finished. While on a weeklong hike in April 2003, I crossed over Fontana Dam as the day's heat gave way to a soft dusk. The *drillzibblers* are now gone, along with their monstrous, concrete-chewing *woggletobblers*. The *slumgullionholes* are now neatly capped with two-foot circular concrete band-aids—46 on the south end and 28 slightly smaller caps on the dam's north end.

I wondered if they ever struck water!

I went looking for Claude Kelly's legacy—the coin impressions. Alas, even that nostalgic milestone eluded me, possibly erased by the relentless assault of time and tourist shoes. After a fruitless half-hour, disappointed, I gave up the search.

Peering down into the empty spillways—slumbering behemoths just waiting for the next flood—I breathed a silent "thanks" to Claude and his co-workers who created this concrete marvel. A lung full of the moist, cooling air, a soft contented "ahh," and I continued on to the "Fontana Hilton"—a showplace shelter at the edge of Fontana Lake—to make my nest for the night.

And I didn't get a glimpse of *Dotsi*, the Cherokee water monster. Because of the *woggletobbler* ruckus, he had probably retreated long ago to the far reaches of the lake. I couldn't blame him!

Chapter Eleven

A Matter of Altitude, Aptitude, and Attitude

At 6,643 feet, Clingmans Dome enjoys the exalted honor of being the highest point on the Appalachian Trail, a mere 41 feet lower than Mt. Mitchell, which reigns supreme east of the Mississippi River. Tourists flock to this alpine aerie, braving the half-mile trek uphill on a paved walkway. At the end of the walkway is an observation tower, which brings to mind a diminutive, futuristic Tower of Babel. From the top of the 54-foot tower, in a sweeping 360-degree panorama, eyes can gaze across 100 miles of rippling mountains into seven states—if the air is clear. On most days, the persistent smoky haze limits views to a mere 22 miles or less.

The Appalachian Trail sneaks past the base of the tower a few yards distant, like a mountain recluse. But the word is out : *The Appalchian Trail! Right down this little path! Gotta get a picture made. The folks back home are never gonna believe this. We've been on the Appalachian Trail!* And if they are lucky, a couple of hikers may stop by for a break. *Wow! Real hikers! Do you mind if we take our picture with you? Cripes! The folks back home are gonna be sooo jealous . . .*

But Clingmans Dome is much more than a grandiose photo op. In 1838, when General Winfield Scott's soldiers began to round up the Cherokees from the western North Carolina mountains, many of the natives managed to elude the soldiers. One band, Tsa'li's group, made their way to *Kuwa'hi*, "The Mulberry Place"—the home of Chief of the Bears, the White Bear—and hid in a cave on the mountain. After all, the Cherokee believed that bears were really humans that had somehow been transformed into bears, and that bears could speak Cherokee, although they seldom did. (Legend has it that a hunter once came upon a mother bear singing to her cub using human words.)

The bears at *Kuwa'hi* had townhouses beneath the great dome of the mountain, where they danced every fall before hibernating for the winter. A perfect place for hiding out. And perhaps the White Bear would befriend the fugitives, even take them to the townhouses beneath the great dome, where they would be safe from "The Removal."

Old Charley Tsa'li was approaching his golden years. He farmed a small plot with his three sons and wife near where the Nantahala River joins the Little Tennessee River. Tsa'li's people were part of the Quallatown Cherokees, a band of about 1000, who lived outside the limits of the Cherokee Nation, as defined in an 1819 treaty. These Cherokees thought they were exempt from the sad upheaval of their brothers further to the east. And truth be known, Old Charley hadn't paid much attention to all the goings on with those Cherokees—being much more concerned if the rains would come before he could harvest the corn crop.

One day in late October 1838, Second Lieutenant Andrew Jackson Smith rode up with three other soldiers and ordered Tsa'li and his family to remove themselves from the property and march to a stockade at nearby Bushnell (one of twenty-five such facilities built to imprison Cherokees in preparation for the displacement to Oklahoma Territory). Tsa'li was confused, to say the least. However, hoping to avoid bloodshed, he and his family went along peacefully.

As the story goes, one of the soldiers prodded Tsa'li's wife with a bayonet because she wasn't walking fast enough. This angered Tsa'li. He spoke in Cherokee to the others, telling them that when he pretended to fall down, they should try to escape. During the melee, one soldier's gun accidentally discharged, fatally ripping a hole in his head. Tsa'li and the others ran into a dense thicket and made their way to the cave beneath the great dome of "The Mulberry Place."

Lieutenant Smith made his report in person to General Winfield Scott: Two soldiers killed, a third grievously wounded, with Lt. Smith barely escaping with his hide because his horse spooked and ran away. Too, according to Smith, the Cherokee women were a walking arsenal, having hidden numerous knives and tomahawks beneath their dresses, which they passed to Tsa'li and the other warriors when the escape attempt was made.

Highly incensed, General Scott ordered the 4th Infantry Regiment, commanded by Colonel William Foster and consisting of ten rifle companies from Knoxville, Tennessee, to hunt down the savages—all twelve—and shoot the murderers.

Much to his credit, Colonel Foster realized how futile it would be to pit his ten rifle companies against twelve "savages" hidden away in the mountainous terrain—the proverbial "needle in a haystack." He enlisted the aid of Chief Drowning Bear and his adopted white son, Will Thomas, along with a band of 60 Quallatown Cherokee, to hunt down Tsa'li's small band of fugitives. He spurred the hunters along with promises of being exempt from "Removal."

Within a month, all of Tsa'li's group had been captured except for the old man himself. Three of the fugitives, including Tsa'li's oldest son, Jake, and brother-in-law, George, were tied to trees and shot. (Mercifully, Tsa'li's youngest son and wife were spared.) Will Thomas convinced Colonel Foster that Tsa'li had played only a minor role in the fracas, so the Colonel declared the incident closed.

The rumors of "Removal" continued to flourish. Alarmed and hoping to further distance themselves from the upheaval, the Quallatown Cherokees captured Tsa'li and let him have a last meal and a prayer with his white neighbor, Abraham Wiggins. Then they led Tsa'li out to a tree and executed the old man.

The following year, 1839, the Commission for the Removal officially declared that the Quallatown Cherokee could remain. Case closed.

Almost. Where "truth" ended, "legend" stepped in. After Tsa'li's death, word quickly spread that he had given his life so that his people might remain in their ancestral lands. However, until the end of the century the Government made repeated attempts to force the Quallatown Cherokee to emigrate westward. But the legend of Tsa'li's sacrifice grew stronger in the face of government opposition and inspired the Cherokees to stiffen their resolve not to be moved. At last the Government acquiesced.

Today, over 10,000 Cherokees roam the mountains of their ancestors. I like to think that Tsa'li's life was not given in vain. His grave lies somewhere beneath the waters of Fontana Lake, guarded forever by *Dotsi*, the Cherokee water monster.

I wonder if the bears still dance in their townhouses beneath the great dome, *Kuwa'hi*, which the white settlers called Smoky Dome, and which would eventually be named Clingmans Dome. During the long fall evenings as the bears prepare for their long winter naps, does the White Bear lament the tragedy of his human Cherokee brothers? And is the cave where Tsa'li and his small band of fugitives hid secretly visited by the White Bear or by Tsa'li's descendents.

And I wonder if mulberries really did grow on *Kuwa'hi*.

*   *   *

Enter Thomas Lanier Clingman: U.S. Congressman, U.S. senator until the Civil War began, Brigadier General for the CSA, twice wounded—the second time severely—duelist, prospector, inventor, scientist, entrepreneur, rich man, and eventually a pauper. A most unusual American.

The man also had an attitude problem. According to Dr. F.A. Sondley, in his *History of Buncombe County,* Clingman was " . . . of most arrogant and aggressive character, greatest self-confidence, unlimited assurance, prodigious conceit, stupendous aspiration, immense claims, more than common ability, no considerable attainments to culture, great boastfulness, and much curiosity." Such was the nature of Thomas Lanier Clingman.

A native North Carolinian, he was graduated from the University of North Carolina at the head of his class. At the tender age of 23, Clingman was chosen to represent his district in the state legislature. He found his niche in politics and went on to serve five consecutive terms in the U.S. House of Representatives. Subsequently, he became a U.S. senator, only to succumb to his southern convictions when North Carolina seceded from the Union. He resigned from the Senate and took up "The Cause."

Even while Clingman rattled the Dome of our great Capitol during the 1850s, extolling his political maxims in his stentorian voice, he had his eye fixed on the vast riches that abounded in the western mountains of his native state. Never lacking in self-confidence, he put his immense energy to work, opening up mica and gem mines, among other endeavors, and he amassed a great fortune. Then one day he cast his eyes upon the massive dome that seemed to dominate the mountains. Clingman proclaimed to the world that "Smoky Dome"—the name given the mountain by local inhabitants— was the tallest of the tall.

"Not so," declared Dr. Elisha Mitchell, a renowned professor of science at Clingman's alma mater. As early as 1835, he had braved the forbidding heights of the Black Mountains, taken their measure with his trusty barometer, and debunked the common belief that New Hampshire's Mount Washington was the highest mountain in the East. Said Dr. Mitchell, "Black Dome is the 'tallest of the tall.'" Hence, a storm of controversy broke out between the soft-spoken scientist and the tub-thumping politician.

In 1857, Dr. Mitchell went back to Black Dome to verify his measurements, but en route he fell to his death in a pool bordering a cascade (now known as Mitchell's Falls). But the question remained unresolved and festered like a nasty sore on Clingman's psyche.

The following year, 1858, Clingman mounted a "scientific" expedition, headed by a well-known natural scientist, Samuel Buckley, to Smoky Dome. Buckley made a few barometric measurements of questionable accuracy, but he got caught up in the awesome beauty and began assigning geographical names to the mountains. With little regard to modesty, he changed Smoky Dome to Mount Buckley, although he did name the second highest after the world famous mountain geographer, Professor Arnold Henry Guyot. The third highest peak he named after his friend, Georgia-born physician-turned-geologist/zoologist, Joseph Le Conte. But the controversy over the East's highest mountain refused to go away, and Clingman was greatly vexed.

Came the eminent Professor Guyot himself to the Smokies in 1859. The perfect solution to Clingman's dilemma! The Swiss-born scientist had been tromping through the northern Appalachians for the past eleven years, measuring the topography and naming mountains. His reputation was impeccable. Clingman engaged Guyot to measure both peaks, and he hired a local guide, Robert Collins, to help.

So in the summer of 1859, accompanied by Clingman and barely able to understand the Professor's fractured English, Collins cut a six-mile path to the top of Smoky Dome. Guyot carried his delicate instruments to the summit on the back of a horse lent for the occasion by Colonel Robert G.A. Love.

When the results had been tallied, Dr. Mitchell won the great debate by a mere 41 feet! Black Dome measured a lofty 6,684 feet—the "King" of eastern mountains; while Smoky Dome rose to 6,643 feet—the highest place in Tennessee. In a magnanimous (and uncharacteristic) gesture, Senator Clingman agreed with Professor Guyot that Black Dome should be renamed Mount Mitchell. Guyot then brushed aside Buckley's claim to fame and gave Clingman his due. He pacified Buckley by letting the Mount Guyot and Le Conte names remain. As a further dangling carrot, he assigned the name Mount Buckley to a knob on the west side of Clingmans Dome. Colonel Love also received a reward for the use of his horse—the next peak to the north became Mount Love. The naming of Mount Collins immortalized even the path cutter, Robert Collins.

After settling the dispute, Professor Guyot returned to his teaching duties at Princeton. He worked with Dr. Joseph Henry, Secretary of the Smithsonian Institute, to set up a meteorological reporting system, which in 1870 developed into the United States Weather Bureau. And he continued to walk the mountains, measuring elevations with his trusted barometer and throwing in a few place names where needed, as long as his legs would take him there. He died at Princeton in 1883.

Samuel B. Buckley followed his star south and west, collecting flora and discovering several new species of plants. His star settled on Texas, and he eventually became the State Geologist. He died at Austin, Texas, in 1884.

And what of Professor Joseph Le Conte, for whom the third highest peak in the Smokies is named? A fluke of friendship, most probably. He had rubbed elbows with both Buckley and Guyot at Princeton University when he took up studies in geology and zoology. Le Conte had very little to do with the Smokies, although he did occasionally hike in the adjacent Black Mountains of North Carolina. His real interests lay in the lofty mountains of the far west. He joined the University of California staff in 1869, where he became a professor so loved by his students that they commemorated his seventieth birthday by decorating his lecture table with an assortment of valuable gifts—a practice that continued until his life's end. Professor Le Conte died in 1901 while on a hiking trip with the Sierra Club in the Yosemite Mountains.

After the Civil War, Clingman's fortune declined as rapidly as it had risen. He embarked on a variety of entrepreneur adventures. His "Clingman's Tobacco Remedies," prescribed for almost anything that ailed the human body, failed just as dismally as his other moneymaking schemes. He died homeless and destitute in Morganton, North Carolina, in 1897.

*   *   *

When young Granville Calhoun first laid eyes on the stranger who lounged on the platform at the small depot at Bushnell, North Carolina, down in the valley of the Little Tennessee River, he thought he had a soon-to-be dead man on his hands. Indeed, Horace Souers Kephart was more dead than alive. His body suffered from prolonged alcohol abuse and tuberculosis, and his mind was assailed by guilt. Granville silently cursed the miner who had asked him to meet Kephart and take him "around" for the next few weeks. He eyed the two mules that would take them the sixteen miles along rough mountain roads to his home far up Hazel Creek on Sugar Fork.

Granville asked, "Can you ride a mule?" Kephart answered, "I'll try anything in the way of horseflesh." Kephart struggled into the saddle and barely managed to keep his seat. They proceeded at a snail's pace, with Granville cajoling, pleading, even threatening Kephart to go faster, while the sick man wobbled atop the sturdy beast like a broken gyroscope. Nothing worked. Desperate, he tied the reins of Kephart's mule to the saddle, grabbed a hickory stick, and with a lot of thrashing and tail twisting, motivated the mule from behind.

It was well after dark when they arrived at the Calhoun cabin. Kephart was in a semi-coma, and Granville had to carry him into the house. He plied his charge with wild strawberry wine and put him to bed. Over the next three weeks, Granville spoon-fed Kephart—first milk, then bread and butter, and finally trout from Sugar Fork, but no more strawberry wine. Kephart slowly recovered from his alcohol withdrawal tremors and mental anguish, and rose from the bed to become a living legend. Thus was Horace Kephart's introduction to the Great Smoky Mountains.

Kephart's all-or-nothing toss of the dice to save himself began a few weeks earlier. Librarian for the St. Louis Mercantile Library, a prestigious position at the oldest library west of the Mississippi, Horace Kephart was also a family man with two sons and four daughters and a writer of some acclaim. But Kephart despised his life.

In fact, he was mentally bankrupt. He detested the confinement of the city and couldn't stand the responsibility of raising a family. His passion for the great outdoors, significantly denied because of his job and family duties, became a cancer eating at his spirit, and he looked to John Barleycorn for relief. On infrequent occasions when he managed to escape to the nearby Ozarks for a solitary camping trip, the experience was always marred by his wife's bitterness. In his words, "She despised me to go on camping trips or to go shooting. She gave me hail-come for not wanting to go to hen clubs." (Now where have I heard that before!)

Then came the toss of the dice. He was caught on a downtown street in the tragic 1904 St. Louis hurricane. As he clung for his life to a lamppost and watched wind-blown bodies crash into storefronts, something snapped. And when the storm passed, Kephart walked away from his job, his family, and himself. As he later wrote, "Knowing nobody who had ever been there, I took a topographic map (of the Great Smoky Mountains) and picked on it, by means of the contour lines and the blank spaces showing no settlement, what seemed to be the wildest part of this region; and there I went."

Horace Sours Kephart eventually settled in near the small town of Sylva, where the mining man who was the recipient of young Granville's silent curses, lived. He came to the Smokies to lose himself in the wilderness. Instead, he found himself in the quiet hollows and wind-blown crags where he roamed.

Over the years, in spite of dark moods and infrequent drinking bouts when grim ghosts of his past rose from mental graves to haunt him, Kephart built a new life and earned the respect of the people who inhabited the mountains that he so loved. He wrote about the mountain people in *Our*

Southern Highlands, which became a best seller. And his book, *Camping and Woodcraft*, became the "bible" for outdoor adventure. But his greatest legacy to the American people unfolded in his unrelenting efforts to save the area from the loggers and to bring the mountains under a protective umbrella by establishing a great national park.

Horace Kephart also had a hand in naming one of the Park's landmarks. In 1929 Kephart, along with local guide Charlie Conner, photographer George Masa, and three others, hiked along a mountain crest to survey the damage done to the slopes and the Oconaluftee River by a monster cloudburst. The party came to a lovely rock outcrop that had been stripped of its foliage by a forest fire some four years earlier. The view was spectacular, and they decided to sit a spell. Charlie grumbled about his foot hurting and took off his boot, whereupon Kephart grinned and remarked, "I'm going to get this put on a Government map for you." And Charlie's Bunion came to be.

Horace Kephart never saw his dream for a national park become reality. In 1931, he was killed in an automobile accident near Bryson City, North Carolina, as he and a visiting writer were returning from a foraging expedition to his bootlegger. His friends laid him to rest in a hilltop cemetery overlooking Bryson City and placed a rock boulder to serve as his gravestone.

But Kephart did live to take his rightful place among the great men of his time. In 1929, the United States Geographic Board, at the urging of Kephart's many admirers and to recognize his unique contribution to the Smokies, gave his name to a mighty mountain with a splendid peak—a most unusual occurrence. (Seldom are geographical features named after a living person.)

But then it is only right that mighty mountains be named for great people. And so it is in the Smokies—by accident or design.

*   *   *

The "birth" of the Great Smoky Mountains National Park (GSMNP) did not come easy. The first stirrings of the embryonic idea went back to the late 1800s. Topping the list of "movers and shakers" who planted the seeds were Horace Kephart; Gifford Pinchot (adviser to President Theodore Roosevelt); Chief Forester of the United States Dr. Chase Ambler, who organized the Appalachian National Park Association in 1899; Senator Jeter Pritchard of North Carolina; and Representative W.P. Brownlow of Tennessee, who caused a stingy Congress to put up the first big dollars and get the financial ball rolling.

But the birthing was long and painful. Defiant, insolent loggers, able to rape the mountains with little regard to existing puny regulations, amassed huge profits and threw up an impenetrable wall that blocked efforts to bring the vast forests under any kind of control. The mountain folk had little inclination to sacrifice ancestral homes and family ties so that the "Gov'mint" could move in. Many politicians were leery of angering the self-serving lobbyists who kept them in office.

Then things began to happen. The pendulum swung mightily to the right and a great hunger swept across the nation for creation of additional national parks across the country. In 1916, Congress bowed to public pressure and created the National Park Service, and brought in Stephen Mather, whom the year before had been appointed as the Assistant to the Secretary of the Interior in charge of national parks, to be the Director. Mather siphoned off a brilliant young lawyer, Horace Albright, who dealt with legal matters pertaining to the parks for the Department of the Interior, to be his assistant. Mather and Albright, both fearless and aggressive leaders, laid a solid foundation for the NPS.

In 1930, when Albright took up the reins of the National Park Service, fortune smiled again. In the course of looking for a suitable place for a national park in the Tennessee/North Carolina Mountains, he visited the Smokies. After that, the outcome was set in stone. Said Albright as he shunted aside political and public pressure to locate a national park elsewhere, "The Great Smokies are destined to join the select company of Yellowstone, Glacier, and the Grand Canyon." He added, "We turn down dozens of appeals for national parks each year, simply because the areas do not measure up to the great scenic standards. But as has been forcefully said by someone, 'National parks are not created by Congress; only God can create a national park.'"

Well, partly so. As always, the bottom line is the almighty dollar. To raise the money needed to acquire the proposed 704,000 acres, schoolchildren gave pennies, nickels, dimes and quarters and raised $1391.72. Together, Tennessee and North Carolina dug into dusty coffers and came up with nearly five million dollars—about half of what was needed. Desperate for a serious money transfusion before land prices became prohibitively high (the word was out!) the Southern Appalachian National Park Committee, formed to administer the nuts and bolts mechanics of putting together the deal, turned to business magnates for help. (The bill establishing the Great Smoky Mountains National Park by Congress and signed by President Coolidge decreed that the Park be acquired by gifts and without cost to the Government.)

As the story goes, a Knoxville delegation sallied forth from their fair town in a flotilla of Lincolns to intercept the auto giant, Henry Ford, at Cumberland Gap. Mr. Ford, known to be an antiquarian, was in the area visiting Lincoln Memorial University. "Would you like to see the real stronghold of yesteryear and meet some authentic yesteryear people?" the delegation asked. "Then come visit the Great Smokies." He accepted the invitation; met some "yesteryear" folks; bought some homespun goodies; and then headed back north of the Mason-Dixon Line. No donation, but he was glad the delegation had come in Lincolns.

Enter Arno B. Cammerer. (Yes, the same Cammerer from which Mount Cammerer takes its name.) Cammerer, on behalf of the NPS, was assigned to assist the Park Committee in determining which lands to purchase first and to set up standards that would be acceptable to the Federal Government. (He would become the federal official most intimately associated with the Park and later become the Director of the National Park Service.)

Cammerer made an urgent appeal to another magnate, a man known for his interest in conservation and beautification of America's resources. Not a problem. Without blinking an eye, John D. Rockefeller, Jr. filled out a check for five million dollars—the amount needed to finish the project—from the trust fund named for his mother, the Laura Spelman Rockefeller Memorial. Now the pieces were in place for the game to begin!

So it came to be, The Great Smoky Mountains National Park. On a warm June day in 1940, 10,000 automobiles carrying a huge throng of 25,000 people drove bumper-to-bumper up to Newfound Gap to hear President Franklin Roosevelt officially open the Park. The Presidential entourage, nearly an hour late, arrived by car from Chattanooga, Tennessee, where the President had just dedicated the Chickamauga Dam. The great benefactor, John D. Rockefeller, was modestly absent, having made his apologies to Secretary of the Interior, Harold Ickes, in a poignant and elegantly worded letter. Ickes spoke for four minutes, the governors of Tennessee and North Carolina briefly addressed the multitude, and the President delivered a diatribe about Nazi Germany and its threat to American security. And so it was done!

It took the 10,000 cars until well after dark to get off the mountain.

*   *   *

The bears were always there. Feral hogs and hikers, both invasive creatures though dissimilar in their impact on the Park, came later.

The hogs, known more popularly as European wild boar, razorback, "Rooshian" (Russian) wild boar, Old World swine—depending on which part of the country you hail from—are seldom seen. But the evidence of their passing is. Nearly everyone who tackles the backcountry of the Smokies comes across long sections of forest floor that have been uprooted, almost as if an army of mechanical trenchers has gone bonkers.

Personally, I have never seen a feral hog, nor do I know anyone who has. But the grunting creatures are there, rooting and rutting—and eating! Acorns, spring beauty corms, May apples, just about any mesic herb in the Park, along with gobs of small vertebrates and invertebrates. Nothing escapes the chomping jowls of these four-legged eating machines. The voracious eating habits of thru-hikers are pretty puny in comparison. But then, it takes a lot of rooting to satisfy the appetite of a critter that can weight upwards to 400 pounds (more than an adult black bear, which usually weighs in at around 300 pounds).

Feral hogs have been gallivanting all over the United States for centuries, back as early as the 1600s. (Just check the commercial "wild boar" hunts all over the U.S. of A. that are advertised on the web!) Settlers en route to a new beginning in the "New World" tucked a few hogs in ships' holds so they could continue to enjoy the delicacies that hid beneath the coarse blackish-gray hide of their Old World porkers. The hogs took to their new homes, often much better than their owners, and proliferated until they became firmly established. And they followed the horse and cattle droppings westward with the pioneers. But the feral hogs (European wild boar as the beasts are called up in the Appalachian highlands) didn't come to the Great Smoky Mountain National Park until the mid-1940s. How, you ask?

In April 1912, the Whitting Manufacturing Company of England introduced thirteen young feral boars onto some company-owned land on Hooper Bald near Murphy, North Carolina, about forty miles south of the Park, with the intention of establishing a hunting preserve. It is believed that the boars came from Russia and were purchased by a company agent in Berlin, Germany. The herd was left undisturbed for eight years to proliferate. (I suspect that at least a smattering were sows since they *did* multiply!) Then around 1920, about one hundred hogs escaped from the preserve and rooted their way into the surrounding mountains, where they "hybridized" freely with Old World feral pigs that had become somewhat domesticated.

When the GSMNP came into being in 1940, Park officials were concerned. The boars' reputation as an invasive threat—an "ecological backlash"—had become widespread. But Arthur Stupka, Park naturalist, reassured the officials. After all, the Little Tennessee River bordered the Park to the south, and no hog could cross that barrier. Yeah, right!

The first hogs appeared near Cades Cove in 1945. They quickly expanded westward at the rate of about 2.5 miles per year (almost as fast as that other non-indigenous invasive pest, the gypsy moth caterpillar). Worse, they reproduced at the phenomenal rate of 12 to 24 piglets per sow per year and lived to the ripe old animal age of up to 27 years. (On the other hand, sow bears usually "bear"—no pun intended—two cubs each year. And while bears go through a prolonged sleep—bears don't hibernate in the true sense—feral hogs forage all winter long.) By 1979, during the prime forage season between April and July, officials estimated hog densities in the hardwood forests of the Park's western half at 79 animals per square kilometer. Something had to be done. The indigenous black bear couldn't exist on the diminished food supply!

Enter the "night stalkers." As early as 1959, a few rangers with a keen eye, steady trigger finger, and the uncanny ability to sniff out the hogs, decided to eliminate the threat. Swinging small subsistence packs onto powerful sweat-stained shoulders and fondly caressing massive guns equipped with night scopes—the critters they sought foraged day and night, but nighttime offered the best hunting—these dedicated men headed into the backcountry to rid the Park of the destructive pests. Shots often fractured the tranquil darkness, echoing across the mountaintops as they mingled with the blood-chilling cries of bobcats and the lingering hoots of the Great Horned Owl.

The rangers did a fine job. Between 1959 and the end of 2001, they "removed" 9,720 hogs from the Park. (Usually the hogs were left where they fell and the bears soon developed a fine taste for pork.)

But in the long run, efforts to forever erase the European wild boar from the Park have dwindled into a maintenance program. The rangers can't get rid of the beasts as fast as they procreate. In the past few years, new contraptions have sprouted up in the dense hardwood forests—trap cages. The "night stalkers" continue to roam the steep high ridges; now and then sporadic shots violate the fragile eventide, evidence of the hunters and the hunted. And goose bumps still tingle the spines of tense hikers who lie in silent shelters, awaiting the next volley. But the feral hogs remain—at least 500 in number—grunting and rooting and wallowing in their dubious glory.

*   *   *

The reader may wonder why I have included so much of the history of the making of our Great Smoky Mountains National Park. Simply put, hikers (including myself) usually breeze through the Park, ooh-ing and aah-ing at the awesome scenery; perhaps cussing at some of the more difficult climbs; and almost always glad to get beyond the restrictive regulations that relegate hikers to shelters instead of the opportunity to tent. (And we always seem to breathe a little easier when we cross beneath Interstate 40, beyond the reach of hungry, uninhibited bears and fierce feral hogs.) Thus, we tend to miss the real significance of what our boots trod on and how it came to be. The GSMNP deserves more.

Granted, what I have included here is greatly oversimplified; and of course, there's much more to the story. Many others played important roles in the Park's genesis and development. Tempers flared, blows were exchanged, back room deals were struck, enemies were made, land was condemned, and families were uprooted. But, like live birth, perhaps labor pains are just part of the process. Even Mr. Rockefeller's generous gift had stipulations.

When all is said and done, though, the Park's history is basically a matter of altitude, aptitude, and attitude.

One final thought. Do the spirits of Cherokee warriors haunt the peaks and ravines of the *Shaconage*, their name for the "mountains of the blue smoke"? Is *Tsistu'yi* still the home of the Great Rabbit, chief of the rabbit tribe, or did he retreat in confusion when the white man bestowed the name "Gregory Bald" on his home? And was the *uktena*, the large snake monster that hid in high mountain passes waiting to pounce on unsuspecting travelers, really killed by the Shawnee magician, Aganuni'tsi, or does it lurk in some secret den waiting for the white man's era to pass? And what of the White Bear, chief of the bears? Is he long gone from *Kuwa'hi*, the Mulberry Place, or does he still lead the bears in the timeless dance before winter's hibernation?

The Cherokee names slip across the tongue like soft candy—words mysterious and difficult to the white ear, yet at the same time enchanting as they evoke pictures of another age, another culture.

So it is in the Smokies.

Chapter Twelve

Hot Springs

I could smell the trappings of civilization well before the sounds wafted up the steep hillside. Greasy food odors mixed with car exhaust and only God knows what else, confused my brain. I tried to sort out the various smells as I picked up the pace, but soon gave it up as an exercise in futility. Hungry anticipation of what lay in the valley below left me with a mouthful of drool, along with the vision of a bustling mountain diner where smiling waitresses catered to my voracious appetite. I nearly doubled over as an immense hunger pain cut through my gut. Excited, I yelled, "Hot dang! Hot Springs, make ready for the 'Model-T'! Ooooga!" The sound reverberated through the leafless trees like the braying of a crazed jackass.

A couple of day hikers on the switchback below came into sight—a man and a woman, forty-something as near as I could tell, sporting matching jackets and daypacks. As I brushed past, they gave me a most weird look, as if I was some kind of freaky critter that had just climbed out of Alice's rabbit hole. No matter! I knew what was at the bottom of the mountain. I'd been there before!

Hot Springs, North Carolina, has it all! Hostels, laundry mat, grocery store, outfitter, post office, bank, restaurants—anything a thru-hiker needs, even a spa! When I got there in 1994, I dropped my pack at the Jesuit Hostel and immediately headed for the Smoky Mountain Diner, where my gluttonous cravings were erased (for a short time) by an incredible quantity of wholesome cholesterol. After all, it was the first "real food" I'd had since River's End Café at the Nantahala Outdoor Center, 130 miles back down the trail. Oh yes! Since it is the first town that straddles the Appalachian Trail on the long trek north, Hot Springs is a hiker's paradise.

Which brings me to the crux of the matter: Hot Springs gets short shrift from hikers. We arrive, hungry and trail worn. While in town, we eat like starved locusts, usually every hour or two, and then we roam up and down the sidewalks in droves, as if we just can't get our fill of sights and sounds. Then, as quickly as we came, we're gone, headed for more adventure and another town up the trail where we can once again amaze the local townsfolk with our capacity to eat.

Then when we begin the long climb from the French Broad to Lovers Leap, we "ooh" and "aah" at the magnificent view of the river as it serpentines along the edge of the picturesque town and passes out of sight beyond the spa—which most of us didn't try. We sweat under a humonguous pack crammed with more food than we can possibly eat; grudgingly, we toss out a few curses as our stomachs begin to churn from the last minute gorging.

We now know all about the great eating places, the best hostels. We've rubbed elbows with some wonderful thru-hikers and a few "locals" whom we hadn't met before. But with a pang of guilt, we realize we really don't know diddlysquat about Hot Springs. Sad!

(My apologies to those readers who don't share my penchant for history or lack any twinges of guilt about kissing off Hot Springs. Burp away the vestiges of the final food orgy at the Smoky Mountain Diner; start the long climb out of Hot Springs; and please feel free to skip this next section.)

*   *   *

Most probably the buffalo came first, great hairy beasts that grazed the lush grass and quaffed the gurgling waters along the smothered banks of the rolling French Broad River, always moving along paths of least resistance as they sought better pastures. On the heels of the buffalo came the Cherokee and Shawnee, the Creek and the Choctaw—unwitting engineers of future roads as they followed the life-sustaining animals across the mountains and through the low gaps. Indeed, Hot Springs may owe its very existence to this symbiotic relationship.

Which makes one question why bovines were (and still are) called "dumb beasts." Indeed, it was a mountain custom of old that, when a new road was needed over the mountains, the settlers would drive a "cow-brute" to the lowest gap in sight and down the other side, following along and driving stakes in its very tracks. Then the new road would be built where the "cow-brute" had walked. Which makes one wonder if the "brute-walker" might not have had a leg up on the stake drivers . . .

Not an easy chore, though, to build the roads. Lots of rock ledges in them thar mountains. Gunpowder wasn't cheap—fifty cents or more a pound—

but the builders used it when they had to. More frequently, they built a huge fire on top of the stubborn ledge, got it fiery hot, and then doused the fire with barrels of cold water. The rock would sizzle and spit, and then crack. Often the planners would bypass the ledge if possible and route the road around and up a "holler." One way or another, the roads were built over-mountain and into the interior of western North Carolina. And quite naturally, early on a road was built along the Indian path that followed the winding flow of the French Broad River, which in due time gave access to the wonderful bubbling heated springs where Spring Creek empties into the French Broad.

Or course the Indians knew about the springs and the strange curative "medicine" that the waters bestowed long before the first settlers came. Then in 1778 (according to legend), Scouts Henry Reynolds and Thomas Morgan stumbled on the springs while chasing a band of Indians, and the word went out. Like flies swarming around road kill they came—the sick, the lame, and the just plain curious—to sample the magic elixir. And like Indians following the buffalo came a tavern, then houses, and soon other accoutrements to establish the inevitable pecking order and a more structured community.

In 1788, two hundred acres, including the springs, were deeded and "Warm Springs" became a place. The tavern grew into a popular hotel, and three years later, William Nelson (no relation to "Willie") bought the springs for "two hundred pounds in solid Virginia currency." Thus began the commercialization of Nature's exquisite gift.

In 1828 came the "superhighway" of the era, the Buncombe Turnpike, which ran from Saluda Gap on the North/South Carolina border south of Asheville, along the French Broad and through Warm Springs, to the Tennessee line. The entire area experienced a huge growth spurt.

The tavern-turned-hotel got an extensive face lift when, in 1832, the Patton brothers, James and John, bought the springs. They created a masterpiece—a 350-room imposing structure with thirteen massive columns to represent the thirteen colonies and capable of catering to 1000 visitors at a time. The ballroom was the State's second largest, and the dining room seated up to 600 diners. As one of the East's most prestigious resort hotels, the Warm Springs Hotel became known as the "Patton White House." Not bad for an out of the way mountain village!

Along came the Civil War. Somehow the hotel, now owned by Col. James Rumbough, survived that grisly affair. Col. Rumbough operated the stage coach line that took mail and passengers over the Buncombe Turnpike from Greeneville (Tennessee) to Greenville (South Carolina)—each town being located fifty miles from Asheville. The Colonel bragged that passengers could have breakfast in Warm Springs, lunch in Marshall, and supper at Asheville. Raisin' the dust!

Mainly through the efforts of Rumbough's wife, Carrie—a lady of some influence—the hotel gained in prominence. In fact, President Andrew Johnson's son, Andrew "Frank" Johnson, Jr., met his bride-to-be Elizabeth "Bessie," the Rumboughs' number two daughter, in the swank ballroom.

When the railroad reached the "Springs" in 1882, people came in droves to "take the waters," and the Rumboughs felt obliged to enlarge the hotel. To the dismay of the Colonel and his patrons, the "Patton" burned to the ground two years later, and that was that. Lacking funds to rebuild, Col. Rumbough sold the property to a northern syndicate, the Southern Improvement Company.

The new owners held a grandiose vision, which saw the light of reality in 1884 in the form of the four-story, 200-room Mountain Park Hotel. All rooms were lighted with electricity and heated with steam. Nearby, golfers could enjoy the Wana Luna, a nine-hole golf course with square tees and greens, which took honors as the first golf course in the Southeast. A grand bathhouse was built to accommodate some new springs discovered during construction, hotter than the old springs by a few degrees.

The bathhouse boasted sixteen marble pools, each nine feet long, six feet wide, and six feet deep. A typical "treatment plan" utilizing the baths and accompanying massage therapy lasted for twenty-one days. And the good citizens, recognizing the value of "one-upmanship" and what just a few degrees higher might do for the local economy, petitioned the State to rename their town, "Hot Springs." Things were booming!

Abruptly, fortune smiled again on Col. Rumbough. The Southern Improvement Company was forced into bankruptcy and offered the property back. The Colonel bought it for a song and dance and once again became the potentate of his magical kingdom.

Then came catastrophe. A macabre monster rose from the killing fields of France and swooped across the turbulent waves, down on the innocent village of Hot Springs. It dug its bloodstained talons into the fabric of idyllic existence and eventually shredded the future into tattered dreams.

When the world's largest ship, Germany's 55,000-ton *Vaterland*, sailed into New York harbor on a bright mid-summer day in 1914, little did her captain, Commodore Ruser, know that he would never again take his ship back into deep water. For when England declared war on Germany on August 4th, transatlantic crossings of vessels belonging to the two nations were cancelled. Commodore Ruser was instructed to remain in New York Harbor and wait for orders—which never came. Not officially interned by the United States—a neutral country—captain, crew, and passengers remained on the ship, day after interminable day, standing regular watches, ice skating on the frozen Hudson in winter, swimming in the murky waters in summer. The ship's band gave stirring shore-side concerts for the New Yorkers. A jolly time was had by all—for three years!

On April 6, 1917, the United States declared war on Germany, and the fun and games came to an end. The Government seized the *Vaterland* as a hostile vessel, along with five other German vessels that were also trapped in New York harbor. So began the weird sequence of events that changed the history of Hot Springs forever.

Some 2200 Germans came as human chattel with the seized ships. What to do with the internees? In an almost comical move, the 300-man crew of the *Vaterland* was taken to Ellis Island and offered U.S. citizenship (refused). Enter Col. Rumbough. Things were not good. His wife had died the previous year. Because of The War, the flow of guests was rapidly drying up, and his sandcastle was steadily crumbling into a cesspool of financial ruin.

Enter the U.S. Government with its fat coffers, and suddenly the pressure was off. The Mountain Park Hotel and surrounding grounds were converted into a prison camp—the largest in the United States at the time—and suddenly the village of 650 increased nearly five-fold. Officers were "incarcerated" in the hotel; rooms in town were "let" for the women and children, and the band continued to play. The German men built a small alpine village out of scrap lumber, driftwood, and flattened cans on the hotel grounds. They even built a chapel out of flattened Prince Albert tobacco tins.

Close relationships sprang up between the internees and the town folk. Guards took prisoners home for dinner. German women, many who were skilled seamstresses in their own right, sewed beautiful dresses for the town ladies. And the two cultures coexisted in easy harmony.

On the eleventh hour of the eleventh day of the eleventh month, 1918, warring powers signed the Armistice. *Vaterland's* band played all night to celebrate. Eventually, the Germans were sent home (although some returned with their families after the war). Several prisoners had come to cherish their little haven away from the *Fatherland* so much that, desperate to remain, they poisoned the wells in an effort to make themselves sick. (Tragically, too much poison was poured into some of the wells and a few died.)

Col. Rumbough struggled to bring elegance back to the tired hotel, but it was not to be. In January 1920, the hotel, like its predecessor, burned to the ground. When the Colonel died in 1924, his daughter, Bessie, acquired the property. In a philanthropic moment she built a smaller version—The Hot Springs Inn—intending for it to become a sanitarium. The plan failed to materialize, so Bessie conveyed the property to the Catholic Church to be used as a retreat and rest home.

This plan also failed. For want of patronage—the Baptists and Methodists far outnumbered the town's Catholics, and Hot Springs was too far removed from high density population centers—the Inn languished as the country smothered in the coils of The Great Depression.

After a short stint as a Jesuit seminary, the property was transferred twice again, but the Inn never regained its former glory. Not even the presence of America's most notorious mobster, John Dillinger, who "vacationed" there occasionally, was enough to attract tourists. Finally, the knell tolled with the coming of Interstate 40, which diverted traffic away from Hot Springs and sent the fragile economy into a tailspin. Like an esteemed samurai who, on "losing face" was destined to commit *seppuku*—the ancient Japanese ritual of disemboweling—the Inn committed its own form of *seppuku*. In 1977, the venerable old building burned to the ground.

About the *Vaterland:* The United States Shipping Bureau seized the ship, renamed it the *Leviathan*, and converted it into a troop carrier. She made 19 trips across the Atlantic, carrying over 100,000 Americans to France's gory trenches. After the war, the *Leviathan* once again became a passenger liner, but The Great Depression spelled her doom and the proud vessel sailed to Scotland, where she was cut into scrap and made into such useful items as razor blades and ice picks.

*   *   *

On April Fool's Day of 2000, I was traveling along Interstate 40 between Asheville and Knoxville, headed for home after a week's hike in the southern Appalachians. As I neared Exit 24, a road sign caught my eye: *NC 209—Hot Springs*. I glanced at my watch—only 8 A.M. Why not? Home wasn't going anywhere. I surrendered to the sudden urge to revisit the quaint town and turned north.

Hot Springs hadn't changed much since my last visit in 1998. I drove down the main drag, slowly, hungrily absorbing sights and smells as if I were again a grubby thru-hiker just come down off the mountain. Familiar landmarks revived memories from three previous thru-hikes. They flooded in, swirling inside my head like a gigantic whirlpool, melding thoughts into a potpourri of blurred emotion.

Over there . . . the shortcut walkway to the Jesuit Hostel, where Wahoola and I had "unwound" in 1990 and I had "worked for stay" in 1994. Dang! There it was! The Smoky Mountain Diner, its small parking lot sprinkled with mud-splashed pickups sporting NRA stickers and an eclectic collection of rifle racks that were displayed in rear windows like sportsman trophies.

Memories of past eating orgies welled up, but I resisted the urge to pull in—the telltale bathroom scales at home was today's reality. I compromised by rolling down the window and inhaling the assorted food odors, which wafted through the window, carried on pristine mountain air that had not yet been sullied by the day's traffic. Diagonally across the street sat Elmer Hall's Inn at Hot Springs—an aged Victorian mansion turned into a "hiker friendly" bed and breakfast and a vegetarian's delight. A bit of unfinished business, that. I felt a sense of regret that I'd never stayed there. Maybe next time . . .

Down close to the river, past the railroad tracks lay another bit of unfinished business before I headed back to the Interstate. Something long overdue, for my first hike I had lacked the temerity to slip past the "No Trespassing" signs to "take the waters"—a favorite escapade for trail-weary thru-hikers. Nor, regretfully, had I taken the time on my other journeys, after the signs had come down and the baths restored. I didn't have the time right now to sample the magical elixir, but I did want to look.

I swung into the entrance of the Hot Springs Spa, now resurrected—a Phoenix risen from the ashes of history—thanks to owner Gene Hicks, who had rescued the overgrown decaying relic. The large expanse of green, where the rich had once frolicked and German internees had marked time, now lay like a giant empty carpet, stripped of its former elegance. High against the sky beyond the river, I could barely make out a rocky crag as it played hide and seek with wispy tendrils of cloud. Lovers Leap, so named by the Cherokees after Mist-on-the-Mountain, a Cherokee maiden, jumped to her death from the spot after her beloved Magwa was killed by Lone Wolf, a jealous rival.

I paused for a moment to view the high ground beyond the green. Here in 1863, Union commander Colonel George Washington Kirk had ordered his 600-man mounted infantry to dig in along a defensive line when he occupied (then) Warm Springs. Here, a short skirmish took place when a smaller force under the command of Major John Woodfin, a prominent lawyer in nearby Marshall, came to liberate the town. Woodfin was killed; and Major Holcomb and James Arrington, Southern soldiers home on leave, were scalped. Seventy-two year-old William Peck fared better. Union soldiers stripped him of his shoes and forced the old man to wander over his farm on a cold, dark night to gather up all of his horses for the Billy Yanks. Before reinforcements could arrive, Kirk and his men slipped away and headed for greener pastures. The thought occurred: Had any of the invaders sneaked down from the trenches and "taken the waters" before the shooting began.

A couple of small white buildings, freshly painted, marked the end of the long gravel driveway. I stopped at the nearest building and went in. Vicki Rathbone changed a harried look into a warm smile and ran stubby fingers through her short blond hair. Both fingers and hair complemented her short height.

"You wantin' a bath?" I looked dubious. "You mean this early?" It was barely 9:00 A.M. and the air temperature couldn't have been above thirty degrees. "Seven, twelve, during business hours," she chuckled. "The water's always hot." I explained that I just wanted to see what all the foofaraw was about, maybe look around a bit. "Sure. I'll go with you myself. Maybe you'll change your mind after you see the setup." A born salesperson!

The baths—twelve hot tubs—were discreetly tucked into the sylvan landscape along the French Broad River, away from prying eyes. Some were enclosed in plastic sheeting to ward off the cold. On the edge of the green, the ruins of yesteryear moldered—the crumbling foundation of the long-gone Mountain Park Hotel and its marble bathhouse, now a roofless derelict. From its innards, steam rose from beneath sheets of rust-stained roofing tin weighted down with broken slabs of marble. Large white plastic pipes snaked out from under the covering, carrying water to the baths.

All that remains of the old Mountain House Hotel and its famous baths.

"You wanna see it?" Vicki asked, almost reverently, like she was about to uncover the Holy Grail. Without waiting for a reply, she shoved a sheet of tin to the side. Brilliantly clear water gushed up from unfathomable depths into the large basin. The mother lode! This was the liquid gold that had put Hot Springs on the map, had made fortunes for some and sent others into financial ruin, had restored health to ailing souls who truly believed in the waters. (Numerous testimonials attest to this fact!)

Fascinated, I stooped and submerged my hand. The soft caressing wetness immediately became a sorceress, conjuring up an image of sheer orgiastic pleasure, and for a few moments my mind lingered in a nearby hot tub. Now I could see why governors and gangsters, gallants and gowned belles, had come to Hot Springs. The temptation was strong.

My watch said otherwise. Alas! Father Time ruled the moment and the vision disappeared into the rising steam.

I thanked my hostess and turned to go. The words bounced off my back. "You sure you don't wanna take a bath?" I turned and waved. "Next time for sure."

Chapter Thirteen

Shelton Graves

On the fourth Sunday in July each year they congregate at the base of the mountain—relatives, friends, and well wishers armed with colorful vinyl bouquets, American flags, and picnic baskets. They come from all sides of the mountain. Some make their way up the Tennessee side by the steep trail along Horse Creek. (This is the same route where Sam Waddle wore out a brand new jeep for well nigh over a quarter century as he breathed new life into Jerry Cabin Shelter and nurtured that section of the Trail for as long as he was able.) Others arrive from the North Carolina side, following the rough trace up through Cowbell Hollow alongside Big Creek. Some even hoof it in on the Appalachian Trail from Devil Fork Gap.

Anyway you cut it, the journey to the lonely glen on the high ridge atop Big Butt Mountain is not an easy one, for the old logging roads have eroded, rutted from the trauma of neglect, until they have become impassable to any kind of wheeled vehicle. Now it's "shank's mare" or the actual horse, for the Forest Service has closed all routes of ingress to vehicular traffic. (In a magnanimous gesture, they allow horses on the Appalachian Trail for this one-day-a-year pilgrimage.) But for these faithful sojourners the trip is fitting and necessary. They come to pay homage to fallen warriors of another age.

Like an Irish wake, the mood is festive as people slowly gather, arriving singly or in small groups, afoot or on horseback. A year's worth of backslapping and hand shaking, hugs and smiling "Howdy's," until three hundred or more are gathered around two plain granite headstones that face each other, separated by the length of a man's body. A small slab of gray granite, incongruously new, lies at the edge of the grave and precisely bisects the short distance that reflects the infinite depth of eternity. Last year's bouquets are now faded and the smattering of flags frayed. But no matter; new decorations will soon take their place.

The Sheltons' grave: Today's remembrance of yesterday's violence.

No dates on the old stones. Just names and organizations, the lettering already eroded and stained by the elements. One stone faces east (according to mountain custom, so that the deceased will face the risen Christ, who will descend from that direction on Resurrection Day) and leans protectively toward its companion. The faded lettering—"David Shelton; Co. C; 3 N.C. MTD INF."—is hard to read. The companion stone, facing west, has been treated more kindly by the ceaseless assault of time (a concession by a higher power because of its obverse position?) This one is easier to read: "Wm. Shelton; Co. E; 2 N.C. INF."

The new marker, recently dedicated by relatives to the memory of young Millard Haire, seems strangely out of place.

Silence descends on the glen as the ceremony begins. The speaker's rich commemorative words rise on tranquil zephyrs that barely stir the late morning air. Eyes stare at the stones, seeking to pierce the fabric of time. Thoughts turn inward as minds relive the horrific act that spawned the stones, which now stand as solemn sentinels for those interred below. Heads bow as a prayer wafts heavenward. Then comes the traditional gun salute for fallen comrades, solemnly rendered by Civil War re-enactors. The old wounds must have healed, for the honor guard is now flecked with butternut and blue. Comes shouted orders, and members of the 12th Tennessee (CSA) and 8th Tennessee (USA) shoulder their weapons and fire in sequence like precise machines. Spectators cringe; some clap hands to ears as the clearing is once again filled with the acrid smell of gun powder.

The final volley is fired. Echoes reverberate across the mountains of two states; then absolute silence descends as onlookers try to lock away disturbed thoughts of the violence that brings them here on this peaceful day. A parson rises and begins to replace the sounds of violence with words of peace and hope. The short sermon ends and the group begins the old familiar words of *Amazing Grace*—a capella, no songbooks needed.

Finally comes the picnicking . . . cloths spread beneath shade trees . . . women unloading baskets filled with good mountain cooking . . . quick glances at other baskets to see how culinary skills stack up against neighbors' baskets . . . the thick odor of fried chicken rising into the still air . . . conversation receding as the eaters get down to business.

As the afternoon dwindles to a standstill, backpacks and saddlebags are filled with the leavings, good-byes are said, and the faithful head back down the mountain. Tribute has been paid. The innocent victims of the violence that laid them here can rest undisturbed for another year.

*   *   *

An oddity that Union soldiers would be recruiting in secessionist North Carolina. But here they were, a detail of twelve grim-faced men dressed in Union blue, in a small cabin on the high ridge of Big Butt Mountain doing just that. But like most things not understood, there was a plausible answer. Mountainous east Tennessee was a strong bastion of Federalism; had been since the old timers who had fought for the Stars and Stripes under Gen'l Washin'ton had come home and put their muzzle loaders aside for axe and plow. And Greene County, a weak tobacco spit from the cabin, was among the strongest.

The elixir of Union loyalty had spilled over Big Butt Mountain, down into the isolated valleys of western North Carolina; down into Shelton Laurel, which had become the staunchest center of Federalism in the region. It was truly a thorn in the backside of "Sesesh" Madison County.

Most of these men called the "Laurel" home. They had been sent by their commanders to recruit their kin and neighbors for the "Cause." The group was a mixed bag: Some of the soldiers belonged to the newly formed Third North Carolina Mounted Infantry with Colonel George W. Kirk at the helm. The others were members of the Second North Carolina Mounted Infantry—Kirk's former command—now commanded by Lieutenant Colonel William C. Bartlett.

Hard times breed hard men, who somehow rise to the forefront of events like larger pebbles in a shaken jar of gravel. Some, like Grant, Lee, and Jackson, glow in the light of God, duty, and country. Others, such as Bartlett, do their job with dispatch and patriotism, and quickly fade away into historical obscurity. And some climb out of the pit of Hell itself, vicious men who feed on the gore of war; men who lack compassion, who worship at the altar of anarchy.

Kirk was such a man. Born in nearby Greene County, Tennessee, when hostilities began he enlisted in the Union's First Tennessee Cavalry to repel the Confederate invasion of his Tennessee homeland. By 1863, he had established a reputation for dash and daring as he led details on bold raids far into enemy territory. His activities soon came to the attention of General John Schofield, who gave Kirk the rank of major and command of the Second North Carolina Mounted Infantry. The audacious major then began to terrorize the citizenry of western North Carolina, who generally supported the secessionist cause. General Schofield was pleased with Kirk's exploits (although turning a blind side to reports of extreme brutality—after all, a war was on) and, on February 13, 1864, authorized him to form the Third Regiment of North Carolina Mounted Infantry.

The General dangled a carrot in front of Kirk's huge ego and made him a colonel, telling him to arm and mount his regiment on horses and weapons taken from the spoils of war. Kirk took in deserters, organized a company of Cherokees, and signed on all "home Yankees" willing to scribble their names on the dotted line. A motley mix for the most part, although the home boys did give a stamp of legitimacy to the organization.

Kirk's reputation as a plunderer and murderer grew until his name soon became the most feared utterance around lamp-lit tables in the cabins of western North Carolina's Southern sympathizers. Thus, in a quest to bolster the ranks, came these men, who tossed in restless slumber in the mist-shrouded cabin high atop Big Butt Mountain.

Lieutenant Colonel James A. Keith, commanding the 64th North Carolina Infantry, CSA, was worse. He hailed from nearby Marshall, the county seat of Madison County, North Carolina. For sure, no love was lost between Marshall and its Federalist neighbor, Shelton Laurel, a few short miles northward at the base of Big Butt. And Keith had it in for the isolated hamlet. Seems that some folks from the Laurel had descended on Marshall sometime around January 14, 1863, to get badly needed salt, which had been denied them because of their Unionist views. They broke into several stores and took the salt and other desperately needed supplies.

On hearing of the raid, North Carolina Governor Zebulon Vance ordered General Hoth at Knoxville, Tennessee, to punish the offenders. Col. Keith and his 200-man force had been operating off-and-on in Madison County. They knew the country and just happened to be in the area. So General Hoth assigned the mission to Keith's 64th Infantry.

On the morning of January 16, the Confederate force swooped down on Shelton Laurel, whipping and torturing helpless women (at the first shots, the men had melted into the hills). The soldiers assaulted and robbed an eighty-five year-old woman and left her dangling near death from a tree in the frigid weather. They also whipped a seventy year-old lady with hickory rods until blood coursed down her back. Not satisfied, they tied the mother of an infant to a tree in a snow-covered yard and laid her baby in the open cabin door, threatening to let them both freeze if she didn't talk. In all, the Confederate soldiers managed to lay hands on fifteen captives—mostly men too old to be conscripted and boys too young to serve.

After three days of despicable treatment, Keith informed the prisoners that they would be marched to Knoxville to stand trial. In the predawn on

January 19th, the prisoners were rousted out into the snow-blanketed landscape for the long march. Amazingly, two prisoners had managed to escape.

Two miles into the march, in near blizzard conditions, Keith ordered the party to stop in a clearing by a small stream. He then ordered the captives to kneel in front of a file of soldiers and gave orders to fire. Some of the soldiers balked at the inhumane treatment, but Col. Keith shouted, "Fire, or you will take their places."

The heinous deed completed, the soldiers dug a mass grave and dumped the still bleeding bodies in. The ground was frozen, and the soldiers were cold and sullen, so the grave ended up as a shallow trench with body parts exposed.

One of the men who had escaped the night before, Pete McCoy, hid nearby and witnessed the entire episode. He made his way back to Shelton Laurel and reported what had occurred. The next day, families came to retrieve their dead. Hogs had already begun to feast on the bodies. The bodies were carried to a family cemetery, wrapped in sheets, and buried in a common grave.

Such was the character of these two rogue commanders who gave the orders that would precipitate the macabre event—soon to unfold at dawn's first light on July 19, 1864, as Keith's men crept up the mountain under cover of darkness.

Inside the cabin, thirteen year-old Millard Filmore Haire couldn't bear to lie on the skimpy pallet another second as his excitement mounted. The others were already stirring and he wanted to be the first one up to show that he had what it took to be a "sojer." His uncle, David Shelton, just might let him sign up and go with them. Or possibly he could persuade his cousin William Shelton, David's nephew. And if they were muleheaded, well then he'd just work on someone else.

Millard felt a small pang of guilt that he might not see his momma for weeks, even months, if he did go off to war. But he just *had* to go give those murderin' Rebs a dose of lead, just like they done to his pa back in September. They'd just rode up and shot him down like he was a mad dog, no excuse, no nothin'. Millard shuddered at the picture that rushed into his mind—his pa lying in the crude pine box just before some neighbors lowered it into that dank dark hole that smelled of death. And the parson's words echoed in his ears, "Robert Nelson Hawkins Filmore Haire was one of us, taken without cause, murdered for what he believed in . . ." Millard forced the memory away as the tears started to come.

Instead, he thought of the small house tucked away in Shelton Laurel down off the mountain. Ma would be setting the table for breakfast about now while Laura, his older sister by a year, would be waking his two younger brothers and two little sisters, telling them to get dressed cause chores had to be done. Millard felt guilty that they'd have to do his work, too. But he'd been sent up to the cabin yesterday afternoon to warn the others that Rebs were in the area. Important work. Yeah, if he was old enough to be given such an important job, he was old enough to wear Union blue.

The picture dissolved in his mounting excitement, and Millard quickly arose and went out into the chill dawn. With childish eagerness, he jumped up on a Chestnut stump and began to crow like a rooster toward the cabin's open door, barely visible in the rising mist.

The first shots cleaved the silence, sending thunderous crescendos through the dripping trees and down into the valleys—and forever ending the exuberant dreams of young Millard Filmore Haire. The next volley cut down David, age 42, and his nephew, William, age 30, as they rushed through the cabin door, fatally wounding both. Acrid smoke mixed with the mist as the firing increased. Martin Norton and W.S. Ray jumped through the back window and ran, somehow eluding the hail of lead. A bullet caught seventeen year-old Ephraim Hensley in the lower back. He crawled into some bushes and managed to hide. His brother, Zachariah, a year younger, wasn't as lucky. He took a bullet and was captured.

Sixty-two year-old Hampton Burgess and his neighbor, Isaac Shelton, fifty-three—both civilians who had come up to the cabin the day before to spend the night with their two soldier sons—managed to make it through the cabin window. They high-tailed it up the trail but were soon overtaken by some of Keith's men and killed. Isaac Jr. escaped but Hampton Jr. was wounded and taken prisoner, as was Alan Lisenbee and two others.

As quickly as it had begun, the firing ceased, quickly replaced by the groans of the wounded and the shouts of the Confederate soldiers as they searched for the Yankees who had escaped. Their grisly business done, the men in gray prodded the captives with curses and rifles and departed the red-splotched glen.

The bodies were left to rot where they had fallen. The following day, the Laurel folk climbed the mountain and wrapped David, William, and young Millard in sheets and buried them in a common grave near where they fell. The two fathers were buried in another unmarked grave a couple of hundred yards further north.

And in Shelton Laurel, the wailing of grief-stricken widows and parents lasted far into the night. None mourned more fiercely than Matilda Shelton Haire, who had lost her husband—and now her young son.

*   *   *

Two war-hardened, ruthless men; both with small regard for human life, both accountable for numerous atrocities. Yet to the victor belongs the spoils—with despicable deeds and unspeakable horrors shrugged off as necessary acts of conquest. To the loser goes the stigma of "war criminal" and trial for crimes against humanity.

So it was. Colonel Kirk rode the coattails of victory and was never called to answer for his plundering and butchery. He and his band of mounted brigands continued to terrorize whole communities in western North Carolina, pillaging at will long after General Lee handed over his jeweled sword to General Grant (which the Union general graciously refused) at Appomattox Courthouse on April 9, 1865. He continued on even after Tecumseh Sherman accepted Joe Johnston's surrender of all North Carolina Confederates at the home of James Bennett near Greensboro, North Carolina, on April 26th. He torched houses and stole horses even after General Richard Taylor (who became the senior Confederate officer east of the Mississippi after Johnston capitulated) passed his not-bejeweled sword to Major General Edward Canby on May 4th.

At last, at Franklin, North Carolina, after he had defeated Major Stephen Walker's 80th North Carolina Infantry, word of the final demise of the Confederate States of America caught up. Kirk took Walker's surrender at Macon County Courthouse on May 14, 1865. This became the last formal act of surrender of Confederate forces east of the Mississippi. (The event is commemorated with a mural in the Macon County Courthouse.)

Kirk and his Third Mounted Infantry, not ready to toss in the towel, continued westward and it was business as usual, although no organized forces existed to oppose them. They quickly became an embarrassment to the Government and were officially disbanded soon after. The soldiers stacked their rifles and went home. The Third Mounted Infantry had ceased to exist.

Lieutenant Colonel Keith wasn't so lucky. He fell into disgrace with Governor Vance after word of the Shelton Laurel massacre spread. The indignant governor wrote to Secretary of War Siddon at Richmond that he would " . . . have him court-martialed, and I will follow him (Keith) to the gates of hell or hang him." At his court-martial, Keith cheated the hangman's noose by maintaining that he acted under the authority of his commander, General Hoth. However, refusing to be appeased, Governor Vance demanded Keith's resignation, and the infamous officer left the service in disgrace.

After the war ended, Keith was arrested by Federal agents for war crimes and lodged in the Madison County jail to await trial. He escaped custody and fled. Post war North Carolina Governor William W. Holden put a price of $500.00 on his head, but Keith managed to elude authorities. He was possibly spotted in California in later years, but he was never brought to justice.

Kirk was also arrested for atrocities committed after the war, while employed as a "strong man" for Governor Holden. The former colonel was hired to raise a force to put down an "insurrection" in Alamance and Caswell Counties after the governor declared martial law. Kirk and his men so brutally treated the civilians that the good governor was sucked into the melee and impeached. Kirk was placed under house arrest in Raleigh, North Carolina, but was "allowed" to escape.

Like his old nemesis Keith, he made his way west after a few years of shady dealings in the mining industry. Kirk died, destitute, in California in 1905 at the age of sixty-eight.

Sadly, in war civilians lose the most and suffer the worst. So it was in Shelton Laurel. Victimized and brutalized by men in gray, whose consciences had been shackled by Keith and others of his knavish mentality, the Laurel residents suffered atrocities time and again. No family escaped the war's horror. Torture—even of women—was commonplace. Death stalked the roads of Shelton Laurel each hour of every day in the form of "Graycoat" patrols, which might swoop down on unsuspecting victims at any time.

Millard Filmore Haire's family exemplifies the severe impact of the Civil War on the tiny community. Killed without cause, his father, Robert, at the "Second Massacre" of Shelton Laurel on September 19, 1863. Killed in action, his uncle, James Haire, 1st TN Cavalry, US, October 17, 1864. Killed in battle, another uncle, Richard "Bevy" Hensley, Co. E, 2nd NC Mtd Inf., US, January 23, 1864. Wounded and captured in the ambush on Big Butt Mountain on July 19, 1863 and incarcerated as a Prisoner of War at Richmond, Virginia, where he subsequently died, his cousin ("Bevy" Hensley's son), Zachariah. His aunt, Mary L. Haire Caldwell, age 25, wife and mother of a seven year-old daughter, tortured and killed by hanging to elicit information during the "Second Massacre"—a scant two months before her brother, Robert (Millard's father) was slain. And this was only small potatoes for the "gray

scourge" that befouled the tranquil life of Shelton Laurel. The Sheltons suffered
even worse!

So there you have it: Two battle-hardened vicious men who managed to
cheat the scales of justice. Men whose mouths uttered the orders that required
men in blue and gray to commit countless atrocities; whose hands ran red
with the blood of slaughtered innocents just as if they themselves had thrust
the bayonet, pulled the trigger. Yet, both are forever doomed to stand as ignoble
symbols of man's depravity.

On second thought, in the long run perhaps justice has been served.

*   *   *

I sat on a fallen oak trunk and munched contentedly on a Snickers bar—
my second of the morning. The day had dawned cold and overcast, but the
sun had chased away the clouds by the time I reached the top of Big Butt
Mountain, giving the day over to an azure sky. Not bad at all for late April
('98). Happily, the weather had finally decided to soften after my previous
week in the snow-wrapped Smokies—almost as if penance were being done
for grievous insult. High above, against the sun, the screech of a red tail hawk
pierced the prolonged silence in the small clearing as it swooped toward some
unsuspecting prey. I thought, *Just me and the hawk—and the grave.*

My eyes kept returning to the two headstones and the small wooden
cross—hardly changed in the four years since my last time here. (A permanent
granite marker has since replaced the wooden cross that memorialized Millard
Haire.) David's stone still tilted slightly toward William's. Last July's vinyl
flowers and small flags, now faded and frayed, blanketed the grave, which
looked in better shape than I remembered.

Peering around the clearing, I tried to make out some trace of the old
cabin—a pile of stones, a depression in the earth, a small clump of irises, a
rotted chestnut stump—but to no avail. Nature and time had erased all signs
of the tragedy that had unfolded nearly 134 years ago. Some of the older trees,
they might have witnessed the slaughter. If only they could speak! And what
of the other grave a short distance up the Trail, still unmarked. Would the old
timers die off before that grave received its due, before the rising generation
got caught up in "other things"?

The hawk suddenly screeched again as it flapped upward from behind a
clump of trees, fighting for air space. A missed opportunity for a quick meal?

A small eddy momentarily stirred the flags and then brushed my face before retreating into the solemn background. I stuffed the last bite in my mouth and pushed the wrapper into a pack pocket with other crumpled castaways. Quietly shouldering my pack, I gave the grave a silent salute and walked from the clearing.

On the high ridge of Big Butt Mountain, in two common graves, the bones of four men and a boy repose for eternity . . .

Chapter Fourteen

The Hermit of Greer Bald

The balds of North Carolina and Tennessee are nothing short of astounding, these phenomena of nature. Earthly giants that long ago shrugged off their woody mantles, they exist among their tree-capped kindred as aristocracy, aloof and patrician—and mysterious. Like well-born nobility, the balds flaunt their charismatic charm; yet, they are an enigma. How did they become treeless vistas of great beauty? Theories abound, but the mystery remains.

Big Bald is unsurpassed in its grandeur. The broad open summit, rampant with knee-high grass that sweeps before the ceaseless wind like a great storm-tossed sea, seems more akin to a high Scottish moor. Standing at the old weather-beaten post that marks the apex, one senses how miniscule the human race is in the universe's pecking order. Pee ants floating on a rotted board in a boundless ocean. The 360-degree panorama is breathtaking! It's all there: The Black Mountains, crested by Mount Mitchell, a mere twenty miles distant . . . the Great Smokies with Clingman's mighty hump—now a tiny bump . . . the Nantahala range against the far distant horizon—a month's walk south by trail . . . the Unakas, where the Trail is headed, resting against the far northern horizon. The sensation is like standing on the rooftop of creation, for all else seems dwarfed.

Such is the majesty of this brushstroke of God's almighty hand on earth's canvas, that Big Bald, a mere 5516-foot hump of one billion year-old rock, can dominate its fifty-four North Carolina and Tennessee cousins that rise above 6000 feet.

(A mote in the eye: Development has overtaken the mountainside facing Big Bald's eastward-looking side. Condo's, get-away mansions, roads, a ski run and golf course now detract from the intense feeling of "standing on the rooftop of creation.")

Aside from its beauty, Big Bald can be holy terror for the unlucky hiker who gets caught in the talons of fierce storms that frequently rack the summit. I well know the fear that creeps up from the bowels and freezes the mind when a storm hits on that exposed expanse. I have hugged the thrashing grass, looking like a fetal blob of hysteria as lightning sizzled the air all around and wind-driven rain and hail slashed and flailed the skin and set it afire in spite of the numbing cold.

But on the first day of May 1998, the bald was benevolent and Nature was kind. The grass swayed beneath a gentle breeze and the sun smiled down a special blessing. I took off my pack, propped my back against the summit post, and slipped a Snickers from the hidey-hole reserved exclusively for the brown gold. (Sorry readers—my secret!)

Ripping the wrapper away, I thought *Only two more things could make a flawless day more perfect. If only I could glimpse a peregrine falcon.* (Big Bald is home to these mighty hunters—"aerial Batmen" with their black bandit masks. These birds, with their 40-odd-inch wingspan, have been clocked at speeds of over 200 mph as they swoop down on airborne prey. A favorite tactic is to slam into the prey and knock it unconscious, and then snare it with razor talons before it strikes the ground. The peregrine may range as far as twenty miles from its nest in search of food. Even as I scanned the sky, a falcon might be soaring in from Mount Mitchell.)

The other thing? *If only I knew the exact location of Old Hog Greer's hermit abode, I'd traipse right down there and poke around a bit.* Swallowing the last bite, I rubbed a grubby hand across my mouth and surrendered myself to the mellow warmth of the sun and gave my imagination free rein . . .

*   *   *

Young David Greer didn't like South Carolina. Too hot for one thing, and too many damned face gnats—the little buggers always wanted to fly up your nose or crawl across your tonsils—and way too many 'skeeters' always trying to suck your veins dry. Not a decent place for man or beast.

As soon as he was old enough to skedaddle out of the sand-rooted pines, young Greer headed for higher ground, gradually working his way toward the distant mountains by herding flocks of turkeys and gangs of hogs to market along rutted, muddy roads. Not bad work, but frustrating at times. None of God's creatures was dumber than turkeys. And the stupid beasts just refused to be herded after dark. Didn't matter where you were, even in a swamp. They'd fly up to the nearest branches and roost till daylight. And heaven help 'em if it rained. The idiot birds would stare up to see where it was coming from, their mouths wide open like empty granny pokes. The dumb birds would just stare and stare until the rain filled their craws and they drowned. The bears loved it when it rained and turkeys were close by cause, by God, they fed right good off'n the carcasses.

On the other hand, the hogs were never a problem—well almost never. Now them was some smart critters. They kept their heads down when it rained and you didn't have to worry about them hanging out in trees when dark came. Only problem with the porkers, they'd hunker down in a mud bog if given half the chance, and ever now'n then one would break ranks and chase after a rattler. Them hogs loved rattlers, which was fine with the youngster.

As fate would have it, one morning David, now grown into a strapping scrapper of twenty-one, passed through the gateposts of Colonel David Vance's farm on Reems Creek to help the Colonel's men run a small herd of cattle over to Asheville. A right pretty piece, the Colonel's place with its five-room log house tucked into a cove near the base of the Blue Ridge, just a spit an' holler from Mount Mitchell. Nary a face gnat and only a few skeeters now an' then—not a bad place to settle down.

And the job was okay. Sheep and cattle were only a couple of steps higher than turkeys on the smart scale, which wasn't saying a lot for the hoofers, but the Colonel paid good wages. He had even taken a liking to David and offered him a steady job after the cattle were delivered.

The Colonel had a daughter—Missy Brank Vance, a pretty lass of eighteen with large blue eyes that could make a man's day with a mere flicker of eye lashes sent his way. And her long flaxen hair with circlets of bouncing curls—a living wheat field ready for harvest that made a man's hands itch to thresh some grain. David Greer was smitten at first sight.

Life at the Vances was pleasant, never harried; and there was always meat on the table and a quaff of "shine" on special occasions, along with some fiddlin' and high steppin'. The weeks became months; corn was shocked and sorghum juice turned into molasses. Finally came the snows and pleasant days filled with time for leisure.

Every waking moment, large orbs of azure magic possessed David's thoughts, and flaxen curls and a princess-like image haunted his dreams. Missy often beamed shy smiles at him when the day's activities brought them together.

By the time the first tendrils of green poked through the melting spring snow, David could stand it no longer and made his move one afternoon as he and Missy strolled down to the ice-covered creek. When he spoke of his love for her, the maiden seemed shocked and her wondrously blue eyes, now set in a face filled only with disdain and pity, spurned his proposal.

How could he have mistaken her kindness for anything else? After all, he was a hired hand, way below her station in life.

Missy's words stabbed deep into David's heart, shredding his soul. Crushed and bitter, he fled to the mountains, resolved to never again open his soul to the opposite sex. Nor did he intend to rub elbows with the human race any more than necessity dictated.

The year was 1802.

David's wanderings took him into the Bald Mountains. At last he found what he searched for. Just below the summit of a wild, untamed bald, at the first trickling of water on the east fork of Higgins Creek, he came to a large boulder field. Perfect! Only slow-witted fools would come to this God-forsaken spot—and definitely no women.

He dug a ten-foot square hole beneath a rock shelf, lined it with stones, and called it "home." By the time the next snows came, David had "collected" a gathering of hogs and built a small moat to keep them handy. He was as snug as a bug in a rug, and happy. No two-legged critters to mess up his life, and the porkers didn't talk back—that is, if you didn't think of their squealing and grunting as backtalk.

The seasons passed—spring storms and winter snow, freeze and thaw . . . old hogs butchered (tough to put a friend down, but it had to be done) and new litters birthed . . . seeds sowed and crops put by. Of course, no person is totally self sufficient, in spite of all intentions, and the time finally came when David had to rub elbows with civilization. He needed salt to cure meat for the winter; now and then a tool broke and he had to search out a smithy; and every few years he had to get a new pair of boots.

Over time his hermit existence clouded his mind, made him mistrustful, indeed made him downright mean. Every trip off the bald meant heated arguments over trifling matters, often accompanied by threats that turned into fistfights. It didn't take long for the lowlanders to take David's measure. "Don't have nuthin' to do with that hog man. He's downright mean." And mothers admonished their children, "Don't go up on Greer Bald (as they'd taken to calling it). Old Hog Greer'll slit yer gullet quicker'n a cat kin blink its eye."

Old Hog Greer proclaimed himself the sovereign ruler of his bald. Indeed, the townsfolk were happy to leave him alone in his mountain kingdom—most of the time. On a late spring day (so some folks said) Old Hog got into an argument with a Mr. Higgins over some cherries in the farmer's orchard. A few hours later Mr. Higgins was found lying in the soft spring grass of his yard, murdered. The "Law" climbed Greer Bald and brought Old Hog Greer down to face the music. But it seems there were no witnesses to the horrible deed and the crazy hermit was turned loose.

In 1834, along about the time Colonel David Vance's grandson, Zebulon (future Civil War governor of North Carolina), was celebrating his fourth birthday, Old Hog Greer went too far. He got into a bitter argument with a smithy over a tool he had taken in to be repaired. Blows were exchanged and the fight turned deadly—no holds barred—as Greer tried to kill the man. Turned out the smithy was the better man. The fight ended with Old Hog Greer crumpled on the hard-packed earth of the blacksmith shop, mortally wounded. "Self defense," the smithy proclaimed, and the "Law" had no trouble believing him.

So ended Old Hog Greer's reign on the bald. Some town men came up to the hermit's stone cave and took the hogs away. They wanted nothing else. The folks in the down-mountain hollers rested easier—although mothers still continued to threaten misbehaving young'uns that "Old Hog Greer's ghost is gonna git you if'in you don't straighten up."

*   *   *

Thunder rumbled in the distance and brought me back to the present. The grass stirred, abruptly wakened by a freshening wind. Yeah, the bald was stretching its limbs, getting ready for the approaching summer storm, which was just gathering on the horizon. (Or maybe Old Hog Greer's ghost was moaning for release from an earthly purgatory!) I got to my feet, scanned the sky once more for peregrines, and headed for Big Bald Shelter.

(Author's note: Fact or fiction? Where does truth end and legend begin? Most of the events in the preceding paragraphs did occur. Colonel David Vance, Revolutionary War hero, did live on Reems Creek; his grandson, Zebulon, did become the governor of North Carolina—twice. German immigrant David Greer, by some accounts, did work for the Colonel for a short time. The maiden who spurned David's romantic advances is in question. By one account, the event happened while David still lived in South Carolina. Another source laid the rejection at the doorstep of Colonel Vance's daughter.

"Hog Greer" did rule supreme over his swinish "subjects" on "Greer Bald." His cavern beneath the rock ledge is still there at the headwaters of the east fork of Higgins Creek, just a short distance from the Appalachian Trail—although it is mostly filled with a century's collection of earthy debris. A trace of the moat can still be seen.

Mr. Higgins *was* murdered in his orchard, and Hog Greer *was* the suspected culprit, but his guilt could not be proven. In 1834, he did try to kill the blacksmith, who turned the tables and killed him. The whereabouts of Hog Greer's grave is unknown.

The legend thrives. Noted historian John Biggs Alderman wrote a play about the hermit in 1955, titled, "The Hermit of Bald Mountain." And any hiker worth his boot soles knows about the infamous recluse.)

Yep, I suspect that the ghostly memory of Old Hog Greer will haunt the grassy summit of Big Bald for generations to come.

Chapter Fifteen

The Hanging

E rwin, Tennessee, is an enchantingly quaint, peaceful town that graces the edge of the Nolichucky River. Here against its red banks on December 29, 1864, Colonel George Washington Kirk and his Third North Carolina Mounted Infantry tangled muskets with Lieutenant Colonel James Keith and his four hundred Confederate soldiers, and sent them hightailing it up the mountain. Here, the Appalachian Trail bids goodbye to the Bald Mountains and climbs up into the Unaka Mountains on its long northward run. A nice place to call home and a good resupply stop for thru-hikers.

Yet, for its 5600 residents, the town—like Mrs. O'Leary's cow, which really didn't kick over the lantern that caused the great Chicago fire of 1871—got stuck with a bum rap. And, like the cow, the townspeople haven't been able to climb out of the abyss of obfuscation that sometimes happens when Fate throws a tizzy. Such is Erwin's cross to bear.

*   *   *

In 1916, the globe made its usual 365 turns around the sun as it had for nearly four billion years. And, as had happened from the time the first Cro-Magnons sat around their nightly cook fires, chewing on half-raw meat and grunting unintelligible attaboys about the day's hunt, 1916 began with man against man, man against beast, and beast against man. In spite of man's evolution, little had changed—except he had become more skilled in ways to fracture the harmony of this magnificent sphere in its celestial orbit.

That tumultuous year, while the German passenger liner *Vaterland* stagnated in New York harbor, the "war to end all wars" raged on the lush, blood-soaked meadows of France. The battles of Verdun and the Somme consumed young Britons and Germans by the thousands in an insane manifestation of power gone awry. The Irish, fed up with servitude to their British lords, rose up on the Monday after that Easter to begin a fight for independence that continues to this day. Woodrow Wilson, the "isolationist President," was elected to a second term but warned the American people that his policy had failed. (The next year, America would leap into the European pool of gore.)

The leviathan battleships, Pennsylvania (BB-38) and Oklahoma (BB37), were commissioned in the early summer of 1916 and sailed "Over There." (Twenty-five years later, early on a peaceful Sunday morning, the Oklahoma would be caught napping on "Battleship Row" at Pearl Harbor. Within moments, she would belly up from her Japanese-inflicted wounds. The Pennsylvania, flagship for the Seventh Fleet, would witness the event from her dry-dock berth. She would suffer only minor damage and would soon be back on the high seas, spitting out death and destruction on her Nipponese attackers.)

Also in 1916, Henry Ford's giant Detroit factory rolled out 730,041 Model-T Fords (all black)—one completed each 43 seconds—and sold them for a mind-boggling $360 each. (By 1927, when the last of 15 million Model-T's rolled off the assembly line, they were coming at the astronomical pace of one per twenty-five seconds!) On November 4, 1916, Walter Cronkite delivered his first commentary—his infant wails piercing the delivery room of a St. Joseph (Missouri) hospital as a doctor whapped his backside to rush new life into his lungs.

And on a drizzly day in September of that same year, Fate turned its contorted face toward Erwin and frowned.

Erwin wasn't much to look at when the planet whirled itself into the new century. The isolated mountain hamlet with its quagmire streets of yellow mud barely sustained a population of 500 hardy souls dressed in flour-sack gingham and Montgomery Ward "overhalls." Originally christened "Ervin," after the village's benefactor, Mr. David J.N. Ervin, who donated fifteen acres for the town, the name was mistakenly recorded on the rolls of the United States Postal Service in 1879 by a careless postal clerk as "Erwin." Rather than wage a lengthy fight against government bureaucracy, the city fathers decided that "Erwin" wasn't such a bad name after all.

Then came the Cincinnati, Clinchfield, and Ohio Railroad—commonly known as the "Clinchfield" and billed as "America's Most Unusual Railroad" because of the way it wound through wild, pristine valleys and penetrated the bowels of Appalachia's granite titans.

Exciting, to say the least! Fire-belching locomotives thundered through Erwin on shiny steel tracks that snaked alongside the Nolichucky, showering stores with soot and shaking mud-brick foundations. Cheerful, grimy-faced engineers waved at snot-nosed kids as cars topped high with black Tennessee coal flashed by, clickety-clacking toward distant markets.

With the railroad came Southern Potteries, a major industry that soon flooded America with delicate hand-painted Blue Ridge China. And the Clinchfield planners liked the looks of Erwin's broad expanse at the edge of town, so they built a large railroad repair facility on the spot. Almost overnight, the town's population swelled to over 2000 and the economy boomed. Things were looking up!

Then in September of 1916, Big Mary came to town and changed the history books!

No question about it, Mary always stole the show. The 10,000-pound Asian pachyderm was the icing on the cake, the attraction that really sold tickets and kept the crowds flocking to the large circus tent. But then Charlie Sparks, owner of Sparks World Famous Show, knew what he was doing. He had been in show biz since he'd worn baggy knickerbockers, and he knew what an audience craved. For sure, when his fifteen-railcar circus filled with lions, clowns, acrobats, and elephants pulled into towns, the people got excited. But "The Largest Living Land Animal on Earth," weighing over five tons and standing "three inches taller than Jumbo," as Mary's billing went, was what caused the crowds to mushroom.

The audiences roared with delight, night after night, town after town, as Mary performed an amazing mixed bag of tricks. She could stand on her head, was able to play over twenty-five tunes on musical horns "without missing a note," and she even pitched a baseball with her enormous trunk in a circus baseball routine. (Her .400 batting average had "astonished millions in New York"—so the posters claimed.) But what really dazzled the crowds was Mary's enormous size—and worth. Charlie Sparks valued his dynamic star at a whopping $20,000!

For Charlie and his wife, Addie (the circus' head cook, roustabout "momma," and *de facto* animal doctor), Mary was more than a performing artist. She had been part of Charlie's life since he was twenty-one, when his father had purchased her as the circus' first elephant in 1898. He had named the four year-old, four-foot high youngster "Mary."

For the childless couple, Mary became the child they could never have. So in accordance with Charlie's instructions, all the circus members gave the elephant the love and care that might have been lavished on an actual youngster. And although the circus did lag behind Charlie's main competitor, the forty-two car Robinson's Four Ring Circus and Menagerie, Mary's fame somewhat leveled the playing field.

In early September 1916, drawn by a puffing Clinchfield locomotive, Sparks World Famous Show rolled into St. Paul, a small mining town tucked into southwestern Virginia's Clinch River Valley. A few days earlier, Charlie's advance team had plastered storefronts and mud-smeared posts with colorful flyers announcing the show's arrival and proclaiming it to be a "100% Sunday School Circus"—meaning no rip-offs and no short-change artists. And of course, the flyers aggrandized Mary's remarkable talents. The countryside resounded with excitement! A circus was coming to town!

As soon as he spotted one of the flamboyant posters, Walter "Red" Eldridge became smitten. A circus job would be perfect to relieve the boredom of his humdrum janitor's existence at the Riverside Hotel. In fact, why not change his whole monotonous life? The circus could mean a ticket out of St. Paul, and for certain he didn't intend to spend the rest of his life pushing a broom in a dingy hotel. On the shy side of thirty, the flame-haired drifter still had a lot of living to do—or so he thought.

As soon as the rail cars were unloaded, Red approached the head elephant trainer, Paul Jacoby, and asked for a job. Late that summer, Jacoby's number one helper, Louis Reed, had departed for greener pastures, which left the trainer short handed. In spite of Red's lack of experience, Jacoby hired him on as an underkeeper and put him to work watering and feeding the large gray mammoths. And he took special care to instruct the new worker about Charlie Spark's "kid gloves philosophy" for handling the animals, especially Mary.

When the circus train chugged out of St. Paul for the next show at Kingsport, Tennessee, Red was on board—his janitor's broom exchanged for an elephant prod. He was headed for fame and glory!

Kingsport looked like something out of the 1880s "Wild West." The recently completed Clinchfield Railroad had linked the town to otherwise inaccessible coalfields and a boom was underway. Workers seeking jobs flooded into the town. Tents were jammed into every nook and wagons clogged the main thoroughfares, which echoed with the curses of unfortunates who had to wade through the ankle-deep mud that formed the town's streets.

As luck would have it, on September 12th, when Sparks World Famous Show came to town, Kingsport's first county fair had just begun. Great timing!

Came the circus parade down the muddy street: Clowns in flashy outfits tossing out bits of candy to the waving crowd that lined the route . . . acrobats in tights bulging with muscles . . . caped performers hinting at marvels that would soon take place in the three rings . . . and the elephants! "Mighty Mary," tail to trunk with her cousin pachyderms Shadrach, Mabel, and another "Mary," dazzled the crowd. The people huzzahed and cheered and rushed to buy tickets for the afternoon performance.

After the show Red and the other underkeepers rode the elephants up Center Street to a nearby pond for watering. On the way back to the circus lot, Mary spotted a watermelon rind by the side of the road and stopped to sample it. In spite of Red's insistent prodding, Mary refused to move on. The self-acclaimed handler, perched high on Mary's shoulders, played to the gathered spectators and jabbed Mary several times with a bull hook—something that he had been warned not to do. The old elephant reacted by wrapping her huge proboscis around her antagonist and tossing him against a nearby wooden drink stand.

Then she calmly walked over to where the hapless man lay and delivered the *coup de grace* by placing her foot on his head and letting five tons of live elephant do the rest. Mary shook her massive head and bellowed a mighty trumpet call at the shocked spectators as Red's head burst open like the over-ripe watermelon she had been denied.

The crowd panicked and ran for their lives. Hench Cox, a sixty-five year-old blacksmith who happened to be working nearby, grabbed up his 32-20 pistol and fired off five quick shots at Mary. The hail of steel bounced off the tough hide like tennis balls on concrete, but the noise did have a calming effect on the elephant, as well as the crowd. Angry shouts of "Kill the elephant" and "Let's kill her" began to penetrate the silence as the wave of spectators surged back.

Charlie Sparks came running and took in the scene at a glance. He'd dealt with similar situations before when a circus elephant had gone "bad," but nothing this serious. And in the past, he had quietly sold the culprit to another circus, as was the custom. But Mary! His pet! Mary had never caused any problems. Never! And one of his folks was killed. His worst nightmare had become a reality.

The throng pressed Charlie for quick justice. He grappled for control of the mob and shouted, "I'm perfectly willing, but there ain't a gun that can kill an elephant." Lucky for Charlie, Mayor Miller and Sheriff Hickman arrived on the scene and "arrested" Mary. Onlookers followed as the official party led Mary to the jail and chained her outside. After a few hours, the crowd grew tired and dispersed, and Mary was quietly returned to the circus. She gave a perfect show that evening.

But a dastardly deed had been committed and rumors began to sweep the countryside: "That elephant done already killed three people." And, "I heard that circus elephant kilt over a dozen." The whispers wouldn't stop. "Yeah, an th' way they kep'it hid. No tellin' how many more done got squashed." Local newspapers, always happy to increase sales, played to the public's mood and fed the frenzy with more rumors. The mayor of Johnson City, where the circus was scheduled to perform the next day, declared Mary *persona non grata*, as did the mayor of Rogersville, next on the list.

Indeed, city fathers all along the Clinchfield route threatened to cancel Sparks World Famous Show "for eternity" if the murderous elephant wasn't put to death. The final blow came when a worker rushed into Charlie's tent and shouted that some vigilantes were on the way with an old Civil War cannon to blast Mary to "Kingdom Come."

Charlie Sparks dearly loved Mary, but he was first and foremost a businessman and had the circus' future to consider. The beleaguered owner and his wife reluctantly decided that Mary would have to be destroyed. But how? Charlie called a powwow between Kingsport and Clinchfield officials and the circus staff. Charlie said, "We could shoot her in the head at her four soft spots. It'd be quick and painless."

The mayor nixed the idea—too risky, what with all the bystanders. One of the circus staff mentioned electrocution. (In 1903, with the help of Thomas Edison, a rogue elephant had been destroyed that way at Coney Island.) Mayor Miller pointed out that there wasn't enough volts in east Tennessee to do the trick. A Clinchfield engineer suggested that a chain be attached from the elephant's neck to a locomotive and that another be attached to her body and another locomotive, and "let'em pull her apart like taffy candy. Or chain'er to th' tracks an let a couple o' engines squeeze'er to death."

White as a sheet at the inhumane thought, Addie shrieked, "That's insane." The engineer, not to be put off, shrugged and said, "We got Ol' Fourteen Hundert" over in Erwin. She can do th' job." (Ol Fourteen Hundert" was Clinchfield's 100-ton derrick, which was used to off load lumber and lift rail cars back onto tracks.)

Technically, since the "crime" had occurred in Kingsport, justice should have been carried out there. But the railroad tracks had suffered from heavy torrential rains and an unusually wet summer. Clinchfield executives were unwilling to send the huge derrick to Kingsport over the Blue Ridge when it might be needed for an emergency in the southern region.

Lacking options, Charlie decided that hanging would be the best solution. With Mayor Miller's blessing and Clinchfield's okay, the circus quietly packed up its gear, loaded the animals, and chugged through the darkness to nearby Erwin.

The drizzly dawn of September 13th found the show resting on a siding in the Clinchfield Rail Yard, not far from "Ol Fourteen Hundert." The tranquil scene was soon spoiled as the curious began to gather. Charlie decided that Mary should go out in style. First, he would treat the good citizens of Erwin to an afternoon matinee—without Mary. And then the show of shows! His pet would become a circus "martyr" and make history.

During the matinee, Mary strained at her chain outside the big tent and nervously swayed back and forth. Why wasn't she inside performing with the other elephants? She had never missed a performance in her twenty-four years. Something ill rode the wind and intuitively she sensed an ominous cloud descending.

The word leaked out into the crowd and spread like wildfire. The killer elephant would be hanged down at the rail yard after the show! Free admission!

As soon as the last bows were taken, excited spectators flooded the rail yard. People crammed into every vantage point, jostling for the best views; boxcar tops and open doors were stuffed. Bodies filled the windows and rooftops of nearby buildings. By five o'clock, the population of tiny Erwin had doubled. Show time!

Tears flowed as Charlie and Addie bid farewell to their beloved pet. Hoping to calm Mary, Charlie ordered Jacoby, the head trainer, to have the other elephants accompany her in the familiar "tail-to-trunk" procession. Down Love Street went the entire circus crew, en masse behind the elephants but silenced by the solemnity of the occasion. Completely out of character, the elephants trumpeted loudly, as if they knew what was about to unfold.

As soon as the procession reached the giant derrick, an underkeeper quickly chained Mary's leg to the track while Jacoby led the other elephants out of sight. Some five hundred feet down the track, near the roundhouse, roustabouts with the help of a Clinchfield steam shovel were busy digging a large hole. At Charlie's nod, a roustabout placed a heavy 7/8-inch chain around Mary's neck and attached it to the derrick's boom, and an eerie quiet descended on the scene. Suddenly, Addie's hysterical wails pierced the drizzly overcast. Mary strained at her leg chain and bellowed. But the grotesque die was cast.

Charlie bowed his head as the derrick wreckmaster, Sam Bondurant, pulled a lever and the chain began to stretch tight. Mary gave a horrendous bellow as the popping and ripping of tearing tendons drowned out the derrick's groaning struggle. The underkeeper had forgotten to unchain Mary's leg from the track! Bondurant cursed and lowered the chain while the elephant's leg was released. Then once again the chain began its life-snuffing rise.

Mary was lifted six feet into the air before the chain gave way with a gunshot crack. The crowd gasped as she crashed onto the rails. The nearest onlookers fled, stampeding the crowd, which became a crush of flailing arms and tripping legs. Old Jim Coffey, totally blind, also ran—toward Mary. A man grabbed his arm and pushed him in the opposite direction. "Whut's ahappenin'?" Old Jim asked. "You crazy or blind?" yelled the man. "Hell, maybe both," Old Jim growled. "I ain't seen a lick in twenty yars. I jist come down to watch'im hang th' elephant."

But Mary just sat there, stunned, her hip fractured. Seeing that they were in no immediate danger, the crowd settled down and a railroad worker produced a heavier chain. A roustabout scrambled up the unresisting animal's back and placed the linked noose around her neck. Then made ready once again, the terrible derrick strained and groaned as Mary rose high in the air. She struggled for a moment, sighed, and was still.

Mary's demise and a town's cross to bear.

T.K. Broyles, a Clinchfield employee, snapped a photo of poor Mary dangling at the end of the chain. She hung there for a half-hour. Finally, an engine snaked the derrick down to the hole and Mary was gently lowered into her final resting-place. The scales of justice had been balanced; the show was over. With nothing else to see, the crowd dispersed. The steam shovel went back to its somber work.

*   *   *

Eighty-eight years later, Erwin still lives with Mary's ghost. Decades after Charlie Sparks and his World Famous Show faded away, the elephant's memory survives, although the city fathers would have it otherwise.

The media periodically resurrects the tragic tale. Mary's hanging has been graphically depicted in *Playboy* and the *National Enquirer*. The TV game show, "Jeopardy," even had a question based on Mary's execution.

But the citizens of Erwin would as soon forget that blemish on their fine town. They have rebuffed efforts to erect monuments *in memoriam*. Even Mary's makeshift grave goes unmarked, and time and civic languor have obscured its exact location.

But who can blame them? The sequence of events that placed Mary in Erwin's front yard was not of their making. By law, Kingsport had legal jurisdiction over the killing and should have resolved the matter. Even now, when out-of-towners snidely ask, "This is where that elephant got hanged, ain't it?" Erwinians are likely to grin sheepishly and reply, "Yeah, can't rightly deny that we hanged it, but dadburned if it was our fault. We got a bum rap." And they did!

Time has a way of altering facts of a given event with the passage of years. Indeed, witnesses, when questioned about a specific recent incident, frequently give different and confusing testimony—a lawyer's dilemma. That's human nature. We all see things differently. So what really did happen on that tragic dreary September 13, 1916?

To give a reasonably clear account, I have drawn from several sources. All agree about the basic facts—the "who, what, when, where, why." After that, things get a bit quirky. Railroader Mont Lilly (who helped hang Mary) claimed that Kingsport did try to electrocute the elephant by shooting 44,000 volts through her thick hide and ". . . she just danced a little." Doubtful.

Also, the rumor spread that on the night after the hanging, Charlie had his roustabouts dig into Mary's grave and saw off her tusks—corroborated by witness M.D. Clark, who claimed ". . . they dug down that night and cut her tushes off." Again, not likely. A close examination of T.K. Broyles' photo of Mary hanging from the derrick boom reveals a dead elephant *sans* tusks. In fact, assuming Mary *was* an Asian elephant, unlike her African cousins she only had rudimentary tusks, if that.

And about the photo: When Broyles submitted it to *Argosy Magazine* for publication, they pooh-poohed it as a hoax. (Allegedly, *Argosy* later approached Clinchfield executives and asked that they allow Mary to be exhumed so that they could get a "real" picture. Clinchfield refused.) Experts now believe the photo is authentic, although it may have been touched up to better enhance Mary's profile through the drizzle.

One stalwart Erwin resident does push for a decent memorial to Mary. Resident Ruth Piper is so dedicated to the idea that in 1995 she petitioned city officials to erect an elephant statue and fountain on the "village green." She also fought for a short documentary of the historical event to be made available at the Visitors' Center, along with a memorial wreath appropriately displayed in the railroad yards.

To date, her efforts have come to naught. In the interim, Ruth has established her own memorial to Mary—in a way. Her store, "The Hanging Elephant Gift Shop" in downtown Erwin, sells T-shirts and other paraphernalia emblazoned with Mary's likeness.

A final irony. In today's society, the event could not have occurred. The Humane Society of the United States, PETA, and other "animal rights" organizations would have been knocking at a Kingsport judge's door even before the train began the 40-mile trip to Erwin. These groups would have demanded an injunction to halt any cruel and unusual punishment to Mary in spite of the heinous deed.

In all probability the judge would have agreed and ordered that Mary be "retired" to the 2700-acre Hohenwald (Tennessee) Elephant Sanctuary to spend her remaining 40-odd years. (This non-profit facility in Lewis County, established in 1995, is a unique place—the only sanctuary anywhere for endangered Asian *female* elephants. Sorry guys, no males permitted. Unlike the ladies, male elephants don't take to herd-style life. They just want to be "out with the guys.")

Mary would have fit in nicely with the eight females that permanently reside at the elephant "retirement home." And as for Erwin and its unsolicited claim to fame? Who knows . . .

Chapter Sixteen

In Memoriam

I hike; I see; I wonder. The thought pulsates inside of my skull like an incessant drumbeat, in near-perfect tempo with the thudding of my dust-choked boots as I approach another trail shrine. I pause out of respect, something that I have done since coming across the first one—a trailside marker in memory of Wade Sutton when I climbed out of the Nantahala Gorge on that first memorable thru-hike in 1990. *Who was this person, so honored, so loved to warrant a memorial in this lonely untamed spot? Why here?* Most are granite markers, small gray-flecked stones with a name and a couple of dates that measure a person's fleeting brush with the planet. The numbers, set in stone—sometimes accompanied by a few chosen words—give the illusion that what you see is the sum total of a life lived. A lifetime of memories is captured in the block of granite with a short grandiloquent epitaph. All that the individual believed, stood for, did, is condensed into a chunk of rock with a name and some nice words.

It's snake oil. A brief glance, a rush of curiosity, and that's usually it. Nothing revealed; nothing explained. You hike on, feeling like a walking puzzle with several pieces missing.

So it is with me. With my imagination running at full throttle but going nowhere, I walk on up the Trail, unfulfilled, craving enlightenment, and the beat goes on: *I hike; I see; I wonder . . .*

*　　*　　*

April 18, 1990. The sign in Rock Gap (three miles south of where the Trail crosses U.S. Highway 64 near Franklin, North Carolina) didn't look very impressive: A small wooden marker (no marble here) that said something about "The John Wasilik Memorial Poplar" being the "second largest poplar in the World." And it could be seen if one was only willing to make the 1.5-

mile round trip down into a wooded hollow (and back up). Yeah, sure! Like I was going to take the time to do *that*!

I had been on the Trail exactly one week today and my appetite was working overtime. Rainbow Springs Campground was within smelling distance, and they had *Pizza*! Naw, I wasn't going to go gawk at some big tree when pizza was so close.

Mentally dismissing the sign's challenge, I dug into my pack and pulled out a Snickers. Now *this* was something worthwhile. Anyway, I needed to let my hiking partner, Wahoola, catch up before we got to Wallace Gap and stuck out our thumbs for the short hitch down to the campground.

Less than an hour before, along with four other depraved hikers, we had "mooned" ol' Albert Mountain. Actually, we had targeted the fire tower, because that's the direction our tushes were bared. And the ignominious deed had been recorded for posterity by Moleskin Meg's able hands as she snapped pictures on an assortment of cameras—seven, including hers—with astonishing dexterity. As soon as I retrieved my camera, I had hightailed it off the summit ahead of the others, hoping to salvage what dignity I had left, but mainly so that I wouldn't have to listen to Wahoola tease me about my skinny butt, which he would have done. (*Walkin'* . . . pp 88-89)

I poked the last bite of bar in just as Wahoola strode into view. He leered like he'd just wowed me with a lewd joke. "Don't say a word," I growled.

"About what?" He straightened up his face and read the sign aloud. "You wanna go see what the second largest poplar in the world looks like?"

"You crazy? It's almost two miles there and back. That's over an hour!" I was almost whining like a dog looking for a place to piss in deep snow. "We could be at Rainbow Springs by then and stuffin' our face with pizza!"

I don't think he heard a word I said. "We won't get another chance. I'm goin' for it," he muttered. Without another word he strode off down the blue-blazed path like he was a sinner rushing to the altar seeking salvation before God Almighty had a chance to renege on the deal. Oh what the heck! I put my pack back on and fell in behind.

The tree more than made up for the unadorned sign. The old titan dwarfed everything around, making the other hardwood trees look like candidates for a toothpick machine. But it had seen better days. Still leafless from winter's squeeze, its massive naked limbs rose stark against the cobalt sky, revealing patches of decay—an early harbinger of the tree's impending fate. As an offering to the wooden god, or perhaps lending credence to its exalted status, two-legged friends had erected a split rail fence, which formed a sizeable enclosure that would have held all of Old Hog Greer's porky friends.

I paced around the trunk. "Twenty steps," I remarked. "Biggest danged tree I've ever seen."

"Biggest damned tree I've ever seen.

"It's big alright." Wahoola gazed from the roots to the topmost branches and shook his head. "Something's wrong. The proportion's not right. It's not tall enough for the girth." Wahoola should know; he had studied forestry. "Look up there at the tip of the trunk. Top's been blown out." Sure enough, I could see the jagged scar.

I grumbled, "Maybe that's why it's number two. Let's go get some pizza."

On the climb back up to the Trail, Wahoola, a few steps to my rear, began to snigger and then laugh. "You wanna share what's so funny?" I snarled, already knowing what was coming.

"You sure got a skinny butt." Give me a break!

So went my first visit to the grand old poplar. Lackadaisical attitude, frivolous, for sure, but no disrespect intended. And in spite of holding off on the pizza, I'm glad Wahoola insisted on going, for most of the Maine-focused thru-hikers just scoot on by. I would have—and did on my 1994 thru-hike.

But in 1998, my conscience rebelled so I swung off of the Trail and betook myself down to the forest shrine. This time I was better prepared, knowledge wise, for my visit—but not for the patriarch's appearance. Eight years of decay had taken a sad toll. Telltale gray fungal whirls had multiplied at an alarming rate and I realized that John Wasilik's tree was in serious trouble. I sat a spell, as I would by the bedside of a sick friend, grieving, reflecting on that first visit and what I had learned since that day with Wahoola . . .

Once this mighty poplar was one of many. Then came the wood sharks, in the early 1930s, wielding axes and saws and swearing at mulish oxen teams that nearly burst their guts as they tried to snake Cyclopean hunks of wood to within reach of gasoline contraptions. And when the loggers came upon two trees that towered above all others, they exclaimed, "Truly these great trees are worthy adversaries. We will save them till last!"

The forest receded before the onslaught until it resembled a dog with a bad case of mange—green scraggly splotches of unwanted scrub interspersed among rotting limbs and bleeding stumps. At last, only the two giants remained. Sweating, gasping for air, with set jaws and straining muscles, the loggers finally brought down one of the trees. They stripped the limbs and sawed the trunk into huge sections, and then gazed at what they had wrought. One said, "Damned if we'll move that sucker." Another: "Biggest sumabitch I ever cut."

The drivers doubled the oxen teams and hooked up. The oxen bawled and lunged as whips split the air above their ears and drivers cursed and fumed. But each section crawled across the forest floor, inch by hard-earned inch, like an oversized fetus struggling down a birth canal toward release, leaving huge scars until they finally lay in a chaotic pile close to the wheezing crane. The foreman eyed the setting sun and scratched his head. "Boys, by damned if we're gonna waste a day on that other poplar. Pack up yer tools."

So the last of the mighty poplars got a reprieve—and a place in local history.

A few facts for the gnarly-brained: John Wasilik's namesake is a tulip (or yellow) poplar and is really not a member of the "poplar" family. Rather, it belongs to the "magnolia" species. Tulip poplars grow tall and wide, attaining heights approaching 200 feet and diameters in the 7 to 8-foot range. This "second largest" poplar sports an eight-foot diameter (which translates into a 25-foot circumference), and it was 135-feet tall before its topmost 21 feet were ripped out by a storm.

At one time the old woody patriarch was listed as the "World's Largest Poplar" in the National Registry of Big Trees—until in 1972 a larger poplar was found in Bedford, Virginia. (This tree still remains the king of the poplars and has been given a place of honor in Bedford's Poplar Park. Its stats: A whopping 10-foot diameter (31-foot circumference) and 146-feet tall.)

Yet, in spite of their great size, poplars are short-lived when compared to some of their cellulose kin. The oldest known tulip poplar is in New York State—estimated at 225 years old. But that's the blink of an eye on the celestial scale when compared to "Methuselah," a Bristletoe Pine discovered in 1957 by Dr. Edmund Schulman high on a slope in California's White Mountains. At *4767 years old* (yep, he counted all 4767 growth rings), the ancient pine is thought to be the world's oldest living tree. Now you know!

What about the man to whom the tree is dedicated? Not a lot remains to mark the passing of John Wasilik, Jr. But then, this is not so unusual. Each day many millions of decent, good-hearted people go about the business of making the world a better place. These folks—all cogs in the wheel of life— suffer through myriad mundane routines, laboring without complaint to pay bills and support families and try to get a little "ahead" so that they can enjoy the trinkets that define "a better life." And when the final time card is punched, when the last sunset brings on infinite nightfall, time begins to feast on lingering memories until the day comes when some aspiring writer strives to resurrect a life and finds only tattered remnants. But that's the way the proverbial cookie crumbles.

Ranger Wasilik fared better than some of "the cogs." He had a tree dedicated to his memory. There are far lesser rewards.

John Wasilik was born in Roselle, New Jersey, during the "Gay Nineties." He graduated from Yale University in 1917 and four days later enlisted in the U.S. Army to do his patriotic duty in the Great War—he didn't even wait to receive his diploma. Pvt. Wasilik spent the next two years in France as an ambulance driver and was decorated for meritorious service. When enough killing had been done to appease the gods of war, all parties signed the Armistice and Pvt. Wasilik returned to the good old US of A. He immediately dug in and earned a Masters degree in Forestry. He joined the Forest Service in 1922 as a Nantahala ranger and never looked back.

Except for a brief stint as a ranger in the Cherokee National Forest (1927), his entire career was spent with the Nantahala National Forest, where he served as the District Ranger from 1939 until his retirement in 1954. Each day he would sally forth from his Franklin (North Carolina) office to nurture and protect the wooded mountains that in turn nurtured his soul. And he was cut from the same fabric as his comrade-in-green, Arthur Woody, the ranger for nearby Chattahoochee National Forest who ruled his "kingdom" with iron-willed righteousness and whose name became a household word as familiar to local inhabitants as "Carter's Little Liver Pills." Both men were wholly dedicated to the conservation of woodlands and land acquisition as a means to preserve the forests for future generations. (Wasilik was responsible for adding over 100,000 acres to the Nantahala National Forest.)

It's not farfetched that these men knew one another; that they cried on each other's shoulder about the pillage of the mountains by greedy uncaring timber barons; that they fought in the trenches together to halt the terrible slaughter.

After he retired, the old ranger continued to live in Franklin at his home on Rogers Hill, filling his days with gardening, tennis (his first love after tree warden) and wowing the local school children with his softball prowess. A devout Catholic, he founded the only Catholic Church in Franklin/Macon County. John Wasilik (age 74) died in June 1968 from a heart attack and was interred at Franklin's Woodlawn Cemetery.

On a solemn gray day a year later, August 31, 1969, family, friends, and fellow lovers of the outdoors—nearly three hundred in all—braved threatening weather and gathered at Rock Gap. The group walked down the steep trail built by members of the Macon Program for Progress, which led to the huge

124 J. R. "MODEL-T" TATE

poplar. (At that time the tree was listed as the "World's Largest Poplar" in the *National Register of Big Trees*. Some say that John Wasilik had "rediscovered" the tree; had loved it as a father might love his firstborn son.)

Family and close friends joined hands and made a circle around the huge base, and a bronze plaque was unveiled: "This Tree Dedicated to John Wasilik, Jr.; District Ranger; Nantahala National Forest; 1939-1954; A Pioneer Forester." Rev. Rufus Morgan then gave the prayer of dedication, and John Wasilik's son, John, Jr., made a few remarks. All then listened with solemn respect as the Deputy Regional Forester, H.C. Eriksson, officially dedicated the tree to its departed guardian.

His words seemed a fitting eulogy: "There is something symbolic about this giant yellow poplar that reminds me of this fine man whom we all respected. It represents strength and ruggedness for the outdoors which characterized John so well."

This is only a thumbnail portrait of a great man's life. But one thing is for sure: The Nantahala National Forest is a better place because of John Wasilik.

Yes, there are far lesser rewards!

(A sad note: Recently Bill Lea, Resource Specialist for National Forests in North Carolina, confirmed what I had suspected when I sat beneath the aged poplar's once-mighty limbs in 1998. The tree is dying.)

A life lesson: Nothing is forever . . .

*　　*　　*

The six-mile climb out of the Nantahala Gorge to Swim Bald could make a Baptist preacher say things that would burn a Methodist's ears. It's a nasty piece of business, this part of the "National Treasure," especially if you've played the fool and partied too much at the Nantahala Outdoor Center. A warm day and an overloaded pack can up the ante to unbearable proportions. Sweat reeking of stale beer pours down into the eyes, blinding sight and making walking treacherous; while sporadic splotches of upchucked food foul the pristine setting and flog the mind with gross images.

So while in this state of animated misery, I nearly walked on past the bronze marker set into a gray marble base. The date, "December 7," penetrated the stinging sweat-blur that clouded my military-oriented mind. From some recess sprang the thought, unbidden: *Hmmm, Pearl Harbor Day. Strange.* Break time!

Weird place for a memorial, out here in "no-man's land," I muttered to myself. *Why not at Grassy Gap where there would be better people exposure?* The gap couldn't have been much further. I studied the plaque. Topped by the NC Forest Service logo, the raised letters read: "ON DECEMBER 7, 1968 783 FEET SOUTHWEST FROM THIS POINT WADE A. SUTTON NORTH CAROLINA FOREST SERVICE RANGER GAVE HIS LIFE SUPPRESSING A FOREST FIRE, THAT YOU MIGHT MORE FULLY ENJOY YOUR HIKE ALONG THIS TRAIL."

A worthy cause, but not at the cost of a life, I reflected as I tried to visualize the scene through the stupor of exhaustion: Frenzied flames where I now stood, whipped into a masochistic demon by crazed winds . . . fireballs leaping from canopy to canopy at lightning speed, causing trees to explode from the intense heat . . . panicked animals fleeing before the dragon's fiery breath . . . Nature's mandate, "survival of the fittest," temporarily put on hold in deference to the falling embers . . . firefighters flushed beet-red from over-exertion, gasping for air with smoke-filled lungs, hearts red-lined as they frantically fight the beast in its lair. And over everything, the choking pall of smoke.

Not a pretty picture! *And just 783 feet from where I now stood, one lonely firefighter gave his life* . . . A fluffy cloud slowly floated across the sun, darkening the shadows and causing a chill to rise through the sweat. I got my feet moving and left my thoughts behind with the plaque. I had enough misery to deal with on this day.

Wade Sutton didn't cotton to grandiose dreams of fame and fortune. As far back as he could remember, all he'd ever wanted to do was fish and be a firefighter, and not necessarily in that order. The fishing was easy. Becoming a firefighter was a mite tougher because Wade had to make a lengthy detour called World War II.

After the war, he returned to Bryson City, North Carolina, and like others of "the greatest generation," the soldier-veteran pushed aside the nightmarish images of battlefield butchery and went on with his life. Wade oiled his old reel and headed for the fishing hole.

After he had made up for five years of angler abstinence and caught a freezer full of fish, he married the gal he'd left behind—a pretty mountain lass by name of Lucille. Soon came a son and two daughters. In a few short years the air was filled with whooping and hollering each evening when their daddy came home to the small cottage on Jackson Line Road, just outside Bryson City, after a hard day's work for a local timber baron. Hard work for meager pay, but somehow the bills got paid and the years slipped by.

Wade never forgot his "dream" of becoming a firefighter. When he heard that the North Carolina State Forest Service had a vacancy for a ranger at Swain County (North Carolina)—his very own county—he jumped at the chance. At age forty he was a mite old perhaps, but he did have a gold mine of experience from his years of timbering. Still . . .

Wade needn't have worried. When he walked into the boss ranger's office for the mandatory interview, it only took a few minutes for the ranger to decide that he need look no further. Topping six feet, plenty sturdy to do the job; respectful, too—the prospect had even removed the faded brown ball cap when he came in. He liked Wade's open, friendly face with grin lines etched around smiling brown eyes. Best of all, his easy manner and confident air said, "mountain bred, mountain grown," which to the weathered ranger's eye spelled resourcefulness and loyalty. And the hands, big and callused, were the truth teller. This fellow was no stranger to hard work.

The interview began. "You ever been in trouble with the Law?" "No suh." Good and to the point. "Why do you want to be a forest ranger?" Wade looked square into the boss man's steely gray eyes, like his daddy long ago had taught him to do, and said with conviction, "I've been cuttin' trees since I got home from th' Army. Don't much like what I see out in th' woods though. Loggers are getting th' forests in a heap o' trouble an' I wanna do something to help save 'em." The ranger stuck out his hand. "You got th' job." It was that simple.

Wade Sutton far exceeded the old ranger's expectations. Over the next twelve years he rose through the ranks and became the head Swain County Ranger for the North Carolina State Forest Service.

At 9:15 on Saturday morning, December 7, 1968, the siren's wail split the tranquil air of Bryson City. The fifty-two year old veteran firefighter called his assistant, R.Q. Canby. "Someone's reported a fire over in the Watauga Creek area. Let's go."

By the time they got to the scene the fire had gotten a good start. Wade said, "I expect it's done burned close to a hundert acres. I'd better call the Graham County (Forest) Office for some help. You go uphill an' see if you can find a place to start a back fire an' I'll head down th' mountain an' see how far it's got."

The contingent from Graham County arrived on the scene at 4:30 P.M. R.Q.'s back burn had kept the conflagration from spreading, so the group quickly got the fire under control. R.Q. was worried. "Wade went off down th' hill hours ago and I ain't seen hide ner hair of him since. We'd better go take a look."

Around 7:30 P.M., the firefighters found Wade's body lying next to a small spring about three hundred yards from where he and R.Q. had parted company. Swain County Coroner Dr. William Mitchell stated that death was most probably due to carbon monoxide poisoning and severe burns. (A rumor persisted that Wade had a heart condition and possibly had died from a heart attack.)

The small Jackson Line Baptist Church was packed with mourners as Reverend Berlin Aldridge eulogized the congregation's fallen member. He was laid to rest in Section D of the Swain Memorial Park in Bryson City.

R. Q. Canby was a hard man to track down. After several wrong turns I managed to find the small slightly run-down house on Schoolhouse Road on the outskirts of Bryson City, where I'd been told that he lived. A grizzled, toothpick-thin old timer wearing a ragged ball cap was bent over in the middle of a large garden plot behind the house and slowly, methodically, created a deep furrow in clod-riddled dirt with an old hoe. Large sweat spots darkened the back of his gray work shirt in spite of the cool morning air of mid-April (2003). Signs of last night's frost still lingered, appearing as a dusty white carpet in the shaded spots beneath several old maples. I walked over to the edge of the garden. "Kinda early to be puttin' taters in, isn't it?" I asked, putting on my best "I'm a gardener, too" smile.

He gave me a once over and snorted like I'd insulted his intelligence. "Had'em in earlier than this before. Later, too." I nodded and tried to muster some respect into my voice at the old man's sage declaration before I dug a hole that might swallow me whole and thwart my purpose for being here. "Yep, I can see you're a man that knows his taters. I shoulda had mine out by now."

He eyed me with tolerant patience, like an animal trainer might look at a feisty cub that needed lots of work. Laying the hoe down to mark his spot, he motioned me toward the small front porch and scowled. "Danged hoe doesn't do half th' work it used to."

We made small talk about gardening and the weather. Like many of the old mountain breed, R.Q. was stingy with his words—born, of course, with a natural distrust of strangers. After he decided that I wasn't from the "Gov'mint" or trying to sell him something, he loosened up enough for me to get around to the subject of Wade Sutton.

I asked him about that day. R.Q.'s face clouded as his thoughts carried him back thirty-five years to an acrid charred hillside and the dismal web that long ago day had spun over so many lives. "Tweren't the best day of my life," he muttered. "I jist don't know how it coulda happened. Wade was a careful man; never took no chances where safety was an issue. It jist don't fit that he got trapped by that fire."

He stopped abruptly, almost as if he were about to reveal a huge secret, then continued. "Orrs (Hughes) said th' same thing. Orrs worked with Wade 'bout as much as I did." R.Q. shrugged. "Now Orrs could probably tell you a thing or two bout what you're trying to find out, but it ain't no use talkin' to him. He's probably out on th' lake fishin'. Besides, he won't talk about it."

I asked R.Q. about the plaque beside the Appalachian Trail north of NOC. He smiled. "Well, me'n Orrs decided that we ought'er do somethin' for Wade, so we had this monument made and carried it up there to where it is now." He paused, struggling for some thought that wouldn't surface. The old fire fighter grimaced. "Dang if that don't beat a fryin' pan." I waited for him to gather his thoughts, but his eyes slowly glazed over, his mind drifting to some far away place where I couldn't go—perhaps he had glimpsed the darkness of eternity. Then R.Q. spoke with soft finality, as if he were delivering an eulogy. Maybe he was. "Wade was a good man."

I promised R.Q. that I would send him the finished article about Wade Sutton. By the time I reached my truck, he was already back in his beloved garden, assaulting the cloddy dirt with the stubborn hoe, planting his seed "taters."

(Author's note: I wasn't able to fulfill my promise to R.Q. Canby. He died in early March 2004 while this manuscript was still being written.)

In 1968, wildland fires in the United States claimed 18 lives. Wade Sutton's name is inscribed on that permanent list.

*   *   *

"We are the dead. Short days ago We lived, felt dawn, saw sunset glow, Loved and were loved, and now we lie In Flander's Fields."

John McCrae's poignant, haunting words, echoes from the past, rose unbidden as I stared at the gray stone. The marble matched the thick mist that wrapped its frigid tentacles around Hurricane Gap (North Carolina)—and my mood—as it stubbornly dominated the noonday sun. The words were a "legacy" from my fifth grade teacher, Katie Blandford, who ruled her classroom like a Marine boot camp DI. Even now I shudder when her scowling freckled face framed by frizzed red hair crashes into my awareness.

Miz Blandford had been obsessed with poetry and had made the whole class memorize tomes of poems, most of which rang hollow inside my insipid thirteen year-old head. But the Canadian surgeon's famous WWI poem, *In Flanders Fields the Poppies Grow*—his bequest to mankind before an untimely death in a dingy French hospital at age forty-five—had somehow etched itself on my youthful soul, and so it will remain until my last breath.

Short days ago we lived . . . Had this man who had gasped his final breath here been affected by McCrae's words, as had I? What meandering along Life's rutted pathway, what unforeseen twists of Fate, had brought him to this lonely place with the unharmonious name of Hurricane Gap?

We are the dead . . . A coterie of subdued bluets and yellow-topped trout lilies surrounded the base of the low memorial. Circled by a bodyguard of irises at rigid attention, they offered a perpetual silent eulogy to the fallen hiker. I read the words aloud, as if the deadened sound might somehow offset the funereal scene: IN MEMORY REX R. PULFORD SEPT. 22, 1920 APR. 21, 1983. *Just ten years my senior,* I thought. For him, *a life cut short; a dream ended in the blink of an eye.* And my fate? *A single heartbeat lies between me and a piece of gray granite.* As it has for each day I have lived; for each mile I have hiked, and always will.

Dorothy Pulford, like most daughters, had a special relationship with her father. They both loved books and the Great Outdoors.

Michigan born, Rex earned his undergraduate degree at Brown University and taught psychology at the University of Detroit for a couple of years. Deciding to spread his career wings, he soared into the field of industrial psychology and spent the next two years giving "ink blot" tests to disgruntled employees. Fate blessedly intervened when Rex and his young wife, Betty, visited the Sunshine State in the early 1950s. Over on the Gulf side, near Yankeetown, they discovered "paradise" on the banks of the Withlacoochee River, disguised as a quaint fishing camp. Surprisingly, the plumbing and air-conditioning worked, the newspapers were delivered on the door stoop (never in the water), and the fish were plentiful.

With Betty's blessing, Rex packed away his battery of Rorschach tests and bought the place. After due deliberation, they named it "The Little Skipper." They catered to the angler crowd for almost a decade, until one day Rex found his true niche—as an elementary school teacher.

The stork swooped low over Yankeetown on a soft Florida day in 1956 and left a rosy-cheeked infant at the fishing camp. It wasn't long before Dorothy was toddling along the docks, waving at the fishermen and staring wide-eyed at the embellished tales of "the one that got away." And then came the day when Rex came home from teaching his sixth grade class and grabbed Dorothy up in his arms. "School's out for the summer," he shouted. "We're going to the mountains!" And so it began.

By the time Dorothy finished college, hiking was in her blood. During previous summers, she and Rex had put many miles on their hiking boots. (Betty liked camping, but hoofing it wasn't part of the deal for her.) During their forays into the mountains, father and daughter frequently encountered weary, trail-tarnished thru-hikers who, for a sandwich or two, would plop down beneath the nearest shade tree and regale them with tales of wonder and delight. So in early 1979, before she leaped into the melting pot of postgraduate studies, Dorothy crammed her backpack with equal amounts of gear and anticipation and stepped off from Springer Mountain to fulfill a long-held dream.

As with nearly all thru-hikers, her Appalachian Trail journey was a life-altering experience. It nearly became a "life-ending" experience. In 1979 the Trail crossed Big Walker Mountain near Bland, Virginia. (The Trail has since been relocated farther north to Brushy Mountain.) On top of Big Walker, Dorothy had the unique (and dubious) experience of becoming a human lightning rod. A black ominous cloud gathered above the horizon, still several miles distant—no immediate threat. Suddenly came a blinding flash and mind-rattling crash, and Dorothy's clothes began to smoke.

But lightning plays a fickle game, frying some to a crisp, electrocuting others with hardly a mark, and letting others live for another day's sport. Dorothy was one of the lucky ones, although she used up her quota of adrenaline for the hike. She walked away with nothing more than scorched clothes, a sizzling backpack frame, and frizzed hair—and a renewed respect for the wily demon. And after a few more million steps, her "dream" became reality when she hugged the terminus sign atop Mount Katahdin.

Enter Jeff Hansen, a tall, handsome, genial gent, who shared her love of Nature. Cupid saw an opening, fired off a volley of zingers, and Nature did the rest. The couple eventually settled in at the Walasi-Yi Center at Neels Gap and opened an outfitter "mecca" and hiker hostel. Soon Jeff attended the National Outdoor Leadership School.

For the next decade, he and Dorothy ministered to the needs of the hiking community—especially for novice "wannabes" headed to Maine (including yours truly) by helping to pare down ridiculously heavy packs and giving advice and a pat on the back. (In 2001, Dorothy and Jeff passed the torch to Winton and Marjorie Porter, who continue to provide the same wonderful service. Dorothy now teaches at North Georgia Technical College and Jeff is the proud owner of a bookstore, the "Book Nut," in Blairsville, Georgia.)

But I digress. This story is really about Dorothy's father, Rex. In early March 1983, about the time Dorothy and Jeff were unpacking boxes and stocking shelves at Walasi-Yi Center, Rex's time came. Now retired, inspired by his intrepid daughter's account of her thru-hike, he sought to catch his own "dream."

On Sunday, March 13th, he spent his first night on the Appalachian Trail atop Springer Mountain after polishing off the eight-mile Approach Trail from Amicalola Falls State Park. And like most of the new "wannabes" headed north, Rex had to slug it out in the trenches, fighting to conquer each interminable mile, each steep Georgia mountain, each blister-plagued, pain-filled day. But he persevered, and his muddy boots and determined stride devoured the miles.

Fortune smiled. In a Heaven-made match, his wife (Betts, he'd taken to calling her) became a willing partner to his hike—in her own way. When she could, Betty would meet Rex at road crossings, where they would share a warm dry tent and hot meals that were a cut above regular hiker fare. And so it went . . . snowy days when the trail disappeared beneath Nature's white blanket . . . shivery days when Winter's breath blasted away excitement and anticipation like chaff scattering before a gale . . . shelter-packed nights where a body became a prisoner, shackled by human morass as surely as if caught in waist-deep quicksand.

And so he plodded on—past the old gnarled tree at Bly Gap as he stepped into North Carolina, his second state on the long push north. On past the colorful kayaks that frolicked in swirling waters near the bridge that spans the turbulent Nantahala. On across the mighty Fontana Dam and up into the mystic fog-shrouded Smokies and over Clingmans Dome beneath an impossibly blue sky. He hiked under Interstate 40 and up Snowbird Mountain.

Suddenly, the calendar flipped a page. Rex's one month anniversary on the Trail happened at Newfound Gap, where Betts met him and ordered a day's reprieve from the daily grind. He and Betty went shopping at nearby Cherokee. They also celebrated his being "smoke free"—nary a single cigarette—since beginning his hike.

Hikers came, and quick easy friendships fostered by the shared goal of reaching Katahdin were formed. Friendships dissolved as quickly when hikers, their excitement ground to dullness, left the small cosmos of the Trail.

In his journal, Rex described Monday, April 18th, as "a day of disasters." He and three companions had reached Groundhog Creek Shelter late the evening before, only to find the shelter crammed. They tented nearby and awoke to heavy snowfall. The group broke camp and headed toward Browns Gap. The snow, whipped by a harsh north wind, brought visibility down to almost zero. Boot prints covered over within seconds and the white blazes that mark the Trail blended in with the snow until they disappeared entirely. By the time they neared Max Patch Bald, the storm had grown into a roaring blizzard.

Enough was enough. Rex and the other hikers, afraid to tackle Max Patch in the fierce maelstrom, turned aside and stumbled along Max Patch Road. They finally hitched a ride into Hot Springs. That afternoon Rex joined up with Betty, who had shown the good sense to make a motel reservation.

April 19th dawned clear and cold. The front had moved its mischief over the mountains into the foothills of western North Carolina. But more misery was in store for Rex. He awoke with an intestinal upset. Fearing *giardia*, the dreaded hiker's scourge, he headed for the local clinic. The doctor took a stool sample (which had to be sent to Erwin for analysis), prescribed plenty of liquids, no solid food of any kind—including ice cream—and no hiking for two days. (Rex recorded in his journal that his blood pressure measured 110 over 65, ". . . not bad for a guy who once had high blood pressure," he wrote.)

Actually, the interlude came as a welcome break for the couple, especially Rex. The early spring storms had trounced him pretty hard through the Smokies. He and Betty drove to Asheville that afternoon to purchase a new pair of boots (size 10 EE—his feet had spread).

Rex's last journal entry is dated "20 Apr, 83 Wed." Beyond that, all is blank. He may have felt too rotten to write in his journal that evening.

Thursday, April 21st. Came time to hike out. Rex felt some better and shrugged off the *giardia* scare. But he still felt weak. Betty suggested that he "slack pack" the fifteen miles from Hot Springs to Allen Gap. She planned to meet him there, and the couple made plans to spend the night at a nearby campground.

During the afternoon came a call from the Forest Service that Rex Pulford had suffered an accident and that she should remain at Hot Springs until more information became available. (Several hours would pass before Betty found out that her husband had perished at Hurricane Gap.)

The "Grim Reaper" had scrawled Rex Pulford's name in the endless sands of eternity.

The aftermath: Like Marines, hikers look after their own. A transient journal in Rex's memory made it to Katahdin, lovingly carried by his thru-hiker friends and returned to the family. (Rumor has it that hikers also carried his new boots and hiking stick to the Trail's end. But if true, these items have mysteriously disappeared.)

Shortly after the tragedy, Rex's friend, Sam Waddle, erected a small cross in Hurricane Gap, and Mrs. Waddle planted some irises. In 1984, Betty received permission from the Forest Service to place a permanent marker there for her fallen husband.

Shuddering, I saluted the irises and cast my morbid thoughts into the flowery cortege. Then shouldering my pack, I surrendered the desolate spot to the clutching mist and walked away. But John McCrae's words continued to haunt my memory for weeks to come.

(Author's note: Sadly, Sam Waddle passed away in early February 2005. Alzheimer's disease had debilitated Sam for several months. The dedicated overseer of Jerry Cabin, whose only title was "U.S. Forest Service Volunteer," made his first trip as a maintainer to the top of Cold Spring Mountain in 1973 in an old gray jeep. The trip up the mountain, eleven miles of rough Forest Service "road" (and that's a generous term), took an hour and a half. And of course, the trip down was equally long and difficult.

Sam Waddle and his old gray jeep. Cold Spring
Mountain is seen on the far horizon just above Sam's straw hat.

Sam spent the next twenty-five years of his life making Jerry Cabin among the cleanest on the Trail. He placed a mock light and telephone in the shelter so that thru-hikers would have something to make them smile.

Sam was my friend. He's gone on, but his spirit lingers. Thanks for the memories, Sam. Rest in peace!)

*   *   *

A long afternoon's hike north of the James River (Virginia), on top of Bluff Mountain's wooded summit, the Appalachian Trail comes to a brief hiatus in the form of a small bronze plaque set into a plain concrete base. In hiker season, the marker is adorned with an assortment of hiker paraphernalia. Small rocks impulsively grabbed up from the forest floor lie scattered at the marker's base. Withered wild flowers, bits of twine, frayed boot laces, and even an odd assortment of coins—whatever moves the person who pauses by the small shrine at mile marker 775.2—are sprinkled among the rocks. Just a few feet away, concrete anchors of a Forest Service fire tower, now gone, rise from the ground like giant mushrooms. And the old Norway pine that casts its late afternoon shadow across my shoulders as I study the wording—a nexus bridging the last hours of a frightened boy a century ago and this day that brings him into my life—it could well have witnessed the tragedy.

I read the faded, eroded wording: *This is the exact spot Little Ottie Cline Powell's body was found April 5, 1891. After straying from Tower Hill School House, Nov. 9 a distance of 7 miles, age 4 years, 11 months*

Sad, graphic words that conjure up mental images best left to Stephen King novels.

Edwin Powell was a goodly man, God-fearing, and a Dunkard preacher. Like many others of his calling, Ed farmed during the week and rode a circuit on Sundays. The Dunkards, more formally known as the Old German Baptist Brethren, were a close sect, not unlike the Mennonites. But there were differences in dress and theology.

For example, the Dunkards took their name from a corrupted form of the German verb "tunken" which meant, "to dip." The Dunkards believed that a person had to be fully immersed face down three times to be truly baptized—a symbolic manifestation of the "Holy Trinity." Dunkard men bobbed their hair and parted it in the middle. Both men and women wore distinctive dress, practiced foot washing, and rendered greetings with a kiss—men with men and women with women.

In 1874, a pretty brown-eyed Dunkard lass by name of Emma Belle caught Ed's eye. The couple soon crossed the gender barrier with the customary "greeting" style, and in a few short weeks exchanged vows. The newlyweds set up housekeeping near Dancing Creek in Amherst County (Virginia) on land shared with Ed's brother, James. Ed was a good steward of the soil and made a decent living with plow and hoe—and on Sundays with his mouth. To his credit, he took seriously the mandate of the Good Book to "be fruitful and multiply." Working diligently to do just that, much to the chagrin of his child-weary wife, he sired eight children. Not a lot, when taken into account that most farmer families counted their progeny on the fingers of two hands plus some toes. But all in all eight was still a respectable number.

One of Parson Powell's circuit churches was the nearby Church of the Brethren in Oronoco (located on present day US Highway 60 seven miles east of Buena Vista). The church had been founded a few years earlier by Spotswood Gilbert. Gilbert's daughter, Miss Nannie, taught the "three-R's" to the neighborhood children at Oronoco's one-room Wood's Schoolhouse, so named because it was built on land donated by the Wood family, who happened to be neighbors of the Powells. The old log building, little more than a drafty shanty, later became known as Tower Hill Schoolhouse because of its close proximity to the prominent Blue Ridge mountain of the same name.

Ottie Cline was the fifth child to bless the Powell household. Naturally inquisitive and a cut smarter than most "almost" five year-olds, Ottie begged to attend school with his brothers, sisters, and cousins. So when Miss Nannie Gilbert rang the bell on the first day of school that September 1891, Ottie took his seat alongside his siblings. The boy, with his questioning blue eyes, blond hair, and fair complexion, quickly won the exalted position of teacher's pet in Miss Nannie's heart. And since he was the youngest one there—and not really a competitor—the other kids didn't tease him.

The snow had arrived early that fall. During the first week of November, four inches fell in nearby Lynchburg—more in the mountains—and the air quickly became thick with winter's chill. Each day Miss Nannie fed the old pot-bellied stove until it glowed cherry-red as she fought to overcome the cold wintry tentacles that crept through the drafty walls and stole the children's attention. A one-sided battle, to be sure—winter's malevolent breath versus the small pile of wood stacked in the corner of the schoolhouse. Over time the pile dwindled until only a few small sticks remained. But mountain folk are resilient in the face of adversity, and the forest was full of provender for the ever-hungry stove. Miss Nannie wasn't concerned, for in past years the boys had always gathered in more wood when they ran out.

Not a lot of noteworthy events transpired on the planet on Monday morning, November 9, 1891. Far to the west, on the flat dark-earth plains near Indianapolis, Indiana, Webb Parmalee Hollenbeck made his way into the helter-skelter world of the emerging Gay Nineties. (At age three, young Webb was whisked off to the "Big Apple" to take dancing lessons. By age eleven he was on his way to stardom, and not long afterwards he took Hollywood by storm—as Clifton Webb.) A couple of months earlier, Thomas Edison had wowed the world with a talking box which he called a radio, and in a few days he planned to unveil the instrument that would carry "young Webb" to fame and fortune—the moving picture projector.

Up in Yankeeland where the snow drifted high on this cold morning, Canadian Dr. James Naismith struggled to put together a game to occupy eighteen rowdy, bored boys at the Springfield (Massachusetts) YMCA. A tough (and fruitless) job it was. In desperation, he borrowed from a game he had played as a kid dubbed "Duck-on-a-Rock." With a once-in-a-lifetime flash of genius, he nailed bottomless peach baskets on poles at either end of the gymnasium, divided the group into two teams of nine players each, wrote down twelve rules, and called the game "basket ball."

But for the folks of Dancing Creek, it was just another day of hard work. Sunny and cold, but not a bad day at all. By the time the children reached the schoolhouse, a frigid north wind had begun to stir the leafless branches, biting fingers and noses and pushing into threadbare clothes. Miss Nannie appeased the ancient iron wood-eater, slowly feeding in sticks from the small pile of wood stacked neatly in an out-of-the-way corner, trying to make it last through the day.

By afternoon recess, the wood was gone and only dull red embers remained. The children shivered as white vapor trails erupted from between chattering teeth and pencils refused to obey cold-numbed fingers. Mountain custom dictated that the boys' recess—usually a five-minute game of tag or "cops and robbers"—come first, followed by the girls' playtime. But they had to have fuel for the stove, especially for the next day, which might bring snow. At least that's what the old timers who knew the signs called for.

The teacher said, "Boys, no games today. I want you to go gather up firewood. But stay within sight of the schoolhouse." In unison, the boys recited, "Yes, Miz Nannie." They'd done this drill before.

Soon the corner was stacked with enough wood to last for a couple of days—more if the weather warmed. The girls had their turn outside, along with the boys—a reward for a job well done, while Miss Nannie fired up the stove with corncobs soaked in kerosene. In no time heat again poured from the stove's innards and the stovepipe turned a deep orange. Then she went to the door and rang the bell. "Time for class. Recess is over." The students came running, glad to be back inside and away from the biting wind and the dark snow clouds that had begun to gather in the north sky.

The children took their seats and class resumed. Some twenty minutes passed before Miss Nannie realized that her youngest pupil was missing. "Where's Ottie?" she asked. Heads automatically turned toward the youngster's seat and shoulders shrugged. "Has anyone seen Ottie?" No one had.

Thinking that the youngster was probably just lollygagging outside, she went to the door and looked. No sign. Worse, flurries had started. Pushing away the first twinge of panic, Nannie Gilbert said firmly, "I want you four older boys to go look around the schoolyard. He probably didn't hear the bell." These last words she mumbled to herself more than to the others.

The boys didn't stay long. Stomping through the door, they shook snowflakes off of their coats and rubbed circulation back into stiff fingers. "Didn't see no sign of 'im, Miz Nannie," the oldest boy said and the others nodded in agreement. "We called 'n called, but th' snow's agettin' harder an' it's hard to see very far." With a sinking feeling, the teacher pointed at Ottie's two older brothers. "I want you to hurry home and see if Ottie is there. He may have decided to go on home."

Reverend Powell soon returned with some neighbor men. They weren't yet alarmed. Ottie had to be somewhere nearby. After all, how far could a four year-old wander in such a short time? But the youngster was not to be found.

As word flashed through the small community, more men came, and then entire families, all walking through the woods, through the intermittent flurries, all shouting at the top of their voices, "Ottie! Ottie Powell! Where are you?" But the forest refused to give up Ottie and the gusting wind threw frantic calls back at worried faces.

Came an excited shout. "Here! Over here!" One searcher had found the place where Ottie had struggled to free a small chestnut pole entwined by some vines. This effort would have required lots of time and intense concentration from one so small, which probably accounted for Ottie falling behind the other boys.

Another frantic yell came a short time later. The pole, about twelve feet long, had been found a half-mile away. The small end had feathered to a point— proof that Little Ottie had dragged it the long distance, probably thinking he was headed for the schoolhouse. But the school was in the opposite direction.

A neighbor, Henry Wood, went to his house and got his dog, and brought the animal to the spot where the pole had been found. The dog seemed to sense that something was awry. The canine put his nose to the ground and sniffed his way out of sight toward the rugged trail that ascended Tower Hill. Thinking that the dog had picked up the scent of some animal—it was headed in the "wrong" direction—the men didn't follow. (On hindsight, Mr. Wood was convinced that his dog had followed Ottie, perhaps even found the lad and licked his face.)

The dog was gone for a long time but finally showed up just before dark. If only they had followed . . . Finally, darkness and a steady rain put a stop to the search.

That night the rain turned into an ice storm. The Reverend Mr. Powell tossed restlessly, staring wide-eyed toward the invisible ceiling of his bedroom as he listened to the muffled sobbing of his wife. He thought of the dream he'd had the previous night, when *all* of his children had been safely tucked into warm beds. The dream had unsettled him to the point that he had awakened Emma Belle and told her about it.

In his dream, he saw a hearse or black wagon. Something compelled him to go inside. An old man sat in the back with his hand resting on a small open wooden coffin. A tiny but bright flame, anchorless, floated above the coffin. Terrified, yet helpless to resist, Mr. Powell approached the man who seemed not of this world. The wizened mouth set in a face shaded with death's pallor spoke with an unearthly voice. "This is my house." The father then awoke, shaken, wondering what sinister message the dream conveyed.

By the time breakfast was over, the dream had diminished to a nagging half-memory that barely dulled the sunny morning. Mr. Powell went out to the corn shocks and began husking corn. Ottie, dressed for school, his blond curls covered by a brown cap, ran to his father. "Papa, can I stay home today and help you husk corn?"

Mr. Powell shook his head. "There'll be plenty of corn to husk this Saturday." Seeing the disappointed look, he added, "Ottie, you're going to be five years old in just six more days. Maybe Ma'll bake a cake and we'll have a party." Ottie laughed and squeezed his pa's stout leg, and then hightailed it after his brothers and sisters.

The Reverend Mr. Powell never saw his Ottie alive again, but the "dream" returned to haunt him for the rest of his days.

The next morning search parties again took to the woods, this time hampered by drooping ice-covered branches and broken limbs. Neighbors came from miles around to search but found no trace of Ottie. Clutching at a flimsy straw on the off chance (or Divine Providence) that Ottie had somehow wandered beyond the Dancing Creek area, Ed Powell ran an ad in the Lynchburg newspaper, describing his son as "a body five years of age, with blue eyes, fair complexion, and light hair." He added, "He is intelligent."

Days turned into weeks, and still they came—by the hundreds—stomping through knee-deep drifts, braving wet, bone-chilling days, shedding coats on afternoons so bright that the snow glistened as if it were on fire. The searchers retraced areas with plodding stubbornness and then moved higher up into harsher climes. Reverend Powell posted a reward for his son, if found alive, in *The Lynchburg Virginian.*

But as the dismal, sullen days of winter gave way to spring's first hint of rejuvenation, hope dwindled and the searchers went home. Oddly, no one thought about climbing the difficult bramble-choked trail that led to the summit of Tower Hill. But then again, how could a five year-old scale such a formidable path that only the foolhardy would attempt in winter?

The Powells despaired of ever knowing what had become of their fair-haired boy.

Five months later, on Sunday, April 3, four young men on a hunting trip—N.M. Coleman, his younger brother, and the two Lipscomb brothers—were traversing the Blue Ridge on the old Bear Trail from Amherst over to Rockbridge County. As they approached the high peak of Tower Hill known as the Bluff, one of the dogs began to bark like he'd cornered a varmint. "That hound's done got somethin' treed," one remarked. "We'd best go see what it is." The other growled, "Get yer gun cocked in case it's a bear." It was neither.

The moldering remains of a young boy dressed in brown clothes, his blond hair still covered by a brown cap, lay curled in a fetal position. The clothes had been snagged and ripped by brambles; otherwise, the body remained as it had lain when Little Ottie, exhausted and suffering from exposure, succumbed to the final sleep—except that his feet were missing. Little Ottie Cline Powell had been found at last.

The Powell family was at church (ironically, the log schoolhouse from whence the tragedy began) when N.M. Coleman rushed inside with the wondrous news. Edwin Powell raised his hands to Heaven in thanksgiving and the family rejoiced. Now their little Ottie could have a Christian burial. Rev. Cline, the minister, dismissed church and the men went up to retrieve Ottie's body.

A physician from Big Island, Virginia, was summoned to conduct an examination of Ottie's stomach in an effort to determine how long the boy had lived after becoming lost. The doctor found three chestnuts, which he thought Ottie had probably eaten on that afternoon before he strayed from Tower School. The doctor surmised that the boy had died from exposure that first night, when the ice storm covered Tower Hill and stole the warmth, and life, from the small body.

Ottie Cline Powell was laid to rest in the Tower Hill Graveyard the next day, Monday, April 4, 1892. Folks said that the small black walnut coffin that neighbor Jack White made was a work of art, his finest ever.

After several weeks, a dark cloud seemed to settle over Emma Belle. She became depressed, so despondent that Edwin feared his wife might grieve herself to death. Despairing, he had the small coffin exhumed and reburied in a field close to the house, so that his wife could see the gravesite from her window. But she refused to be consoled.

In an act of desperation, Ed moved his family to Rockbridge County and bought a house in the small hamlet of Cornwall, not far from Buena Vista. There, he opened the Crossroads General Store.

Emma Belle never recovered from the tragedy. Still grieving for her son, she died in 1897. Edwin Powell never preached again. He eventually remarried and moved from the area. Some say he sired another son, which he named "Otye."

"Progress" finally reached the top of Tower Hill. The US Forest Service built a fire lookout tower on the summit around 1917, just a few yards from where Little Ottie's body was found. The fire tower jutted up from the summit like a giant skeletal finger pointing toward Heaven's door, a grim reminder of what can befall careless children who wander away from home. Concerned teachers and parents resurrected the story of Ottie, telling it again and again to wide-eyed frightened kids.

Over time the story grew until it became a powerful tool of intimidation—right along with "the Boogey Man" and threats of "If you don't straighten up, you ain't gonna get nuthin' fer Christmas 'cept a lump of coal!" Frequently, screams would pierce the tranquil night air as a youngster awakened from a hideous "Ottie-induced" nightmare, in which the child wandered helpless and alone in a deep dark forest.

Eight years later, Buena Vista teacher J.B. Huffman made an attempt to "set the record straight." He authored a small booklet, which he titled *Little Lost Boy in Mountains of Virginia*. Wanting to do more, he made a concrete cross and carried it up to Ottie's "site," where it remained until 1968. Came more progress in the form of the Blue Ridge Parkway and the Appalachian Trail. Tower Hill became Bluff Mountain, and the fire tower came down as airplane spotters and weather satellites assumed the role of fire wardens.

With the Trail came myriad hikers, all curious about the concrete cross that blocked the path atop Bluff Mountain. Mr. Huffman decided the time was ripe to do more for Ottie. He resurrected his book, sold copies, and stipulated that the proceeds go toward erecting an appropriate memorial to replace the original cross.

But the job wasn't finished. What had happened to Ottie's grave? Was there a marker? In fact, where was the grave? No one seemed to know.

Then in the mid-1990s, Rufus Parker, a member of the Natural Bridge Appalachian Trail Club began to search. His quest led him to an overgrown corner of Cecil Foster's cow pasture—the old Powell homestead—near present day Madison Heights. Three scattered broken boulders marked Ottie's final resting-place.

Appalled, Mr. Parker led a campaign to raise funds for an appropriate stone. His plea to local residents produced about as much money as he could have gotten from selling pencils on a street corner in Buena Vista. So he turned to the hiker community. Wallah! In a few months, donations swelled to over $2100.

Today, the corner in Mr. Foster's cow pasture has been transformed. Nicely decorated with perennial shrubs, the site is enclosed by a chain link fence. On June 21, 1996, the first full day of summer, a headstone of black granite, as fine as any you'll see in the big cemetery over in Buena Vista, was set at the head of Ottie's grave, and the broken stones were carted away. The front of the memorial is decorated with a serene pastoral etching of trees, mountains, and clouds, with birds circling overhead. On the bottom right, beneath Ottie's name and the words and numbers that reveal the vital statistics of a life completed ("Born on or about Nov. 15, 1886; Died on or about Nov. 9, 1891), a small boy perpetually wanders among rocks and trees. Inscribed on the back of the memorial are the words of Mr. J. B. Huffman—a fitting eulogy:

THE LEAVES HAD FALLEN FROM THE TREES,
   THE MOUNTAIN CAPS WERE WHITE,
WHERE LITTLE OTTIE LAY DOWN TO SLEEP,
   THAT CHILLY AUTUMN NIGHT.
HIS LITTLE BODY WAS TIRED AND WORN,
   FROM CLIMBING THAT LOFTY PEAK,
A ROCK HE HAD FOR HIS PILLOW,
   WITHOUT MOTHER TO KISS HIM "GOODNIGHT."
JUST HOW LONG HE SLUMBERED AND SLEPT,
   THE LORD ABOVE ONLY KNOWS,
BUT WHEN HE OPENED HIS EYES,
   HE WAS IN THE SWEET HOME OF THE SOUL.

From the grave, the eye is naturally drawn upward along the long wooded slope that terminates on top of Bluff Mountain. A closure of sorts, for this was the route that Ottie stumbled along to his tragic death. Down here he was born; up there he died. Here his remains will dwell until the earth finally consumes the last vestiges of bone and wood, and time erases the ornate tribute. But the mountain will remain as witness through the endless ages that on an icy day long past, a small boy died on its icy crest. Alpha and Omega!

(Author's note: Records reveal that Ottie Cline Powell's remains were discovered at the site on April 3, 1892, not April 5, 1891 as detailed in Mr. Huffman's book and on the plaque. Too, Ottie's funeral was held on April 4, not April 6, 1892, as Mr. Huffman recorded. But then, mistakes do happen . . .)

Hence, the bronze plaque on this lonely spot that has my undivided attention. The questions come like fat drops of rain. *How did Little Ottie wander away from his schoolmates? Did he simply become so intensely interested in the chestnut pole that he failed to realize he no longer could hear the voices of his classmates? Did the deteriorating weather cause him to become disoriented? Why did he wander up such a difficult trail instead of taking a less arduous route? What were his last moments like? Did Mr. Wood's hound actually find Ottie and give the terrified lad a small measure of comfort, however brief? At the end, did he simply lie down, frightened and whimpering for his mother, and give up on life like an antelope caught between a tiger's jaws?*

No answers; just a deep sadness—as sad as "sad" can be. I can only hope that he simply went to sleep.

I search my pack for a suitable tribute to Little Ottie's memory but come up empty handed. (No extraneous gear in my pack.) Picking up a tiny pebble, I carefully position it at the end of "*months*"—a stone "period" for the sad words; a symbolic closure for a family's long-ago grief.

Then as the shadows lengthen toward infinity, I mouth a brief prayer for the boy's soul and head down the mountain for Punchbowl Shelter, a mile away, to spend the night—well within the range of a roaming restless spirit.

And the beat goes on. *I hike; I see; I wonder . . .*

Chapter Seventeen

Uncle Nick

Why would anyone want to pay homage, however slight, to an eccentric hermit who was willing to squander a goodly part of his life in self-imposed exile—never mind spending nearly a month researching and writing about the man? Yet, I did. Why, you ask?

A fair question, indeed. It's like this. Most of us have a "past" that lingers after our passing (at least for a generation or two, depending on what fields we plowed and crops we sowed). The individual who bedazzles John Q. Public with his or her deeds, famous or infamous, always seems to attract a small army of biographers, reporters, or historians who work diligently to preserve that person's past for future generations.

Not so with Nick Grindstaff.

His past is as elusive as a magician's bag of tricks. Most of Nick's life is hidden in the ground alongside his decaying bones and in the graves of folks now long dead who knew him. In fact, aside from the eroding monument on the high ridge of northeast Tennessee's Iron Mountain that marks his final resting-place, little is known about the man. Hard to believe that in this wild, forsaken place now broached by the Appalachian Trail, a man lived for nearly half a century isolated from the human race. Here Nick eked out a meager existence in rocky soil hardly fit for earthworms, sharing his days and nights with four-legged critters and slithering companions while the world passed him by.

But Nick wasn't a mean person. Unlike Old "Hog" Greer, who ruled the heights of Big Bald in the early 1800s and terrorized anyone who dared trespass on his kingdom, Nick welcomed the occasional visitor and shared his scant provender without complaint. He just didn't want to live among the lowlanders.

So Nick ended up much like he lived—with little more than a widow's mite in worldly possessions. And the sparse epitaph scrawled into the rock headstone of his grave paints a sad, lonely picture: *Lived alone, suffered alone, died alone.* But there is much more to Nick's story, because one biographer did care . . .

During the turbulent years before the Great War, while Mr. Henry Mock was busy siring the next volley of six Mocks with his second wife Mary over in nearby Mock's Mill, Virginia (years later it would become Damascus), Nicholas Grindstaff came to Bethel Doe, a small, modest community in northeast Tennessee's Johnson County. Granted, the tiny wiggling bundle arrived a day after Christmas of 1851. But for Issac and Mary Heaton Grindstaff it was close enough, and they named their son after the holiday's patron saint. Catherine and Sarah, his sisters, and his brother John, were delighted they had a younger brother to coddle over.

When Nick was barely three, tragedy struck the Grindstaff family. Mary died in 1853, and a year later Isaac passed on. Relatives in Bethel Doe took Nick and his three siblings in and raised them with patience and love. And Nature, rarely penitent, took pity and compensated for the boy's loss by endowing him with a strong body, good looks, and a quick brain. At an early age Nick joined Bethel Baptist Church and was later baptized (at age 23) by Reverend Jessie Cole, one of the pioneer ministers of east Tennessee. Friends and acquaintances held Nick in high regard.

When Nick, the youngest of the orphaned children, attained the legal age of 21, the relatives divided their parents' old farm into four equal parts, with one section going to each child. For the next five years, Nick worked hard to wrest a living from the stubborn red clay of Doe Valley.

Then something seemed to take control of young Grindstaff's mind. He became possessed with a single idea: *Head west to seek his fortune.* The itch became unbearable, so Nick sold his farm and the log house he had built to his neighbor, E.S. Jordan. On a frost-blanketed morning in the autumn of 1877, he rode off into the unknown with the rising sun at his back.

Little is known about his journey to the West. Rumor has it that he was robbed and became disillusioned with the human race. Another rumor persists that Nick fell in love with a woman during his travels and that she jilted him. He never spoke about the misfortune that befell him, what catastrophic event so poisoned his mind that he fled from civilization. His brother, "Chimney" John, when asked about that blank spot in Nick's past, simply said, "He don't never talk much about it. Tain't none of our business nohow." And that was that.

When the disgruntled man returned to Doe Valley, his westward six-year trip was sealed in a vault of silence. Iron Mountain, the majestic height that cast its morning shadow on the folks down in Doe Valley, beckoned. The mighty mountain would become the balm that would soothe his tortured soul for the next forty years.

Nick Grindstaff, Hermit.

Nick built an eight-foot square cabin, stout enough to withstand the fiercest winds, on the mountain's west slope, a short distance down from the summit. No windows—not necessary—and the doorway was an oddity, only three feet high and just wide enough to accommodate Nick's broad shoulders. Too, the slanted oak-stave roof barely allowed enough room at its highest point for the hermit to stand erect. Nick put the finishing touches on his cabin with a short rock and mud chimney. But a dirt floor would suffice.

He furnished his home with a pot, a baker, and a large cast iron skillet, in which he cooked and ate. A couple of wide chestnut boards nailed to short logs and topped with a leaf-filled tick served as couch and bed. It was sufficient for Nick's simple lifestyle.

Over the next forty years, the hermit thrived in his mountain aerie. He built a barn not far from his cabin and bought a steer, which he trained to work as an ox. (The 1200-pound beast actually had better accommodations than his master, for the barn was larger and better ventilated.) The valley folk kept an eye on their reclusive neighbor, frequently making the long walk up the steep mountain trail to sit a spell and chat or to bring Nick some decent home cookin'. He welcomed all that came to call. At some point they bestowed on Nick the term of affection reserved for kindly bachelors: "Uncle."

But the wild animals that roamed the woods became his true kindred, for they asked for nothing except the right to live free—as did Nick.

One hot day the snake came, seeking the dark coolness of the cabin. A fine rattler it was, too, with eleven rattles and a button. Seemed a shame to kill such a grand specimen, so Nick took the serpent in and made it a pet. The pair coexisted in an easy relationship of avoidance, with the rattler keeping to a dim corner or hiding in some hidey-hole in the rafters. On cold winter evenings, the snake would slither out and lie full length by the dancing flames of the fireplace near Nick's feet.

One day Sam Lowe, Nick's friend since childhood days, trekked up the mountain from Doe Valley to hunt bear. He passed by the shanty and decided to pay a visit. When Sam entered through the low doorway, he spotted the rattler coiled in a corner. Instinctively, he raised his old smoothbore to dispatch the reptile. But Nick said, "No, you shall not kill my pet."

Sam kept a wary eye on the critter all the while. The urge to shoot the snake was almost more than he could stand. Folks in their right mind knew that the only good rattler was a dead'un. When Nick went out to the barn to do a chore, Sam shot the snake and hurriedly left with the evidence. Nick never had much to do with Sam after that. Folks down in Doe Valley said that Sam, a fiddle player of some repute, hid the rattles in his fiddle so that every time he drew the bow across the taut strings he would recall the trick he had played on his old hermit friend.

Nick's dog, Panter, became his best friend in later years. Where the dog came from remains a mystery, but an old photo has survived. Panter showed a generous blending of mountain canine genes, probably topped by Mountain Cur with a fair dose of Blue Tick hound and beagle in the DNA soup. Short-haired, blackish brown with white paws, a "cross" of white on his chest, and floppy ears, the dog stood about "thigh high" and probably weighed in at about fifty pounds—all muscle. Panter was totally devoted to his master.

On top of Iron Mountain, just up from Nick's cabin, stood an old hickory tree that had survived the onslaught of the timber barons. Old Nick loved that tree and often went there to sit and enjoy the cooling breeze. His closest friend (of the two-legged variety), a nephew named R.B. Wilson, stopped by one day and found his uncle propped against the tree, taking a break from a round of chores. Panter, sprawled beside his master, wagged his tail in greeting. Nick remarked, "Ain't this is just about the prettiest place a man could ever flop his carcass down on? Not a bad place for a man to spend eternity." Little did he know . . .

On Saturday, July 21, 1923, Baxter McEwen went up the mountain to check on some of his cattle that ranged the area. He approached Nick's cabin and shouted a greeting. Not getting a reply, he looked inside. The old hermit lay on the crude slab bed, stone cold dead. Panter, grieving and half-starved, and loyal to the end, sat on his master's chest and guarded against all intruders. He would not let McEwen near the body. Nick had been dead for three or four days. His shoes were off and he probably died in his sleep.

Word quickly spread that Uncle Nick had passed. The next day, Sunday, over two hundred folks from Doe and Stoney Creek, toting a fine casket, climbed the mountain to pay their last respects to a man whom all had admired in spite of his eccentricities. R.B. Wilson and another friend, Asa Shoun, selected Nick's final resting-place beneath the stately old hickory, and the grave was dug down into the red sandstone.

When some men went inside to retrieve the body, Panter refused to let them come near. The men finally overpowered the dog and tied him up. They cut away Nick's ragged coveralls, wrapped him in a clean sheet, and carried him outside and placed him in the coffin. Not an easy task, manhandling the load two hundred yards uphill to the grave, but the men were strong and determined. The Honorable John Stout, who had befriended the hermit in earlier times, gave the eulogy; and then the crowd departed.

All that Uncle Nick possessed was left on the mountain, except for the steer, its harness, a bell, a currycomb—and Panter. The dog never recovered from Nick's death. Panter became vicious and finally had to be put to sleep.

"Uncle" Nick Grindstaff's tomb just off the Appalachian Trail.

R.B. Wilson, with the help of neighbors and Nick's friends, raised $208.07—a considerable sum in 1924—for a memorial. Vaught Grindstaff and Asa Shoun built the monument from fieldstone taken from the mountain. When finished, it somewhat resembled the small fireplace and chimney that had warmed Nick and his "pets" for almost a half-century. A slab of mountain granite was set into the stonework and inscribed with the sad epitaph that captured the essence of Uncle Nick Grindstaff's life: *Lived alone; Suffered alone; Died alone.*

On July 4th of the following year, friends and relatives gathered again at Nick's grave to dedicate the memorial and to bid a final farewell to the man whose life in some unfathomable way had touched theirs from this alien place. A small band played "America"; Asa Shoun spoke about the life of Uncle Nick; Reverend R.M DeVault preached a fine funeral sermon (Nick's second "send off"); and Professor D.M. Laws lectured on the nature of mankind. Friends and relatives reverently placed a few flowers beside the concrete slab that plastered the grave, and then the people departed.

As the footsteps faded, a maverick breeze stirred the branches of the old hickory, and then silence returned to the glen. Nick Grindstaff now belonged to the hollow echoes of the past.

*   *   *

Three thru-hikes—three times I had stopped in the small glen and stared at the chimney-like protuberance; had wondered about the man buried beneath the aging concrete slab whose life had evoked the tragic words etched in the faded granite. Each time the questions flooded in like a rip tide, tugging at my imagination and thrusting my mind against an impenetrable barrier of ignorance. *Who was this man? What events brought him to this lonely end?* And the greater question: *Why?*

Each time the frustration of not knowing grew, until it raged like a huge cankerous sore in my innards. In the months after returning home from that last hike, I had searched endlessly to find answers to those questions, which refused to let go. I had spent fruitless hours in libraries, had sat hunched over my computer keyboard like a poorly programmed robot while I surfed the web until my eyes resembled those of someone just dragging home after a three-day drunk. The quest became an obsession. Like panning for gold—sure to strike color in the next wash; or like the fisherman's addiction, the next cast would surely hook the big one.

But it never happened. Uncle Nick Grindstaff's past was as slippery as raw oysters. And then "Fortune" smiled. The town librarian at Damascus, Virginia, said, "See Paschal Grindstaff."

I found Mr. Paschal (that's what his friends call him, and I soon found myself addressing him likewise) at Trail Days 2004—a "must attend" hiker celebration held in mid-May each year at Damascus. He sat in a lawn chair among the huge crowd of sweating fans (the thermometer hovered near the ninety-degree mark) at the town's gazebo. A bluegrass band polluted the air with nasal twangs that tried to mimic Bill Monroe and Hank Williams but came out as a hybridized teeth gritter. After asking a dozen people, an elderly lady pointed him out.

I knelt beside the lawn chair and shouted in his ear, "I'm looking for some information about Uncle Nick Grindstaff. Do you know anything about him?" Mr. Paschal smiled and shouted back, "I might have something at home. Let's give our ears a break." He folded his lawn chair and we walked to his car.

Turns out that Mr. Paschal was a walking encyclopedia when it comes to local history. Retired from the US Postal Service since the late eighties, the former postmaster of Damascus had served up packages and letters to several generations of hikers during his distinguished career, not to mention enough words of encouragement to weary hikers to fill several spiral notebooks. On the way to his home about four miles outside Damascus, he regaled me with tales about the town and some of the hikers he had met over the years.

Mr. Paschal led me down to his basement (neater than most peoples' houses) and rummaged through some boxes filled with hiker memorabilia. "I know it's here somewhere. Saw it not too long ago." Sure enough, he soon pulled a tattered booklet from the assortment.

The faded orange cover had a dim, slightly blurred picture of a big man with a large black mustache and heavy black eyebrows. He wore a bearskin greatcoat and a cap made of animal fur, and oversize earflaps covered his ears. But the facial feature that jumped out was the lower jaw—large, square, and thrust out against the world's adversities. The title beneath the picture read, *NICK, THE HERMIT.* In smaller letters beneath the oversized title were the words, *The South's Most Famous Hermit.*

I'd finally struck gold!

(Author's note: It was all there: Nick's childhood, his life as a hermit, pictures of his cabin, the barn, his dog Panter, his brother "Chimney" John, the account of his death and burial. In 1926, Nick's lifelong friends Asa Shoun and R.B. Wilson commissioned Adam M. Daugherty of Bakers Gap, Tennessee, to write Nick's story. Mr. Daugherty, Johnson County's (Tennessee) Poet Laureate, after interviewing the old hermit's family and friends, recounted Nick's life in a lengthy poem simply titled, *Nick, the Hermit.* Oddly, details about Nick's trip west are lacking.

The festering sore of not knowing that part of Nick's life still irritates my soul.)

Chapter Eighteen

Mock's Mill

You might say the story of Mock's Mill began over in Surry County, North Carolina, along about 1760 when Daniel Boone first pushed westward from his home in nearby Yadkin Valley, headed across the Appalachians toward the irresistible hunting grounds of Kaintuck. Or maybe even later, in 1775, when the intrepid woodsman and thirty others blazed the Wilderness Road through the Cumberland Gap and opened the area to settlement—for those who had the moxie to live in prime Indian country. Over the years, Daniel Boone's "Indian savvy" and prowess as a mighty hunter spawned numerous larger-than-life legends that set many a young man's imagination on fire. Among these was young Henry Mock, Jr.

But to go back a couple of generations:

In 1752, ten year-old Peter Mock had emigrated with his parents from Germany to North Carolina by way of Pennsylvania, eventually ending up in the lush rolling hills of North Carolina's Davie County. Peter became a successful farmer and businessman and eventually married comely Barbara Martin. The couple had two sons, Peter, Jr., and Henry A.

Being the younger son, as Henry grew older he came to realize that, according to custom, the older brother stood to inherit the family fortune. Mocksville, as the small community became known, had been Henry A's home since birth. But it had nothing to offer a burgeoning young adult without prospects. So with much sadness, a small bankroll, and his parent's blessing, Henry A struck out for greener pastures.

In nearby Surry County he found what he was looking for. The land lay gentle and the soil tasted sweet. Here a man could make a good home. Henry bought a farm and built a cabin. In time he married a local lass by the name of Catherine Black and started a family.

Henry Jr. arrived in 1794. Like his father, he had the misfortune of not being the firstborn son. Two older brothers, George and Peter, preceded him, so the family fortune was ordained to pass on to George. Unlike his father though, Henry Jr. stayed and tilled the crops alongside his brothers. Not an easy task, keeping his feet planted while his head soared with youthful fantasies about Kaintuck, put there by no less than Daniel Boone himself when the living legend had passed through on his way to the golden land. Why, Dan'l had actually eaten at their table! And Henry had heard the gospel truth direct from the mighty hunter's mouth! The boy's imagination seared his mind and he resolved to some day follow in Boone's footsteps.

He kept putting the dream on hold. Another crop year loomed as spring approached; harvest time ruled the lives of everyone as fall came on. More spring plantings, more harvests, and the years crept by until the dream faded into a dim memory. But hard work and perseverance paid off. By the time he reached twenty-five, Henry had saved enough money to wed the young lady who had stolen his heart, pretty Nancy Gibbs. In December 1819, they set up housekeeping in a small cabin on his father's farm.

One spring day in 1821 a group of settlers passed through on their way to Kaintuck. Excited talk filled the air (and the head of Henry, who hung onto every word like it was a message from The Almighty Himself). Tales of the bounteous land over the mountains—"where a man kin walk all day an' never see another soul an' th' dirt'll grow turnips bigger 'n watermelons," as one of the migrants boasted. The flame that had consumed Henry Mock, Jr. in his youth, which had been reduced by responsibility over the past years to a smoldering ember, now flared into a full-fledged firestorm.

Henry went looking for his wife. "Git packed, Nancy. We're goin' to Kaintuck!"

The couple never made it to the land where turnips grew "bigger'n watermelons." Over in the Blue Ridge of Virginia, at a water gap where two gushing mountain streams met, they came across their own version of "Paradise." The place was already fairly settled with friendly folks like the Wrights, Larimers, and Hands.

Henry bought ninety-one acres from John Larimer, who had been granted considerable acreage in the area for his service in the Revolutionary War, for the hefty sum of $405. He erected a dam across the Laurel Fork of the Holston River, just below where Beaverdam Creek converges, and built a gristmill.

The next year his brother, Peter, who also got short shrift in the inheritance pecking order, arrived to make his fortune. Henry bought another thirty-eight acres from Larimer (which made him the owner of what would eventually encompass most of Damascus). Soon the community became known as Mock's Mill.

For the next sixty-three years, "Mister Henry"—he had achieved a modicum of respect—ground the neighbors' corn. He also wore out three wives and sired thirty children (some say thirty-three)!

In 1886, some three years after young disillusioned Nick Grindstaff shook the dust of humanity from his coattails and stalked off to Iron Mountain to begin a hermit's life, John Daniel Imboden came to Mock's Mill—and changed the community and the lives of its citizens for generations.

The former Confederate general had been one of General Lee's right hand men and had "shone" in numerous important Civil War engagements. But he had failed to excel in post-war civilian life. Reeling from failed speculations in coal and steel in Big Stone Gap, Virginia, the entrepreneur chased his "rainbow" to the small town tucked between the tall mountains where the Laurel and Beaverdam Creeks met. He'd heard that unlimited deposits of iron ore abounded beneath the reddish hematite soil. That, along with the area's vast hardwood forests, spelled "steel" and untold riches.

Excited, Imboden bought up most of old man Mock's landholdings, rolled up his sleeves, and chased after his dream of building a "steel city" on the site. He flatly stated that here was ". . . the very best in the United States for a modern 'Damascus,' destined to become as famous . . . as its ancient namesake in Asia." And since he owned nearly everything for miles around, including the community, Imboden changed the name of his "dream site" to "Damascus."

The huge deposits of iron ore turned out to be a pipe dream, for the only ore to be found was on the surface. It was a bitter pill to swallow for the sixty-three year-old former general. There'd be no "steel city," but all was not lost. The virgin timber that covered the slopes heralded great wealth.

At his beck, the tree cutters came by the hundreds. From all over the country, they crowded into the tiny town, roughshod timber jacks anxious to wield axes for a day's wages. And with the influx came moneymen from the north, equally anxious to gild their pockets with the cellulose gold. In a few years, Damascus had become the Nation's timber capitol. (In 1912, Washington County—mainly Damascus—produced more sawn boards than the entire state of Pennsylvania.)

But as always happens, uncontrolled greed comes with a price. In twenty-five short years after the lumber boom began, for as far as the eye could see, the forests had been raped and the denuded mountains resembled peeled onions.

General John Daniel Imboden didn't live to see the monster that had crawled out of the "Pandora's box," which his failed dream had unleashed. Probably a good thing, or else he might have taken up residence on Iron Mountain with Nick Grindstaff. The founder of Damascus died in the town he had named on August 15, 1895. His body was interred in the "General's Section" of Hollywood Cemetery in Richmond, Virginia.

Old "Mister" Mock sired his last child, Isaac, at Damascus in 1873, when he was seventy-nine. He lived long enough to see the boy become a man, and then gave up the ghost at the unusually ripe age of ninety-eight. Between Henry Mock and Isaac, they lived under every President of the United States from George Washington to Dwight Eisenhower. Isaac was still thriving in Phoenix, Arizona, in 1956.

Chapter Nineteen

Sarver Hollow

E ven on a good day Sinking Creek Mountain can be five miles of pure misery—as it was on that unseasonably hot second day of June 1998 when I staggered across the rocky torture device. An indifferent sun beat down, heating the exposed crest to egg-frying temperature—not that I would have fried any eggs on that tilted stretch of agony. Heck, they would have slid right off into the valley a thousand feet below.

Thick sweat oozed from overworked, overloaded pores, drenching my stinking shorts and tee-shirt with sour-smelling brine, making me wonder if this is how it felt to ferment in a vat of cucumbers on their way to becoming pickles. Actually, the stench had become part of my permanent aura. The sweat just magnified the odor. Worse, patches of ankle-high poison ivy covered whole sections of the slanting crest, springing out of dirt-packed crevices—anywhere roots could grab a hold. More agony to be endured on an already misery-saturated day.

I thought of my two previous passages along Sinking Creek Mountain, in 1990 and 1994. Wind-driven rain that whipped right into my eyes, along with a nasty fog, had been on the weather menu both times. I shuddered, remembering the lichen-covered rocks, how they had become slick as ice in the rain; how I had nearly slid off the slippery crest into the misty void several times.

The memory triggered another thought, even scarier. The stormy night I had spent alone at the old Sarver cabin ruins down on the east slope of this irascible hunk of rock on my second trip crowded in like a bad 3-D rerun. I had garnered enough phantasmagorias *that* night to supply Edgar Allen Poe with material for three novels.

I had made my bed beneath a leaky tarp hastily thrown up in a corner of the dilapidated corncrib. *Any port in a storm*, but I had been scared enough to pee in my shorts because of wily serpents that I *just knew* were slithering toward me, looking to cozy up with me in my damp (but warm) sleeping bag. The blackness reeked of bloodcurdling terror because of what sounded like odd **dragging** footsteps on the fallen, rotted boards. Not to mention ghostly **murm**urs just beyond the feeble reach of my flashlight.

Sarver Cabin ruins where I spent a rainy night beneath a leaky tarp—just about where David "Wahoola" Jones stands.

My heart hammered against my chest until I feared it might actually burst through the ribs and run off into the night. Real or imagined, it didn't matter. I left at first light and ate breakfast miles away.

(Much later I found out that the Sarver ruins were supposedly haunted by a ghost, which had affectionately been dubbed "George" because of a large stash of empty George Dickel bottles discovered in the old corncrib where I had spent the night. In fact, a few years back one hiker went so far as to swear to his companions that the mischievous spirit had quaffed most of the communal bottle of George Dickel while they all slept. Yeah, right!

Other hikers since have claimed to experience weird happenings while bedded down in the ramshackle ruins.)

On second thought, maybe today wasn't so bad after all. At least I had a view.

Squinting into the glare, I tried to see my future through the shimmering heat waves and prayed for a shady spot to take a break. Way up ahead, a couple of gnarled trees wavered like cheap props for a stage setting. Not the best place to stop, but this mountain was stingy with its shade. It would do. Besides, why hoard all of this wonderful misery? Gold Bond and Thirty Seconds couldn't be too far behind. I'd wait and share some with them.

Gold Bond had entered my life a couple of weeks before at Knot Maul Branch Shelter, a few miles south of Pearisburg, Virginia. Three other hikers and I had already settled in for the night when Gold Bond strode in. I sized him up: College age, stocky, long hair that terminated in a short pony tail, loud grating voice that rasped against the senses, and an extroverted manner that rubbed salt into my trail-weary mind—in a word, "obnoxious." He took off his pack, bragged that he was "gonna put on a show," and proceeded to do just that.

First, he pulled a dirty plastic coke bottle out of his pack that he'd carried from the last highway crossing. Then he dumped some powdery stuff from an MRE (Meals Ready to Eat—military food) heating packet, and then poured some water into the bottle and brandished the bottle cap. All the while Gold Bond explained what he was doing but not why. He faced us and gave a smug, knowing grin as a weird milky haze began to escape from the dingy bottle, just like the Genie stirring after centuries of hibernation when Aladdin swiped his hand across a tarnished lamp. He gave the top a quick twist and shouted, "Show time. Watch the top take off like a rocket."

All eyes turned skyward—then back toward the bottle when Gold Bond blurted a panicky "Uh-oh." That sucker had started to swell like a balloon. "Must've got the top on too tight," he muttered. Fascinated, we watched the bottle expand until it took on a grotesque, almost obscene look. Holy cow! I had no idea a Coke bottle could get *that* big! The thought went poof as Gold Bond yelled, "It's gonna blow! Hit the deck!"

Mesmerized, we continued to stare at the bottle, now the size of a half-gallon milk container and still growing. Jayzus and Mary! We couldn't move, couldn't take our eyes off *the thing*. With a humongous bang it exploded, a plastic hand grenade that sent wispy shreds of "shrapnel" all over the clearing and into the shelter. I emitted a long low whistle into the static silence and chuckled. "Sumabitch, Gold Bond. Now *that* was entertainment!"

In the space of several days, we leapfrogged back and forth and I got to know Gold Bond like a brother. He was actually a nice guy, sort of a "hands-on" type who enjoyed fiddling with new things. (He didn't try the Coke bottle act again, though.) A few days later we spent the night together at a shelter and I asked him how he came by his trail name. He reached inside his pack and pulled out a big container of Gold Bond powder. "From this," he explained. "I love this stuff. I sprinkle it all over me—crotch, feet, under my arms, in my hair, just all over." Well, that was a twist.

Thirty Seconds just showed up one evening like a little lost puppy. She was a picture of youth, short and shy, with big brown eyes that mirrored a naïve trust in all living creatures and enhanced her short coal-black hair. I asked how she came by her name. Her eyes twinkled as she explained, "An old hiker back in Georgia said I wasn't as big as a minute; just barely thirty seconds." It fit.

They finally caught up and we walked single file until the slanted ridge moderated into a flat wooded section. Suddenly we were in the midst of an incongruous arrangement of rock piles. Small piles; larger ones the size of small houses; some round, others oblong. "Downright strange," I muttered, still as curious and fascinated as the first time I had laid eyes on the puzzle. "Has to have been done by the Sarvers, but I don't see for what purpose." The rock heaps were without rhyme or reason; they were just there, hunkering beneath the trees like stone igloos in a surreal Siberian village.

We soon came to a blue-blazed trail leading down the mountainside. I said, "This goes down to the old Sarver cabin. Anyone want to go visit 'George'?" By now, all thru-hikers knew about the thirsty alcoholic ghost. "I'll wait here if you want to go." I had no intention of going *down there,* even if the spring was supposed to be five-star. I eyed my water bottle—a little less than half full, enough to get me to Cabin Branch about five miles away if I was careful. "Just keep an eye out for rattlers and copperheads. Probably be lots of 'em hanging out by the spring."

When I offered this bit of sage advice, Thirty Seconds opted out. And when I mentioned that it was over a half mile down and back, Gold Bond quickly lost interest.

A missed opportunity in hindsight—foregoing a daylight tour of Sarver "Hollow," for I had no idea that six years later I would be writing about this very place.

*   *   *

Except for a giant "hiccup" of Nature, the Sarvers would never have settled up on the east side of Sinking Creek Mountain. It happened this way—more or less.

A billion years ago, give or take a few millions, the Appalachians were birthed in the central bedrock of a giant supercontinent, Pangea, which contained the earth's landmass and was surrounded by a single ocean. Alas, nothing is forever, and about 750 million years ago the supercontinent began to stretch and thin like warm taffy. Some 200 million years later came a colossal happening. The supercontinent split into continents, which began to drift away from each other. Over eons, the continental plates spread until, as if captured by giant rubber bands, they began to retract toward each other.

Then a mere 270 million years ago, the unthinkable happened—the continental crusts of Africa and North America collided, and the African crust subducted beneath the North American crust. Elasticized folds of bedrock were thrust thousands of feet up into the air. Thus were the mighty Appalachians created.

(It is interesting to note that North America and Africa were connected before Pangea broke apart, so the Appalachians belong to the same mountain chain as the Atlas Mountains in Morocco.)

But Nature is never static. About 30 million years later, just as the dinosaurs were crawling out of the primordial swamps, the continental plates began to drift apart again, forming the Atlantic Ocean. (Even today, these plates continue to separate at the mid-Atlantic Ridge.)

Erosion quickly began its persistent gnawing. Over the course of a hundred million years, the Appalachians were reduced to mere nubbins of their former grandeur. Eventually rock-gnawing wind and rain undercut Sinking Creek Mountain, a mammoth ridge of limestone capped with sandstone. And then came the "hiccup."

Ten to twenty thousand years ago, a gargantuan landslide—a "rock-block" slide (where huge slabs stay intact, as opposed to a "rockslide", when the slabs break into pieces) occurred. In fact, the entire twenty-mile length of Sinking Creek Mountain is the site of one of the largest landslides in North America, with one rock-block area stretching over three miles. The entire crest tilted southeastward toward Craig Creek Valley and, as the mountain slid downward, a "bench" of a few acres was formed on the mountainside.

(Can't stand genealogy? Feel free to move on.)

Sarvers have inhabited Sinking Creek Valley, Virginia, for generations. Genealogy records of Botetourt County (and later of Montgomery and Craig Counties, which were formed from Botetourt County) fairly burst at the seams with Sarvers. Old documents list Gasper Sarver as having lived near land inherited by Magdalin Runnills (wife of John Reynolds, a large landowner in the Sinking Creek area) as early as 1772. In 1791, a John Sarver was named Constable of Botetourt County. Patsey Reynolds, granddaughter of John and Magdalin Reynolds, married another John Sarver in the early 1800s.

Other Sarvers entered the records: Henry (wed in 1801), John, (wed in 1815), another John (wed in 1812), George (wed in 1838), and John (George's son, born in 1841). More "John's": John (married in 1873), John (wed in 1892)—on and on, and all from the Craig County area. (John seems to have been a favorite Sarver name.) And then Henry Sarver strode into the limelight.

His story is simple, not unlike thousands of others of that era. Henry Sarver was born around 1829—just about the time that Davy Crockett committed political suicide by condemning the popular "Indian Removal Act," which sent the Cherokee Nation reeling toward Oklahoma. It also sent Davy to a peeling stucco mission in Texas for his famed date with destiny. Like most of his Sarver kin, Henry lived and farmed in Sinking Creek Valley (near the present day Ross Cemetery, the final resting-place for several of his offspring.) He married a local girl, Sarah Caldwell, in 1853.

That same year, three events of lasting impact occurred. English surgeon Alexander Wood invented the hypodermic syringe. George Crum, a chef at the Moon Lake Lodge in Sarasota Springs, New York, furious at magnate Cornelius Vanderbilt, who had sent his fried potatoes back because they were too thick, vented his wrath. Spitefully, the chef redid the dish by slicing the potatoes too thin to be eaten with a fork—and by this simple bit of skullduggery invented the potato chip.

The third? Who could have dreamed that the union of Henry Sarver and Sarah Caldwell would impact on the history of the Appalachian Trail well over a century and a half later!

Losing no time, the couple produced their first born, Andrew Jackson, just ten months after wedding vows were exchanged. Other children soon followed: George Washington born in 1856; Mary A. in 1858 (she died in 1862 at four years of age); and William J. in 1863.

Then chaos! On April 12, 1861, Brigadier General Pierre Gustave Toutant Beauregard gave the order that sent the first rounds streaking toward Fort Sumter to unleash the horrific conflict, in which two mighty armies would battle for the next four years in a bloody contest of ideologies. Less than a month later, on May 1st, Henry Sarver enlisted with other Craig County boys in Company C of the 22nd Virginia Regiment and went off to do his duty for his native state.

(Author's note—for the "history buffs": At the start of hostilities, the 22nd Virginia Infantry was part of a West Virginia militia organization, the Kanawha Riflemen, originally formed by Captain George Smith Patton [great-grandfather of the famous WWII general, George Smith Patton, Jr.] in 1856 as the Kanawha Minutemen. When the first shots were traded, the 22nd Infantry was reorganized under the command of newly commissioned *CSA* Colonel Patton and officially became part of the Confederate Army in June 1861.

The 22nd Regiment participated in at least thirty-four battles or campaigns over the next four years, until it was disbanded on April 15, 1865, soon after a telegram was received telling of Lee's surrender at Appomattox. The 22nd was nearly wiped out twice: By the Army of the Ohio at Droop Mountain, West Virginia, in 1863; and as part of the Army of the [Shenandoah] Valley, commanded by Jubal Early, at the Battle of Cedar Creek, Virginia, in October 1864, when Phil Sheridan broke Early's army in a crushing counterattack. The 22nd also participated in the bloodletting at New Market, Virginia, and Cold Harbor.

On September 19, 1864, the 22nd's commander, Colonel Patton, suffered a leg wound at the third battle of Winchester, Virginia, and was taken prisoner. He refused to have the infected leg amputated and died six days later. Colonel Patton was only 32. He is buried alongside his brother, Tazwell—killed in Pickett's Charge at Gettysburg—in the Stonewall Cemetery in Winchester. The marker reads ". . . here asleep in one grave, the Patton brothers.")

Henry Sarver's war record, like many of his peers, is sketchy. That he participated in many of the 22nd Virginia Infantry's campaigns is highly likely. He was captured on September 19, 1864, at the third battle of Winchester and sent to the Union prison camp at Point Lookout, Maryland, located at the tip of the peninsula where the Potomac River joins the Chesapeake Bay.

That he survived the prison is no small feat. Of more than 53,000 Confederates incarcerated at Point Lookout while the camp was in operation from August 1863 to June 1865, at least 4,000 died (some estimates go as high as 14,000) from malnutrition and disease. But Henry was one of the lucky ones.

He was released on June 20, 1865 when the camp shut down. He returned to Sinking Creek Valley and got on with the serious business of hewing out a life for Sarah and his fledgling family. Sarah's widowed sister, Elizabeth Caldwell Elmore, and her young son Fleming, came to live with the Sarvers. Elizabeth's husband, James, had been killed in Pickett's Charge at Gettysburg.

Sometime around 1880 Henry bought a small plot "over the top of the mountain" (Sinking Creek Mountain on the Montgomery County side). He cleared the land and built a fine two-story cabin from the inexhaustible supply of huge chestnuts that covered the mountains and stretched as far as the eye could see. He, Sarah, and Elizabeth lived, labored, and raised their families on the isolated bench, which in due time came to be called "Sarver Hollow."

Seasons passed, the years evaporated like spilled gasoline, and a new generation took its place in the cycle of life.

(Author's note: Henry Sarver's grave lies in a small cemetery a short distance from the cabin he built—and where I spent that fear-clogged evening in 1994! A Civil War tombstone with his name and unit inscribed marks the grave. Records indicate that Sarah is also buried there, along with a granddaughter, Mary Alva, who died at age two; and Sarah's sister, Elizabeth, and her son, Fleming. The other graves lack markers except for Mary Alva's, which was hand-hewn and is barely legible. But it is plausible to assume that Sarah lies beside her husband. The dates Henry and Sarah died and the circumstances of their passing have not surfaced as of this writing.)

Andrew (Andy), the firstborn, stepped up to center stage. (Little is known about Henry Sarver's other sons, George and William.) Andy attended the Givens School near the base of Sinking Creek Mountain on the Craig County side, a hard walk of nearly a mile over the mountain from Sarver Hollow. Crockett B. Givens—grandfather of Clarence Givens, whose account of the

Sarver history is chronicled herein—was born some five years after Andy but attended the two-room school during Andy's time. He recalled that young Andy tried to correct the speech of the other students by saying, "Don't say 'ain't', 'cause 'ain't' ain't right." In time, Andy married a lass eight years his junior—Mary A. The couple had five children.

James P. (Jim) was born to Andy and Mary in 1879. This first child was very talkative and a voracious reader, who made the arduous trip down the mountain (no road accessed Sarver Hollow) to get the daily paper. Jim was also a German sympathizer, which sorely vexed the neighbors. He never married and died in 1965.

Then the gene pool seemed to shift. Nettie, born in 1881, was a lady of few words and always kept her real self hidden deep within the close confines of her mind. She, too, never married and silently bore her spinsterhood to her grave. Nettie died in 1959.

John Henry came along in 1886. Like his sister, he was not given to long sentences—almost to the point of being taciturn—but he was a worker, and a strong one at that. Clarence Givens recalls that John Henry was always the one who tossed the hay up on the stack, the hardest job. Clarence also said that John Henry was the only man he ever knew who wore long johns twelve months of the year. To his credit, the man was thorough. Often when someone made an extra fine job of something, that person would jokingly be called "John Sarver," a high compliment.

And the man was a hustler. John would spend long stretches in the mountains, looking for ginseng roots to sell. (Folks said that although he couldn't read, he had a gift for saving money.) John Henry left the mountain several times, but he always came back. Restless and yearning for something "more," he eventually left Sarver Hollow for good and settled in nearby Montgomery County.

Along about 1918, Cupid fired a volley of arrows his way and he took a direct hit. He married Amy Lee Hughes, some fifteen years his junior. In 1919, the couple had a child, Roy Leon. But the marriage turned sour and Amy ran off with the baby. Later, Roy went to live with a kindly neighbor woman, Hattie Reynolds Ferrell. (He returned to live with his father when Amy died in 1937.) John Henry died in 1968; Roy followed in 1982.

W. Mason (Mace) entered the world in 1897. Like his older brother John, Mace eventually traded the isolation of Sarver Hollow for the busier valley below. There, he married and in 1931 had a son, Mason Lee. Mace survived his son by seventeen years and died in 1970.

The last child, Mary Alva, lived two short years and died in1902. She is buried in the cemetery in Sarver Hollow near her grandparents.

Based on the memories of Carl Givens (Clarence's uncle), when Andy died in 1911, the remaining Sarvers left Sarver Hollow and moved to a house on property belonging to Carl's uncle, John Alexander Reynolds, just below the mill on Sinking Creek. But when Andy's wife, Mary, died in 1933, some of the Sarvers (most probably Nettie and Jim) returned to Sarver Hollow. They mostly lived hand to mouth. But with a good garden, hogs fattened on acorns, a fine apple and peach orchard, plus the never failing spring, they managed to survive.

In the mid-1950's, with the timeworn buildings disintegrating and no longer capable of meeting the physical demands of a mountainside livelihood, Jim and Nettie had to face the inevitable. They left Sarver Hollow for good and went to live with Mace in the valley below.

Sarver Hollow changed hands at least once more before the US Forest Service purchased the property.

Andy, Mary, and four children, along with grandsons Roy Leon and Mason Lee—all closer in death than in life—lie near each other in the Ross Cemetery near the site of the old Maywood School on Virginia Highway 42, close to Simmonsville, Virginia.

And high up on Sinking Creek Mountain, in the old cemetery now overrun with weeds, near the old ruins that molder among the tangled undergrowth and occasionally, when the breeze stirs, sigh with memories of yesteryear, the others rest in isolated solitude. And that's as far as the frayed fabric of time and space, which connect the past and present, will stretch . . .

*   *   *

I'd be lying straight out if I said that the story of the Sarvers hasn't eaten away at my mind like a hungry mouse in a hiker's food bag. Since that abominable night at the old Sarver ruins, I had frittered away countless hours on the web surfing for Sarver information, to no avail. After four years of frustrated effort, I finally called it quits.

Then in late March 2004, I stopped by Blacksburg, Virginia, to visit my close friend, David "Wahoola" Jones and his lovely vivacious wife, Lori. Wahoola had been my "sort-of" hiking partner in 1990 on that first thru-hike. In the course of our chitchat, I asked him if he knew anything about the Sarvers who had lived just off the Appalachian Trail on Sinking Creek Mountain (only a few miles from where David now lived). "A little," he replied, "but I can put you in touch with a couple of gents who know a lot more."

In about the time it takes to cook and eat a box of mac-n-cheese, we were sitting in the warm living room of Blacksburg resident Bob Ross. We exchanged small talk while we munched on Mrs. Ross' delicious homemade cookies and waited for Bob's distant cousin who lived nearby, Clarence Givens, to join us.

Of medium height and somewhat stocky with thinning hair, Bob had retired from Virginia Tech, where he worked in the metal shop of the Physics Department. He bore his seventy-four years like an old comfortable sweater in spite of a slight limp from a years-ago motorcycle accident. Twinkling eyes set above a salt and pepper beard immediately put me at ease.

On the other hand, Clarence, 67, was tall, thin, clean shaven, and sported a bumper crop of grayish-blond hair. I quickly found out that he and I shared a common bond: We were the same age, and both of us had retired from military service (he from the Air Force and I from the Marine Corps) in 1980. But Clarence showed more sense than I did—he farmed full time instead of chasing after words to fill a page.

After pleasantries had been exchanged, I asked the magic question: "What can you tell me about the Sarvers of Sinking Creek?" Bingo!

It turned out that as boys, Clarence and Bob had lived a couple of miles from the Sarver family. They would take the "Givens Trail" that led up from Sinking Creek and crossed the mountain at the Sarver's peach orchard before winding down to the old home place. There, the boys ate Nettie's cookies, listened as Jim expounded on matters of great interest to young ears, and drank cold pure water from the spring after they tired of chasing the hogs.

The rock "igloos"? Bob scratched his beard and thought hard. "Seems like there were two open fields on that mountaintop that the Sarvers farmed." Clarence nodded agreement and offered, "And there was the peach orchard on top, too. When they cleared the fields, they had to do something with all the rocks. I guess they just stacked them up and left them." Riddle solved. And two new friends made!

(Author's note: During the spring and summer of 2001, the Roanoke Appalachian Trail Club, with help from the US Forest Service, built a shelter a few yards from the old Sarver cabin. The parents of Scott Marshall Riddick, a special education teacher who was also an avid Appalachian Trail hiker and a voracious volunteer trail worker, funded Sarver Hollow Shelter. Scott died of a heart attack at age 34, before he had a chance to realize his dream of doing a thru-hike of the Trail. The shelter is built in his memory. Sarver Hollow Shelter was dedicated on October 20, 2001.

The five-star spring is still there, along with the tumbledown ruins, the cemetery, a few apple trees, and presumably the occasional wandering snake. Word has it that "George," disgruntled by the encroaching "civilization" on his antiquated abode, has packed his spectral bag and gone looking for a new home.

Thankfully, the rock piles on the broad crest of Sinking Creek Mountain remain to excite the imagination of passing hikers.)

Chapter Twenty

To Hell and Beyond

Brush Mountain, my lunchtime goal on this sultry, wet morning of May 28, 1994, rose above Craig Creek Valley, a scant eleven miles by trail north of the Sarver Hollow side trail. Dang, it looked high! Remembering the mountain from 1990, I could already feel my muscles groan in protest against the stiff climb and I was still a good four miles away. Worse, I was still sore from yesterday's slip-slide spine-tingling trek across the tilted crest of Sinking Creek Mountain in pelting rain. A five-mile slanted ice rink that spelled disaster, what with the plate-size lichens that lay there like innocuous off-color splotches of chocolate pudding but actually oozed with slick goo, just waiting to ambush a careless boot and send boot and body tumbling off into the mist-filled void.

In spite of the mounting heat, I shuddered, remembering last night's miserable "digs" at the old Sarver Hollow ruins by myself and the ghostly "imaginings"—or was it! Whichever, it had caused me to move out at first light and eat breakfast far away from the reach of anything that might not be of this world. A plain nasty experience. Heck, "Nasty" didn't even begin to describe yesterday's misery.

Today was the antithesis of yesterday. The sun, only half way through its morning climb, beat down with a personal brutal vengeance, as if I had flagrantly violated some immutable law of physics. Sweat ran into my eyes, stinging like the dickens, then down my nose and into my mouth, where it became a salty snot-tainted cocktail.

And that was the good part. Every pore had become a sweat gusher. I felt like a walking puddle of DNA as my life force spilled out onto the rain-soaked ground. Dang, but I dreaded climbing that mountain!

Too soon, I left the lush rolling meadows of Craig Creek Valley behind and stood glaring at the path that led up Brush Mountain. Strange. It didn't look as steep as I had remembered. A trick of time? In fact, the trail eased upward like a giant sleeping serpent, switching back and forth in gentle sweeps as it crept toward the long summit. Lickety-split, and I was on top, trudging along a dirt road pockmarked with miniature pond-size mud puddles in which four-wheeler tracks had played an indiscriminate game of hop-scotch.

Somewhat to my amazement, no puddle seemed too small. Everything was fair game because the four-wheelers got'em all. Even stranger that the mechanical beasts ruled the mountaintop, for they did. Old tracks went every which way—in and out of trees on each side of the road before circling back to make "wheelies" around the miniature lakes, then disappearing in the muddy water and out again. A straight shot down the middle. And the "crisscrosses," gobs of'em, obviously made by high-flying "fishtailers" cruising back and forth, their antics forming innumerable wavy squares in which games of tic-tac-toe could be played.

In a couple of words, the old mountain road had been gang raped. And it had happened again—sometime this morning.

I stared at the fresh tracks—at least three sets, although I couldn't tell which way the four wheelers had gone. Away from me and off the mountain, I hoped.

Wishful thinking. Five minutes later I heard the alien, angry whine of motors gone crazy. Here they came, right toward me—four of the buggers, all covered with mud and their caps flipped backward in the best redneck tradition. They hooted and yelled as they lurched in and out of mud puddles, and then chased each other in and out of trees, finally circling in the middle of the road in a tight wheelie spin that slung mud all over creation. That little trick finished, they pounded each other on the back like they'd won the Indy 500, "high-fived" several times, and slowly let the circle collapse. Then while the engines idled, the riders contemplated their next bit of devilment.

Slowly, four pairs of eyes were raised toward the lone hiker who stood gawking at the redneck party from fifty yards away. I stood exposed beside a large puddle, next to some trees at the edge of the eviscerated road. A finger pointed my way, heads nodded, and engines revved up amid some "yahoo's" and "hot damns." Wheels slung mud and stinking fumes filled the air. As one, the group roared straight at their prey. Too late to make a run for it! I stood my ground and waited for the axe to fall.

The four wheelers roared with throttles wide open, increasing speed at an exponential rate. Too late, I saw what was coming. Muddy water flew in all directions as they crashed into the puddle. Then they were gone, hooting and hollering like they'd just bagged a rare animal—which I guess they had. I heard one yell above the hammering exhausts, "We nailed that motha." Another screamed back, "Yeah, we got his ass good." And in unison, just like it had been rehearsed, four "bird" fingers shot into the air. A final salute from the kings of the mountain.

I was too shocked to even muster up a good cussing at my assailants, just stood there and watched until the group disappeared around a bend and the engine noise abated. Nasty brown liquid drenched my skin and skimpy outfit. I spit a few times, in case I'd gotten some of the stuff in my mouth.

Then came the cussing, some good old Marine venom, even some stomping. Then the relief that all I'd gotten was a mud bath slowly soaked in. Heck, women even paid to get that done to their faces in beauty shops. I returned their "salute" and walked on up the Trail, not realizing that soon my day would change from the bizarre to a soul-stirring experience.

The fairly large clearing off to my left was totally unexpected. I couldn't remember it being there in 1990. For that part, I couldn't recall being on this part of Brush Mountain before. Curious, I turned into the clearing and walked the few yards uphill to a granite monument.

The words fairly leaped out. "Audie Leon Murphy June 20, 1924—May 28, 1971." Now what was the marker doing on this isolated mountaintop? And what did it have to do with Audie Murphy?

Like most everyone else of my generation, I knew that Audie was America's most decorated hero of WWII (and probably one of the luckiest persons on the entire planet); also, that after the war he became a movie actor. I'd seen his autobiographical movie of his war experience, *To Hell and Back*—the only film I could recall in which the main character was played by the main character. I read on: ". . . died near this site in an airplane crash . . ."

The words crashed into the solitude like an intense bolt of lightning without thunder, and then the date, "May 28." Coincidence, that Fate should lead me to this lonely spot where Audie's luck finally ran out—exactly twenty-three years to the day after the tragedy? Goosebumps rippled my skin as unbidden images assaulted my mind. A plane violently ripped apart, littering the forest floor near where I sat . . . bodies twisted and mangled, lifeless forms scattered about the wreckage like discarded rag dolls . . . the warped smell of things unnatural burning in combination . . .

I gritted my teeth and pushed the morbid thoughts away. Beyond the granite marker, a blue-blazed trail led up to a magnificent overlook. While I ate lunch and let the view ease the unsettled feelings that clung to my innards, I swore a silent oath to get closer to Audie Leon Murphy when I got home. He deserved more; much more.

*   *   *

In hindsight, the Marines shortchanged themselves big time the day they turned Audie Murphy down. "Too short," the recruiter growled, then added, laughing, "Hell boy, a strong fart would dump you on your ass." Audie, barely 5'-5," tipped the scales at a skimpy 111 pounds. He next tried the Navy and the Paratroopers and got the same treatment. But the Army, frantic to quickly expand its ranks for the war effort, let Audie sign on the dotted line on June 20, 1942. The new recruit swore that he was eighteen years old that very day.

Reliable evidence exists that Audie altered his birth certificate to enlist. He was probably seventeen—or possibly even sixteen by some accounts. His peers promptly named him "Baby Face," because that's exactly what Nature had doled out to the diminutive lad. During his basic training phase at Camp Wolters, the scorching Texas sun got the best of Audie one day while he was doing close order drill and he passed out. The Army in its abundant wisdom decided the soldier didn't have what it took to be an infantryman, so he was offered a job as a cook. Audie resisted, insisting that he was a fighter, not a bean slinger. Just before he went overseas, the Army offered him another great deal—PX (Post Exchange) clerk.

Audie laughed in the Army's face and went off to war.

Audie Leon Murphy, the seventh of twelve children, was born into poverty on June 20, 1924 (some say a year later) near the dying town of Kingston, Texas. But poverty and hard times were the norm in the scrub-covered plains of northeast Texas where "King Cotton" faced abdication. Three of Audie's siblings had already died by the time he uttered his first squeals in the small clapboard tenant house on the W.F. Boles farm where his father, Emmett Berry Murphy, worked as a sharecropper. The mother, Josie Bell, would strap the toddler in a swing while she worked alongside her husband in the stifling cotton fields. As soon as Audie was old enough to carry a bucket, his world became hard, backbreaking work— milking the cows and carrying wood for the cook stove. Soon afterwards, he went into the cotton fields to do grownup's toil.

When the Great Depression hit, "worse" got "worser." In 1934, Emmett left to find work. He never returned. Ten-year-old Audie, the eldest child still at home, suddenly found himself playing the role of surrogate father. He quit fifth grade and went to work chopping cotton for a dollar a day. Faced with the task of putting meat on the table for his mother and eight siblings, he became an expert shot, sometimes having only one bullet for his old .22 caliber rifle to do the job at hand. A missed shot and the family went hungry. Dark days had descended on the Murphy family, and for a time they lived in an old railroad car on a siding in Kingston.

Then came catastrophe. Poor health from hard work and countless days of worrying finally got the best of Josie Bell. She died on a warm day in late May 1941, when the cotton bolls were swelling. Audie laid her to rest beside her parents in Aleo Cemetery south of nearby Farmersville, Texas. She was only fifty. (Audie's father, Emmett, fared much better. He died in 1976—five years after Audie—at the ripe age of 90.)

Stricken with grief, the man-boy, only sixteen, faced the inevitable: He couldn't take care of the three siblings who still remained at home. With his heart ripping in two, Audie placed Nadine, Billie, and Joe in the Boles Home Orphanage outside of Greenville and went to work at a close by service station. He made a solemn vow that someday he would reunite the family.

When the bombs fell on Pearl Harbor, Audie's boss said, "Son, here's your opportunity. Go make something of yourself." He did!

The War moved slowly for "Baby Face" Murphy. At Ft. Meade, Maryland, where he was sent for advanced infantry training, the lowly private had a flash of fame, which in a way heralded far greater things to come. At the 500-yard line on the rifle range, all the shooters sprawled on the ground in the prone firing position like they'd been taught. And when the loud speaker blared out "Commence firing," in about ten seconds Audie zinged ten shots into the bull while the other shooters were still wrestling to get into firing position.

The soldier in the "Butts" who scored Audie's target pushed up a white disc (signifying a bull's eye) ten times in rapid succession, which caught the line coach's attention. The coach, a grizzled sergeant with a wad of tobacco packed into his left cheek walked up behind Audie, spat a glob of brown juice between the prone private's legs and swore. "Dammit, Joe (all the recruits were called 'Joe'), I don't know what that clown in th' Butts is doin', but yer s'posed to git one disc spotted fer each shot, not ten fer one." He yelled at the corporal who had line communications with the Butts. "Tell th' Butts Sarge to have that numbnuts on Target 19 to rescore the target. And no more clownin' around or I'll have his ass fer breakfast."

Again, the white disc quickly rose ten times into the center of the target. The coach's eyes bored into Audie. "Joe, how many shots did you fire?" Audie replied, "Ten, Sar'int, just like I was supposed to." Without another word the coach handed Audie ten more rounds. "Do it again." In rapid succession came ten shots, followed by ten white discs.

The coach gave a long low whistle. "Summabitch. Son, where'd you learn to shoot like that?" Audie said, "Back home in Texas, Sar'int. Twern't nothin'." Maybe not for him, but the word got around. Don't mess with "Baby Face."

(Guns were part of Audie's daily regimen. As kids, Audie and his friends would take "aimed-to-miss" pot shots at one another during "Cowboys and Indians" or "Cops and Robbers." Or, to add a little more spice when that sport got boring, they would act out a modern day version of "Willian Tell" by placing bottles on each others heads and shooting them off. Make no bones about it, Audie Murphy was a crack shot; also, he knew what the working end of a bullet sounded like—two attributes that would serve him well later on, when the "games" were played for keeps.)

In February 1943, Audie was assigned to Company B, 1st Battalion, 15th Infantry Regiment, 3rd Infantry Division, which was engaged in the "mopping up" phase of the North Africa campaign. (He would remain with Company B throughout his military service.) In just two years, the soft spoken, baby-faced Texan would have won a "battlefield commission" as a second lieutenant. He would have been wounded three times; and he would have received every medal the United States awards for valor.

His extraordinary heroism, which had earned him a Distinguished Service Cross (second only to the Medal of Honor), along with his two Silver Stars and two Bronze Stars, reached a blazing climax on a snow-blanketed field near Woltzwihr, France. Close to midnight on January 25, 1945, in near zero weather Company B assaulted a heavily defended position as part of an offensive to push the German army out of France. By the time the attack was over, except for Second Lieutenant Murphy, all of the officers and 102 soldiers of the decimated company's enlisted strength of 120 had been killed or wounded.

Lt. Murphy suddenly found himself in command of an 18-man company with orders to hold his position at all costs. Company B straddled a critical piece of terrain—the only road that led into the 3rd Infantry Division's area and made the Division highly vulnerable to an expected German counterattack. The next morning, the Germans attacked in force and all hell broke loose. Realizing that his men could not withstand such overwhelming numbers, Lt. Murphy ordered his small command back into the woods and for the next hour single-handedly held off six German Tiger tanks and waves of infantry. In an all-or-nothing gamble, he directed artillery barrages on his own position.

When the Germans closed to ten yards, Audie jumped on a burning tank destroyer and, hidden by smoke, fired its .50 caliber machine gun, mowing down wave after wave of the enemy. A nervous lieutenant at regimental headquarters got on the phone and asked Audie how close the Germans were. He yelled back, "Hold the phone and I'll let you talk to one of the bastards."

Only seconds after Murphy abandoned the burning tank destroyer, it exploded in a massive fireball. Not done, although he was bleeding from a reopened hip wound, the boy-soldier led his small band in a daring counterattack. The Germans threw in the towel and withdrew.

A few weeks later, Major General Alexander Patch, 3rd Infantry Division's Commanding General, pinned the Medal of Honor, the Nation's highest award for gallantry in battle, on "Baby Face" Murphy's chest.

The youthful fighter received thirty-three awards in all, including five from the French and one from the Belgians—all by the ripe old age of nineteen (or was it eighteen)! Sadly, of B Company's 235-man roster when Private Murphy joined the unit, by war's end only two of the original soldiers remained—a supply sergeant and Audie. The rest had been killed or wounded.

The final tally by the time First Lieutenant Murphy (he received a promotion) was released from active duty in September 1945: Wounded three times, he had participated in nine major campaigns, including one amphibious assault, and was personally credited with putting away at least 240 of the enemy enemy.

But valor sometimes comes at a hefty price.

As the most decorated soldier of WWII (and in his country's history at that time), Audie Murphy stepped back on American soil a true hero. Soon came star-spangled parades in large cities. The good citizens of Farmersville, Texas, held a big celebration for their local hero. (Kingston was too small to host such a "doin's.") The Brooklyn Dodgers even staged an "Audie Murphy Day" at Ebbets Field.

Then a seemingly innocuous event happened that would have a major impact on the hero's life. Movie star James Cagney saw Audie's photo on the front cover of *Life*. Cagney stared at what he thought was an actor's face hidden beneath the war-weary eyes that gazed back from the glossy black and white. On a whim, he invited the soldier to Hollywood as his guest, hoping that this unique American would be welcomed with open arms by the movie moguls.

The trip was a bust. "Don't call us; we'll call you," became Audie's swan song. He stuck it out for several weeks, even slept in a friend's gymnasium after he wore a hole in Cagney's welcome mat. But nothing came of his attempt at stardom. Frustrated and disillusioned, the fledgling actor finally shook the dust of fickle Hollywood from his shoes and went back East.

After three years of spinning wheels, Audie Murphy had run the gamut of opportunity, working menial jobs such as a parking garage attendant. The fifth grade dropout had no business skills, and the classified section had no job listings for a "crack rifleman with fearless ambition." He returned to Hollywood determined to have another go at the silver screen. Then fortune grudgingly bestowed a slight smile on the struggling veteran.

James Cagney called in some favors and managed to land Audie a bit part in a major motion picture, *Beyond Glory*, which starred heavy hitters Alan Ladd and Donna Reed. Critics, somewhat parsimonious with their words, said that Audie Murphy ". . . does right well for himself. You'll recognize him. He's the one with the southern drawl." It was enough to give the aspiring actor a whiff of "what might be" and barely enough to land him a bit part in another movie. But "bit part performer" didn't appeal to Audie Murphy.

His big break came from an unexpected source.

With a little money in his pocket, he decided it was time to make good on the solemn promise he had made before he went off to the killing fields of Europe. Audie bought a large two-story house in Farmersville, Texas, for his oldest sister, Corinne, and her husband and three children, with the understanding that the three younger siblings left in the orphanage would live with them. Six children under one roof didn't work out, so Audie arranged to have Nadine and Billie live with his older brother, "Buck." But what to do with Joe, the youngest?

Audie turned to James "Skipper" Cherry, a wealthy theater owner in Dallas, Texas, who had once befriended him. Cherry belonged to a consortium of Texas theater owners.

"Easily done," remarked Cherry in response to Murphy's dilemma. "The Boys Ranch can be his home." Then Cherry inquired about Audie's movie career. "Not good," he confessed. "Nothing but bit parts." Then came the words that would change Audie's life forever. "You want to be a leading man?"

Cherry's consortium had worked a deal with Allied Artists, by which Variety Club, the consortium's charitable involvement with such worthy enterprises as Boys Ranch, would put up the money for a major motion picture about a fictional Boys Town called *Bad Boy.* The entrepreneur decided that he would give his actor friend's career a boost by insisting that Audie get the leading role.

When Allied Artists balked at using an untested, little known actor, Cherry said, "No Audie, no money." The reviews were terrific and Audie's acting career was made.

Apparently the war hero-become-actor had a face that brought out the maternal instinct in women, and for some strange reason, the macho syndrome in men. Audie Murphy went on to make forty-four films over the next twenty years. Most were movies in which the actor wore a uniform of sorts or had a horse between his legs. He once remarked that the many Grade B westerns in which he starred all had the same plot; only the horses changed.

But on the "up" side, Murphy did bank nearly three million dollars. And his acting was good enough to earn him a "star" at the corner of Vine Street and Selma Avenue on Hollywood's "Walk of Fame."

In 1949, at the urging of his good friend David "Spec" McClure, Audie wrote his autobiography, *To Hell and Back*—not to glorify himself, but rather to tell the story of his comrades of Company B. The book was an instant best seller. In 1955, Universal-International, which had negotiated a seven-year contract with Murphy after his huge success with *Bad Boy*, released the movie of the same title. Audie, age 31, played himself as a 19-year-old. (The movie became Universal's highest grossing picture until 1975, when *Jaws* hit the big screen.)

When Audie's autobiography hit the streets in 1949, at the Army's behest the most decorated soldier returned to France on a goodwill tour. He revisited the site near Woltzwihr where he had won the Medal of Honor. The M-10 was still there, right where he had last seen it. A pastoral, peaceful scene on this day, though—unlike that wintry hell four years before when the demons of war had unleashed such maniacal fury on the nineteen-year-old who had stood his ground on 31 tons of burning tank destroyer and defiantly laid his life on the line.

Audie gazed in awe at the burned-out hulk and surveyed the damage. The M-10 had been struck three times by German Tiger 88-millimeter rounds, not to mention numerous dents and scratches in the armor made by enemy bullets seeking to bring down the man who wouldn't die.

Audie's acting career wasn't all work. Romance blossomed when starlet Wanda Hendrix saw his poster on a movie billboard (as sometimes happens in Hollywood) and came calling. He married the petite film star in January 1949, but the marriage failed after two years (also a common occurrence in the movie capital). Audie married Braniff Airline hostess Pamela Archer on April 23, 1951, only three days after his divorce became final. But this union persevered and the couple produced two sons, Terry and James.

When the hordes swept south of Korea's 38th Parallel in 1950, Captain Audie Murphy (promoted by the Texas National Guard, which he joined with high hopes of getting into the thick of things) turned in his cowboy outfit and again donned soldiering clothes. Alas, the Thirty-sixth Division never got out of the States. Disgruntled, Audie returned to acting, but he retained his commission in the Texas National Guard. He remained with the Thirty-sixth "T-patchers," eventually attaining the rank of major. He was transferred to the Inactive Army Reserve in 1966, where he remained until his death.

And the cost of valor? For Audie Murphy, it came high. Twenty-five years after the war, soak-sweated nightmares still plagued his nightly dreams. Came nocturnal episodes so violent that he couldn't bear to sleep in a dark room and insisted on having a loaded pistol under his pillow. Came crying spells, when he sobbed for his lost comrades. Audie was constantly assailed by memories so vividly soul-ripping that he became dependent on Placidyl—a sleeping pill his physician had prescribed to get him through his nightly horrors. Swamped by dammed-up emotions that surged against his psyche and ravaged his ego, he sought escape in fortune-busting activities such as gambling, women, horses, and shaky business ventures. (He was forced into bankruptcy in 1968.)

Belatedly, doctors recognized that America's most decorated soldier suffered from "battle fatigue." (During Vietnam the condition was elevated to the twaddly status of "post traumatic stress disorder." Same disease; different war.) Audie finally admitted that he had a problem. He locked himself in a hotel room, went "cold turkey" with the sleeping pills, and for a week, endured withdrawal symptoms until he had dried himself out. He found a personal catharsis as an outspoken advocate for the needs of veterans. Further, he broke down the old taboo of publicly discussing "battle fatigue" by candidly talking about his war-related mental problems.

Audie never totally purged the nightmares, but he tried—partly in his poetry and song writing. The poetry was pretty fair, and he could have made a decent living as a songwriter. Between 1962 and 1970, he wrote seventeen songs. Several made the top ten list, helped along by recording artists such as Dean Martin, Teresa Brewer, Eddy Arnold, and Charlie Pride. And he found another soul-cleansing outlet as a Freemason. Encouraged by his friend and benefactor, James Cherry, Audie joined the Masonic Order in 1955. In just two years, he had received the 32nd Degree, the highest level normally achieved.

Audie's last film, which he produced, was made in 1971. In *A Time for Dying*, Audie played an aging Jesse James. On a rainy Friday morning, May 28, 1971, Audie took a break from the movie set and, along with three friends and the pilot, boarded a twin engine Aero Commander 680E at Atlanta. The group intended to visit a manufacturing plant in Martinsville, Virginia, which had attracted Audie's attention as a possible business investment.

A few hours later, folks in Grayson and Carrol Counties in southwest Virginia saw a plane dancing in and out of the low-hanging clouds ". . . like it was on a yo-yo string" one observer remarked. Within minutes, the plane crashed into the fog-shrouded side of 3100-foot Brush Mountain, nearly fifty miles north of its intended flight path. Rescuers finally reached the crash site on Memorial Day and retrieved the bodies. For weeks thereafter the curious made their way to the gruesome scene and toted away souvenirs in the form of pieces of twisted, scorched metal. (When the plane crashed, Audie still had twenty minutes of filming left in *A Time for Dying,* part of which featured himself. As a result, he only appears in one scene in this, his final movie.)

Audie Leon Murphy lost his fortune, but never the respect of his countrymen. The Medal of Honor winner was interred with full military honors at Arlington National Cemetery near the Tomb of the Unknowns on June 7, 1971, a few days shy of his forty-seventh birthday. In accordance with his wishes, his government-issue grave marker is unadorned, lacking the gold inlaid MOH crest normally set into Medal of Honor winners' stones. He never looked on himself as a hero; rather, he strongly believed that all who faced the enemy and stared death squarely in the eyes were heroes. Only President John Kennedy's grave receives more visitors each year.

In 1996, Audie Murphy was inducted into the National Cowboy Hall of Fame's Hall of Great Western Performers at Oklahoma City. There, his fame rubs elbows with other great stars such as Gregory Peck, Barbara Stanwyck, and of course that acclaimed actor who never saw a day of war but sure knew how to act it, John Wayne.

Somewhere along the way a brilliantly red hybrid tea rose was propagated and named in his honor. The United States Postal Service issued an Audie Murphy commemorative stamp (after many petitions and several Congressmen were called into action) on October 16, 1999. And the following year, the Masonic Order posthumously bestowed its highest accolade, the 33rd Degree, on their heroic Freemason. Pamela Archer Murphy accepted the award in her husband's name.

Not a shabby bottom-line for a Texas sharecropper's son who once made his bed in a railroad siding boxcar.

On Veterans Day, 1974, one hundred and fifty persons made their way up a winding Forest Service road to the summit of Brush Mountain. The object of their pilgrimage? A large square hunk of granite with a slanted top and some words chiseled into the gray-flecked stone. The twisted, burned metal "souvenirs" had long since disappeared. A fair tradeoff though—a monument for some airplane wreckage.

It had taken Blacksburg VFW Post 5311 three years and a day after the crash to get a permit from the Forest Service, who laid claim to the mountaintop. And then came the arduous task of hauling the multi-ton rock to the mountaintop. But there it sat, resplendent in the sun-drenched glade. After the unveiling and a brief ceremony, the visitors departed, leaving the memorial to commiserate with the lingering ghosts of unfulfilled dreams.

(Author's note: A spokesman for the United States Army said about their most decorated hero after his untimely death, "There will never be another Audie Murphy." Hollow words, indeed!

Came Ronnie Hooper. Different war; same blood, guts, and glory.

No mountaintop monument for Joe Ronnie; no link to the Appalachian Trail. And unlike Audie Murphy, no accolades fell his way. But he deserves his moment in the sunshine of public awareness. Never heard of him?

Joe Ronnie Hooper, too, was a soldier but his war—Vietnam—had quickly become a blight on America's national conscience. Out of sight; out of mind. Best left buried in the political graveyard of all-time "boners." A shame!)

*   *   *

The strawberry-haired six-footer—a charger who had excelled as Washington State's former football scoring champ at Moses Lake High School outside Yakima—enlisted at age nineteen. But unlike runt-like Audie, Joe Ronnie was a big man. When he walked into a Navy Recruiting Office, the chief petty officer quickly signed him up and counted his blessings. Joe Ronnie gave it four years and his best shot, but he just couldn't march to the humdrum beat of the sailor's lot. So when the time came to reenlist in 1961, he changed over to the Army and soon became a "Screaming Eagle" in the 101st Airborne Division.

Joe Hooper barely survived his first (of two tours) in Vietnam. He packed a lot of living into those hell-filled months. Joe got a battlefield commission as a second lieutenant. And along the way, he received 37 awards, including the Medal of Honor, two Silver Stars, six Bronze Stars, and eight Purple Heart Medals—a tally that by some accounts make him the most decorated soldier in America's history.

To take the measure of this remarkable man, consider this. On February 21, 1968, near Hue during a nasty bit of business called the Tet Offensive, Joe Hooper found out what he was made of. (Then) Sergeant Hooper was leading his six-man squad on a recon patrol when the unit came under intense fire from a heavily defended bunker position on the opposite bank of a river. The squad followed Hooper 's charge across the river and overran the bunkers.

For 6 ½ hours Hooper and his squad fought against overwhelming odds. Time and again, their leader ran through exposed areas rank with withering fire to take out fortified positions that sought to annihilate his men. He put his life on the line at least half a dozen times that day to save wounded comrades, even though he himself had been severely hurt (the medic counted seven wounds). Sergeant Hooper refused to be evacuated until all his men had been pulled to safety, at which time he passed out from loss of blood.

Two days later Joe regained consciousness in a field hospital. He stole a rifle, hitched a ride back to his unit, and jumped into the thick of battle. Technically he was Absent Without Leave (AWOL), but by the time the Army found him forty-eight hours later, he had been wounded again. (In a few months, President Richard Nixon would hang the Medal of Honor around Joe's neck.)

In the end, like Audie Murphy, Joe Ronnie became his own worst enemy. After his second Vietnam tour, Joe was assigned to Fort Polk, Louisiana, to train troops. But he couldn't fit into the tedium of Army life without combat. So in 1974, disgruntled, severely afflicted with arthritis, and sixty percent disabled from war wounds, the battle-hardened veteran resigned his commission and walked off the military reservation with a $12,000 "farewell" check hidden in his shoe.

From there it was all downhill—straight to rock bottom. Unable to cope with his inner demons, he brushed aside the comfort offered by his wife and two children and turned to John Barleycorn for release from his private hell. Came divorce, then years of nightmares and alcoholic binges that stretched into weeks. Night after night friends would carry the senseless hero out of Seattle bars on their shoulders—just as Joe had whisked wounded soldiers to safety across his shoulders that bloody day near Hue. But members of the Medal of Honor Society take care of their own, and somehow they managed to keep Joe Hooper employed by the Veterans Administration in spite of his frequent absences.

Finally came the day that the fallen hero had enough of being a bottom feeder. Like a phoenix rising from the ashes of despair, he decided to regain control of his runaway existence.

In his pre-Army days, Joe had worked with racehorses, a job he had relished. So off he went to faraway Kentucky to learn the tricks of the trade, to find the big break. Excited, the would-be equine entrepreneur traveled down to Louisville's Churchill Downs to watch the 104th running of the Kentucky Derby on May 5, 1979.

But Joe never got to see "Spectacular Bid" flash across the finish line 2 ¾ lengths ahead of "General Assembly." He had died alone in his hotel room during the night. A brain aneurysm had taken down the 40-year-old veteran, accomplishing in a brief flash what the North Vietnamese had been unable to do in countless battles.

Joe Ronnie Hooper was buried in Arlington National Cemetery with full military honors, close to Audie Murphy's grave and just a short stone's toss from the Tomb of the Unknowns. But sadly, it took a year for someone in the media to recognize Joe Hooper for what he was—possibly America's most decorated hero—certainly the Vietnam War's most decorated. A few sparse articles were written; there was even some talk of making a movie of Joe's life as had been done with Audie Murphy and WWI's most decorated hero, Sergeant Alvin York. But the words "Vietnam War" and its progeny were not popular subjects, so nothing ever came of it.

So there they lie in America's most hallowed ground—two mighty warriors; two kindred spirits, whose sacrifice shouts out at their countrymen, "Freedom comes with a high price." If we will only listen . . .

*   *   *

Recently, I spoke to a class of high school seniors about my Vietnam War experience. On a whim, I asked if anyone knew who Audie Murphy was. A couple of arms hesitantly rose into the air. Said one pimple-faced lad with an eyebrow ring and green hair, "He's that dude who played *The Nutty Professor*." Heads nodded knowingly.

Contemptuous of her classmate's gaffe, a pretty gal with long blond hair haughtily corrected the mistake. "I *believe* that was Eddie Murphy. Audie Murphy was his younger brother."

No one was willing to take a stab at Joe Ronnie Hooper.

How sad! And how fast America forgets. Other than the Medal of Honor gravestone, Joe Hooper's life barely lingers in a few tattered newspaper clippings and a couple of well-meaning web spots.

And like an old sepia photograph, Audie Murphy's memory is fast fading away. Reruns of old Grade B westerns; a scuffed star on a Los Angeles sidewalk;

a few scattered musty museum rooms with Audie paraphernalia; some commemorative stamps hidden away in collectors' albums; a hunk of granite sitting on Section 46 of Lot 366-11, Grid O/P 22.5 in Arlington; and the lone marker atop Brush Mountain—that's about all that's left.

There's nothing special about Joe Ronnie Hooper's final resting-place; it's just another stone lost among the sea of white granite that covers Arlington's solemn landscape.

On the other hand, thanks to high media coverage, which spawned a mass influx of sight-seekers to Audie's grave and caused the turf to be worn down past the roots, Audie got a sidewalk. Yet one wonders how long the curious will continue to seek out his simple grave on the hillside above the swirling waters of the Potomac.

But then, perhaps the "Audie Murphy rose" will linger for a few more generations . . .

Chapter Twenty-one

Mosby's Confederacy

On a sun-drenched Sunday afternoon in late June 1990, the minute I hiked beyond the "Trespassers Will Be Eaten" sign that warned hikers to steer clear of the goings on inside the National Zoological Park Research compound north of US Highway 522 near Front Royal, Virginia, I knew something had changed. Not given to superstition (I can't say the same thing about my flighty, unpredictable alter ego Model-T), I tried to shrug off the feeling of "things" unseen skulking in the shadowy depths of the dense scrub oak thickets that crowded the Trail. But try as hard as I could, the uneasy feeling persisted. Now and then I sensed movement behind me, even eyes boring into my back. But after turning around several times to check and finding only the yellow-splotched facade of the silent forest, I gritted my teeth and willed myself to hike on, refusing to give in to the overpowering urge to turn and shout, "Who's there?"

Something kept nagging at my mind, a tidbit that lay just beneath the surface but stubbornly refused to rise into cognitive sunlight. The mental straining threatened to implode and short-circuit my brain, so I took off my pack and surrendered the moment to the fourth Snickers of the day.

Slowly, like cold molasses oozing from a Mason jar, it came—a vague recollection about a Mosby campsite and an old structure that had been used as a trail shelter until it rotted into the soft forest turf a few years back. Sucking the last shreds of peanut from my teeth, I consulted my tattered *1990 Trail Data Book* and there it was—Mosby Campsite, 3.4 miles north of the highway. The site had to be close to where I now brooded, straining to detect any sound that penetrated the crushing silence, any clue to the sinking feeling that threatened to turn the day into a rancid aftertaste.

I hurried on, casting anxious glances at the trees for the blue blazed trail that led to the old campsite. But if it was there, I missed it.

As the shadows lengthened to near ridiculous proportions, which tweaked my overworked imagination with otherworldly images, I finally reached my day's destination. Hikers had dubbed the new Jim and Molly Denton Shelter built by the Potomac AT Club the "Hilton" because of its beautiful layout complete with an upper deck, skylights, a cooking pavilion, and best of all, a chain-operated shower that fed off of a nearby spring. I quickly unpacked, ever mindful of the overwhelming silence and hidden eyes, and made my nest on the shelter floor. That done, I shivered through a wonderfully exhilarating icy shower, which seemed to somewhat ease my apprehension. Feeling almost human again, I started supper, all the while keeping my ears tuned for hikers who would undoubtedly be coming in for the evening. After all, I had been on the Trail for seventy-five days and had yet to spend a night by myself.

And there it came, just as I was savoring the first bites of mac-n-cheese. The gosh-almighty marvelous sound of footsteps! I'd have company again this night!

My hope soon turned into a pipe dream. After the exchange of perfunctory greetings came the bombshell. The hiker told me that he had just begun his yearly section hike back at Highway 522 and planned to do more miles before dark. Disappointed, I growled, "Nasty bit of trail ahead, especially if you get caught by the dark. Plus, th' snakes, you know." (Now that was an outright fib, for I'd never hiked a step north of where I now sat. The desperate flailing of a drowning man going down for the second time.) Pushing hard, I added, "Bad night to be in a tent, cause it's gonna come one hellacious storm tonight."

He stared at me like I was a sniveling cur—or a blathering idiot, reader's choice—which I realized I was beginning to sound like. "Not for a couple of days, according to the weather forecast I heard this afternoon." He put special emphasis on "I heard," and I knew then and there that I'd been caught in my small web of deceit. The hiker shouldered his pack and stalked toward the trees, apparently in a hurry to be rid of this lie-monger. Didn't even say goodbye or good luck.

But at the edge of the clearing he turned and gave me a parting shot. "By the way, you'd best watch out 'cause this is Mosby's Confederacy. The local folks say that they've actually seen his ghost and that the whole area's bad haunted. Strange happenings."

For a brief moment it seemed like his eyes actually glowed red like some maniacal demon, and I shuddered as he continued. "Yep, mighty strange happenings. They even camped right down there by the spring." He pointed a long finger toward the sound of trickling water, where I had to go and fill water bottles before I went to bed. Then without another word, he strode off into the deepening gloom. Going down for the third time! Lordy, send hikers!

Thinking back, I remembered a few things about Mosby from American History 101. Actually, it was more of a blurred memory mixed with the cute well-endowed brunette who sat two rows across from me, and of Ms. Robertson, the teacher, blabbing something about a "Gray Ghost" to the class. I seemed to recall that Mosby and his partisan rangers roamed across the northern Virginia countryside during the Civil War and gave Union Army commanders peptic ulcers. And that was all I could recall.

The sun dropped below the trees. I waited in vain for some hikers to show. Dang, but how I hated to make that trip down to the spring. I procrastinated, waiting for hikers that never came, and the twilight deepened. Nothing stirred; the inside of a crypt couldn't have been more silent. Finally came a short croak from near the spring, then another, and then a full chorus of reverberating "ribbits." I faced the inevitable. No more hikers were coming.

With my heart pumping like the steam-driven pistons of Casey Jones' fire-belching engine #382, I picked up my water bottles and headed for the spring, mumbling with each faltering step, "No such things as ghosts."

I slept very little that night. Around midnight, the privy door began to bang sporadically, causing heart-stopping spasms of clammy chills to rack my body with each explosive crack. And then came the pre-dawn pee call, which I put off until the pain turned to nausea; and then the near heart attack on my way to the pee-tree when a nearby bush erupted as a doe bolted from the clearing.

But the greatest shocker. I went to the privy in the safety of the bright morning sunlight. The door was securely latched!

(Author's note: For the complete account of this, my first night alone on the Trail, please see page 328 of *Walkin' on the Happy Side of Misery*. Just for the record, by the time I reached the Trail's northern terminus in Maine three months later, I had spent many nights by myself. Thankfully, I had long since gotten over the "willies" and felt totally safe embraced in the friendly arms of the nurturing forest.

But then, Mosby didn't range north of the Virginia border, or so I've been told . . .)

So what's the big deal about Colonel John Singleton Mosby? Well, for starters he was the clichéd proverbial thorn in Mr. Lincoln's butt, not to mention Old "Unconditional Surrender" Grant and his hell-bent subordinate destroyer of the Shenandoah Valley, Phil Sheridan. With a small band of local partisans, Mosby so disrupted Union operations in northern Virginia and became such an embarrassment to the Army that Grant assigned an entire division to get the "Gray Ghost"—dead or alive. President Lincoln (who gave Mosby his descriptive nickname) so feared the raider would sneak into Washington some dark night and kidnap him that he ordered the planking removed each evening from the Chain Bridge, which spanned the Potomac. In retrospect, Lincoln probably made a wise move, for Mosby's reckless daring raids had hauled in some mighty big fish!

The "Gray Ghost".

For example, take the midnight raid at Fairfax Courthouse on March 8, 1863. Mosby with a band of twenty-nine men brashly entered the quarters of Brigadier General Edwin Stoughton, who commanded the 9th Vermont Brigade. The Gray Ghost roused the sleeping general with a slap on his rump and said, "Get up General and come with me."

Growled the General, "What is this? Do you know who I am, sir?" To which Mosby replied, "I reckon I do, General. Did you ever hear of Mosby?" The General snorted. "Yes, but have you caught him?" Mosby laughed and said, "No, but he has caught you."

When Lincoln heard that Stoughton had been captured, along with fifty-eight horses, he sighed. "Well, I'm sorry for that. I can make new brigadier generals, but I can't make horses." (Legend has it that Mosby sent a lock of his own hair to the frustrated President, along with a note bragging that Mr. Lincoln would soon be kidnapped and have his own head shaved—just prior to Mosby slipping a hangman's noose around his Presidential neck.)

*   *   *

John Singleton Mosby, like Audie Leon Murphy, got short shrift when Ma Nature passed out the sizing genes. He was born in Edgemont, Virginia on December 6, 1833, and raised in the shadows of the Blue Ridge near Charlottesville. As a youth, he was "delicate" and often heard adults prophesy that the frail boy ". . . would never live to be a grown man." But the prophets were wrong and the youth grew into an adult who barely tipped the scales at 125 pounds—yet managed to outlive most of his contemporaries.

With his slender build, short height, clean shaven face, and sandy blonde hair combed in the style of a young Jeff Davis, he could easily have faded into the drab background of a small crowd—except for the eyes. The keen gray eyes, which seemed to flash with fire. They captured people like moths fluttering before a flame and mirrored an inner firestorm and restless determination that bespoke of greatness to come—if given the chance.

The chance did come, but barely, and with a whimsical twist of Fate at that.

When he reached the turbulent age of seventeen, young Mosby began his studies at the University of Virginia. He soon became a natural target for bullies because of his small size. But his fiery spirit usually allowed him to give back as good as he got, and he was able to "callithump" with the best of the school's revelers. On at least two occasions during his first year, Mosby took part in this bizarre event, during which students would gallop hell bent for leather around the campus and through neighboring streets on horseback, all the while whipping up all the ruckus they could manage.

(Sound familiar? During my college days, an impromptu panty raid on the girls' dorm usually sufficed as a relief valve for the full head of steam we sometimes built up from the stress of academia. And of course, the mass protests of students in the '70s and '80s carried more dignity than slapping riding crops against sweaty horse flanks or thrusting ladders up toward giggling, hopeful girls who waved nylon trophies from second story windows. Now, *those* were the days!)

In his third year Mosby somehow incurred the wrath of George Turpin, a medical student who had established a reputation as a notorious knife-wielding bully. Only days before, Turpin had practiced his surgical skills on a fellow student who had rubbed him the wrong way. Now he spread the word that ". . . he would eat Mosby 'blood raw'." The following day, Turpin confronted Mosby and pulled out his hog sticker, ready to make good his threat. The sprightly Virginian quickly decided that southern honor didn't require him to reciprocate in kind, so he pulled a borrowed pepper-box pistol from his jacket and calmly fired a single shot into his assailant's neck.

Turpin lived, but Mosby got the worst end of the deal—at least one might think. He was expelled from the university. On May 25, 1853, the young perpetrator was convicted of "unlawful shooting," fined $1000 (later rescinded), and hauled off to the Charlottesville jail to serve a twelve-month sentence.

"Fate," that fickle arbiter of man's comeuppance, can take some strange turns. In John Mosby's case, the jail sentence proved to be one of those spurious twists that ultimately took him on a long circuitous road to fame. He decided to study law while incarcerated.

Oddly, the attorney who had vigorously prosecuted the case now came to Mosby's aid and prevailed upon Virginia's Governor Johnson to grant the young offender a pardon, which he did on December 23rd as a "Christmas present." As soon as he was released, Mosby continued his law studies under the tutelage of his benefactor. In a few months, the State of Virginia admitted John Singleton Mosby to the Bar, and he set up practice in nearby Howardsville.

A year later, Cupid fired off a volley of pheromone-tipped arrows at Howardsville's newest attorney when pretty Pauline came to town with her father, Beverly L. Clarke, an accomplished attorney and noted politician visiting from Kentucky. After a spirited courtship that sent the heart-struck man traveling to the Bluegrass State several times (which cut deeply into his business hours, not to mention his wallet) he moved to Bristol, Virginia, and opened his law office—the only one in town.

John and Pauline were wed in Nashville, Tennessee, on December 30, 1857. Among the dignitaries who attended was U.S. Senator Andrew Johnson. In the spring of 1859, as war clouds began to darken the eastern skies, Pauline gave birth to the couple's first son. Turbulent times, those, but the Mosby household flourished.

Just prior to 4:30 A.M. on April 12, 1861, debonair Louisiana-born General Pierre G.T. Beauregard donned his trademark kepi and stepped from his headquarters as the first hint of dawn began to soften the lead-tinged waters of Charleston Bay. Only three months before, the career Army officer had finished his first day as superintendent of the U.S. Military Academy at West Point—and had been relieved of his command just four days later because of his outspoken secessionist views. With a deeply ingrained sense of duty, Beauregard felt obligated to watch the beginning of the Armageddon he was about to unleash. Turning to an aide, he spoke softly, and his quiet command sent the first shells flying toward Fort Sumter. The reverberations echoed across Charleston Harbor and into every household in the divided nation.

Including Mosby's. The lawyer didn't hold with secession, but he *was* pure Virginian to the core. So, like his fellow Virginians, he cast his lot with his native state—for better or worse. In January of that fateful year, Mosby joined a local cavalry company, the Washington Mounted Rifles (later incorporated into the Virginia Volunteers), as a private. He donned butternut garb and marked time drilling and speculating about the rumors of war that smothered the hills and hollows of isolated Bristol.

Then came the specter of things to come when Union Major Anderson surrendered Fort Sumter to the Rebs. Huge armies maneuvered toward a small hamlet few had heard of—Manassas (the Yanks called it Bull Run)—to settle the contested issue of dissolving the Union. John Mosby closed his business, kissed his wife and son farewell, and rode away with his enthusiastic comrades toward the sound of battle, afraid that the war would be over before he reached the firing line.

Mosby needn't have worried, for there was plenty of action to go around. In this first major clash of wills, he and 32,000 other gray-clad men helped Joe Johnston rout Irvin McDowell's boys in blue and sent them scurrying from the wooded slopes of the Manassas countryside, back toward the Potomac. The message was clear: The war would be long and the bloodletting terrible.

After the First Battle of Manassas, the Virginia Volunteers became part of the 1st Virginia Cavalry. Mosby suddenly found himself elevated to the rank of lieutenant and assigned duties as the regimental adjutant—and sitting square in the sights of the new commander, Colonel (soon to become Brigadier General) James Ewell Brown Stuart.

"Jeb" Stuart, impressed with Mosby's feisty manner, promoted the 27-year-old to first lieutenant and made him a scout on his personal staff. Mosby soon distinguished himself by planning and leading Stuart's daring sweep around the whole Union army during General McClellan's ill-fated Peninsula Campaign, an event that much embarrassed The Little Napoleon.

Came a ten-day stint in Washington, D.C.'s Old Capitol Prison when the lieutenant-scout was captured while dozing under a shade tree after the desperate hard-fought action of Seven Days Battles outside Richmond. The Feds made the mistake of hauling Mosby through Newport News on his way to be exchanged. He took in every detail of General Ambrose Burnside's flotilla, which was loading troops and supplies for the move north to join up with General John Pope's army near Manassas in preparation for another go at the Rebs—this time commanded by none other than "Old Granny" Robert E. Lee.

During this second battle of Manassas, General Lee and his Army of Northern Virginia out-smarted, out-maneuvered, and out-fought Pope's Army of Virginia, 63,000 strong, and sent the Union forces reeling out of Virginia and forced Lincoln back to the drawing board.

Mosby saw an opportunity in northern Virginia and approached his boss. "Give me a few good men and free reign, and I can do more good for the Confederacy than a division of infantry." Stuart gave the nod in December 1862, and the legend of the Gray Ghost took root.

A slow beginning for the eager captain (Jeb promoted him) and his small band of fifteen strong-willed men. But soon the Mosby Partisan Rangers, as they were known, were eighty strong. When the band grew to 240 partisans, it was incorporated into the regular Confederate Army as the 43rd Virginia Cavalry Battalion, and its fearless leader was again promoted.

Capitalizing on the growing legend he and his potent blue-bashers stoked, Lieutenant Colonel Mosby outfitted himself with a gray plush felt hat topped with a curling ostrich plume (much like the one his mentor, Jeb Stuart, wore). The rakish hat enhanced the gray cape lined with scarlet that he wore thrown dashingly over his shoulder, as became the iron-fisted potentate of Mosby's Confederacy.

Roughly encompassing the five counties of northernmost Virginia, the area was almost a tiny kingdom unto itself. Here, Mosby was sole judge and jury, and his authority extended into every backwoods hollow. He even forbade his men to leave Mosby's Confederacy without permission, on threat of "exile" to the regular Confederate Army. By the end of 1864, the Gray Ghost, now a full colonel, was able to marshal a formidable force of 800 battle-hardened rangers. (Promotions came quick in the battle-thinned officer ranks of both sides!)

Mosby's tactics were simple: Split his command into small groups and boldly attack in several places at the same time to cut the Federal supply lines and disrupt communications. It worked! Finally Phil Sheridan, who had been ordered by General Grant to destroy everything in the Shenandoah Valley that could be used by the Confederates—down to the last sheaf of moldy grain and old gimpy rooster—had had enough. He formed a special task force of two hundred soldiers armed with new Spencer repeating rifles and gave them simple orders: "Kill or capture Mosby."

By the time it was over, the Gray Ghost had turned the tables and killed or captured all but two of his pursuers—and enhanced his own arsenal considerably. Highly incensed that *his* side always seemed to end up sucking hind tit when it came to the arrogant raider, the youngest general in the U.S. Army, cocky 23-year-old George Armstrong Custer, embarked on his own plan. All of Mosbys' men would thereafter be treated as outlaws and summarily hanged when captured. Custer managed to get his hands on six of Mosby's partisans and made good on his threat. Mosby promptly hanged seven of Custer's troops in a game of high stakes "one-upmanship." The yellow-haired commander ate crow.

Livid at Mosby's impudence, Grant "suggested" that Sheridan seize family members of the partisan group and hold them hostage in Ft. McHenry as a guarantee against further depredations by the raiders. But Sheridan had had enough and sloughed off his superior's tirade. To the very end, Mosby continued to thumb his rebel nose at the blue-frocked generals, giving Sheridan chronic indigestion and Grant skull-splitting migraines—not to mention more gray hairs for the troubled head of "Honest Abe."

But the boys in blue almost got their man on several occasions.

For instance, on the night of June 8, 1863, a detachment of the First New York Lincoln Cavalry heard that Mosby was in the area. They stormed into the northern Virginia home of James Hathaway, where Mosby's wife, Pauline, had taken up residence so she could be near her fugitive husband. Outraged at the intrusion into her bedroom, she clutched her bedclothes to her neck and indignantly denied any knowledge of her husband's whereabouts. The soldiers finally caved before the vehement icy glare of the wronged wife and rode away. Clad only in his longjohns, Mosby left his perch on the branch of a walnut tree outside her open bedroom window and went back to bed.

A year later, he wasn't as lucky—or was he?

On December 21, 1864, Mosby and one of his lieutenants, Tom Love, had been out reconnoitering a large force of Yankee cavalry that had been discovered in the area. The two men tracked the enemy until they settled into a bivouac near Rectortown and began to build their nightly cooking fires. Mosby dispatched a man to his main force with orders to prepare to attack the encampment at daybreak the next morning. Then he and Love rode off to collect more men in nearby Loudoun County.

A freezing rain mixed with sleet had begun to fall and soon covered the road. Eventually the two riders came to the house of Mosby's friend, Ludwell Lake, where suppertime aromas wafted through an open window. Wet, chilled to the bone, and overcome by the delicious smells, the pair dismounted and invited themselves in, much to the delight of Mr. Lake and his family who were already eating.

Mosby and Love dug in. But before coffee and dessert could be served, a Yankee cavalry troop, three hundred strong, dashed into the yard and surrounded the house. Captain Brown, under orders from the troop commander, Major Douglas Frazar, took a detail and rushed into the dining room.

Mosby had the presence of mind to conceal the rank insignia on his jacket collar with his hands, hoping to pass himself off as a simple private or lieutenant until he made his break. For though the situation seemed desperate, he quickly decided that he would make every effort to escape. Then, as Brown's men strode toward Mosby to take him into custody, a trigger-happy trooper in the courtyard fired through the open window, which unleashed a hail of bullets from others. Mosby was struck in the abdomen, but in the confusion he managed to crawl into a bedroom and hide his uniform jacket with its incriminating rank insignia beneath a washstand.

Major Frazar managed to get the firing stopped and dismounted to take charge inside. By the time he and Brown's detail came into the room, Mosby had smeared blood from his wound to the area around his mouth. He gasped that his name was Lieutenant Johnson, 16th Virginia Cavalry, asked for mercy, and then feigned the "death rattle."

Frazar examined the wound to see if the Reb was worth taking prisoner, but he quickly decided that the wound was mortal and predicted the victim would die within twenty-four hours. Frazar ordered his men to strip the boots and trousers from the mortally wounded "lieutenant." He claimed the plumed hat as his personal booty. The troop returned to their company area with Love and Lake in ropes. However, in their excitement the soldiers left Mosby's horse standing at the front gate, with his holstered pistols hanging across the saddle.

Major Frazar showed off the unusual hat and bragged about the Reb lieutenant he had bagged. His gloating was short-lived though, for some old timers recognized the famous hat. Quickly, rumors flew across the land that the Gray Ghost was finally dead. The newspapers printed it as gospel truth, and Mosby's men encouraged the rumors, which bought their leader valuable recovery time.

The Gray Ghost lived to fight again, much to the embarrassment of Frazar's superior, Colonel W. Gamble, who had rushed to send the good news of

Mosby's demise up the chain of command to General Sheridan. When recriminations flowed back down the chain, Colonel Gamble asserted that after investigating the blunder, it became evident that Major Frazar was "too much under the influence of liquor to perform his duty at the time in a proper manner." (Mosby, a teetotaler, gleeful stated in his memoirs that he owed his near-miraculous escape to whiskey!)

No doubt that John Singleton Mosby led a charmed life. He narrowly managed to evade the permanent clutches of the Grim Reaper on at least three occasions (gut shot twice, which almost always spelled doom for the victim) and came close to being captured a like number of times. Just two months before Mosby received his near-mortal wound at the Lake home, he became pinned beneath his horse when the animal was shot dead during a furious battle. One of his stalwarts, Capt. Montjoy, charged the converging Federals, driving them back so that he could pull Mosby from the equine wreckage.

But finally came the day of reckoning at Appomattox Courthouse, when General Lee offered his sword to General Grant in the time-honored tradition of gentlemanly surrender (which Grant graciously declined) and negotiated terms for his starved, mangled Army. The Union commander included Mosby's men in his general parole. But he excluded Mosby, declaring that the man was nothing more than a fugitive outlaw, and he ordered that the $5000 bounty remain on his head.

In the end, the Gray Ghost refused to formally surrender his command. Instead, twelve days after Lee's capitulation he gathered his troops for the last time at Salem, Virginia, in the heart of "Mosby's Confederacy," and told them, "I disband your organization in preference to surrendering it to our enemies." After a few appropriate remarks, he finished with, "I am no longer your commander . . . Farewell." The men simply faded into the countryside.

In mid-June, the elusive Mosby finally waved the white flag after he was granted a parole. But his troubles didn't end. The word quickly went out among the victors, "Pay back time for Mosby," and hostile authorities used any petty (or trumped up charge) to get their man. Mosby endured his private hell, but after a few months Pauline had enough. She marched into the White House and sought help from the long time friend of her family, President Andrew Johnson. He refused to get involved, even rudely asked her to leave. Undeterred, she went to the office of her husband's wartime adversary, Ulysses Grant, and complained about the injustice. Grant was moved by her plea and gave her a handwritten note exempting Mosby from frivolous arrest.

The family moved to Warrenton, Virginia, where John formed a law partnership with James Keith. Came several years of harmonious existence, but in 1876 Pauline died from complications caused by childbirth. The newborn died soon thereafter. Devastated, Mosby farmed his seven children out to relatives and left Warrenton, never to return until forty years later when he was laid to rest beside his beloved Pauline.

During the ensuing years, Mosby forged a close friendship with Grant and became a campaign manager for Grant's run for the White House. On Grant's recommendation, in 1878 President Rutherford Hayes appointed Mosby as the United States Consul to Hong Kong.

When he was recalled seven years later, Mosby asked Grant to secure another position for him. Although soon to take to his deathbed, the former president managed to secure Mosby a position with the Southern Pacific Railroad, which took the former cavalryman to San Francisco. There, he became a friend to the Patton family, especially young George. Often he recounted tales of Mosby's Rangers to the youth, and before long he and "Georgie" were galloping across the California hills, reenacting Civil War episodes, with Mosby playing himself and young Patton relegated to the role of none less than General Robert E. Lee.

(George Smith Patton, Jr., would become one of the great generals of WW II. Undoubtedly, Mosby played a significant role in shaping the future general's voracious craving for battle.)

An unlucky horse kick fractured Mosby's skull, causing loss of sight in one eye and putting an end to his career with the Southern Pacific. President McKinley got him a job with the Department of the Interior, enforcing Federal fencing laws near Omaha, Nebraska. But Mosby was too zealous for the local politicians, so he was "demoted upward" as an assistant attorney with the Justice Department. After his retirement in 1910, the old veteran continued to live in Washington until his death on Memorial Day, 1916. The Grim Reaper would not be put off any longer.

*   *   *

When I passed through that history-burdened area still known as "Mosby's Confederacy" on my two subsequent thru-hikes, hidden eyes still bored into my back. Unexplained noises again shattered the stifling silence of taciturn forests in cahoots with some deep unrevealed mystery. And with each timid step I wondered, *Do I tread on ground cursed by tainted blood, spilled in vain for a hopeless cause? Do gray-clad ghosts linger here, wraithlike shades that rise out of secluded dark hollows to ride gentle evening breezes across the mountains and through the gaps, ever seeking the unattainable? Do the dead ever truly rest?*

Oh Lord A-Mighty! Please let me have some company tonight!

Chapter Twenty-two

The Legacy of "The Hole"

T hru-hikers live for the day they cross the bridge that spans the wide Shenandoah, for when they step onto the soil of Harpers Ferry, West Virginia, they're apt to brag, "Half done already." But it's really a psychological quirk. Sure, they've racked up a thousand miles or so, but do the math. The real midpoint lies some eighty-odd miles further north, just beyond Pennsylvania's Pine Grove Furnace State Park. But there *is* some comfort, not to mention the ego scratching, in just saying the words.

The real brain-jerker? Harpers Ferry is the home of the hiker "holy of holies," the Appalachian Trail Conference! (The name was changed in July 2005 to the Appalachian Trail Conservancy to better conform to its mission, which has "mutated" with progress over the years.) No serious hiker would pass through Harpers Ferry without paying a visit to this hallowed shrine from whence the magic of the Trail emanates. So thus it was with me.

As had happened on my first thru-hike (and was now happening again on this, my second journey), I paused in mid-bridge and admired the swirling rapids of the Shenandoah River's postcard panorama. The breath-taking beauty once again overwhelmed me, forcing thoughts of aching muscles and sweat-drenched skin to the far reaches of my mind. Reluctantly, as if trapped in a dream where nothing obeyed my will, I continued on across the bridge, now drawn by the noises of civilization that heralded pizza and ice cream, even a hot shower if I were lucky. The images became stronger and I quickened my pace, salivating like Pavlov's dog from the culinary delights that were almost within my grasp!

I had forgotten a lot in the four years since I had last crossed this bridge. The surge of déjà vu caught me by surprise, for as I stepped off the concrete and onto the soft alluvial soil, I seemed to slip into another dimension rift with the musty odor of history. It seemed to permeate the air, invading my mind like a sorcerer's potion. Visions of pizza and ice cream dissolved as somber images of clashing armies and a maniacal insurrection rushed in. With subdued reverence I swung my dusty boots from the white blazes of the past thousand miles and followed the blue-blazed trail that led away from the river.

The dirt path eventually intersected a sidewalk that led past the old Storer College, now part of the Harpers Ferry National Monument; then along a street sagging with peeling antebellum houses ulcerated by time and filled with restless ghosts of a long-gone era. Then down the last block, spanned by an old cracked sidewalk that teeter-tottered from years of wrestling with the insistent roots of ancient trees, there it stood. The tired stone building still squatted unceremoniously at the intersection of Washington and Jefferson Streets, still looking exactly as it had in 1990 when I first cast awe-struck eyes on it. The "Mecca" of the hiker kingdom: The Appalachian Trail Conference!

Actually, the ATC is more like a hiker's visitor and information center. When I walked inside, a gray-headed lady, a volunteer, greeted me. Her genuine smile and kind face put me at ease. "Is this your first time here?" she asked, taking in my trail-worn appearance with a quick, knowing glance.

I puffed up like a politician who had just been given the keys to the White House. "Nope. I stopped by in '90. I'm on my second thru-hike."

The lady tried her best to look impressed but it didn't fly. She'd seen too many grubby hikers come through the door. Thankfully, Jean Cashin, a motherly facsimile for hikers, walked over and rescued me from making a complete fool of myself. "I haven't taken your picture for the ATC book yet, have I? Let's go outside and see if I can corner another hiker or two for the camera, and we'll save some money." It didn't take long.

(After twenty-four years of wiping away the tears of failed dreams and applying band-aids to the trail-bruised egos of hundreds of discouraged, frustrated hikers, Jean retired in 1996. Her role was aptly assumed by veteran thru-hiker Laurie Potteiger.)

I browsed through old photo albums and magazines, and chatted with other hikers until a close friend, three times A.T. thru-hiker Bob "Rerun" Sparkes, who lives a short distance outside of Harpers Ferry, arrived to haul me off to his home for three days of heavy eating. It was tough trying to avoid the jealous eyes of the other hikers when I tossed my pack in the back of Rerun's small Isuzu pickup. But I managed.

As soon as I climbed inside the cab, by tacit agreement both windows came down. And honest injun, what I really meant to say was, "Man, Rerun, it's sure good to see you." But what popped out was, "Say Rerun, is that pizza place over at Charles Town still open?" He chuckled. After all, what's a little *faux pas* between hiker buddies . . .

*   *   *

(Author's note: An apology to the reader. What follows seems like a compilation of disjointed, disconnected events. But in the end, I do tie it all together. Just hang on to the eclectic parts and you'll get the whole picture!)

Any account of the lore and legends of the Appalachian Trail would be incomplete without delving into the fluvial past of "The Hole"—at least that's what trapper and ferryman Peter Stephens called the rugged water gap where the Potomac and Shenandoah Rivers converge when he squatted there in 1733. Eventually news of the trespass reached the aristocratic ears of Thomas, Sixth Lord Fairfax, who lived on an estate near Winchester, Virginia.

The Baron had inherited from his mother, Catherine Culpepper Fairfax, something in excess of five million acres in northern Virginia, which amounted to nearly a quarter of the colony's entire area. His vast empire, which was ". . . bounded by and within the heads of . . . Rappahanocke and Patawmoeck Rivers, and the courses of said Rivers and the Cheaspayoke Bay" was officially known as the Northern Neck. The area included the paltry acreage grabbed off by Stephens. "Wasteland," His Lordship grumbled when told about the squatter, and he shrugged the matter away as if it were little more than a blowfly trying to make off with a piece of his kidney pie.

In 1747, English emigrant Robert Harper, a millwright and architect, was engaged by a group of Philadelphia Quakers to erect a meetinghouse near present day Winchester. When he arrived at "The Hole" on his way south, Harper immediately recognized the potential for industry if he could harness the powerful waters of the two rivers, not to mention the easy money to be made by ferrying travelers.

After finishing his obligation to the Quakers, Harper bought Stephen's "squatter's domain"—cabin, corn patch, and ferry equipment—and set about making his dream become reality. Four years later, with things coming together, Harper decided to "go honest" and obtained a patent (a form of lease granted for "three lifetimes": husband, wife, and youngest son) from Lord Fairfax for 125 acres of "waste and ungranted land" at the confluence of the two rivers.

Sniggered the aging baron to his manservant as he pocketed the modest sum, "The dullard. Can't tell wasteland from a tinkers damn."

But the Proprietor of "The Hole" would not be deterred—not even when floodwaters swept through his holdings a year later and foreordained the disasters that would plague the future of the small community.

(In the next two centuries, at least a dozen "memorable" floods would disrupt the stability of area, washing away bridges, mills, and changing the entire economic focus of the town. The all-time record crest—36 ½ feet— occurred in 1936, double the 18-foot flood stage. In 1996, Harpers Ferry Lower Town was inundated twice, first by snow-melt from the "Great Blizzard," and later by heavy rainfall from Hurricane Fran—the first time in recorded history that the town got dunked twice in one year.)

Before long, Harper had built a thriving gristmill that hummed to the rushing waters of the Shenandoah. Lastly came a large stone house (that today is the oldest building in Lower Town and bears his name, although he didn't live to see it completed). As suspected, the ferry proved to be a real moneymaker, for "The Hole" became a major jumping off point for scores of settlers seeking land in the fertile Shenandoah Valley. Some stayed and the area grew. In 1762, Harper obtained an additional twenty-five acres of "wasteland" from Lord Fairfax.

Eventually the town folk became fed up with the name that had been foisted upon them, which detracted from the natural beauty of the place. They petitioned the Virginia General Assembly in 1783 to change "The Hole" to "Shenandoah Falls at Mr. Harper's Ferry." But soon after the request had been granted, the city fathers belatedly realized that it took a mouthful of words to identify their small piece of paradise, and the name was soon shortened to Harpers Ferry. They even dropped the apostrophe.

Then things began to jump like sizzlin' frog legs in a red-hot skillet when the highly esteemed Thomas Jefferson visited the village. Naturalist, author of the Declaration of Independence, and armchair explorer, the venerated statesman had heard about the magnificent view that could be had from the mountain above Mr. Harper's ferry. Filled with anticipation, the future president traveled from Monticello to see for himself. He wasn't disappointed.

On a soft October day in 1783, surrounded by gold-tinted trees, he perched near a delicately balanced rock that seemed to almost touch the lazy clouds that drifted toward the far horizon and gazed with hushed reverence at a scene of great beauty. The two mighty rivers that cleaved the ageless Blue Ridge with impunity held his attention hostage. The colliding waters wrestled for dominance until they joined to become a raging giant, spreading frothy tentacles, which clawed at myriad obstinate rocks that rose out of the swirls like miniature Poseidons as the torrent swept toward the sea.

Jefferson wrote a long flowery account about the trip two years later, and the town folk showed their appreciation of his eloquent appraisal of their village by naming the delicately balanced rock after the famous man and inscribing it with his name and date of the visit.

(Author's note: Jefferson Rock rests near the Appalachian Trail on a rise above St. Peters Catholic Church in Old Town. Or at least a part of it does. As usually happens during a hard fought, bitter presidential campaign, the candidates acquire an assortment of detractors. The campaign of 1800 was no different. Republican candidate Thomas Jefferson took on the incumbent Federalist President, John Adams, with whom he had mixed it up in the previous campaign and lost. In the heat of the race, Jefferson collected his share of enemies.

One happened to be a Captain Henry, who was in charge of the small United States Army detachment sent to Harpers Ferry to guard the new Armory. During the midst of the campaign, Henry, who had probably been quaffing more than his fair share of the rum ration, ordered some men to trade their flintlocks for pry bars and follow him up to Jefferson Rock, whose image festered in his mind like a pestilent boil. Urged on by their embittered leader, the soldiers pushed their pry bars beneath the delicately balanced rock and heaved.

As the huge boulder went tumbling toward the valley below, the soldiers cheered and Captain Henry shook his fist at the sky while shouting that the defilement was symbolic of what the electorate would do to ". . . him whose name is carved thereon." The disgruntled captain thumbed his nose at the topless base and promised an extra ration of ale for the men. With his rage vented, Henry marched the detail back down the hill, where his own rum keg beckoned.

However, the ill-tempered captain proved to be a bad prophet, for Jefferson licked Adams and became the third President of the United States. The State of Virginia demanded satisfaction from the United States Government for the grave discourtesy shown to their favorite son, but Jefferson played down the incident and cooler heads managed to avert an unpleasant situation. Captain Henry's fate was not recorded, but the rock with the hand-carved inscription still lies where it came to rest over two centuries ago.)

Before he became president, George Washington had likewise toured the hamlet as a representative of the Patowmack Company and liked what he saw. Soon after he took the oath of office, the topic of arms production arose. Washington knew just where to go. He urged the Government to purchase 118 acres at Harpers Ferry for a Federal armory and arsenal.

In 1820, New England gun maker John Hall signed a contract with the War Department to manufacture 1000 of his newly patented Spencer breech-loading rifles at the Harpers Ferry Arsenal. Even as the ink dried on the contract, the stage was being set for tragedy. In a few turbulent years, the sleepy town would be thrust into the national limelight. The bloodletting would begin and the ghosts would come to stay.

*   *   *

About the time Captain Henry went tromping up toward Jefferson Rock to display his dissatisfaction with Jefferson, in far off Connecticut a midwife wiped the blood-smeared mucus from a squealing baby and then laid the newborn near its mother's swollen breast. Only then did the midwife open the door to the anxious man outside. With a voice as coarse as her hands, the old crone grunted, "It's a boy. He got a name yet?"

Owen Brown gazed at the squirming bundle of flesh that whimpered as it rooted at a distended nipple. "We'll call him John. John Brown." And so it was.

Owen, a tanner, moved the family to an abolitionist stronghold in Ohio when John was five. A staunch Calvinist, Owen imbedded his strong anti-slavery views in his son's fragile mind, thereby laying the foundation for John's zealous behavior in later life. He also taught his son the tannery trade and eventually made him foreman of the family business.

John Brown married at age twenty and had seven children by that marriage. When his wife died in 1831, he soon wed a 16-year-old, who bore him thirteen more children, though only half of the full brood of twenty lived past childhood. During the next twenty-four years, John Brown wallowed in failure, failing as a tanner, land speculator, wool broker, and sheep farmer. In fact, the visionary leanings instilled by his father overwhelmed his business acumen and he eventually had to declare bankruptcy.

As his financial burdens multiplied, John Brown sought refuge in a metaphysical world where he fancied himself the savior of the oppressed black population. And by the time he turned fifty, Brown was firmly trapped in his delusional creation, entranced by visions of slaves rising up en masse against unscrupulous masters, with himself commissioned by God Almighty to lead the charge. He had to act!

The Kansas-Nebraska Act paved the way. Passed as a compromise by a divided Congress in 1854 to ease the tensions between pro and anti-slavery factions in new territories in the country's rapid westward expansion, the bill allowed residents to decide if their territory would be free or open to slavery. John Brown cast a worried eye toward the western horizon, where Kansas was already becoming a hotbed of dissention. "Our friends out in Kansas need help," he growled in a voice filled with the power of righteous conviction.

So the aging abolitionist and five of his likewise abolitionist sons saddled up and rode off into the setting sun to help the good slave haters tip the scales of Lady Justice.

Things didn't work out as he had planned. Brown set up housekeeping on the bank of the Osawatomie River, where he organized a small militia unit. When the kettle finally boiled over, as it must when passionate men collide, he armed four sons and two other followers with long swords and they spilled into the small pro-slavery community on Pottawatomie Creek. In a show of force, the assailants dragged six unarmed inhabitants into the night, where they proceeded to hack the helpless victims to death.

This atrocity earned John Brown the nickname "Old Brown of Osawatomie" and led to a price being placed on his scalp. Brown and some of his men fled to Canada, where he regrouped and redefined his grandiose strategy to free the slaves, down to the tiniest detail. Finished at last, on the day before his fifty-eighth birthday he convened a "provisional constitutional convention." The "convention," which consisted of the few men who fled with him to Canada and what resident free blacks he could lay hands on, adopted a provisional constitution complete with a preamble and executive, legislative, judicial, and military branches.

At last John Brown was ready to fulfill his "Great Commission." There were rifles aplenty in the Federal Armory at Harpers Ferry, and plenty of slaves to use them when the uprising began!

Around July 1, 1859, John Brown, using the alias "Isaac Smith," rented a small farm from the Kennedy family over in Maryland, about four miles from Harpers Ferry. He passed himself off as a farmer from New York and expressed interest in buying a farm in the area. He and two of his sons even farmed a little while they secretly finalized plans and waited for arms and men to assemble at the Kennedy farm.

On October 10, "General Order No. 1" was issued from "Headquarters War Department, Provisional Army, Harpers Ferry; John Brown, Commander-in-Chief." The order provided for division, brigade, regiment, battalion, and company organizations, as well as a general staff. (Oh yes, the man had a plan!) Then came the day for the "invasion"!

At 11 P.M. on Sunday, October 16th, the "Commander-in-Chief" quietly led his "army"—*all twenty-one of them, which included five free blacks*—across the Potomac River and commenced hostilities against the slave mongers of Virginia. At first, operations went as planned. Brown's men seized key points, including the B&O Railroad Bridge and the Federal Armory and Arsenal. Guards, posted at street corners, summarily arrested about forty of the town's citizens, including the mayor, when they appeared on the streets in the early dawn.

Brown ordered the citizens incarcerated in the thick-walled gatehouse at the Armory, which also housed the fire engine, where he had set up his command post. Then he perched on the high seat of the fire engine and waited for the slaves to revolt.

It didn't happen. By the time the sun was well above the horizon, the town was in an uproar. Able-bodied men grabbed rifles and whatever else that might be used as weapons and rushed to defend their town.

Nearby towns quickly dispatched militia units. Post haste, the citizen soldiers forced Brown's entire "army" into the Armory gatehouse. "General" Brown released all but ten of the hostages and fortified the building, and then he ordered his men to fire on "anything not black." By evening, the streets of Harpers Ferry were awash in uniformed men who milled about, careful not to get within the sights of the rifles that jutted out from makeshift loopholes like angry porcupine quills. Stalemate!

Then came the Marines! Lieutenant Colonel Robert Edward Lee and his aide, Lieutenant James Ewell Brown Stuart happened to be in Baltimore when word came that Harpers Ferry was under attack. The (real) War Department dispatched a detachment of Marines from Baltimore to Harpers Ferry and ordered Lee to take charge. Lee sent Stuart under a white flag to offer terms for surrender, which Brown spurned. Then, simply put, Lee told Lieutenant Green, the officer in charge of the twelve grim-faced Marines, to storm the gatehouse, free the hostages, and kill or capture the insurgents.

No sooner said than done. The Marines bashed in the door, freed the hostages (except for the mayor of Harpers Ferry and a prominent citizen, whom Brown had killed), captured Brown, and captured or killed the insurrectionists. When the smoke cleared, Brown's "army" had ceased to exist. Twelve had been killed, two were unaccounted for, and Brown was wounded. (A casualty rate of nearly 75 percent!)

One Marine was killed. Mission accomplished.

John Brown was taken to nearby Charles Town, tried, and hanged at noon on December 2, 1859. The bloodstains that splattered the walls of the Armory gatehouse, which the people had taken to calling John Brown's Fort, soon faded into dingy blotches, and a semblance of calm returned to the village. But things would never be the same. Harpers Ferry had lost her virginity.

Among the spectators in the crowd who watched John Brown's body drop through the gallows trapdoor were members of the Cadet battery from Virginia Military Institute. They had brought cannons to protect the proceedings in case any Brown supporters showed up to attempt a rescue. As the noose was placed over the would-be savior's head, the cannoneers were called to strict attention by Major Thomas Jonathan Jackson, an instructor at the school who had been charged with command of the battery for the event. (In a few short months newly promoted Lieutenant General Jackson would have become General Lee's trusted right-hand man. Jackson's troops would nickname him "Stonewall" for his unflappable poise in the thick of battle and would follow him to the pits of Hell and back. At the zenith of his brilliant career, he would be mortally wounded at the Battle of Chancellorsville after he was felled by a bullet fired by a friendly sentry.)

Madman, monster, martyr—reader's decision—but in the north, bells tolled and guns were fired in memory of John Brown. Church services and public meetings were held to glorify his life and deeds. Sadly, Brown's parting words, written shortly before the noose wrought its tough justice, proved highly prophetic: ". . . crimes of this guilty land will never be purged away but with blood." Nearly a million Americans would be killed, wounded, or die from war-related disease before the purging was finished.

War came to Harpers Ferry, sawing through the fabric of the peaceful community like a gigantic crosscut saw, ripping back and forth as Blue and Gray wrestled for control of the strategic piece of ground that Lord Fairfax had called "a wasteland." The village had become strategically important as an access route through the Blue Ridge and into the unbloodied North. Now "The Hole's" true worth would be measured in lives lost and blood spilled.

In fact, the town changed hands *eight* times. The day after Virginia seceded from the Union, panicked soldiers destroyed the Federal Armory and Arsenal, along with 15,000 rifles, to deny approaching Confederate forces the huge arms trove.

The men in gray didn't stay long. They took a lesson from "Billy Yank" and burned manufacturing buildings and the railroad bridge on the way out of town. Like leaves being sucked into a vortex, the Federals rushed in 14,000 troops to garrison the town. But General Lee had big plans to carry the war into Maryland and points north, and a strong Union force at Harpers Ferry, blocking his supply line from the Shenandoah Valley, just wouldn't do.

The short of it: The General sent three quarters of his army, about 23,000 men, under the command of Major General Thomas J. "Stonewall" Jackson, to take the town. This he did, bagging 12,500 Union troops in the process—the largest single act of surrender during the war. Opening Harpers Ferry paved the way for Lee to get his nose bloodied by George McClellan at a place called Antietam.

Harpers Ferry eventually wound up in the hands of Union General Phil Sheridan, who used the town as a base of operations to carry out Grant's order: To strip the Shenandoah Valley so clean that "even a crow will have to fly beyond its borders to find something to eat."

Finally, the gods of war had their fill of good American flesh. Their voracious appetites temporarily satiated, they looked elsewhere on the planet for other diversions. And Peace returned to Harpers Ferry.

All over the country people began to patch up lives put on hold and communities that had been fractured by the insanity that had brought an entire nation to its knees. Many shrugged their shoulders in exasperation and muttered to no one in particular, "What waste. How could it have happened?" Bodies of loved ones hastily buried in makeshift cemeteries even as the smoke of battle cleared were disinterred by families and brought home for the final rest.

The Government sought to ease the Nation's grief by establishing great national cemeteries adorned with larger than life heart-rending monuments. And on ground that only months before had hungrily soaked up the blood of thousands, politicians tried to make the soil hallowed through flowery dedications. But the thousands upon thousands of re-interred corpses that moldered beneath lush sod in neatly lined graves, which stretched far beyond mortal comprehension, rendered the true hallowing.

And in the bustling cities and quiet hills and hollows of the healing Nation, a rallying war song metamorphosed into a hymn of hope and began to play in the heads of the living, giving a measure of ease and healing.

*   *   *

About the time that John Brown was packing his saddlebags and heading off to Kansas to lock horns with the pro-slavers, William Steffe, an insurance salesman of modest means, left his native city of Philadelphia to visit South Carolina. One evening he was drawn to a patched up circus tent where an old time Methodist camp meeting was in full swing. Imagine Steffe's surprise when the congregation began to sing the first hymn. *His song*, the one he had penned a couple of years before (was it '55 or '56?) for the Good Will Engine Company of Philadelphia! How well he remembered!

The firemen had used it as a song of welcome for the visiting Liberty Fire Company of Baltimore. He had written the first verse as "Say, Bummers, Will You Meet Us." Now here it was, in a Methodist songbook, with "Bummers" changed to "Brothers." Otherwise, the same words and same simple tune.

His song! By Gads! How that chorus—*his chorus*—stirred the soul! He hadn't the slightest idea how it came to be in the songbook. But heck! If the Methodists wanted to use it, who was he to put a damper on their fire? Steffe's chest stretched to the bursting point as the words of the chorus, "Glory, glory, hallelujah," filled the air from a hundred rejoicing voices, swelling into a tidal wave of praise that nearly lifted the frayed top from the tent. The hell-fire-and-brimstone circuit rider who stood behind the makeshift pulpit, champing at the bit to blast the sinners in the crowd to Hell was going to have a heck of a time topping *his* song!

Steffe returned to Philadelphia and continued to sell insurance. He hadn't written any more songs, but no bother. All over Philadelphia people were singing the song (mostly to hear the rousing chorus, he suspected). It had even been published in the popular *Lee Avenue Casket*.

But Steffe didn't have long to enjoy his brief stint in the public eye. War roared across the land, and suddenly selling insurance didn't seem like a very high priority. Steffe hired on as a dispatch courier for Union General Benjamin Butler.

A bigger surprise awaited the amateur composer when he carried some dispatches to Boston. A friend invited Steffe to attend a review of the Second Battalion, Boston Light Infantry, known as the "Tiger" Battalion, at nearby Fort Warren. The band began to play and the soldiers' voices rang out in unison, singing—*his song*! Only it wasn't. Came the words from a thousand crisp voices, "John Brown's body lies a-moldering in the grave," repeated three times just like he had written his verses and followed by the same soul-rousing chorus.

Steffe couldn't have halted the ground swell that swept through the ranks of the entire Union army even if he had wanted to. For the bastardized version (with *his* tune and chorus) soon became the rallying song of the North, and many a boy in blue died with old John Brown's name clinging to his swollen tongue.

Before long, verses were added or changed to glorify the life of the soldier, to vilify the despised Jeff Davis, to deify the martyred abolitionist Brown, even to honor President Lincoln's Emancipation Proclamation.

But how did a hymn metamorphose into a battle anthem?

In far off Maine, in the mid-1840s, another John Brown was born. His staunch Calvinist father instilled a love of country and sense of patriotic duty in the growing youth. So when the cannons roared at distant Charleston, like others of his kith young John Brown kissed his weeping mother and shook his father's callused hand and marched south to do his share to preserve the Union.

He eventually ended up on the marshy salt flats of Fort Warren on Georgia Island in Boston's outer harbor, where his hard work and steadfast devotion to duty soon got him promoted to sergeant.

On a brisk spring day in 1861, Sergeant Brown's "share" consisted of supervising a detail of privates who had been assigned to pick up debris on Fort Warren's new parade ground. As the men worked, a soldier began to hum the popular Methodist camp meeting hymn and soon several were singing, "Say, Brothers, will you meet us, on Canaan's holy shore . . ."

Sergeant Brown took a lot of ribbing from other soldiers of his battalion because he carried the same name as "Old Brown of Osawatomie." So when one of the detail, Private Harry Hallgreen, suddenly changed the verse to "John Brown's body lies a moldering in the grave," the others joined in with gusto. Sergeant Brown protested, but the damage was done. He shrugged his shoulders at the inevitable, grinned, and joined in.

Hallgreen's version quickly became the rallying song of the "Tigers."

On Sunday, May 12, 1861, the "Tigers" stood with the rest of the Massachusetts 12th on Fort Warren's manicured parade ground, listening as the chaplain, Reverend George Hepworth, addressed the new recruits. At the end of the speech, William J. Martland, leader of the regimental band, raised his baton to assist the soldiers of "Tiger" Battalion in carrying out the special surprise they had prepared for the regiment.

As the familiar notes of the old revival hymn rose into the air, the men of the "Tiger" Battalion began to sing, "John Brown's body lies a moldering in the grave." Amid ear-splitting cheers, Private Hallgreen and Sergeant Brown took bows.

The song quickly spread to other units until "John Brown's Body" ran rampant like an unstoppable flood throughout the rank and file of the whole Union army and spilled over into the civilian populace. However, the Scotsman's brief claim to fame rapidly faded as new verses were added that glorified the life and death of the martyred John Brown, whose name had become a household word in the north. Hallgreen made no waves, and the song's origin was soon forgotten. But not the song.

As the spirit of abolitionism took root and grew in northern minds, "John Brown's Body" was sung as part of every public rally. Indeed, Colonel Fletcher Webster's 12th Massachusetts Regiment sang the song in July 1861 as they paraded through the streets of New York on the way south to the killing fields of Virginia. The huge crowd responded with wild enthusiasm, and thereafter Webster's regiment became known as "The Hallelujah Regiment." On March 1, 1862, "The Hallelujah Regiment" halted at the exact site in Charles Town where John Brown was hanged. The entire regiment formally sang "John Brown's Body" *in memoriam.*

*   *   *

Samuel Gridley Howe couldn't understand his wife's obsession with writing poetry and plays. In fact, he considered it a downright waste of time, a detractor from the sanctity of marriage and a hindrance to his important position on the President's Sanitary Commission. Sure, they worked together to further the abolitionist effort and had even met the great John Brown. But with two young children, his wife should be a full time mother instead of an unknown author.

Julia Ward Howe put up with her husband's occasional tantrum with stoical resignation. She told herself that she would gladly roll bandages or serve in a hospital, or do other volunteer work with the Sanitary Commission, but with two young children she couldn't get far from the children's nursery. Nay, she didn't even have the practical deftness to prepare and package sanitary stores for the war effort. Some insidious inner voice told her, "You would be glad to serve, but you cannot help anyone; you have nothing to give, and there is nothing for you to do."

So she kept her silence and stayed close to the pen and paper that lay in a neat stack on the desk in their wartime suite at Washington's Willard Hotel.

On a pleasantly sunny day in November 1861, the Howe's minister, Reverend James Freeman Clarke, invited Mrs. Howe to accompany him and some friends to observe a review of Union troops being conducted in nearby Virginia. The spectators were watching the activities from a distance when a large Rebel force approached. The commander feared that the troops might be trapped and ordered the regiments to retreat back across the Potomac *post haste.*

The only road quickly became clogged with soldiers, which created a tremendous roadblock and made it impossible for the carriage in which Julia Ward and her friends rode to proceed. The group began to sing songs to break the tedium of the long wait, finally concluding with the popular "John Brown's

Body." Reverend Clarke asked, "Mrs. Howe, why do you not write some good words for that stirring tune?" To which she replied, "I have often wished to do this but have not as yet found in my mind any leading toward it."

Julia slept soundly that night and awoke in the predawn twilight. As she lay there waiting for the dawn, words began to twine themselves into verses, which became stanzas. Quickly she jumped out of bed, grabbed a pen, and in the dimness began to write, "Mine eyes have seen the glory of the coming of the Lord . . ."

In February 1862, the poignant words were published on the front page of the *Atlantic Monthly* under the title *Battle Hymn of the Republic*, which was coined by the magazine's editor, James T. Fields.

That same year, Ditson and Company published the poem as a song, but it was overshadowed by the specter of war. The song slowly gained in popularity until, like its patriotic well-worn ancestor, at last it raced across the Nation and became a healing balm for thousands of grief-stricken, disquieted lives.

Julia Ward Howe stepped into the annals of history. Her meteoric rise to the lofty heights where the likes of Longfellow and Whitman dwelled somewhat bedazzled her obdurate husband. He pouted for awhile, but after coming to grips with his wife's brilliant talent and realizing the extraordinary gift that she had bestowed on the Nation, he pursed his lips and grumbled no more.

And what of the young Scotsman whose name fanned the embers of a comrade's spoofed imagination and gave birth to a song that touched millions of lives? Sergeant John Brown would not live to hear the "Battle Hymn of the Republic." Early in the war he drowned in the Shenandoah River near Front Royal, Virginia.

(Author's note: There were other "pretenders to the throne," although most historians now attribute *Say, Brother, Will You Meet Us* to William Steffe. *The Methodist Hymnal* simply lists the music as coming from a 19th Century USA camp meeting tune.

Most Civil War buffs credit Sergeant John Brown of the "Tiger" Battalion as the original "John Brown" of the song. And to give credit where credit is due, Julia Ward Howe owed a great debt of gratitude to one Chaplain Charles McCabe of the 122nd Ohio Volunteers for the success of *Battle Hymn of the Republic*.

McCabe became captivated when he first heard the stirring hymn and began to sing it in his magnificent baritone voice at every opportunity. Briefly held as a prisoner of war, he sang the song for other Union prisoners in Richmond's Libby Prison until silenced by Confederate guards. Exchanged after a few months, McCabe had opportunity to sing the hymn twice for

President Lincoln. The President remarked, "Take it all in all, the song and the singing, that was the best I ever heard." McCabe's lofty rendition of *Battle Hymn of the Republic* became famous throughout the land, as did the hymn itself. The rest is history!)

*   *   *

Now to wrap the "Legacy" of the Hole up in a tidy, credible package.

Funny how Fate has a way of meandering through the affairs of men, collecting here, tossing aside there, sometimes tying events together to make something really good. In this instance, had George Washington not visited Harpers Ferry, chances are the Federal Armory might have been built elsewhere, perhaps in the free North, where there were no slaves to support an uprising.

Given that possibility, the insurrection that ended with John Brown's hanging might not have happened, and there would have been no John Brown's "body lying a-moldering in the grave." Folks would still be singing "Say, Brothers, will you meet us on Canaan's holy shore" at camp meeting revivals. And arguably, Julia Ward Howe's early morning harvest of immortal words would be just another bit of beautiful poetry in dust-catching tomes—if in fact she would have written it at all, given different conditions.

But out of this series of seemingly unconnected events came a rare genuine gift—a grand patriotic anthem that still stirs the soul and makes one proud to be an American.

So "The Hole" has left us a legacy through its vivid contribution to America's heritage—the essence of our country's continuing existence. From "wasteland" to National Historical Monument; from "John Brown's Body" to the poignant, yet rousing words of *Battle Hymn of the Republic*; through devastating floods and horrific violence to the quiet sobering reverence that is bought with blood, sweat, and tears, Harpers Ferry has stayed the course. Old Harper would be proud!

Chapter Twenty-three

John Brown's Fort

A lot of history in Harpers Ferry. Volumes have been written about this town that was once a strategic passageway between Southern rebellion and Northern resolve. But here's a little historical gem, which I'll bet the historians have either missed or shrugged off as insignificant.

Amazingly, the thick-walled brick gatehouse, soon dubbed "John Brown's Fort," survived the bloody conflict—the only building in the Federal Arsenal and Armory to remain intact. Of course, the fire engine was long gone, a victim of some dogged contest between Yanks and Rebs. And the dingy splatters that bespoke of a violent episode had disappeared beneath coats of whitewash and cankers of mildew when the building served as a prison and guardhouse for whoever held the grounds of the river town.

After the war, people came for a while to worship at the martyr's shrine. But folks soon realized that if a body really wished to stand on hallowed ground, then the true pilgrimage had to be made to the Brown family farm at North Elbe in New York's peaceful Adirondacks. For that's where John Brown's corpse had been taken shortly after he was hanged. If a body were lucky, one might even get a peek at Brown's wife, Mary, who still lived there.

So the famous building became a derelict—a storage place for the town's junk—although the townsfolk still looked on John Brown's Fort as part of the glory of Harpers Ferry.

In 1892, excitement began to mount for the residents of Chicago. The World's Fair (some called it the World's Colombian Exposition) was to be held in their city that summer! Bingo! A flashbulb exploded in the brain of Civil War veteran and former Congressman Adoniram J. Holmes of Boone, Iowa. Why not buy John Brown's Fort, move it to Chicago, and make it into an exhibit for the Fair!

In spite of objections by the residents of Harpers Ferry, negotiations were completed and the old structure was disassembled, brick by brick, numbered, and shipped to the windy city. Holmes' workers reassembled it at 1341 Wabash Avenue, just outside the Fair's boundary. The Fort was enclosed in a neat frame building and opened to the public—for a fee of course. Holmes tried to enlist Annie Brown Adams, Brown's daughter who had cooked and helped with her father's subterfuge at the Kennedy Farm before the raid on Harpers Ferry, as a guide and lecturer for the exhibit. She declined, writing to Holmes from her California home, "I may be a relic of John Brown's raid on Harper's Ferry, but I do not want to be placed on exhibition with other relics and curios, as such."

In spite of a fine display of John Brown relics and a rousing lecture by an eyewitness to the raid, Colonel S.K. Donavin, the attendance faltered and the enterprise flopped. When the Exposition ended in 1893, John Brown's Fort went into receivership. The sheriff auctioned the building from the courthouse steps to the highest bidder, which happened to be a consortium who wanted the property as a location for stables for a department store. So once again, the old fort's bricks and timbers were disassembled and stacked on the site. To what end, nobody knew or really cared.

Except for Kate Field. Back in Washington, this remarkable lady, who published *Kate Field's Washington*—a weekly magazine of criticism and current affairs that enjoyed a modest national readership—began a two-fisted campaign to return the fort to its former glory. For many years she had promoted John Brown's martyrdom as a noble cause. In fact, in 1870 she had persuaded a group of wealthy influential men to purchase John Brown's North Elbe farm, which had fallen into disrepair after the Widow Brown died. At Miss Field's urging, the consortium presented the property as a gift to the State of New York to be preserved as a state park.

Now she set her sights on the pile of unwanted rubble, once a fine historical building, now just waiting to be carted to the garbage dump. It wasn't hard for the esteemed publisher to convince the consortium to let her have the pile of junk—for free. The rub was in raising the money to haul it back to Harpers Ferry and to reassemble the structure.

For several weeks she and a friend, attorney Robert McCabe, tromped in and out of Chicago establishments, pleading for donations from tough-minded, uninterested businessmen, more often than not feeling their ears burn as they were ridiculed for getting involved in such a "crazy scheme."

One day, after being subjected to a particularly demeaning attack, Kate Field sat on a park bench with her attorney friend and faced the reality of failure. She stared with tired eyes at the smoke-belching chimneys that rose above Chicago's many breweries, which bottled the frothy liquid that satiated America's thirst. A random thought coursed through her mind: Those chimneys were symbolic of the cause for personal freedoms for which she had long advocated, including the right to drink as one chose. Her liberal goals had put her at odds with hatchet-wielding Carrie Nation's Temperance Movement, but they had also endeared her to America's booze barons.

Suddenly Kate cried, "What is the matter with me? I have not used my wits." The couple made their way forthwith to the office of Mr. McAvoy, the owner of Chicago's largest brewery. She presented her card and was immediately ushered into the inner sanctum. With his usual directness, McAvoy asked, "What do you want?" Kate Fields explained the purpose of their visit. The beer baron laughed and asked, "How much do you need?" With her heart skipping beats, she replied, "Two thousands dollars should get the job done." Then came the magic words, "I think I can get that sum for you."

A few phone calls later, Kate Field had the money in hand. A lesson in perseverance and determination!

Work began in earnest. The Baltimore and Ohio Railroad offered free transportation for material and persons connected with the project. The Associated Press fell in line with free wire service for business transactions. The B. & O. also offered the original site for the restoration, but Kate Field preferred the seven acres on a bluff overlooking the Shenandoah River, about three miles outside Harpers Ferry, which had been donated by farmer Alexander Murphy.

Now Kate Field needed someone to oversee the actual work. But it would not be her, for she had developed serious health problems. Kate closed down her magazine and turned over the job of finding a contractor to her trusted companion, Robert McCabe. Then she left for Hawaii and its more favorable clime.

Chicagoan Edward Cummins had what McCabe described as an "affadivit face," so sincere and honest that he gave Cummins free rein in carrying out the restoration. Cummins gathered up his family and moved to Harpers Ferry to begin his "altruistic mission," as he described it. But the milk of good intent soon turned into clabbered hog slop.

Word reached all the way to Hawaii that the Harpers Ferry townsfolk were up in arms about the Fort's restoration. Well aware of Kate Field's fanaticism about things related to their old nemesis, Brown, the residents feared that once the Fort was restored, Brown and his sons and henchmen would be disinterred and reburied at the site. Supposedly, they had sworn to tear the Fort down as soon as it was built. At least that was the message that reached the beach at Oahu where Kate Field sought to restore her health.

Shocked, she sent McCabe an urgent message, asking him to go to Harpers Ferry and find out what was going on.

Turns out the problem didn't lie with the Fort at all. Cummins was the culprit. He had outraged the community by referring to the inhabitants as rebels and scum and had not paid his laborers a single penny. Worse, the laggard spent his time fishing instead of working. The residents were fed up.

McCabe confronted Cummins, who laughed in his face and declared that he had a signed contract and could do whatever his Yankee heart desired, although he did intend to finish the job—eventually. Frustrated, McCabe turned to the town's stationmaster, E.B. Chambers, for help.

The old gentleman, known for his no-nonsense approach to problem solving, had a solution. "Throw his lazy arse in the river." It seemed like a plan!

About midnight Mrs. Cummins, quite hysterical, awakened McCabe at his hotel. She wailed, "My husband got throwed in th' river by some men. Twern't hurt, but scared'im t'death. He 'scaped and got back to our place. Lordy, what we gonna do? He's scairt t' death."

McCabe got Chambers and they went to the Cummins' lodgings, where they found the culprit hiding in a closet, shaking so hard his false teeth rattled. "What can I do?" he cried.

"Best to get out of town," McCabe replied. "I would if I had train fare," Cummins declared. "We'd be on the first train outta town." McCabe yanked the original contract from his vest pocket and proffered a pen. Cummins scribbled his name and invalidated the document. The attorney escorted the man and his wife to the railroad station, where he bought them a train ticket to Chicago and then watched as the man with the "affidavit face" and his teary-eyed wife climbed on the 4 A.M. early bird special that waited on the northbound tracks.

McCabe asked Chambers to help him find a new contractor, someone from the area that the people would respect. "Look no further," said the stationmaster, chuckling. "I know just the man." A simple handshake sealed the deal, and Mr. Chambers took on the challenging job and completed it without delay. John Brown's Fort had come home.

Well, almost.

In far off Hawaii, Miss Field's health continued to deteriorate. She died on May 19, 1896, soon after Mr. Chambers had completed the restoration. A planned building boom and park in the vicinity of John Brown's Fort failed to materialize. Soon interest (and visitors) dwindled to nothing, and farmer Murphy began to store hay in the building and use it as a makeshift stable for livestock.

But the Fort wasn't finished.

In 1903, Storer College—a black co-educational school established on Camp Hill at Harpers Ferry—began its own fundraising effort to purchase the building. Six years later, on the fiftieth anniversary of John Brown's raid, the school had the necessary funds in hand. The building was again torn down and rebuilt on the Storer campus lawn, where it served as a shrine and museum for the martyred Brown

In 1954, the United States Supreme Court ruled against segregation in the landmark decision—*Brown vs The Board of Education*. A bittersweet victory for the trustees of Storer College, to be sure, for the decision brought an end to federal and state funding for the institution. A year later Storer College closed its doors for good, and the facility was conveyed to the National Park Service.

Over the next few years, John Brown's Fort took on a new role, when sky watchers of the Ground Observation Corps used its belfry as an observation tower during the Cold War days of the late fifties. But the wandering building still lingered in limbo. There was one more move to be made.

In 1960, the NPS brought John Brown's Fort back to Lower Town. Since a railroad embankment now covered the original location, the Park Service sited the building 150 feet east of the original location, where it now rests.

John Brown's Fort as it appears today in
Harpers Ferry Lower Old Town. Home at last!

Fire station , prison, junk house, stable, observation platform, World's Fair exhibit, and museum; the old building had traveled all the way to Chicago and back! After a 72-year absence, like a prodigal son, John Brown's Fort was finally home!

Now you are a leg up on the historians!

*   *   *

I can't let Harpers Ferry go without writing about *those other inhabitants.* They're not directly related to John Brown's Fort. Then again, maybe they are . . .

Those who deal in such things firmly hold to the premise that there are more ghosts in Harpers Ferry than almost any other place on the continent. In fact, it has been opined that the town's disembodied spirits are so numerous they have to book appointments to spook the public. Perhaps.

Truth be known, I've never seen a spook. When I was a kid, about nine or so, one evening my grandfather, "Pap," pshawed at my reluctance to go up to the dairy barn in the pitch-black early winter night and fetch a jug of milk out of the milk cooler for supper. Now that in itself isn't so bad. But I had to walk right past a couple of old neglected graves with unreadable tilted headstones!

Shivering, I croaked, "Them ghosts in the graveyard will get me. I seen'em!" (I hadn't, except in some nightmares.) No way!

Pap shook a gnarled finger in my scared face and spit the words out like he was the world's foremost authority on haints. "Now you listen to me youngun. Ain't nary such a thing as 'unnatcherals.' If you don't believe in'em, you sure as hell ain't gonna see'em." Which meant to my fragile mind that if you did believe in'em, *you sure as hell was gonna see'em*!

Fearing the wrath of Pap's old razorstrop more than ghosts, I ventured out into the dark, heart going lickety-split, trying to fend off the haints by mumbling half-remembered Bible verses that somehow got garbled by a vision of Pap laying the razor strop across my bare butt. I probably broke a local track record in my dash to the barn and back. (The Bible verses must have worked, because no haints waylaid me.)

So I make it a practice *not* to believe in'em, in the hopes that it'll keep the infernal spirits in their place!

But consider Harpers Ferry, with its "Myths and Legends" Ghost Tour. Enthusiastic guides, dressed in period costumes, know where the real spook action is! They hasten with their excited ticket holders to 221 Potomac Street, where sometimes they can hear the sounds of the lifeless body of a Confederate spy banging down the main staircase where he met his demise from a well-placed Yankee bullet.

And of course there's the free lancers. Almost every evening in decent walking weather they come out in droves to roam the streets in search of unnatural quarry. Occasionally, they are able to talk their way into an old ghost-infested house, where they tippy-toe across creaking boards and quietly listen for telltale signs of spectral activity. And sometimes they bag a ghost or two.

Some tell of meeting an old man, gaunt, white-haired, with an uncanny resemblance to the stern-faced statue of John Brown in the nearby wax museum. He limps slowly down the sidewalk with a small black dog that matches his gait. The resemblance is so striking that tourists suspect the Park officials have hired the old man to act as a living historical prop. Often, people ask if they can have their picture made with him and the man gives a grim nod. Trouble is, when the film is developed there is no man or dog. *And on several instances the John Brown look alike has been seen walking to the door of the old fire engine house, and then simply melting into thin air.* Or so they say . . .

Then there's Hog Alley. Supposedly that's where the outraged residents dragged the body of African-American Dangerfield Newby, who took part in Brown's raid, after he was shot in the throat by a well-aimed six-inch spike fired from a powder-loaded musket. Old timers said the free-roaming hogs had their fill. Some folks have observed an old black man in baggy trousers up in Hog Alley. He wears a tattered slouch hat and clutches at his horribly scarred throat as he wanders aimless along the cracked sidewalks crying out for his family's freedom. Or so they say . . .

And what about Saint Peters Catholic Church? Now *that* place has more "presences" than a medium can crowd into a séance. This building, the only church in Harpers Ferry to survive the Civil War intact, was used as a hospital. According to historical archives, one young soldier, a Catholic, whose wounds were not as severe as some of his comrades, lay in the churchyard waiting his turn to be carried inside for treatment. All the while, his life's blood slowly seeped into the ground until he became too weak to cry for help. But the young man had faith that he would get help. And when at last the stretcher-bearers carried him across the threshold into the church, he rejoiced in a barely audible voice, "Thank God I'm saved." And then he died. Some visitors claim to have seen a golden glow on the threshold and hear a weak voice whisper, "Thank God I'm saved."

A few even claim to have witnessed eerie glows floating high above the altar and on the ornate walls—spherical manifestations of restless spirits caught in a dimensional warp not of their making. And then there's the sound of a baby crying, but not seen, on the church's time worn steps. And the vacant-faced aged friar that people on the way up to Jefferson Rock sometimes meet near the church's Rectory. He never returns their greetings, just strides on down the path and *walks through the wall of the old church.*

Even Robert Harper got into the act. When the American Revolution came, Harper was in the throes of building his large home. But the project stalled from a shortage of laborers. Fearing the bands of roving renegades that preyed on such out of the way places, the old man had his wife, Rachel, bury the family gold and made her swear not to tell a living soul.

Harper died before the house was finished. His valiant widow attempted to complete the job herself but fell from a ladder and was killed instantly, taking the secret of the gold's whereabouts to her grave. The Harper House, the oldest building in Harpers Ferry, still stands. Visitors passing beneath its high walls sometimes are amazed to see an old woman dressed in 18th century clothing staring down toward the old Harper Garden, where it has long been rumored that the gold is hidden. Or so they say.

But enough about ghosts. *If you don't believe in them . . .*

Chapter Twenty-four

The Gaps of South Mountain

G athland State Park could be compared to a refreshing seltzer after tackling a gut-popping meal. Or like the mints placed beside the check at an expensive restaurant to lessen the shock when you sneak a glance at the damage—if you know what I mean. It's certainly not what a body might expect to find tucked away in a gap atop Maryland's South Mountain; but then, Crampton Gap couldn't be a better setting for a park.

I look around. Soft serenity saturates the air like an invisible mist, cozily covering the manicured grounds and well-kept buildings, and lingers to soothe the souls of car-weary tourists. And best of all, Gathland State Park is a great place for a sweaty thru-hiker to take a break after hustling the ten or so miles from Harpers Ferry along the long spine of South Mountain. (Gads! There's even a soda vending machine by the *bathrooms*!)

But Gathland State Park is also a place of contradictions. For instance, take the strange Moorish Arch that rises out of the soil like Arthur C. Clarke's imperturbable Jovian monolith, only this structure is real. It can be examined by the eyes and touched by inquisitive fingers.

And then there are the large tourist-friendly cast iron plaques that have been strategically placed in roadside pull-offs to snare curious eyes, obviously to recount some significant past event.

So on that day in 1990 when I first laid eyes on Gathland's oddities, my curiosity was immediately aroused. But first things first! I dropped some coins in the soda machine, chugalugged the can's contents, and moseyed over to the plaques. Civil War doings. I recognized some names from American History 101 and vaguely recalled a few details about Lee's Maryland Campaign, but the little gray cells couldn't spit out anything about the Battle of Crampton's Gap. For that's what the combined plaques described in lots of words, which protruded from the oxidized surfaces like educated pimples—way too many for my mind to grasp.

Perhaps another time, I muttered to myself, leaving any lingering curiosity crumpled on the dusty ground near the word-clogged shrine. Besides, Crampton Gap Shelter was less than a half-mile away and I was getting hungry.

The tall Moorish Arch didn't fare much better. *The Philosopher's Guide* referred to it as a "war correspondents' monument." A few imbedded statutes that reeked of Roman mythology and some fancy, altruistic quotes that embellished long lists of engraved names—none that I recognized—gave the monument a bizarre effect. Nearby, an old foundation that competed with a host of weeds bespoke of better times, better days. Weird. The "monument" had meant something to someone, somewhere, and perhaps it still did; but not for me, not now. Crampton Gap Shelter (and a big pot of mac-n-cheese) was just fifteen minutes away.

I gave the strange monument a last look and hurried on my way, assuaging the fleeting guilt with a perfunctory *Perhaps next time.*

Perhaps another time . . . Two more times now I have rested beneath the old trees at Gathland State Park. Each time, as before, I plunked coins in the soda machine and drank its cold liquid while staring at the Arch and the small crop of cast iron tablets, which stuck out of the roadside pull-off like pop art lollipops. Each time little twinges of guilt tugged at my sweaty noggin. I didn't know any more about Crampton Gap than I did on that warm early July afternoon in 1990. Hollow words, those, the shallow excuse I'd mouthed that day to take me away from this place. And with each visit, the words returned to haunt my mind like a zealous prosecutor pursuing an indictment.

In 1998, I actually started to get up and go read the blasted plaques. Anything for peace of mind. But the afternoon was fast fading and I was famished. And the shelter was so close! I caved, growling to myself *Okay, not now. Perhaps another time.*

However, I did extend an olive branch to my conscience. I dug into my pack and wrote a note in my journal: "Crampton Gap, check it out."

Now, *Perhaps another time* has come! (Warning! More fodder for the history sleuths!)

*   *   *

"Damn Rebs sure made a mess of this place," Corporal Barton Mitchell, Company F, 27th Indiana Infantry, griped to his companions, Privates David Vance and William Hostetter. The three men lay in a small grove of trees that bordered a large field beside the Monocacy River, some two miles south of

Frederick, Maryland. The field was a mess, little more than a garbage dump—the telltale leavings of a large Confederate bivouac area. An arm's length to Mitchell's right, Company F's First Sergeant, John Bloss, lay on his stomach and scanned the field and woods beyond. "Keep a sharp eye out boys, 'cause the Rebs can't be long gone."

He was a little short in his estimate. Lee, along with Longstreet and his part of the Confederate army, had departed the area three days earlier, marching north toward Pennsylvania. McClellan had gotten wind of Lee's latest mischief and was hard on his heels.

Almost. For General McClellan (also called the Little Napoleon by various admirers and Little Mac—though never to his face—by his detractors) was a superb organizer. He had pulled together a demoralized bunch of troops and made them into the magnificent Army of the Potomac. But the man failed miserably as a warmonger, tending to err badly on the side of caution.

Bobby Lee knew his opponent, right down to the color of underwear he preferred. He had capitalized on McClellan's timid nature when he had formed his battle plan to invade Pennsylvania. Now, thirsty to taste more Union blood after the licking he gave the boys in blue at the Second Battle of Manassas, Lee had convinced Jeff Davis that neutral Maryland was a ripe plum ready for plucking, what with its bounteous crops, which Lee's army badly needed.

Too, Maryland was filled with southern sympathizers. The people just might rally around the "Stars and Bars." By the time his Army of Northern Virginia reached Pennsylvania, they'd be well fed and sassy. But the main selling point for Davis: Lee stood a good chance of sucking the Little Napoleon into a gray-lined vortex and whipping him good. A major victory on northern soil could pave the way for England and France to recognize the Confederacy as a separate nation and possibly force Mr. Lincoln to face the reality of a dissolved Union.

Thus came the men of the 27th to the clover-padded field outside Frederick on Saturday, September 13, 1862. The troops had been hard at it before dawn, acting as the XII Corps' advance skirmish line. Still wet from wading across the Monocacy River at Crum's Ford, the men just wanted to rest and dry out, not watch for butternut bumpkins who were probably miles away. All up and down the skirmish line, hundreds of foot-sore troops slumped beneath shade trees or sprawled on the soft carpet at the edge of the open field and waited for the next commands that would send them off again, most likely on another wild goose chase. Or keep them here. Who knew, except the generals, and they weren't likely to confide in the likes of Sergeant John Bloss.

Satisfied that his men weren't likely to be overrun by hordes of Rebs in the next few minutes, he shouted down the line, "Okay fellows, take a break. But stay in place." Bloss uncapped his canteen and took a long swig of tepid water. Then he noticed a yellowish package lying in the grass between Mitchell and Vance. "What is that, Mitchell?"

The corporal answered, "An envelope, Sar'int." The First Sergeant growled, "Well hand it to me." As Vance passed the package over Mitchell's body to Bloss, three small cigars wrapped inside a folded two-page letter fell out. Astonished, Mitchell gasped, "By damn, Sar'int. Cigars!" He grabbed the cheroots off the ground and handed one to his first sergeant. As the excited corporal reached for a match, Bloss picked up the letter, which was filled with sentences penned in a neat, precise handwriting, and began to read.

The words sprang at him like a striking rattler. *Special Orders 191; Headquarters, Army of Northern Virginia; September 9th, 1862.* First Sergeant Bloss nearly fainted. For he held in his grimy hands a copy of General Robert E. Lee's battle plan for the invasion of Maryland. The document was signed by Lee's Adjutant General, Colonel R.H. Chilton, and was addressed to General D. H. Hill. Dumbfounded, Bloss growled, "Mitchell, put out that match and give me the cigars. We've got a tiger by the tail." He stuffed the cigars and letter back in the envelope and rushed down the long blue line in search of his company commander, Captain Kop.

A staff officer who had been a bank teller where Chilton had banked prior to the war recognized Chilton's signature. The document was authentic! Three hours later, the envelope and its contents had traveled up the long chain of command to McClellan's headquarters at Frederick. The Commander of the 87,000-man Army of the Potomac quickly devoured the contents and could hardly believe his luck.

So this is what Bobby Lee is up to. Dividing his army so that Jackson can capture the Union garrison at Harpers Ferry and keep his supply line from the Shenandoah Valley open while he invades the North. The slippery cuss and Jimmy Longstreet are holed up at Hagerstown, waiting for Jackson to join up so they can invade Pennsylvania. A bold plan, worthy of Bobby Lee's brilliant mind—except that now I know what that rascal's got up his gray sleeve. By damn, he'll not set his Rebel boots on good northern soil. I'm going to catch Old Bobby with his pants down.

Exuberant, McClellan turned to his staff and waved the document in the air. "Here's a paper with which, if I cannot whip Bobby Lee, I will be willing to go home. Now I know what to do!" As an afterthought, he pointed at his

Chief of Staff, Major General Randolph Marcy, and added, "Telegraph Mr. Lincoln and say that I have in my hands the complete battle plan of the rebels. And tell the President to pass my respects to Mrs. Lincoln and that I will send him trophies." Turning to his adjutant, he crisply ordered, "Have all Corps and Division commanders report to me immediately."

The President didn't get overly excited when he received McClellan's news. As a matter of fact, Lincoln had recently remarked to a cabinet member that "McClellan has a bad case of the 'slows'." But this time the President was wrong, for Little Mac intended to cash in on his remarkable luck.

The general and his senior commanders gathered around the map and came to the same conclusion. Push the Union army over South Mountain as soon as possible. Send Joe Hooker's First Corps—then bivouacked beside the Monocacy River—and the other four Corps, which were strung out for miles, along the National Road and through Turner's Gap to the north. Send Jesse Reno's Ninth Corps along the Old Sharpsburg Road through Fox's Gap, a mile south of Turner's Gap. And have William Franklin's Sixth Corps move through Crampton's Gap, some six miles further south, along the Burkittsville Road.

The army would then reunite in Pleasant Valley west of South Mountain. From there it wasn't much more than a stone's throw to Hagerstown. Armed with the element of surprise and vastly superior numbers, the army would annihilate Longstreet's forces, capture the wily Lee, and then march south and destroy Jackson's forces at Harpers Ferry. The war would be over!

Asked one of the generals, "What if South Mountain's passes are defended?"

McClellan had already taken that into consideration. "Not likely; and if so, there'll only be minimum resistance. No, the main battle will be at Hagerstown."

Within the hour, the mighty Army of the Potomac was on the move.

But McClellan was wrong all three counts. South Mountain would prove to be his nemesis. There would be no trophies for his President. And Robert E. Lee would escape to fight other battles.

(Author's note: How a copy of General Lee's Special Orders 191 ended up in a clover field on the Best farm near Frederick has defied history scholars since the errant envelope was discovered. At first, suspicion centered on General Hill, whose headquarters was located near the Best farm. But Hill's copy of Special Orders 191 hadn't come from Lee's headquarters. Instead, it had been hand copied by Jackson's staff and passed to Hill separately. Fortunate for Hill, he had mailed this copy home with instructions for his wife to preserve it. He was later vindicated, as the copy that went missing was the original sent to him from Lee and signed by his Adjutant General. When Hill failed to become the scapegoat, the Adjutant General fell under suspicion because of his strong pre-war ties to the North.

Sloppy handling or an act of treason? After all, generals, both Union and Confederate, had managed to lose or capture each other's battle orders *five* times in the twenty-six days that preceded the confrontation at South Mountain. In the end, even though they've dug down to historical bedrock, the seekers of truth have had to shrug their shoulders in frustration and swallow the bitter pill of failure. The mystery of Special Orders 191 will likely never be solved.

A stroke of luck for Little Mac, that First Sergeant Bloss happened to be the one to spot the yellow envelope. Educated at Hanover College, John Bloss had the intelligence to recognize the importance of his find. He rose from sergeant to commanding officer of Company F. Wounded in four different campaigns, he survived the war and climbed the ladder of success as an educator, eventually becoming president of Oregon State University.

And the cigars? Their fate is as elusive as the mystery itself. But I'd lay money that they didn't go to waste!)

McClellan had seriously misjudged his adversary. True, General Lee had taken a calculated risk in dividing his forces, but he wasn't about to be caught with his pants down. The brilliant strategist assigned General Daniel H. Hill's division to "form the rear guard of the army." For Hill, this meant fortifying the three southernmost passes on South Mountain. Thus, the stage was set for America's bloodiest tragedy, which patiently waited for three little known mountain passes to alter history and cause giant armies to meet at a small stream with the strange Indian name "Antietam," which flowed near the sleepy village of Sharpsburg.

Early on Sunday morning, September 14, 1862, Confederate Colonel Alfred Colquitt quickly combed the tangles out of his heavy black beard, buckled on his sword, and motioned for his aide, Lieutenant George Grattan, to follow him. With his stride full of piss and vinegar, as befitted the commander of the 6th Georgia Regiment, he walked through the door of Mountain House— at least that's what the locals called the wayside tavern in Turner's Gap. Colquitt had commandeered the inn as his temporary headquarters.

As the colonel headed out into the misty dawn, he growled, "Come on Lieutenant. I want to take a look at what I couldn't see last night." They hurried to the previous evening's vantage point, which offered a panoramic bird's eye view of the vast plain that extended east toward Middletown, Maryland. In the fading light of last evening, the battle-wise eyes of the middle-aged colonel had watched hundreds of campfires appear as the sun descended behind South Mountain. Concern had twisted his face as he turned to the young officer and said, "It can't be McClellan's army. They're supposed to be over at Frederick, holding a line between General Lee and the Capital. It must be those two Union cavalry brigades hot on Jeb Stuart's heels that he told me about when he happened by this afternoon."

That had been yesterday's worry. Now he waited with poorly concealed patience as the mist slowly dissipated and retreated before the rising sun. "Good God A'mighty," Grattan gasped. "Just look at that, Colonel! Must be the whole God-awful Union army!"

The large orange orb reflected off of the shiny buckles and clips that marked the rifles and canteens of thousands of troops lined up in Corps' formations—all moving toward South Mountain like some grotesque organism. Colquitt squinted into the sun, trying to get his brain to accept what his eyes saw. He drew a long breath and let it whistle out between his teeth. "Son, hightail it back to General Hill and tell him he needs to see this. We've got a battle on our hands!"

Lieutenant Grattan mounted his saddle and sped off but soon encountered General Hill and his staff riding hell-bent toward the crest. General Lee had already gotten word that things were heating up and had sent Hill to investigate. The general's heart caught in his throat as he watched the vast army move up the Middletown Valley. But in his disciplined mind, fear quickly gave way to awe and admiration. He turned to Colquitt and swore, "By damn, Colonel, I've never seen such a glorious spectacle. And probably never will again."

But the soaring moment quickly soured as nasty reality struck. Lee's divided Army of Northern Virginia was in serious trouble. If he, Hill, failed to halt the Army of the Potomac at South Mountain, there'd be hell to pay. McClellan's army would gobble up Longstreet like a hungry fox in a hen house and have Jackson for dessert. Hill quickly gave the orders to realign his 5800 troops to face the threat. Then it was wait and pray.

On they came, uncountable numbers arrayed as bluish strings that stretched back to the horizon. About 9 A.M., the main thrust began when General Jacob Cox's Kanahwa Brigade, which had steadily pushed up the Old Sharpsburg Road to Fox's Gap, ran into a fusillade of minnie balls from Brigadier Sam Garland's Reb pickets. The bullets whined into the advance Union skirmishers like angry hornets, drawing first blood, and then the no-holds-barred fighting began in earnest.

Union commanders launched all-out attacks, and the determined Rebels fought back like inhuman machines. Decidedly outnumbered, the defenders soon scattered, carrying their wounded with them, including Sam Garland, who had taken a minnie ball in his chest. Desperate, General Hill ordered two howitzers from Turner's Gap down the old woods road to face the Yankees, and he gathered up all the staff officers, teamsters, cooks, and stragglers he could find to defend the guns.

In an unparalleled act of intimidation—or misjudgment—the small show of force caused General Cox to halt his advance, giving Hill time to bring up reinforcements.

Vicious fighting again erupted, but the strengthened Confederate line managed to regain some of the blood-soaked ground and stall Cox's advance.

Down in Frederick, General McClellan couldn't believe the reports that winded couriers delivered: "Massive resistance at Fox's Gap. Unable to advance." As the day wore on, reports of attacks and counterattacks continued to flow into the headquarters. But the Rebels, although vastly outnumbered, managed to hold the gaps.

Confused, the Little Napoleon scratched his head and wondered. *Could he have totally misjudged Lee? Was the copy of Lee's battle plan a well-orchestrated subterfuge designed to ambush the ambusher? Could it even be that he faced the intrepid Longstreet at South Mountain?*

McClellan decided to force Fox's Gap with Reno's entire Corps. Once the Rebels were driven off, the IX Corps would then swing right and attack north along the mountain's spine, where Reno would join Hooker in a combined attack on heavily fortified Turner's Gap.

But Sam Garland's men at Fox's Gap, crazed at their commander's death, had other plans. (Shortly after General Sam Garland had been carried from the battlefield and placed on the steps of Mountain House Inn, he died.) When the guns fell silent several hours later, Jesse Reno had joined Sam Garland in death. Hundreds of Billy Yanks would never go marching home again, nor would hundreds of Johnny Rebs ever look away again to the cotton fields down south.

Superior numbers finally forced the determined southerners to retreat, and by mid afternoon Union flags waved in Fox's Gap, but the cost in lives shocked commanders on both sides. Defiantly, Turner's Gap still flew the "Stars and Bars." What was left of Garland's brigade hobbled back up the woods road to help defend Turner's Gap.

Longstreet rushed two brigades, numbering 3300 men, to Turner's Gap, trying to beat Hooker's Corps, which was marching at double quick from the

Monocacy. Finally, about 4 P.M., Hooker had his Corps in place and the attack began. Ridiculously outnumbered, the Confederates yielded each foot of ground with crazed fury. But somehow they managed to hang on.

When darkness descended, Hooker's and what remained of the dead Reno's men had surrounded the stubborn Rebels on three sides, but they still held Turner's Gap. Exhausted Union troops dropped to the ground, rifles askew where they fell, and oblivious to the cries of hundreds of wounded, slept side by side with their dead comrades.

But General Lee knew what he was up against. The butcher's bill was too high. Unwilling to sacrifice more men to a hopeless cause—the combined Union forces at South Mountain outnumbered the Confederate defenders nearly five to one—as the hour hand approached 10 P.M., Lee ordered Hill to give it up and bring his troops back into the fold.

But Hill had done his job, and superbly. His division had delayed McClellan's army, buying precious time for ammunition and supply trains to roll to safety and, most importantly, giving Lee time to reassemble his disjointed army.

Meanwhile, miles away at Crampton's Gap, General William Franklin was being afflicted by his own case of the "slows." McClellan had given him his marching orders the day before, when the whole army had been sent scurrying toward South Mountain in high hopes of nabbing Bobby Lee in his hidey-hole at Hagerstown. The VI Corps commander was to attack the Rebels at Crampton's Gap—back door to Harpers Ferry—as soon as he heard the first cannons boom to his north, which would signal the start of the battle. His orders were to crush the defenders with his far superior force—his Corps against a skinny brigade—and rush south to relieve the besieged garrison at Harpers Ferry.

With that mission finished, he was to drive a "wedge" between Jackson and Longstreet in Pleasant Valley west of South Mountain, preventing the two "halves" from reuniting.

But instead of marching directly toward Crampton's Gap on the 13th, so as to be in place for an early assault the next morning, Franklin remained where he was and bedded his troops down for the night. When the cannons began to boom at Fox's Gap the next morning, the VI Corps wasn't even close to their objective. Worse, when Franklin reached Burkittsville around noon on the 14th, he suddenly realized he had a problem. From which side of Burkittsville should he launch his attack? The general ordered his 12,800-man Corps to break out rations for the noon meal while he and his staff spent the next four hours formulating a battle plan.

Ready at last, he aligned his Corps along Burkittsville Road's north side and gave the command to attack. The Confederates met them head on at the base of the mountain and fought with furious intensity. But it wasn't enough. Outnumbered six to one, the Rebels slowly retreated up to Crampton's Gap, leaving behind large numbers of dead and wounded.

In the gap, the Rebels fought savage battles in the cultivated fields once owned by Joshua Compton, but the effort became hopeless. Around 6 P.M., badly outnumbered, their units decimated, surrounded on three sides, those Confederates who could walk faded into the approaching twilight and descended the mountain. General Franklin had carried out the first part of his mission—a day late and a dollar short.

But the "slows" still plagued the man. Instead of following through with the "wedge," he bedded his troops down in Crampton's Gap. Early the next morning word came that Jackson had taken Harpers Ferry. Wracked with indecision—to march on Jackson or stay put—Franklin decided the best course of action was no action at all, and the "wedge" got hopelessly tangled up with the "slows."

So the timid general remained at Crampton's Gap until routed out of his reverie by an angry McClellan, who ordered him to Sharpsburg when the bullets began to fly across Antietam Creek on the morning of September 17th. But by then the fat was in the fire.

Ever pragmatic in spite of his bold nature, after South Mountain fell General Lee decided to abort his goal of invading Pennsylvania and to retreat back south of the Potomac. But news that Jackson had taken Harpers Ferry put a new spin on things.

Lee determined to hold his ground at the small stream near Sharpsburg and give his army time to regroup. That's where McClellan finally cornered the gray fox with half an army. And then the unforeseen happened. General Jackson force-marched his men from Harpers Ferry and managed to join Lee just in time for the opening gambit.

So McClellan, the master braggart, had to eat crow again, for there would be no surprise assault, no taking of Bobby Lee, and no trophies to send back to the President. And instead of Hagerstown, America's bloodiest day would happen at the small creek called Antietam.

The Little Napoleon won his gaps at South Mountain, but at a horrific cost to both sides. Over 51,000 Union troops engaged 11,000 Confederates (which included Longstreet's reinforcements to Hill's division). The "butchers's bill": The Union lost 2,329 killed, wounded, or missing. The Confederates lost an estimated 3,558 men.

"Peanuts," some might say when compared to the terrible tragedy that unfolded three days later, when the war machine ground up entire units and casualties were numbered in the tens of thousands—and the sluggish waters of Antietam Creek ran red. The men at South Mountain who felt the Grim Reaper's scythe would argue otherwise.

Two future presidents, both members of the 23d Ohio Infantry, were present at Fox's Gap that day. A Rebel bullet ripped through the left arm of Lieutenant Colonel Rutherford B. Hayes, leaving a gaping hole but narrowly missing the bone (otherwise, he would likely have left an arm at the Wise cabin, which was used as a makeshift hospital, along with his political future). With his men pinned down by heavy fire and unable to come to his aid, Hayes lay where he had fallen while minnie balls whizzed overhead. Suddenly a lieutenant risked all and dashed through the deadly hailstorm to drag his commander to safety. A hospital detail evacuated Lieutenant Colonel Hayes to the house of Jacob Rudy in Middletown, and within a couple of weeks he had recovered sufficiently to return to his command.

Commissary Sergeant William McKinley's duties that day kept him out of the line of fire and he didn't participate in the fighting. Of interest is the fact that McKinley was assassinated while in office—on September 14, 1901, thirty-nine years to the day after the battle at Fox's Gap.

After the bloodbath at Antietam, the Army of Northern Virginia, though still dangerous, had been badly hurt. Outnumbered and suffering from staggering losses, General Lee stood to lose everything if McClellan chose to renew the attack. Reluctantly he abandoned his plan to invade Pennsylvania. Indeed, the only way he could save his army was by evading any further action and pulling back to the safer ground of Virginia.

Then came one of history's most masterful bluffs. Playing on McClellan's timid nature, the wily general kept his army on the battlefield, as if he held a "royal flush," just daring his opponent to raise and call. It worked! Unable to accept the obvious, the overly cautious McClellan again got a bad case of "the slows" and ordered his army to wait for reinforcements, which never came.

A missed opportunity, for as the Army of Northern Virginia piled up on the north side of the Potomac, waiting for high water to subside, the gullible general could have cornered Bobby Lee and annihilated the retreating army, thus hastening the war's end. But unable to overcome his timidity, McClellan failed to press forward, much to Mr. Lincoln's chagrin.

McClellan did telegraph the President that he had won a "great victory" by preventing Lee from invading Pennsylvania, but the President wasn't buying and ordered McClellan to pursue Lee's weakened army south and destroy it. When McClellan failed to budge, Lincoln journeyed to Antietam in early October to take stock and found his "supreme commander" hopelessly bogged down again by "the slows." Mr. Lincoln received assurances that his wishes would be carried out expeditiously.

Somewhat mollified, the President returned to the Capitol and waited, but the Union commander continued to stall. After several weeks of sending harsh threats that were countered with lame excuses, the exasperated President reached the end of his patience. He fired the Little Napoleon and turned command of the Army of the Potomac over to Major General Ambrose Burnside.

During Lincoln's war of words, Lee licked his wounds and ten months later, after soundly whipping Burnside at Fredericksburg, led his army back north, this time into Pennsylvania for another date with destiny at a small hamlet called Gettysburg.

(Author's note: After the war, a spiteful government stripped Lee of his citizenship, although he was never tried as a traitor, and confiscated his Arlington estate, turning it into a national cemetery. The humiliated general mounted his favorite war horse, Traveller, and rode the 110 miles from his Richmond home, where his family had resided during the conflict, to Lexington to assume the face-saving position offered by a grateful, albeit defeated, Virginia. Bolstered by his beloved Mary, he quietly served as president of Washington College until he succumbed to a fatal heart attack in 1870. Lee was buried on the campus, and the College was renamed Washington and Lee University as a lasting tribute to the great "non-American." The circle was finally closed when President Gerald Ford restored Lee's citizenship a century later. But too many white crosses had been planted in the rolling hills of his wife's family lands, and Arlington National Cemetery remains the property of the United States Government.

During Lee's funeral, Traveller, the iron-gray war horse that went through Hell with his master, followed behind the General's hearse. After the solemn event, Traveller was put out to pasture. Shortly thereafter, a rusty nail that protruded from a rotten board did what four years of bloody battles had failed to do. Traveller, age thirteen, contracted lockjaw, for which there was no known cure, and had to be shot. The animal was laid to rest outside Lee Chapel, not far from his master's grave.

J.E.B. Stuart, Lee's young aide during the crisis at Harpers Ferry, achieved the rank of major general. He commanded Lee's cavalry, acting as the far-reaching eyes of the Army of Northern Virginia. His admirers called him

"Beauty" because of the dashing figure he cut with his scarlet-lined cape, flowing yellow sash, and rakish plumed hat. Stuart's daring exploits behind Union lines gave rise to tingling goose bumps many a night as blue clad soldiers sat around cooking fires and sneaked wary glances into the inky darkness.

The legendary general, only thirty-one years of age, was mortally wounded in a battle with Union cavalry near Richmond in May 1864. He lies with other brothers-in-gray in Richmond's Hollywood Cemetery.)

*   *   *

By 1810, the year that Joshua Crampton was born near the gap that bore his family's name, the Cramptons had already been long established there. And they weren't the only settlers on South Mountain. Arthur Nelson bought a 575-acre tract seven miles further north on the mountain, as the crows fly. His purchase must have been a zinger, for the locals began to refer to his holdings as "Nelson's Folly." In 1750, Robert Turner offered to buy the property, and Arthur jumped at the chance to unload the white elephant. But beauty is often in the eyes of the beholder. Turner liked the place well enough to build a fine stone house, which folks called the Mountain House at Turner's Gap. In 1769, Jacob Young, who listed his occupation as innkeeper, bought Mountain House and turned it into an inn.

By the time President George Washington pushed the National Pike through Turner's Gap to Boonsboro (in 1810) to open up western Maryland, Mountain House was already old with a well-established reputation. Ten years later the National Pike was extended on to Hagerstown, which brought many travelers—and dollars—to Boonsboro. The grateful citizens of Boonsboro erected the first monument in the United States in honor of their benefactor, George Washington. Sometimes as many as twenty stages a day would stop at Mountain House for food and lodging, and the tavern-turned-inn prospered.

In the turbulent years before the Civil War, South Mountain was host to another kind of traveler, for the mountain's long spine leading north from Harpers Ferry into free Pennsylvania became a main avenue for the Underground Railroad. Fugitive slaves passed through the isolated wind gaps that soon would soak up the scarlet cost of their freedom, headed toward the "Promised Land"—often only to be caught by bounty-hungry slave hunters who combed the area for easy prey.

Enter George Allen Townsend, born in 1841 on Maryland's Eastern Shore. His father, Stephen Townsend, an itinerant Methodist preacher with itchy feet, moved the family from parish to parish throughout Maryland and Delaware until, when George turned fourteen, the parson finally found his niche in Philadelphia. The lad entered school there and graduated in 1860 with a Bachelor of Arts degree from Central High School.

Young Townsend gained full-time employment as news editor for the *Philadelphia Inquirer.* A year later he moved up, becoming the city editor for the *Philadelphia Press,* and that's where the opening salvoes at Charleston Bay found him. The twenty-one year old journalist marched toward the sound of the cannons as a reporter for the *New York Herald,* becoming the war's youngest correspondent. By war's end, Townsend's name was as familiar to northern households as was John Brown.

After the cannons had been oiled and put away, with his reputation now well established, Townsend continued to write like a well-oiled machine, feeding the public a copious diet of news columns, plays, and books, with several on the "best seller" list. At some point during the Reconstruction Era, he began to write under the pen name "GATH," which he took from his initials, along with an "H" that he borrowed from the Holy Writ: "Tell it not in Gath, publish it not in the streets of Askalon." (II Samuel 1:20)

In 1884, the famed author and lecturer came to Crampton's Gap in search of descriptive material for a book about slave runners. Townsend was so taken with the beauty of the place that he purchased 110 acres, which amounted to nearly all of the Crampton's Gap battlefield. He quickly set into motion his dream for a grand estate, which he would call "Gapland." A modest building, "Askalon," soon rose out of the soil near the roadside. Gapland Lodge quickly followed. As royalties from his many books fattened his bank account, he built Gapland Hall, a magnificent manor with three-foot walls of natural stone and over eleven rooms.

Five years later Gapland Den, a twenty-room architectural fantasy with a large ballroom and library, was completed. And a final touch: He had the workers build a fine mausoleum. The entrance was covered by a slab of snow-white marble that bore the inscription "Good night Gath," and the tomb was guarded by a large bronze rendition of his Great Dane, who kept eternal vigilance from its perch on the roof.

Gath's voracious appetite for building was temporarily appeased, and he took to gracious—if somewhat eccentric—living. He assigned Askalon to his two children and their nurses and tutors. The servants stayed in Gapland Lodge, while his wife Bessie resided in Gapland Hall. Townsend reserved Gapland Den for himself. However, the family did dine together—and very well indeed! The affluent writer imported a French chef for their dining pleasure!

Gath's fame spread, and post offices, knives, horses, even cigars, bore Townsend's pen name. Distinguished visitors flocked to Gapland Den to taste Old World *haute cuisine* and to waltz evenings away in the grand ballroom. Life was sweet in Crampton's Gap's idyllic setting.

Gath had one more structure to build. In 1896, he traveled to Hagerstown to see the unusual Romanesque arch that fronted the new Antietam Fire Station. During the 1890s it had become vogue for cities to pay tribute to their heroic firemen by building ornate fire stations patterned after a "castles and palaces" motif. Townsend was taken with the Hagerstown design. He called the workers together and told them, "I want to build a memorial to my fellow war correspondents." He handed the supervisor a copy of the plans his architect had carefully drawn up. "Make it just like this." And the men went to work.

The finished memorial was startling. Standing fifty feet tall and forty feet wide, the structure was heavily embellished with symbols. A large Moorish arch was topped by three Roman arches, which according to Gath, represented "Description," "Depiction," and "Photography." To the right of the arches, a square crenellated tower jutted above the entire structure, much like an unfinished prop for a King Arthur movie. Niches sheltered symbolic terra cotta statuettes of mythological Mercury, Electricity, and Poetry. And oddly, two horse heads, inscribed with "Speed" and "Heed" stared out from their lofty nooks above the arches.

The Greek mythical creature "Pan" also made the cut, capturing a place on the tower, where he stood transfixed in stone (instead of chasing through the woods after virginal maidens). The goat-man held his traditional seven-reed Syrinx in one hand while he drew a Roman sword from a stone scabbard with his other hand. On the side opposite the tower stood a small turret, topped with a more appropriate symbol akin to the memorial's purpose—a gold weather vane depicting a pen bending a sword.

At various places on the monument, quotations appropriate to the journalistic endeavors of war correspondents, including verses from the Old Testament, were inscribed. And to give legitimacy to the work, he caused to be set into the memorial two tablets inscribed with the names of one hundred and fifty-seven war correspondents, which he had himself compiled.

On a chilly mid-October day of that year, just weeks after the last dabs of finishing mortar had dried, Maryland's newly-elected Governor Lloyd Lowndes came to Crampton's Gap and gave a fitting dedication for the new War Correspondents' Memorial. Distinguished visitors came from afar to "ooh" and "aah" over the strange creation that had sprung from the dark crevices of the famous writer's brain. Guests offered congratulations and handshakes as they munched on hors d'oeuvres at the lavish reception that followed in Gapland Den's grand ballroom.

When the last visitor had left, Gath strode out into the deepening twilight to fill his lungs with pristine air and to walk among the trees and buildings of his half-million dollar kingdom. Aah! How the blissful solitude of Gapland stirred his soul!

His walk eventually led him to the monument, his masterful creation and his tribute to those who had bent the sword with the pen, as he had. A cloud floated across the giant harvest moon, just peeking above the trees, then scurried away, leaving the ghostly structure outlined in pale moonlight. Gath drank in the sight for several minutes, impervious to the freshening wind or the sudden stirring of leaves. "Perfect," he murmured into the dusk. "Just perfect."

Gath returned to his writing, but his star had begun its descent. The $100,000 annual income that supported his mountain kingdom began to dwindle. In 1904, the Civil War Correspondents' Memorial was turned over to the War Department and later transferred to the National Park Service to be kept as a National Monument. Royalties continued to diminish or disappeared altogether, and Gath reached a point where he was unable to maintain Gapland. Helplessly, he watched as the grounds lost their manicured appearance, and he anguished as the wilderness encroached and the grand buildings began to deteriorate.

Now desperate, Gath began to sell valuable paintings and furnishings in an attempt to stall the inevitable. But came the day when he had nothing left to sell. George Alfred Townsend, the man widely known as Gath, was pauperized by his Gapland, the place he loved best in the world. Gath died in 1914 at age seventy-three and was buried in Philadelphia, far from the beautiful mausoleum that bore his name.

Townsend's daughter couldn't hang on to the property either. Soon after her father's death she sold Gapland for a fraction of its cost. The new owners tried to operate Gapland as an inn, but the attempt failed and the place became a derelict, assaulted by vandals and strangled by an uncaring wilderness.

Over the next several years as ghosts came to roost, the bronze mastiff disappeared, along with the marble slab, and the mausoleum crumbled into rubble. Hungry for more detritus, the earth reclaimed the magnificent Den and Library, reluctantly leaving the jaded foundation for a future meal.

In 1943, a church group acquired the land for a summer conference site. Eventually, Gapland ended up in the hands of the Frederick Chamber of Commerce, along with the Historical Society of Frederick County, Inc. These organizations deeded the property in 1949 to the State of Maryland to be administered as a State Park. Park officials renamed the old estate "Gathland State Park" as a tribute to its famous founder. Gath would have been pleased. His Civil War Correspondents' Memorial, the only such in the Nation, now had a permanent home.

(Author's note: Gapland Hall, Bessie's "house," was restored in 1958 and now houses the Park's Visitor Center. Gapland Lodge, the servants' quarters, now serves as the Park's Museum, where the "pen that bent the sword"—the gold weather vane—is on display.)

A careful study of the roster of war correspondents listed on the memorial will reveal that thirty-three cannot be identified, and twenty-two were Townsend's personal friends or large contributors to the memorial, not correspondents. Several prominent Union journalists were omitted altogether— as were some Confederate journalists, but then they were on the losing side!

And since the original 157 names were compiled over a century ago, more names have been recently added. On Wednesday, October 1, 2003, an entourage of official and celebrated dignitaries converged on Gathland State Park to unveil a plaque dedicated to four journalists who lost their lives in a different kind of fight—the war on terrorism. Their names are familiar to those of us who grit our teeth when nightly news anchors announce the grim costs of waging war: Daniel Pearl, *Wall Street Journal;* Elizabeth Neuffer, *Boston Globe;* Michael Kelly, *Washington Post;* and David Bloom, *NBC News.* And the beat goes on . . .

*   *   *

Today, the guns have long since been silenced on South Mountain. Folks, working under the umbrella of "Progress" have dropped the apostrophe and "s" from the names of the old history-packed gaps—although for some lost reason "Turner Gap didn't sound right so they kept the "s."

The march of time has forced other changes. Burkittsville Road, which became a point of departure for General Franklin's assault on Crampton's Gap, is now called Gapland Road (officially Maryland Highway 572, which winds over the mountain and connects the small hamlets of Burkittsville to the east and Gapland to the west). Burkittsville remains pretty much as it did when Franklin's VI Corps passed through on September 14, 1862. Most of the heavy fighting that day took place in the large field at the north edge of the Gap, which is now bisected by the Appalachian Trail. No scattered bones here to greet the curious, though, for such gruesome reminders were long ago removed to more decorous ground.

The Sharpsburg Road (alternately referred to as the Sunken Road where it passes through the broad saddle of Fox Gap) has been rechristened the Reno Monument Road. Here in this forlorn place General Jacob Cox's Fourth Division of Reno's IX Corps swept up the slopes at mid-morning on that tragic day and clashed with General Sam Garland's tenacious brigade. Here, bodies fell on top of each other until piled in tangled stacks like dead limbs atop a beaver's lodge. And here, before the sun fell beneath the western horizon, two gallant leaders met their untimely end.

But Reno Monument Road is somewhat of a misnomer, for now other memorials and metal markers have appeared near the Reno Monument, which stands by the field where the most vicious fighting at the Battle of South Mountain took place.

Daniel Wise owned the land then and lived with his son and daughter in a cabin, now gone, which rested by the edge of Sunken Road some fifty yards west of the present site of Reno's Monument. Wise had the good sense to hightail it to safer ground when the bullets started to whine that Sunday morning—a smart move, for Sunken Road became a Confederate strongpoint early in the battle, and the cabin itself became a focal point in the furious contest of wills.

Two days after the battle, a Union burial detail tossed fifty-eight Confederate bodies down Daniel Wise's well. Four days later, even as the waters of Antietam Creek mingled with tarnished red seepage, burial details still dug shallow graves in the thin mountain soil for the multitude of gray-clad corpses.

And with the spring plowing and beating rains came a new harvest. Bones, glistening white in the brilliant sun, protruded from the freshly turned earth, so plentiful that children could walk from one end of the field to the other without stepping on bare soil. (Confederate remains from the Battle of South Mountain—all that could be found—were interred in Rose Hill Cemetery at Hagerstown. By the end of 1874, 2240 bodies had been recovered.)

Major General Jesse Lee Reno personally directed his Corps at Fox's Gap after Cox ran into an immovable Rebel wall. As twilight neared, he rode to the front to see what was holding up the advance to Turner's Gap, just in time to join the melee as John Bell Hood's Texas Brigade made the last attack of the day. A bullet caught him in the chest, and troops hastily carried him to the rear where he died soon after. Friends took the body to Washington, D.C., and Jesse Lee Reno, at the blooming age of thirty-nine, was laid to rest in Georgetown's Oak Hill Cemetery.

On September 14, 1889, twenty-seven years to the day after the battle, surviving veterans of Reno's IX Corps erected a monument at Wise's Field to mark the spot where their valiant leader had fallen. Like its namesake, the memorial is tall, erect, and somber.

Brigadier General Samuel Garland, Jr., like his counterpart, took a minnie ball in the chest. But unlike Reno, Garland 's mortal wound came early in the battle. His staff carried him to Turner's Gap and laid the bleeding officer on the steps of Mountain House, where he soon died. A detail carried his body down the steep road to Boonsboro. Less than a week later, Garland's remains were returned to his native Lynchburg, Virginia, and buried in the Presbyterian Cemetery. Like Reno, Sam Garland's star burned out during his prime. The General was only thirty-two years old.

On September 11, 1993, Maryland's Sons of Confederate Veterans dedicated a memorial at Wise's Field to the courageous general. Perhaps not as big as Reno's nor as ornate, but sometimes magnanimous gifts come in small packages.

Just two weeks after the latest plaque was unveiled at Gathland, on October 16, 2003 another memorial came to Wise's Field, this time to honor the North Carolina Confederates who bore the brunt of the fighting at Fox's Gap. The monument shows a young Confederate color bearer lying on the ground with his regimental flag in his hand. A strong lesson in "death before dishonor," for the lad took a Yankee bullet rather than surrender his flag.

A few words about the unlucky man whose farm was raped by the onslaught at Fox's Gap. His story goes back a few years before the bullets began to fly.

German immigrant John Fox, with his wife Christiana and son Frederick, settled in the gap in 1751. When his parents died, Frederick and his four siblings inherited the farm. Frederick married and continued to add to his holdings until he owned all of the land from Fox's Gap to Turner's Gap. When his wife died in the early 1800s, Frederick sold his holdings and moved to Ohio.

In 1858, Daniel Wise paid $46.96 for some acreage in Fox's Gap, cleared a four-acre field, and built a small but stout log cabin. There he lived, beside Sunken Road, with his children John and Matilda, eking out a living as a subsistence farmer, day laborer, and "Root Doctor" of some repute. Then came the despoilers.

Well before daybreak on that Sunday, Daniel Wise gently shook his children awake and went out into the soft dark with his sleepy-eyed son to slop the hogs while Matilda fried some fat back and got the biscuits going. He kept a wary eye out for the strangers in gray homespun who had dug in on the downside slope of the mountain the previous afternoon.

Don't like the looks of this, he thought. *Strangers with weapons. Has to be Rebs by their looks, but what in the dickens are they doing up here on the mountain? Well, it's the Sabbath and surely they won't go firing off them muskets on the Lord's Day. But that don't mean they mightn't try to get their hands on my chickens.* He kept his thoughts to himself . . . no need to worry his young son.

Chickens! He maneuvered the son toward the slab-sided hen house to take inventory. Satisfied with the count, the farmer and his son headed for the open cabin door. *I'd best hide the silver and have the kids pack a few things just in case. At least till them Rebs leave. No siree, I don't like the looks of this at all.*

Sabbath or not, Daniel Wise decided to forego church and stay close to his cabin. About 9 A.M., he was sitting outside the door, repairing the old mule's harness, when the flop-eared mutt sprawled at his feet suddenly growled and took off lickety-split through the field, barking like he'd gotten wind of a deer. Wise stood and peered toward the far tree line. *Now what has got that dog's dander up?* Curious, he walked out into the field to get a better view. And then all hell broke loose.

Wise grabbed his children and fled as the first shots filled the air down on the east slope. The family scurried down the mountain to the only safe haven Daniel could think of, the old Mount Caramel Church. For the next four days, he and others waited until a man in a filthy blue uniform came to the church and told them that they could return to their homes.

Daniel Wise couldn't believe his eyes. The landscape of his farm was completely changed. Shallow graves flanked his cabin and defiled the field where he had recently picked a pitiful crop of corn. The cabin, bullet-ridden, had weathered the storm; but inside, splattered walls and the plank floor, made slick by reddish gore and covered with soiled bandages, told of the violent carnage that had come to his mountain and cursed his home. Spoiled air pregnant with the coppery smell of recent death hung in the room, and large green blowflies buzzed through the fetid space, gorging on the fruits of battle.

(The carnage was so horrific that several Union burial details dosed themselves with quantities of John Barleycorn to deaden the senses. Only then, when staggering drunk, did the men go about their grisly task, armed with picks and shovels, and canteens replenished with whiskey. The pick served a twofold purpose: One, to dig into the rocky earth. The other? If a drunken soldier could get the pick snugged beneath a corpse's belt, then he didn't have to dirty his hands. Sometimes it took four or five swings before an alcohol-dimmed brain could get erratic hands to insert the pick where it had enough purchase to drag a body to a shallow trench. Hard times, even for tough men!)

The children, at first numb with shock, began to wail, then scream hysterically. Daniel Wise took them outside and sat them down by the well, and held them close until the hysteria subsided into sobs. "It'll be okay," he said. "We ain't dead like those other poor souls. Yeah, we'll be okay. First thing we've got to do is get our home cleaned up. John, go draw some water."

The boy lowered the wooden bucket into the round hole. The bucket hit something, and the lad peered into the well. His scream was halted by a rush of vomit. All Daniel Wise could make out as he grabbed his son was "Dead. They're all dead."

Eventually the nightmares subsided, although they never disappeared. How long the family remained at the mountaintop farm has been lost to the years. Daniel Wise never received any compensation from the U.S. Government for damages to his property as a result of the battle. The unlucky man, whose name will forever be associated with the Battle at Fox's Gap, died in 1876 and is buried in the Middletown Reformed Cemetery. The fate of his children is unknown.

The Wise cabin, unprotected and unregistered as a historical site, was suddenly and inexplicably torn down by a new owner in 1919. The well had already been filled in. And no, it is not a grave. The Confederate bodies were removed soon after Daniel Wise reclaimed his cabin. But I imagine the Wise family drew their water from the nearest spring—however far they had to walk.

Four years after Daniel Wise's death, the 21st Massachusetts Infantry, a unit that had fought at Fox's Gap, published a regimental history. In it, they accused Daniel Wise of dumping the Confederate bodies down his own well. The unfounded accusation became a part of the several legends that sprang from the Battle of South Mountain. But the dead tell no tales . . .

The Appalachian Trail Conference now owns the site where Daniel Wise's cabin stood, as well as the field just to the north. Here, the untested, raw recruits of the 17th Michigan Infantry Regiment, only two weeks in uniform, received their baptism of fire as they charged across open ground with a single purpose, to dislodge Confederate Brigadier Thomas Drayton's brigade from behind the stone wall that shielded the gray purveyors of death. History decrees that this field forever be known as the 17th Michigan Field.

The ten acres directly south of the 17th Michigan Field contains Wise's Field and the solemn stone memorials to fallen heroes. Here, desperate men of the 45th Pennsylvania labored northward through a wall of steel to help their beleaguered comrades from Michigan—and suffered more casualties than in any other battle in which the unit fought during the Civil War. This ground is now owned by the CMHL.

The Appalachian Trail skirts these fields that have seen enough violence and bloodshed to outlast mankind's imagination. The Trail brushes the north edge of the 17th Michigan Field.

The National Pike (also called Boonsboro Road by local residents), over which most of McClellan's army passed through Turner's Gap on the way to Sharpsburg, was a major artery connecting Frederick and Hagerstown by way of Boonsboro. It is now known as U.S. Highway Alternate 40.

Today, the big draw at Turners Gap is the Old South Mountain Inn, for tourists and hikers alike, for the Appalachian Trail goes right past. And if you choose your day (the Inn is closed on Mondays) you can sit in the grand dining room and feast on such delicacies as Duck Mousse Pate with Hazelnuts, or even sink your teeth into a brace of quail—while you ponder the history that clings to the place like a coating of very old dust.

Oh, by the way, the Inn's Maryland Crab Cakes are simply mind-boggling!

*   *   *

A platter laden with South Mountain's bountiful past would not be complete without a thumbnail sketch of the Dahlgren family, who built the quaint chapel in Turners Gap that sits by the edge of the Appalachian Trail, across the road from the Old South Mountain Inn.

John Adolphus Bernard Dalgren was born in 1809 at Philadelphia, the son of the Swedish Consul. He never wanted to be anything other than a blue water sailor. After being turned down as a midshipman, he persevered and entered the United States Navy in 1825. Young Dahlgren sailed the seven seas until1847, at which time he was promoted to lieutenant and assigned to the U.S. Navy Yard in Washington D.C. He rolled up his sleeves and went to work to upgrade the Navy's outmoded weaponry.

He first established an ordnance work shop (later designated the Navy Gun Factory). Then over the next few years, Dahlgren invented bronze boat guns, rifled guns, and most notably, a class of cast-iron smooth bore "Dahlgren" guns that had a most unusual "soda bottle shape" because of the heavily reinforced area at the butt end. His 11-inch Dahlgren smoothbores became the standard armament on U.S. warships.

During his time at the Navy Yard, "Commander" Dahlgren (success brings promotions) became a close friend and confidant of Abraham Lincoln, whose natural curiosity led him to such out-of-the-way places. So when the war began, Commander Dahlgren was promoted to captain and on the President's recommendation given command of the Navy Yard. The following year he became the commander of the Navy Department's new Bureau of Ordnance.

But dissatisfied and frustrated with the bureaucratic bull dooey that came with the job—and the enemies he had a tendency to make in high places—Dahlgren prevailed on the President to help him escape the Washington morass in which he was drowning. In 1863, his sympathetic friend had him promoted to rear admiral and assigned to the prestigious position of Commander, South Atlantic Blockading Squadron, which had the task of blockading Charleston Harbor.

Unfortunately, although his courage was never called into question, the admiral got snagged in the flubbed campaign to capture Charleston, and his reputation suffered. He continued to lead the squadron for two years and aided in Sherman's capture of Savannah, but he never climbed any further up the rank structure. After the war, he served respectively as commanding officer of the South Pacific Squadron, the Bureau of Ordnance, and the Washington Navy Yard. Rear Admiral Dahlgren died there in 1870.

His excellent work at the Bureau of Ordnance earned him the title of "Father of United States Naval Ordnance." As a further, albeit belated, tribute, Dahlgren Hall at the United States Naval Academy and Dahlgren, Virginia, home of the Naval Surface Warfare Center, were named in his honor.

Sarah Madeline Goddard, daughter of Ohio Senator Samuel Vinton, awoke one morning in 1862 to find herself a war widow. When the war ended, she married Admiral John Dahlgren, himself a widower with two children (one deceased, the victim of Kil-Calvary's ill-fated raid on Richmond). The couple lived in Washington—when the Admiral wasn't at sea—and theie union prospered. The couple had three more children.

When the Admiral died, the wealthy widow assuaged her grief by writing several works, among them *Memoirs of Admiral Dahlgren*, and by immersing herself in missionary work, which eventually led her to Turner's Gap and Mountain House. A devout Catholic, in 1881 Mrs. Dahlgren decided to build a chapel across the road from her home.

The result was a picturesque church built of native stone quarried from the hill behind Mountain House. Rare stained-glass windows and an altar of white marble imported from Italy reflected the love and faith of its benefactor. And when the 400-pound bell tolled in the belfry, believers donned their

Sunday best and came to worship at "The Chapel of St. Joseph of the Sacred Heart of Jesus" with the gracious lady.

Madeline Vinton Goddard Dahlgren died in 1898 and was interred in the church's crypt with other family members. (However, in 1959 her body was exhumed and re-interred at St. Michael's Catholic Church in Poplar Springs, Maryland.)

Between 1922 and 1925, the Sisters of the Holy Cross at Notre Dame owned the chapel and used it as a summer retreat. The property was returned to the Dahlgren family in that year, but it remained vacant until 1960, when Joseph Griffin purchased it. The latest owner, the Central Maryland Heritage League (CMHL), is in the process of restoring the chapel to a condition approaching its former elegance. Equally important, the organization has also given the chapel something it has always lacked—protected status as a registered historical site.

(Note: A more famous Dahlgren Chapel exists on the campus of Georgetown University. John Vinton Dahlgren, the surviving son of Madeline and John senior, was a member of the Georgetown class of 1889. He and his wife, Elizabeth, had this chapel built in memory of their son, Joseph, who died in infancy. It has also claimed a small moment in the limelight. The facade that beautifies the building's front was the setting for a ritual desecration in the movie, *The Exorcist*.)

In October 2004, the CMHL held a raffle for a painting donated by world-famed artist P. Buckley Moss in order to raise funds for a new slate roof. And if you feel the need to kneel before the marble altar—or the urge to exchange nuptial vows in the quaint church—it can be done. Just call the CMHL. Of course, they would appreciate a donation!

*   *   *

One wonders what might have happened if a copy of Lee's Special Orders 191 hadn't gone astray. McClellan would probably have reacted too late to stop the Army of Northern Virginia from invading Pennsylvania. Once there, Lee might have won a significant battle on northern ground of his own choosing, which most likely would have ultimately led to the Confederacy's recognition as an independent nation. Certainly the battles of South Mountain and Antietam would not have occurred. Nor would President Lincoln have had the "perceived" victory of Antietam, which he used to launch the great Emancipation Proclamation. And likely there would have been no epic tragedy among the rolling fields at Gettysburg.

But then, the sorriest game in town is "What If."

Lastly, to my readers, if I have gotten carried away in my recounting of the history of South Mountain—especially the digressions—I apologize. Yet, this ground along the long spine of South Mountain is surely hallowed, as much so as Gettysburg, or the Alamo, or USS Oklahoma in her watery grave, or the crumbled rubble of a Marine Barracks in distant war-torn Lebanon.

In the gaps of South Mountain, all is now peaceful, as befits sacred soil. The guns have done their gruesome work and are now relics in musty museums. Brutalized flesh and bones have long since been removed, and the birds again fill the air with melodious chirping.

Were it not for the distant metallic grinding noises of a nation at work, which snakes upward into the solitude like a poisonous adder, one might hear the phantasmal whispering admonitions of restless spirits that stand eternal vigilance in the high gaps: *Remember, the butcher's bill must always be paid.*

Lest we forget . . .

Chapter Twenty-five

A Case of One-upmanship

T he Alter Ego tried to lay the blame on yours truly, but it was really his hissy-fit. In fact, the whole rotten night at Dahlgren Back Pack Campground (1990) that had brought on the miseries camped on his doorstep, not mine. The jerk had tried to save a couple of ounces by shipping a perfectly good weatherproof tent home and "making do" with a skimpy tarp not much larger than a belly dancer's thong. To make matters worse, the idiot didn't know a granny knot from a square knot, which caused the whole blamed contraption he called a shelter to collapse during a humdinger of a thunderstorm. Damned wonder I didn't drown, no thanks to him.

But one good thing did come out of that sordid affair.

As soon as it was light enough to see, "we" stuffed the tangled muddy mess into the backpack and walked away from the mucky hell. The rain tapered off to a drizzle and soon stopped, and before long the sun began to tease me with a few hints that it just might come out of its hidey-hole and play. An hour or so later, the Trail turned onto a paved road, which was barred by iron stiles and a sign forbidding entrance to "Washington Monument State Park" until visiting hours began—at least another hour, if my watch hadn't drowned in last night's melee. *Danged long way from Washington, D.C., to have a state park for old Georgie,* I remarked to "Old Fumble Fingers," but he was still hanging onto his hissy-fit and giving me the silent treatment. *Well, that sign surely doesn't apply to thru-hikers.* No reply. Screw him! I squeezed through a narrow opening to the stile's right and continued up the deserted road.

A right pretty place, even in the depressing early morning dampness of a day that couldn't make up its mind what it wanted to do. The road wound upward and soon passed a low cottage. As I sneaked past, feeling like a trespasser, a loud bang from a slammed door announced the resident park ranger, who walked outside and watched as I passed by. All the while he eyeballed me suspiciously, as if I were fixing to make off with the vending machine that stood near the bathroom building.

The weird stone structure squatted beside the "Trail."

I rearranged my features into a reasonable imitation of flippant innocence and pointed to my backpack. "Thru-hiker," I called. His grim-faced silence was enough to scare me from pushing my luck, so I bypassed the restroom, which contained the ultimate luxury of thru-hikers—a real "john." I could feel his steely gaze eating into my back until I finally passed around a bend.

The good thing? Actually, there were two. By the time I reached the crest, the sun had pushed the clouds away, bathing everything with its golden rays, including a weird-looking stone structure that squatted beside the Trail. I pondered the bottle-shaped tower, then read the prominent marble tablet: "Erected in memory of Washington; July 4th, 1827 by the Citizens of Boonsboro." *Now this is strange, Model-T,* I mumbled. *I didn't know Georgie Boy had any famous relatives.*

The Dorkhead was still in high mute, which was okay with me. Curious, I took off my pack and went inside. A stone circular staircase led up to an observation deck. Neat! I went up for a look-see and caught my breath, struck speechless by the sheer magnitude of earth and space that stretched nearly to infinity. After I could drink in no more, I descended to the tower's tiny stoop and cooked grits (the other "good thing"). And then out of the clear blue, as I stirred the grits to just the right consistency, Model-T decided to end his sulking.

Nice view, huh? I budged a little. *Sure is.* I sampled a spoonful. Almost perfect. Came the next salvo. *Think it'll rain again today?* I squirted a big glob of squeeze margarine into the pot and stirred it in. *Maybe, but not likely.* I took another taste. *You have'n grits?* What a dumb question. It almost tied his stupid tent trick. *Yep.* He was over his hissy-fit. The power of grits!

(For a somewhat slanted account of that miserable night, read pages 340-346 of *Walkin' on the Happy Side of Misery.* But beware. The Alter Ego put a heck of a spin on the truth.)

*   *   *

The stone tower where I had eaten breakfast that soggy Saturday morning on the last day of June 1990 has a history almost as turbulent as the thunderstorm of that previous evening. But to get the whole picture, one has to ramble a bit.

Along about 1788, two brothers, George and William—cut from the same restless cloth as their more famous cousin, Daniel—broke off from the Boone clan in Pennsylvania and sought less settled surroundings with their families. Holding high ambitions, they acquired some land in the unsettled valley at the western base of Maryland's South Mountain, near the route that

General Braddock's army had followed some thirty years earlier when they marched west to fight the French. The Boone brothers named their holdings "Boones Berry." ("Berry" was an old English word for "citadel," later "estate.")

Around 1792, in hopes of attracting others to the isolated wilderness, the brothers set aside two tracts, which they called "Beale's Chance" and "Fellowship," and they laid out a town in one-half acre parcels. Then they pulled out the cash box and waited for people to come.

They did, and soon the brothers were faced with a small dilemma: What to name the fledgling village. The men flipped a shilling and George won. Hence, "Margaretsville," named after his wife, Margaret, claimed a place on the map of "Terra Maria"—Mary Land. Somewhere along the way, Margaretsville became Margaret Boone's Ville, but that proved too much of a mouthful. So around 1805 the town fathers voted to change the name to honor their founders and came up with Boons Borough. (For some reason the "e" became a literary casualty.)

The next metamorphosis came in 1841, when the town's newspaper editor found he couldn't fit "Boonsborough" into the paper's masthead. He immediately saw what had to be done. "Boons'boro" fit perfectly. The no-nonsense residents, most with good parsimonious Yankee genes, soon realized they could save time and effort by doing away with the apostrophe altogether. With no place left to cut, "Boonsboro" stuck.

The good folks of Boonsboro had a special affection for the "Father of Their Country." After all, young George Washington had surveyed the route that would eventually become the National Road when he passed through the area with General Braddock. And after his presidency had ended, George Washington had strongly lobbied the Jefferson Administration for a road to open up the western part of the new nation to settlement, including the small village of Boonsboro. Said a prominent businessman, "We should do something to honor this great man," and others echoed his wish.

At 7 A.M. on July 4, 1827, all of the village residents who were able—about five hundred—gathered in the public square. The mayor aroused the people with a stirring speech about the grand service rendered by the great leader on their behalf. When the last jubilant huzzahs had melted into the sweltering heat, the fifers began to fill the air with lilting tunes. Then with "Old Glory" waving to the beat of drums, the crowd marched two miles to the top of South Mountain where a one-acre plot had been purchased—selected for its close proximity to the blue-tinted granite rocks needed for the business at hand. The people rolled up their sleeves and went to work, stopping only for a short dedication service at noon, followed by a quick lunch.

When work ended at 4 P.M., the townsfolk had erected a stone tower fifteen feet high on a circular base fifty-four feet in circumference. The mayor read "The Declaration of Independence" and three aging Revolutionary War veterans fired off a three round salute from the tower's top. Plans were made to raise the tower an additional fifteen feet after the "busy season" was finished in the fall, which they did.

Thus came into being the country's first "monument." It also became the nation's first monument to George Washington—much to the chagrin of the good citizens of Baltimore, a world away to the east.

In spite of its isolated location, the Washington Monument became a popular place for picnics and romantic pursuits—and as an instrument of war. Union forces used the tower as a signal platform during the battles of South Mountain and Antietam. But the remoteness of the site proved the monument's downfall, for it also became a haunt for vandals, who took great pleasure in prying the granite stones loose and rolling them down the steep slope. In time, the structure was reduced to a pile of rubble, and the patriotic residents of Boonsboro threw up their arms in disgust.

By 1882, members of the Boonsboro Odd Fellows Lodge had taken all they could of whining complaints by irate residents about the desecrated memorial. Armed with determination—and dollars arm-twisted from the loudest of the complainers—the Odd Fellows rebuilt the monument and went one better. They capped the structure with a canopy and built a road to the site so folks could keep an eye out for no-gooders. But watchful eyes couldn't deter the massive crack that developed in the wall during the next decade, and the Washington Monument again toppled to the ground.

And there it lay for the next twenty-odd years.

In 1920, the Washington County Historical Society purchased the one-acre plot. Came the Great Depression, and a wonderful opportunity in the guise of the Civilian Conservation Corps. In 1934, the land was deeded to the State of Maryland for a state park. The CCC, always on the lookout for good projects, ordered their boys to South Mountain. They anchored the original cornerstone and raised the tower to its former height. With a final touch, the workers set into place a copy of the first marble tablet, which had disappeared years before.

The Washington Monument received its third dedication on July 4, 1936, 109 years after the determined citizens of Boonsboro had marched up the mountain to honor the great American.

(The original one-acre plot has now grown to 108 acres, lovingly nurtured by the Friends of Washington Monument State Park, formed in 1993 to help with the Park's support. As with their other projects, the CCC built the monument to last. Today it stands like a rock, impervious to insult and injury.)

The National Road was authorized by a heavily lobbied Congress in 1806, during Jefferson's presidency, and became the first road to be built with Federal funds. Actual construction began in 1811 and continued until the 1830s, when funds ran out. By then it had reached Vandalia in central Illinois.

Unable to feed the monster they had created, Congress transferred ownership of the road to the individual states through which it passed (which were in worse financial shape than the Federal Government). By 1870, the National Road had become an embarrassment. The states, having learned a lesson in financial irresponsibility from the United States Congress, relegated responsibility for the road to the many counties through which it passed, which spelled the pot-holed road's doom.

All but abandoned, the National Road languished at the mercy of financially strapped counties, until Henry Ford began pumping black Model-T's out of his factory in smoke-choked Detroit by the thousands. America opened her arms to a new form of transportation. And the National Road received a reprieve.

*   *   *

The one-upmanship? The residents of Baltimore couldn't believe what one of their own, just back from an overnight trip to Hagerstown, was claiming. Boonsboro had erected a monument in honor of President George Washington! Tiny insignificant Boonsboro—really not much more than a hole in the road! The structure was only about thirty feet high! But nonetheless, it was a monument.

Heavy thunderstorms had forced the stagecoach passengers to spend the night at Boonsboro's dilapidated hotel, and the man had heard some of the local residents bragging about the town's achievement. "Preposterous," Baltimore's mayor yelled when the rumor reached his office. He promptly commissioned a delegation of three prominent citizens to investigate and report back with all haste!

Two days later the harried appointees returned with hangdog looks and told the mayor, "It's true, Yer Honor. Boonsboro's got themselves a monument to George Washington. It's only a little thing, no taller than a ship's mast. But by gads, they beat us to the draw." The mayor glared at the purveyors of bad news as if they were responsible for the blight on Baltimore's good name and spat, "Well now, we'll just see about that." And he summarily dismissed the men with an imperious wave of his honorable hand.

The source of the mayor's irritation? Baltimore's city fathers had come up with the idea of a majestic monument to George Washington in 1809, only ten years after the leader's death. They had promptly petitioned the Maryland General Assembly for the right to hold a lottery to raise $100,000 for the monument. Then the monument's managers offered a $500 prize for the best design. Robert Mills, an architect from Charleston, South Carolina, submitted the most grand (and expensive) plan, which the managers selected with the mayor's blessing.

With funds in hand and a design on the drawing board, construction began in 1815. A crowd of 30,000 assembled at the work site and witnessed the cornerstone being laid. By 1826, most of the work had been completed, except for the magnificent statuary of George Washington dressed as a Roman warrior in a horse-drawn chariot, which Mills had designed to cap the high tower.

The grandiose monument had already cost double the planned $100,000, so the apoplectic mayor ordered the harried managers to come up with something less expensive. They finally commissioned Italian sculptor, Enrico Causici, who had sculpted several of the panels in the Capitol's Rotunda, to complete the job. Causici's design depicted George Washington resigning his commission as Commander-in-Chief of the Continental Army in 1783—most apropos, as the United States Congress had temporarily sat in the senate chambers of the Maryland State House in Annapolis at that time.

Then came the upsetting news that Baltimore had been "out-monumented" by little Boonsboro.

It would take another two years for Causici to complete the sculpture, and for the multi-ton sixteen-foot tall resemblance of Washington to be raised to the top of Mills' 162-foot tower. At the formal dedication on November 25, 1829, the mayor beamed as he bragged to the governor, "We got ourselves the first *architectural* monument in the United States."

No one mentioned Boonsboro's "first monument"; in fact, the town's name was taboo in the city chambers for some time.

Baltimore's Washington Monument rose above everything else, jutting 178 feet into the smog-filled air and giving the citizens—at least those willing to climb the tower's 228 steps—a birds-eye view of their part of "Terra Maria."

Baltimore's awesome monument created a national sensation. "Shame!" screamed the residents of the Nation's capital. "Two monuments to the illustrious American for whom our city is named, and we have done nothing. Shame!"

Four years later, in 1833, a group of influential Washingtonians formed the Washington National Monument Society and began to raise money. Taking a lesson from their neighbor, in 1836 the organization solicited designs from America's leading architects. It took a while, but nine years later the Monument Society, seduced by Robert Mills' remarkable talent, chose his magnificent design—an obelisk over 500 feet high, which would become the world's highest freestanding structure.

In true Mills' style, the architect added an ornate statuary of Washington driving a chariot pulled by Arabian stallions. (If at first you don't succeed . . .) As the *piece de resistance*, he included a large Greek temple with abundant colonnades. (Alas, no cigar for Mills. "Too costly," the power brokers quipped, and that part got scratched.)

By 1848, the Monument Society had collected $230,000 and work began with a patriotic July Fourth dedication of the cornerstone. (The cornerstone contains a time capsule with memorabilia of the city in the 1840s, along with notes on the Washington family history, some coins, and a Bible—surely a thorn in the butt of today's "Separation of Church and State" extremists.)

The project stalled in 1854 at a height of 153 feet, first over controversy caused when Pope Pius IX donated a papal stone, then by the looming political turbulence of a nation about to be divided, which led to apathy for the project. Contributions dried up and vandals practiced their vile trade on the abandoned eyesore.

Came the Civil War, then a decade of recovery, during which residents cringed with embarrassment every time they looked at the uncompleted structure. Again, cries of "shame" punctured the tranquility of early evening as strollers passed the White House. The outcry reached into the deepest corridors of the Capitol, and the legislators heard. Congress dug into the (seemingly) endless coffers of the US Treasury and appropriated funds to complete the monument.

Work resumed in 1876, this time by the US Army Corps of Engineers—a fitting undertaking as the country celebrated its first centennial. The Washington National Monument was formally dedicated on February 21, 1885, the day before Washington's birthday.

The final cost of the 90,854-ton structure came in at $1,817,710. But at $3,272 per linear foot, the 555' 5 ½" high obelisk was a bargain. And unlike the other Washington Monuments, this one provides a choice: The visitor can either climb the 896 steps to the top or zoom up in a flat sixty seconds.

One-upmanship now rests at the top of the magnificent obelisk's dome. But just like the song from *Oklahoma*, "It's gone about as fer as it can go" . . .

*   *   *

Should you find yourself lingering at the base of the "first" Washington Monument some sunny day, cast your eyes skyward and you just might get a glimpse of a hawk, or a bald eagle—even a golden eagle. The odds are stacked in your favor.

During selected months of the year, "birders" come to count those rare coursers of the heavens. In the fall months of 2004, they counted well over 2000 hawks of varied species, along with forty-seven bald eagles and nine golden eagles. Not too shabby for a narrow section of Maryland sky.

And chances are, if the timing is right, you'll be able to sink your pearly whites in an apple or two. Washington County grows some 400,000 bushels of the delicious fruit. A hiker's dream!

Chapter Twenty-six

To Perdition and Back

T he intent was noble, albeit tinged with greed. But history hounds would be among the first to validate the old cliché: "The road to Perdition is paved with good intentions." For the new Republic, wracked by growing pains and stretch marks, had a ravenous appetite and cried to be fed. Lumber, iron, and coal—essentials of the industrial food chain—topped the grocery list.

Heeding the wails of the hungry nation, powerful men of purpose stepped forward, anxious to nurture the Democratic miracle their forebears had created. So what if vast profits, generated by facile brains that were driven by unleashed ambitions, gilded the pockets of the nurturers in the process? New jobs would be created; the standard of living would rise. Everyone would benefit. And America would become a world power to be reckoned with!

So honorable *noblesse oblige* knelt at the throne of almighty *cause celebre.*

The appetite was horrific. By the 1880s, over 30,000 sawmills were ripping magnificent chestnuts and oaks into coarse boards to assuage the country's cravings. (In the East, armies of axe-wielding men had already been hard at it for decades, reducing whole forests to cordwood to make charcoal for coke-starved iron furnaces.) A few forward-thinking individuals looked at the pillaged forests and began to voice their concerns. "Not to worry," countered the timber barons. "There's trees enough to last for generations to come. And hells bells, they *do* grow back."

The worriers had no argument against *that* truism, so they shrugged their shoulders and returned to their silent vigil.

The timber barons had spoken the truth—up to a point. The trees did last for generations—two—and they did grow back, but not in the braggarts' lifetimes. By 1900, South Mountain, like many of its kin, was little more than an eroded, obscene blemish that defiled Pennsylvania's pastoral landscape. (Shades of Virginia's Iron Mountain!)

Farmers, seduced by promises of easy money—the sugary drooling that dripped from the slick tongues of unscrupulous front men—grasped their thirty pieces of silver and secretly gloated at how they had outfoxed those dumb city slickers. Then after the lumberjacks had descended like a pestilent nightmare and ravaged the land, reality struck like a thunderbolt. The money was long spent; the land wasted. Nothing was left but erosion and desolation. Good solid men who had owned their mountain domains since the Revolutionary War wilted before the accusing eyes of bewildered wives and sought refuge in John Barleycorn's siren song of bliss.

But came the moment of truth, as it always does. Property taxes, like death, are mankind's lot. When they came due, such folks had little choice but to abandon their farms. Likewise, timber corporations that owned huge tracts of pillaged land found it more advantageous to abandon holdings than to pay property taxes. So the cast-off property—some *four million* acres—was sold at sheriffs' auctions, often for as little as two dollars an acre.

By 1885, Perdition reigned supreme on the disfigured mountains of William Penn's woods, and a shocked population rent their clothes and cried for absolution.

*   *   *

The stone iron blast furnaces did their share to help Perdition ascend its nefarious throne. Mind-boggling, the enormous quantities of lumber and iron needed to supply the growing country. Absolutely necessary, but the nation paid a dire price for its progress. No controls, no measures to reforest or reclaim the land. In effect, a blank check was handed to an industry in chaos.

On South Mountain the raping started early, way back on July 23, 1762, when Samuel Pope received an original land grant of 137 acres. Pope didn't keep the property for long. Three months later he conveyed the land to George Stevenson, Robert Thornburg, and John Arthur, who wanted to build a blast iron furnace there. The hematite was rich and plentiful; lots of money could be made.

For the next few years the furnace turned out cast iron plates for stoves and kettleware, even made firearms for the American Revolution. But the profits had to be split three ways, which made for slim pickings, and eventually the furnace owners faced bankruptcy. So when Michael Ege offered to buy the ironworks at the price set by Court-appointed referees—15,565 pounds sterling—the trio jumped at the chance to get out from under.

Michael Ege hailed from a long line of ironmasters. When his father died, Michael and his brother were raised by one of the great ironmasters of the time, their uncle, Baron Henry Steigle, who owned the Elizabeth Furnace in Lancaster County, Pennsylvania, and became the first manufacturer of glassware in the United States. So Michael Ege took to Pine Grove Furnace like a blowfly to an outhouse.

Before long, the ambitious ironmaster had acquired two other furnaces. And when Michael died in 1815, his eldest son, Peter, inherited Pine Grove Furnace. (Second son George received the Mt. Holly Iron Works and daughter Mary got Cumberland Furnace.) Like father; like son. Peter immediately went to work amassing more land and furnaces. But, as befitted the owner of a major iron works, he first built himself a stately brick English Tudor Mansion. (Peter's mansion is today's American Youth Hostel at Pine Grove Furnace State Park. It sits right beside the Appalachian Trail and is a favorite drop zone for passing hikers.)

By the time the Panic of 1837 sent the financial world into a tailspin, Peter had added Laurel Forge, which could turn the pig iron from his Pine Grove blast furnace into malleable wrought iron, and some 35,000 acres of timber-rich land to his small empire. But trapped by the Panic, overextended and deeply in debt, Peter was forced into bankruptcy.

At a sheriff's sale the following year, thirty-seven year-old Frederick Watts and his partner, Charles Penrose, bought the ironworks at Pine Grove for $52,000. By 1843, Penrose had had enough and sold his share to Watts. (When Frederick Watts died, or how long he retained ownership of Pine Grove Furnace, is submerged in mildewed books in dank library basements; but it is known that his grandson William Watts, lawyer and medical doctor, inherited one-half interest. Indications are that he eventually became sole owner.)

Came a period of stability and prosperity for the furnace in 1864 when a group of investors bought the property from William Watts and formed the South Mountain Iron Company. The principal investor in the company was Jay Cooke, who carved his niche in the history books by creating the radical concept of selling war bonds—which financed the lion's share of the Union's cost for the Civil War. (In 1873, Cooke found himself deep in debt and declared bankruptcy, which created a financial panic so severe that it took the Federal Government nine years to recover.)

South Mountain Iron Company, anxious to make some big bucks, mortgaged the property to the Cumberland Valley Railroad Company for funding to build a connector railroad from Pine Grove to the Cumberland Valley Railroad. Came a slump in iron demand though, which prevented the Company from meeting its mortgage obligations, and in 1877 the mortgagor foreclosed.

By now the Furnace old-timers knew the routine only too well. Another sale! However, this time the sheriff got a break, for the dirty deed was done by the Merchants Exchange in Philadelphia. Jackson Fuller bought the Furnace for one hundred dollars, subject to the liens against the property; and Thomas Kennedy paid $10,000 for the old railroad and its franchise.

Enter Jay Cooke again—forgiven for past transgressions—along with his son Jay, Jr., and several other investors. They incorporated as the South Mountain Mining and Iron Company and bought the furnace from Fuller. The new owners gave the old furnace a facelift, heightening the stack, installing a steam hoist to raise raw ore to the top, and replacing the old water wheel-turned bellows with one that was steam operated. Most important, new technology made it possible to mix anthracite coal with coke without reducing the quality of the pig iron, which kept the furnace glowing when coke became scarce. Efficiency bred efficiency, and soon the Corporation had three ore mines connected by railroads and a fuel source of 25,000 acres of prime woodland.

In 1883, Pine Grove Furnace tapped out 6,000 tons of iron. Easy profit for the owners, but a dog's life—or worse—for those who dug the rouge-colored hematite ore. A shifty lot who had to be controlled with an iron fist, wholly irresponsible and mostly a bunch of drunken brawlers, according to Horace Keefer, who served as superintendent of the South Mountain Mining and Iron Company. But it's a proven fact of life that you get what you pay for.

So it was with the ore diggers. They worked eleven hours a day for eight cents an hour. The furnace's Company Store provided everything and ran a tab, which became a noose around the workers' necks, for they never made enough to clear the books. Like their black lung brothers in the anthracite fields off to the west, they "owed their souls to the Company Store." The only ways out of the quagmire: Pray that the company would go bankrupt; become so ornery mean that the Company would flog the miscreant and run him off; or die.

But progress, always indiscriminate, breeds on itself. With expanding technology came the Bessemer furnace with its cheaper output, which spelled doom for the stone blast furnaces. Pine Grove Furnace went "out of blast" in 1895, ending 131 years of iron making on South Mountain. A good thing, too, for South Mountain had become balder than a turtle's noggin.

In 1913, South Mountain Mining and Iron Company sold the defunct works to the Commonwealth of Pennsylvania, along with 17,000 acres of forest that remained. Most of the acreage became part of the Michaux State Forest, but enough was set aside to create the Pine Grove Furnace State Park.

Some of the historic buildings still stand: The Ironmasters Mansion, as previously stated, is now an AYH Hostel and caters mostly to the hiker crowd. The old company store, just inside the Park, sells half-gallon cartons of ice cream to grungy thru-hikers who seek to fill their bellies and scratch their egos simultaneously. A hiker thingy, becoming a member of the famed "Half Gallon Club." You've got to eat it all at once, and "fastest eater" is a title hard sought after.

The gristmill became the Visitors Center. The old ore quarry is now Fuller Lake—swimmers welcome, but beware. The edge drops off to an eighty-foot abyss, and the water down there is reported to be ice cold!

And the old furnace, which gave the Park its reason to exist? It squats close beside the Appalachian Trail, patiently waiting for an ironmaster's lit match.

*   *   *

Unlike its elderly neighbor some twenty miles to the north, Caledonia Furnace suffered an early death, felled by the terrible swift sword of retribution against its owner, Thaddeus Stevens—lawyer, senator, *provocateur*, abolitionist zealot, and master of political hardball. Quite a resume, but historians have unleashed a litany of unsavory adjectives, enough to fill a small Thesaurus, to describe his irascible, somewhat eccentric behavior and his post-Civil War legacy.

(Of late, historians have softened the adjectival lambasting and elevated Stevens from "grim-faced executioner of Lincoln's Reconstruction plan" to "a more prosaic figure . . . exerting little influence." Reader's choice.)

I'm ashamed to admit that I had it all wrong from the "get-go." In 1990, when I first hiked into Caledonia State Park and laid eyes on the quaint building and the sign that let me know I was looking at Thaddeus Steven's Blacksmith Shop, my first thought was: *I didn't realize he was a blacksmith.* The next fleeting rush of brain activity came on the heels of that admission: *Now let's see. Thaddeus Stevens. Wasn't he one of those free blacks who shared the advocacy pulpit with Frederick Douglass?*

Boy, was I a mixed bag of fluff! But in my defense I have to plead partial insanity, having been mightily distracted by the yells of people at play in the Park's *swimming pool*, which had just come into view! Visions of ice cream sandwiches, hot dogs, and thousands of gallons of clear, cool water, just waiting to pleasure my sweaty carcass! Need I say more . . .

But back to Thaddeus Stevens.

*   *   *

"We are surely cursed by God," Joshua Stevens moaned to his wife when he first cast eyes on his second born son. Only minutes before, the aged midwife had cleansed the infant and wrapped him in a clean gingham blanket before gently tucking him in his mother's arms. Quickly, the wrinkled crone left the accursed house afflicted with the "Mark of the Devil" before some of the "curse" rubbed off on her. As she walked, the midwife shuddered and wondered what atrocious secret sin the Stevens must have committed that would bring down the powerful wrath of the Almighty on their heads.

The mother, Sarah, drained by the ordeal she had just endured, wept silently and averted eyes filled with guilt from her husband's shocked face. "First a son with two clubfeet, and now this one also," the man groaned as the tears began. He frantically searched his mind for past sins, anything so enormous that might have brought about such a disaster. But even as the tears flowed, a secret part of him rejoiced that this son only had one clubfoot. The babe's older brother had two!

So amidst guilty anguish and recriminations and bearing the "Mark of the Devil," Thaddeus Stevens arrived into the world on April 4, 1792, in the small Episcopalian village of Danville, Vermont.

Joshua Stevens, the father, took to the bottle, unable to cope with his guilt—whatever it was—and soon became the village sot and chief flunky. He took to long absences and finally abandoned the family when clubfooted Thaddeus was a young adolescent. In a magnificent gesture to his family, the man managed to get himself killed in the War of 1812.

On the other hand, Sarah Stevens was a dedicated mother. Although the family lived in abject poverty on a small farm outside Danville, she knew that the only hope for her two clubfooted boys lay in a good education. The stalwart, determined mother took in washing and cleaned up others messes, and somehow scraped up enough money to enroll them in nearby one-room Peacham Academy.

Thaddeus had most everything going against him—frail, poor, a "limper," unattractive—and the kids teased him mercilessly. But the lad showed remarkable resilience against the taunting. And he had brains!

A miracle, given his adversities, but in time the lad made it to Dartmouth College. More hard times followed the luckless student through the hallowed halls, though. A sad fact, but Thaddeus was poor, the poorest student at Dartmouth, and never had enough money for the books he needed. Nor did he have the time, money, or desire to socialize with his rich classmates. As a result, his superb intellect and self-esteem suffered from the constant snubbing and ridiculing.

The ultimate insult came when Phi Beta Kappa, an honors fraternity, showed him the door when he attempted to become a pledge. A bitter pill to swallow, this public humiliation, which burned a huge hole in his ego. The "political" Stevens would ever after resent secret fraternities and lodges and become a staunch anti-Mason—the worst enemy of the Masonic order before or since, some say. But he did graduate from Dartmouth in 1814.

Stevens tried to better his luck in far off Pennsylvania, teaching in a one-room schoolhouse at York while he studied law in the evenings. Again his brilliant brain served him well. He passed the Bar in one year and hung out his shingle in the modest borough of Gettysburg, where he became an overnight success. During his first year as a lawyer, he successfully argued nine of ten cases before the Pennsylvania Supreme Court, an unprecedented feat, which brought him success and fame. And the money followed, lots of it; enough to have him recorded one year as Gettysburg's highest taxpayer. He even accumulated enough money to buy his sainted mother a 250-acre farm and fourteen cows. (An act that gave him "great satisfaction," Stevens once remarked. I wonder, though, for that's a hefty bit of work for an old lady to tackle!)

And like any wise investor, the lawyer diversified. He decided to dabble in stone blast furnaces, even built one over in Adams County in partnership with James Paxton, which he named "Caledonia" after his home county in Vermont.

Thaddeus Stevens was a virtual two-legged paradox. He entered the political arena in 1833 when he was elected to the Pennsylvania House of Representatives, riding in on the coattails of the popular Anti-Mason ticket. During his tenure over the next nine years, Stevens would be cast as villain and hero, sometimes in the same paragraph of whichever newspaper had him in its sights. The bulldogged Anti-Mason led a witch-hunt against Pennsylvania's freemasons, scattering them like dry leaves in a strong breeze.

Yet, he single-handedly saved the state's fledgling public education system from being abolished. He used his position to advance his business interests, bribed newspaper editors, and may have manipulated elections. He fought (and lost) a bitter battle against his adopted state over the right of black males to vote.

In 1839 the Anti-Mason party fell in disfavor, and with it went the dynamic Stevens. Out of power, outcast and shunned, he was soon out of money. When his term expired, he quietly left the Pennsylvania political arena. His nose had been bloodied and his character impugned, but his indomitable spirit yearned for more. The fifty-year-old ex-public servant shrugged off the public humiliation and swallowed the bitter bile of failure; then he set his jaw and moved to Lancaster in search of better days.

At first they came slowly, like tentative steps on an ice-coated pond. He had managed to hang onto enough of his busted bankroll to buy a lot with two rundown houses for $4,000 at a sheriff's sale. He moved into the better of the two, rented the other, and then he went looking for a housekeeper.

His search led him to the Gettysburg doorstep of Lydia Hamilton Smith, a mulatto with two small children. Stevens convinced her that she would profit from the position, so she moved to "Old Thad's House," as the locals had taken to calling it. Of course, the henny-cluckers in deeply religious Lancaster had a field day with the delicious rumors of sexual impropriety that spread like wildfire. A bachelor and a widow living under the same roof!

(Stevens and his housekeeper ignored the malicious whispers, and Lydia Smith remained at her position until his death over twenty years later. To the end he insisted that she be addressed as Mrs. Smith, and he left the loyal widow $5,000 in his will.)

Then the better days came in a rush. "Old Thad" may have suffered a political death, but there was nothing wrong with his fine lawyer's brain. Like a phoenix rising from acrid ashes, he soon had the local lawyers and courts cowed with his legal razzle-dazzle, and gold began to flow into his coffers again.

Then came the big break. In 1848, he again tossed his hat into the political ring, campaigning for the U.S. House of Representatives—and won! Congressman Stevens took his seat and promptly found a new mission in life: Take on the slave-dealing South. He quickly learned the Washington game of dirty politics and back room dealing, which served him well in pushing his radical anti-slavery agenda.

But his views were too far right for the gentle folk of Lancaster County, and he lost his bid for reelection. Biding his time, the aging lawyer dusted off his shingle and then settled into his Lancaster home—and waited.

The wait took six years. As rumors of coming war over threats of Secession spread across the land and smothered men's minds like an odious wet blanket, talk of political subjugation to "slave power" and domination by Southern aristocrats infected conversations throughout the North. Suddenly "Old Thad's" radical anti-slavery rhetoric didn't seem so far fetched.

In the election of 1858, he was swept along on a ground swell of public indignation (not to mention considerable back room finagling with the new powerful anti-slavery Republican Party). Voters deposited him once again on the floor of the U. S. House of Representatives, which had become a malevolent breeding ground for radicalism—just Steven's cup of tea! He soon became the leader of a faction known as the Radicals, hard core warmongers whose members scoffed at compromise with Secession and ached to place their collective boots on the long neck of the Confederacy. Moreover, he became a vexing thorn in the presidential butt of the newly arrived rail-splitter from Illinois.

Stevens, the quintessential devil's advocate, detested Mr. Lincoln's "malice toward none and charity for all" approach to Reconstruction. Stevens wanted to defrock the Southern aristocracy, redistribute the wealth, and give each black man a mule and forty acres. It didn't fly. The leader of the Radicals would have gladly sought to impeach the Great Emancipator if he could have gotten away with it. Instead, he bit his tongue and flexed his muscles as Chairman of the powerful Ways and Means Committee.

As much as he detested Mr. Lincoln, Stevens abhorred Andrew Johnson. (When the Republican Party named Johnson, a Democrat from Tennessee, as candidate for Vice President on Lincoln's re-election ticket in 1864, Stevens asked, "Why Johnson? Couldn't the party find a candidate without going down into one of those damned rebel provinces to pick one up?")

After Mr. Lincoln's assassination, the querulous old man didn't hesitate to launch impeachment proceedings (greased with a slathering of trumped-up charges, as it turns out) against the new president when Johnson tried to continue Lincoln's plan of benevolent forgiveness. The impeachment failed by a single vote, but the damage had been done. Johnson's wings were clipped and his power base demolished.

Stevens was so ill during the impeachment trial that he had to be carried into the House chambers on a bed. Bitter to the end, he decried his life's work in a gasping deathbed groan of self-condemnation, just weeks after Johnson's acquittal: "My life has been a failure."

But had it?

The brilliant lawyer and political strategist drafted the Thirteenth (officially abolishing slavery) and Fourteenth (equal rights of citizens) Amendments and pushed for their ratification. As his wealth increased, he became a philanthropist, giving to the needy and defending many blacks in court, always *pro bono*. (When he died, over $100,000 in notes for unpaid loans, owed him by those he had helped, were found among his personal effects.) Stevens had standing orders with his personal physician and cobbler that any deprived or disabled

WALKIN' WITH THE GHOST WHISPERERS 261

child they encountered was to be helped and the bill sent to him. When slack markets turned his iron furnaces into financial liabilities, as they frequently did, he absorbed the losses rather than lay off his workers.

The dying congressman's last act reinforced all that he had said and done in his many attacks on the inequality of man: He arranged to be buried in Lancaster's Schreiner Cemetery, the only one in his adopted home town that allowed blacks to be interred with whites. The epitaph inscribed on his gravestone, in his own words: "I repose in this quiet and secluded spot . . . that I might illustrate in my death . . . equality of man."

Villain, slick-tongued scoundrel, or American hero? Marked by the "devil"? An enigma, for sure. One thing he was not, though, and that was a *blacksmith*.

Stevens' Caledonia Furnace had the misfortune to be at the wrong place at the wrong time. Early in the summer of 1863, "Bobby" Lee convinced Jeff Davis that an invasion into Pennsylvania would take some of the pressure off of besieged Vicksburg and tempt Joe Hooker's Union army to fight a decisive battle on northern soil—where Lee would surely prevail and gain great glory for the South. As soon as the Army of Northern Virginia marched across the Mason-Dixon Line, Lee zeroed in on the outspoken Yankee who was planning the destruction of his homeland, namely one Thaddeus Stevens who just happened to own an ironworks on nearby South Mountain.

Came the order down the line: Destroy Thaddeus Stevens' Caledonia Furnace. The official reason—destruction of a site that produced iron for the Yankees. But some close to the General whispered that it was a vendetta, a payback for "Old Thad's" abolitionist fomenting tirades against the South.

On a sultry afternoon in early June 1863, a young cavalry officer and his troop rode into the Caledonia Ironworks and carried out the orders. When they left, the furnace lay in ruins and buildings blazed, and the terrified workers had scattered into the woods. The furnace died a swift death—as did the young officer who carried out the order. Less than a month later at Gettysburg he was killed by a well-placed Yankee bullet. (One would like to think that the bullet didn't come from iron produced at the Caledonia Furnace.)

After the battle, the fields at Gettysburg were so overrun with casualties that the able carried the wounded to makeshift field hospitals in the pastures at Caledonia. (Today, children romp and play in these same fields, now part of Caledonia State Park, blissfully unaware of the gruesome events that unfolded a century and a half earlier.)

The property changed hands several times after Stevens's death, but the furnace remained in ruins. In 1902, the Commonwealth of Pennsylvania acquired the property and leased it to the Chambersburg and Gettysburg Trolley Company, which built a trolley to Caledonia and added amusement rides to attract people. (A prime example of *If you build it they will come.*) The Commonwealth designated the site a state park in 1903. In 1927, the Pennsylvania Alpine Club brought a modicum of historical respectability to the Park by rebuilding the stack of the original furnace on a reduced scale.

The crowds continue to flock to Caledonia State Park, the most visited and oldest of Pennsylvania's operating state parks. (Those in the "know" will say I have committed a *faux pas,* but not so. I concede that the *very first* was Valley Forge, designated a state park in 1893; but it is now a national historic site administered by the National Park Service.)

All in all, I think "Old Thad" would have been pleased with the end result of his Caledonia Furnace—all things considered.

*   *   *

The means to escape from Perdition's clutches was already being set into place long before the harsh rasping of crosscut saws began to violate the gentle peace of the high mountains, in the form of one André Michaux. In the late 1700s, he came from France to the Blue Ridge's South Mountain in search of botanical treasures. The dauntless explorer departed with specimens galore, but he left behind a precious legacy, albeit unforeseen, which eventually became a knife that sliced away the steely tentacles of Perdition and penetrated its ugly heart.

Michaux's official title was "King's Botanist," a Court appointment awarded the Frenchman by King Louis XVI for "botanical services" rendered to France. The King then dispatched Michaux to America to search for trees that might be suitable to restore France's war-depleted forests. The King made a good choice in Michaux, for the man had a green thumb larger than the head of a twelve-pound sledgehammer and a remarkable eye for the unusual.

The King's Botanist, along with his 15-year-old son, Francois, journeyed deep into the American frontier. (Michaux's young wife had died in childbirth.) Father and son climbed some of the highest peaks in search of new plants, including Grandfather and Roan Mountains. Along the way he made friends with another intrepid explorer, William Bartram; even exchanged seeds and notes and followed several of the routes taken by the great man. Later, after an ambitious exploration of the Hudson Bay region in Canada, Michaux proposed to statesman Thomas Jefferson that he, Michaux, and his son undertake an exploration of the great Missouri River to its source.

In fact, Jefferson drew up a contract; however, France got in a huff so Michaux withdrew from the proposal. (A decade later, when Jefferson, now president, commissioned Lewis and Clark to explore the Missouri, he dusted off the same proposal that had been submitted by Michaux and used it as the basis for a new plan. The Michaux contract is now on display at the American Philosophical Society in Philadelphia. It is unique in that it bears the signatures of President George Washington and the men who would be the next three successors to the presidency.)

Among Michaux's several discoveries as he tromped through the Blue Ridge were the Bigleaf Magnolia, the Catawba Rhododendron, and Ginseng, which he recognized as having some medicinal value. He taught mountaineers about the worth of the plant's roots and unwittingly became the "father" of a mountain enterprise that flourishes today. In return for the generous hospitality of his host country, Michaux introduced several rare plants into the United States, including the mimosa, crape myrtle, and camellia.

With his personal funds exhausted (the King's Botanist hadn't been paid in seven years), in 1796 he returned to France. A dark cloud seemed to float above his penniless ears, for the ship, swamped by a fierce gale, was driven aground on the Dutch coast. Michaux nearly drowned and most of his notes and specimens were lost or severely damaged. The bedraggled botanist stepped onto French soil to find his ungrateful King and the King's extravagant wife, Queen Antoinette, already rotting in their graves, their heads snipped off by the Revolution's guillotine.

More bad luck waited. Michaux discovered that the Queen had given many of the rare specimens he had sent to France to her father, the Emperor of Austria. Further, although the new Republic's administrators acclaimed his work, they had no intention of honoring the disgraced King's promise to pay. The only bright spot: He was reunited with Francois, whom he had sent back to France several years earlier.

Financially ruined, Michaux placed his few remaining specimens in a Paris museum and set about writing two books about his travels and discoveries. But he couldn't support himself and abandoned the nearly finished drafts when, in 1800, an opportunity arose to accompany an expedition to the Spice Islands in the South Pacific. After an argument with the ship's captain, the botanist left the expedition at Madagascar to study the copious flora on the large island. In the middle of his exploration, he died from malaria.

As sometimes happens, a man becomes larger in death. When word reached France that Michaux had died, his colleagues eulogized him. Someone even suggested that a statue be erected, but the effort died a quick death from apathy. No matter, for in his absence his drafts had been completed and published. (They still whet the appetites of botanists all over the planet—a lasting memorial to the great man.)

Francois followed in his father's footsteps and returned to America, where he became a celebrated botanist and author of the first comprehensive work on North American trees, *The SYLVA of North America.*

André Michaux's name is forever attached to hundreds of plants that grace the trails where he once walked—and where we now hike.

*   *   *

At last came the day that André Michaux's legacy to South Mountain, the way back from Perdition, would bear fruit.

John T. Rothrock was a man of many talents: Botanist, Union cavalry officer (who was seriously wounded at Fredericksburg), medical doctor, university professor, and a "mover and shaker." Equally important, he was dedicated to the reclamation of Pennsylvania's four million acres of ruined landscape that had been pillaged by uncontrolled timber barons.

In 1877, when Dr. Rothrock taught botany at the University of Pennsylvania, he was selected to give a series of lectures on "forestry," based on the three volumes authored by André Michaux and his son, Francois. These lectures, highly prized, became known as the Michaux Lectures and covered various aspects of forestry. Professor Rothrock's rousing call to action endeared him to conservationists throughout the state, indeed the country. Over and over he thundered at his audience, until the words were engraved in the convolutions of spellbound brains, ". . . unless we reforest, Pennsylvania highlands will wash into the oceans."

The governor heard, and in 1895 he appointed Dr. Rothrock as Commissioner of Pennsylvania's spanking new State Forestry Commission. Over the next several years, the indefatigable "forester" acquired some 500,000 acres of despoiled Pennsylvania landscape. Through a vigorous program of reforestation, he turned vast tracts into sylvan islands of recreational pleasure and protected forests. It came as no surprise that among the first of the State Forestry Reservations (later called State Forests) he established was the Michaux Forestry Reservation, a tribute to the remarkable man whom he so admired.

When Dr. Rothrock resigned from the State Forestry Commission at age eighty in 1914, trees again graced the mountains. Their beauty lent credence to Joyce Kilmer's newly penned poem with its hauntingly beautiful words, "I think that I shall never see, a poem as lovely as a tree." (Kilmer wrote the poem in February 1913. The young poet, only thirty-two, was killed in France during WWI.)

Largely through Rothrock's untiring labor, Pennsylvania had a system of state forests and parks unequaled in the country, and over two million acres of Commonwealth land had been reclaimed. Little wonder that he earned the title, "Father of Pennsylvania Forestry," especially since he never professed to be a "forester."

Perhaps he should also be remembered as the "knight in shining armor who slew the evil dragon, Perdition."

*   *   *

Nowadays, Michaux State Forest is a rip-roaring 86,000-acre tourist Mecca, crisscrossed by hiking trails, including the Appalachian Trail, which runs along the entire longitudinal axis, and is home to Caledonia and Pine Grove Furnace State Parks. And just off the A.T., barely a mile south of Pine Grove, a hiker can sink his teeth (or should I say booties) into more of South Mountain's vivid history—that is, if a few briars and an occasional rattler doesn't put a damper on the enthusiasm.

Case in point: The A.T. kisses the north edge of old Civilian Conservation Corps (CCC) Camp, No. S-51—one of 113 such camps in Pennsylvania during the early 1930s. So what if you've got to do a little bushwacking to see the sights? A lot of history there, and the trip is worth the effort—in spite of the wiggly thingys.

Or, you can read all about it right here!

Camp S-51 was a child of the Great Depression, born in a flash of inspiration from Franklin D. Roosevelt's harried brain. America floundered in deep water. Its destitute masses huddled in soup lines or rode the rails to any place the trains slowed enough to let them make a safe exit. No jobs, millions out of work. The obvious answer, really a no brainer: Make jobs; put the people back to work. Someone, probably a former Marine, suggested, "We could set up boot camps and run 'em just like the Marines do." An afterthought, "Just the young'uns though. The old geezers couldn't stand the heat."

So the CCC was born. Unmarried males between the ages of 18 and 25 (later 17 and 23) were eligible for six-month "tours," which could be extended for up to two years. The "recruits" came dressed in rags and hungry. Their benevolent "Uncle" gave them all the food they could eat, a place to sleep, a uniform, and $30.00 a month (of which most was sent home to needy parents). The United States Army ran the camps in true military fashion. Up at 6 A.M.; breakfast at 6:30; by 7:15 trucks were loaded, and then came the bellowed order, "Move'em out."

Experienced civilians acted as "supervisors" . . . lunch on the job . . . return to camp at 4 P.M. for cleanup and inspection, followed by dinner . . . at dusk, the lowering of Old Glory. Then came free time until "lights out" at 10 P.M. Each camp typically consisted of 200 "boys" and staff, and a small village-worth of buildings.

Camp S-51, the first in Pennsylvania, began in May 1933 when a group of "boys" from Philadelphia disembarked at the Pine Grove station. They lived in railroad coaches until they had cleared enough area on the old Bunker Hill Farm, acquired by the State years earlier, to set up tents, which proved unpleasant and dangerous.

(Early on, lightning struck a tent during a thunderstorm and killed two men. The bolt fused the coins in one victim's pocket into a solid ball, and for years it remained in the District Forester's office. It may still be there for all I know, a grim reminder of Nature's fury.)

Sturdy buildings were finished by Christmas and the CCC'ers moved into their permanent home, which soon became known as Camp Michaux. The "boys" fought forest fires, reforested barren land, and built roads, buildings, picnic areas with swimming pools, campgrounds, and a plethora of state parks. There wasn't anything the CCC boys couldn't—or wouldn't—tackle!

And talk about camp entertainment! One of the favorite pastimes, a contest of sorts with a money prize, called for the "boys" to assemble in a long line at the base of a nearby mountain and proceed to the summit—in search of *snakes!* Rattlers, copperheads, blacksnakes, rat snakes, even rattleheadedcoppermoccasins; it didn't matter. Cash on the barrelhead for each snake, dead or alive, plus the winner got a bonus. Although the "contestants" caught thousands of the wrigglers, they missed a passel. When a rock fence that extended down the mountain and through the camp was removed, thousands of snakes slithered out of the cracks. (Serpent offspring still infest the rocky crevices of this area, so watch your step!)

When wobbly bombs decorated with "Rising Sun" emblems rained down on Pearl Harbor on a sunny Sunday morning in December 1941, the CCC boys exchanged their uniforms for military garb, traded their axes and hammers for M-1s and bayonets, and went off to war. Camp Michaux soon had a new name—and new tenants.

Camp Pine Grove, formerly Camp Michaux, was one of the country's best kept secrets, rivaling the super hush-hush Manhattan Project, a smokescreen name given to the nearly impossible task of making the atomic bomb. Even the International Red Cross didn't know about the camp; it didn't officially exist. Activated in May 1943 and officially known as Pine Grove Prisoner of War Camp, it had a single purpose: To act as a triage station for POWs who might possess information that could significantly aid the war effort.

As part of the process, Nazi extremists were identified and sent to special holding camps where they couldn't inflame or intimidate the regular POW population. Separate the chaff from the grain; send the "no-nothings" on to regular POW camps and sneak the "got-somethings" into Camp Hunt, Virginia, one of the country's two Strategic Defense Interrogation Centers, where their brains could be picked dry by interrogators who knew all the tricks.

Camp Pine Grove hired no civilians (too risky) and only used carefully screened soldiers as guards for the 2000-odd prisoners that filled the camp at any given time. Only about twenty percent showed any promise for future interrogation, and the weeding out process was a "fly by the seat of the britches" operation, taking anywhere from a few days to several months, depending on how tough a nut they had to crack. But the interrogators at Camp Pine Grove had a few tricks up their sleeves.

Although unconfirmed, the rumor persists about a German Naval officer who had dug in his heels and refused to cooperate. One of the interrogators found out that the officer had a thirst for good American whiskey. Forthwith, the obstinate German was placed in a cell with another prisoner, along with two bottles of good Jack Daniels Tennessee bourbon. Soon, the words gushed from his loosened tongue, and the ceiling Dictaphone recorded everything. A few days later, a German submarine pen—its exact location a closely held secret by the Third Reich—was bombed to rubble. One for the home team!

Another rumor, also unconfirmed, claimed the inventor of the German "buzz" bomb was a "guest" of the camp for a while.

A question comes to mind: Did the interrogators use force? Probably, for POWs had an insufferable dread of the Camp's "sweat box." But no one escaped over the six-foot high fence that surrounded the camp, nor was any POW shot during the Camp's brief history. Really quite remarkable, since there were 2,803 escapes from the various POW camps across the United States. Fifty-six prisoners were shot during escape attempts, of which thirty-four died.

After six years, on May 7, 1945, Germany's "reign of a thousand years" came to a wretched end in an underground bunker in Berlin. Japan's war mongers followed suite three months later, when the end result of the Manhattan Project—two strange looking bombs—rained down unimaginable horror on a defeated people. The world rejoiced and plowshares once again replaced swords, and America's fighting machine was dismantled.

Camp Pine Grove closed in May 1946, an obsolete trinket best forgotten, a victim of its secret past and best left to the snakes.

A year later, members of the Presbyterian and Evangelical and Reformed Churches signed a ten-year lease for the old POW camp, whereby they agreed to pay the Commonwealth $600 per year and keep the buildings and grounds in good shape. So Camp Pine Grove got a facelift and again became Camp Michaux, with Church Camp added to define its new status. Briars were cut, buildings repaired, and the snakes evicted.

For twenty-five years children came in the summertime to frolic, swim, sneak first kisses behind the leaders' backs, and learn Christian moral values. But "Progress" has a way of bringing an end to idyllic pleasures, and in 1972 the property reverted to the Commonwealth. The buildings were torn down, fences removed, and Camp Michaux, the late Camp Pine Grove, returned to the wild—much to the delight of the rattleheadedcoppermoccasins and an occasional disoriented bear.

*   *   *

It's all gone now, except for the remnants of rocky foundations and what remains of an old stone barn, which probably dates back to Revolutionary War days. (Hessian prisoners captured at the Battle of Trenton may have been used to build the barn.) If you look closely, you might see the foundation of the high guard tower that stood in the POW camp's center.

But the forest is quickly reclaiming its own. Not a bad thing, really, because *Perdition* is always *Out There*, always looking for a way back!

Chapter Twenty-seven

The Dark Side

July 6, 1990: Thelma Marks Memorial Shelter, circa 1960. It wasn't much to look at, the old log derelict with its rusty tin roof and the ridiculously high stone fire pit, nearly as tall as the sagging shelter floor— because hikers just kept adding rocks to the sides over the years instead of removing the ashes. Typical! And what of the rat-gnawed, tilted floor that had served as a graffiti board for thirty years of hiker vulgarity? The whole thing was an obscene relic that should have been pushed over the side of the mountain years ago, in my humble opinion.

I almost didn't stay. As it turned out, I wish I hadn't. I sneaked a quick glance at my tattered Timex—nearly 7:30 PM—and studied the encroaching shadows, which had been pushed by the low sun to near-impossible lengths. The Alter Ego sneered at my hesitation. *C'mon Ace, Duncannon's only four more miles. A quick hour's hike if we hustle, then it's the Doyle Hotel, beer, bath, and real food. Put it in high gear and let's get outta here.*

Tempting, but I'd left Boiling Springs at 5:30 AM and had come nearly twenty-three miles to get within striking distance to meet Skate and Eco-Warrior at the Doyle for breakfast at 8 AM the next morning. Several days ago we had made plans to meet there in case we got separated, which we had. I gave the battered floor another look and grimaced. But I didn't have any juice left for a four-mile rush to town. *No way, Jose. A fool's journey. Two hours at best, and we'd most likely break a leg in the dark. Besides, we've already got the beer.*

Gospel truth, we did! I'd found a plastic grocery bag hanging on a tree limb at a road crossing several miles back. Inside was the last can of what had begun the day as a full six pack, along with a short handwritten note from Lagunatic (a 1989 thru-hiker now on a video project that involved thru-hikers and their experiences). The scribbled note told thru-hikers to ". . . enjoy, but pack out your trash." I had grabbed that baby off the tree, bag, note, and beer, and made it disappear inside my pack quicker than a magician could hide a trick rabbit inside his tuxedo jacket. Oh yes!

I pacified Model-T by taking the beer down the steep trail to the spring so it could cool while we ate supper. I dipped water out of the shallow pool, filling both bottles, and then placed the shiny can in the icy water. That's when I first felt the "eyes."

Pinpricks needled my back, causing me to shiver in spite of the heat. I peered into the thick scrub that surrounded the spring and searched the shadows for the source of this sixth sense, which had suddenly raised the goose bumps and triggered the uneasy feeling of being watched. *No Mosby ghosts this far north,* I mumbled, wracking my brain for anything else that might have caused any phantasmagoric wavelengths to linger.

But the forest refused to reveal any secrets, wouldn't even give up a bird's chirp. I grabbed the water bottles—and the beer—and hurried back up the hill to the safety of the shelter. I'd drink the stuff warm before making a trip back to the spring and whatever lurked there, imagined or not. Model-T's petulant comment, *Big bad-ass Marine scaredy-cat's gonna drink it hot,* rankled; but he could shove it.

The uneasy feeling persisted while I ate. After supper, I sat at the edge of the shelter and watched the thickening blackness smother the remaining light while I drank the prized beer. But the fizz seemed to stick in my throat, just one continuous gag as the lukewarm bitterness wrecked havoc with my taste buds. Determined and slightly nauseated, I finally got the vile stuff down. Came the inevitable burp, followed by the feeling that somehow I had been shortchanged. *Damn nasty stuff,* I remarked, which opened the door for Model-T to start with his cockamamie taunting about my manhood and intelligence.

Turning a deaf ear to his blathering, I stomped the can into a misshapen disk. *Dribblebrain,* I muttered, determined to have the last word, but he couldn't let it be. *Snorkledick,* came the retort. Snorkledick? I bit my tongue and crawled beneath the mosquito net, and relinquished the night to "whatever" owned the unseen eyes, the irrational entity that transcended rational dimensions and managed to fracture the peaceful evening and keep sleep at bay.

The "whatever" didn't sleep either. Several times during the endless night I heard "things" rustling in the bushes behind the shelter, strange sounds that sizzled my synapses and froze my blood. I nearly suffocated from holding my breath as I tried to hear past the blood pounding against my eardrums. As soon as dark eased into morning twilight, I packed up and got the heck out of Dodge!

In retrospect, I've often wondered if the "entity," if such a thing existed, had tried to convey a warning of impending disaster, a message that got mixed up with goose bumps and warm beer and "dimensional interference." You can be the judge.

I met Clevis and Nalgene a month later at the Kay Wood Leanto (same as a "shelter" for us boys who hail from below the Mason-Dixon Line), which sat on the edge of benign ravine a couple of miles south of Dalton, Massachusetts. Unlike Thelma Marks Memorial Shelter, this one exuded friendly vibes. It was also one of the newer type shelters and had a loft.

I had settled in and just put the water on for a pot of mac-n-cheese when they walked up to the leanto. I soon learned that Clevis was really Geoffrey (Geoff) Hood from Signal Mountain, Tennessee, and that Nalgene, his hiking partner, was Molly LaRue from Shaker Heights, Ohio. Boy friend, girl friend, I assumed, which turned out to be correct. A nice couple, even if they were southbounders.

For those of you who have led sheltered lives, a "clevis" is a pin that holds two items together, whether it be the small pins that connect the pack to a backpack frame, or a large pin that joins a pair of mules to a plow. And "Nalgene" is the brand name for wide-mouth plastic water bottles favored by most hikers.

Clevis reminded me somewhat of a young Abe Lincoln—tall, thin, prominent brow and captive eyes—except that his voice came out an octave higher than what I imagined the long ago president's might have. Nalgene, on the other hand, was semi-short, blond, and had an engaging smile that lit up her rosy cheeks. I guessed both to be in their mid-twenties. Clevis mentioned that he and Nalgene had been outdoor therapy counselors for troubled teens in Salina, Kansas, until the agency lost its grant money, which led to layoffs and opened the door for their southbound thru-hike. The couple planned to return to Kansas after they finished their hike and hopefully resume their outdoor therapy work with kids. At some point in the conversation I heard the "M" word. Well, these two were certainly made for one another!

(Years later, I would learn much more about this remarkable pair, although I wish it were otherwise!)

Clevis paused the conversation and climbed the short ladder to check out the small loft. "It'll do for us, if you don't want it." Far be it from me to intrude on blossoming romance, so I granted them proprietary rights to the loft.

Just as I started to dump the macaroni into the boiling water, a shadow fell across the entrance. Another man, this one much older and definitely not a hiker, introduced himself as Tom, the leanto's caretaker. In his grizzled hands he held a plastic bowl filled to the brim with *cold macaroni salad!*

"Kay sent it in case there were any hungry hikers up here." (The same Kay Wood, as it turned out, for whom the leanto is named. This dedicated lady, herself a "2000-miler," had hiked the entire A. T. over two summers in the late 1980s, and she lived almost within spittin' distance. That the shelter had been named for a living person attested to her firm commitment to the Trail and its hiker brood.)

Tom grinned at our wide-eyed faces. "She woulda come herself, but she had a meetin' to attend. If you want, I can leave the bowl." Was he kidding? Lickety-split, and we had that bowl cleaned spic-n-span and back in his hands. Our shouts of thanks to Tom and our benefactor followed him far beyond the shelter clearing.

Thinking back over the nearly fifteen years since we shared that delicious macaroni salad, two things stick out in my mind: First, Clevis, who spooned the salad into our three pots, took great pains to make sure the portions were equal. Second, he liked to call Nalgene "Little Mouse," used it several times as we chatted the last hours of the evening away. And when his whispered "Good night Little Mouse; sleep tight Little Mouse" and muffled giggles drifted down from the loft and floated through the soft darkness, I smiled a silent blessing on the two lovers.

The next morning I awoke early and ate a quick breakfast, anxious to get the eleven miles to Cheshire under my boots. Leaden rain clouds hung in heavy folds and distant thunder groaned promises of a nasty day for those foolish enough to be out and about. As I packed up, I heard Clevis gently murmur, "Wake up, Little Mouse." Came her sleepy retort, "Mice don't get up this early. Go away." I put on my backpack and softly called, "Have a great trip." Clevis replied, "Each day is a great trip."

As I walked away from the leanto toward the approaching storm, my trite words seemed only a hollow echo alongside his reply, so filled with life yet to be lived. I pushed the thought away and focused on Cheshire's waiting bounty. My destiny lay to the north, theirs to the south, and they were soon forgotten.

Five weeks later, at Bald Mountain Pond Shelter in Maine, everything changed. Several hikers, myself included, were rooting in our mac-n-cheese when Slim Chance, another thru-hiker, arrived from Monson, Maine, about three days to the north. Immediately he asked, "Have you heard the news about the two thru-hikers who were murdered on the Trail in Pennsylvania?" We paused, staring, waiting for more.

"Two southbounders named Clevis and Nalgene . . . at the Thelma Marks Shelter . . . the murderer still on the loose."

Slim Chance's terse words tumbled into the dank Maine soil as memories rushed in like a giant tsunami, crashing against the senses and leaving in its terrible wake the soul-searing words, *"Each day is a great trip."*

(Now our paths have again converged in the pages of this book; our destinies are once again drawn together, this time not by macaroni salad but by the written word. And Clevis' words still echo in my mind, never to be forgotten . . .)

During the next few weeks, the media had a feeding frenzy. "Facts" surrounding the murders clogged the airways and filled newsprint space ordinarily allocated to ads. Rumors spread up and down the Trail like a virulent disease, leading to wild speculation and misinformation. Terrified hikers, fearing for their lives, left the Trail for home and didn't return.

And all the while, the gruesome graphic details spat out by a frenzied media overwhelmed the real tragedy: Two lives had been abruptly extinguished as if a lighted match had been blown out in a single loud "whoosh." There would be no marriage, no children for Geoff and Molly to cuddle and nurture, no grandkids for grandparents to spoil, no rosy future, no "anything." Only the final oblivion of the grave for pretty vivacious artistic Molly and gregarious altruistic Geoff. They are surely owed more!

Geoff and Molly met in Salina, Kansas, in 1989. They hit it off right away, for both shared the same love of the Great Outdoors. Both had strode parallel paths that converged when they signed on as counselors for Passport for Adventure, a program that took teens at risk on extended camping trips and taught them self esteem, confidence, team work, and social interaction.

From the first toddler steps, wee Molly was bubbly and outgoing (as ministers' daughters often are). Early on she showed a natural bent with the crayons, and by the time she graduated from high school, Molly was an accomplished artist. Small wonder that she won a national student contest to design a U.S. postage stamp! She left her Shaker Heights, Ohio, home to attend Ohio Wesleyan University, where she earned an art teaching degree.

The vivacious artist taught in an Ohio school for a short period of time, but her love of the outdoors took her into other climes, including Outward Bound. She sought to combine her passion for teaching and wilderness adventure into one experience; hence, Passport for Adventure seemed like a God-sent opportunity.

Geoff, too, answered the call of the wilderness and eventually found his way into Outward Bound and other outdoor leadership schools. Somehow, he managed to curb his insatiable desire to head to the hills and graduated from the University of Tennessee in the late 1980s with a degree in secondary education. But according to his mother, Glenda, Geoff never expected to be confined to a classroom. "He wanted to work in nature, teaching kids. He was outdoors all the time."

So when the woodsman-cum-teacher heard about the job in Salina, Kansas, it was just his cup of tea! For Geoff (and I suspect for Molly, too), *each day was a great trip*! But sometimes life comes at you fast—too fast.

The following account of the horrific tragedy is drawn from hikers' notes, newspaper accounts, and court records:

On Tuesday, September 11, 1990, the day I reached Stratton, Maine, for a much needed "zero day," 846 trail miles off to the south in Duncannon, Pennsylvania, Clevis and Nalgene were doing likewise, luxuriating in the old Doyle Hotel's hospitality and doing hiker chores. Fifty-cent draft beer and reasonably priced food more than offset the $11.00 a day dingy threadbare rooms—no air conditioning—and the communal bathtub with its prehistoric dirt ring.

Geoff called his mother and arranged to meet for a family reunion at Harpers Ferry on September 21st, stressing for her to bring soap and brushes so that he and Molly could scrub down their packs. That evening they sat in the Doyle's tattered pub and exchanged trail talk with bartender Tim Yeoman while they enjoyed a sumptuous dinner of shrimp, fries, and mushrooms, and drank the fifty-cent beer.

At some point during the meal, they signed the "Hiker Register" that Tim kept on top of the groaning beer cooler and scoffed at the previous entry, authored by "Greenhorn," who claimed the dubious honor as last of the 1990 southbounders. Nalgene penned a rebuttal: "Hey, Greenhorn, you most certainly are not the last entry of the season. As you can't read this, we'll tell you when we catch you! As we hear it, we're about mid-slip of the south-bounders moving down. Oops. Getting food on the book. Good food; time to go. (signed) Clevis and Nalgene."

But "catching up" wasn't in the cards!

That same day, some twenty-five miles to the south, Karen Lutz, the ATC's chief administrator for the Mid-Atlantic Region, drove out of Boiling Springs, Pennsylvania, and noticed a peculiar looking hiker walking along the highway that carried the Appalachian Trail across the Cumberland Valley. (The

Trail has since been relocated off the road.) The man, outfitted in soiled baggy generic trousers and a long-sleeve shirt that appeared to come from the same dumpster, plodded along with his head down, as if he didn't want to be recognized. The small daypack on his back and two red gym bags, one tucked under each arm, labeled him as a drifter and definitely not a backpacker.

Karen dismissed the man from her thoughts until an hour later, when she spotted him again. Startled by the incongruity, she thought, *He's following the Appalachian Trail!* The drifter had followed the white blazes off the main highway and onto the side roads, exactly as the Trail did. Karen, a seasoned hiker and no stranger to spending nights alone in the backcountry, shuddered as a chill brought goose bumps. *This guy's heading for Darlington Shelter for the night!* The thought was unsettling, and she suddenly realized why. She would be absolutely terrified if she had to sleep at Darlington Shelter that night.

The sun ushered in Wednesday, September 12th, by quickly peeling away the early morning fog along the Susquehanna River. In late morning, Geoff and Molly met her elderly great-aunt and two other relatives. Lunch followed, along with a ton of trail stories, which dragged into mid-afternoon. By the time the pair had said their goodbyes and loaded their backpacks, the sun was already brushing the western horizon.

Geoff and Molly stopped to buy some munchies on the way out of town and then began the hot four-mile climb up Cove Mountain. When they reached the side trail to Thelma Marks Memorial Shelter, the deepening shadows convinced them that here would be a good place to halt for the night.

The next morning, southbound thru-hikers Brian "Biff" Bowen (a jeweler) and his wife Cindi (an elementary school teacher) hiked into Duncannon. They did chores and grabbed a pizza, and were on the way out of town by late afternoon, headed for Thelma Marks Memorial Shelter where they hoped to overtake their friends Clevis and Nalgene.

(Another friend, Gene "Flatfeet" Butcher—an Army "lifer"—had left Duncannon nearly three hours earlier, but "something" pulled him past the turnoff [the "entity"?] and he pushed on to Darlington Shelter, another seven miles to the south.)

When Biff and Cindi scrambled down the steep one hundred-yard side path, they too experienced a strange sensation. Bill felt his hackles rise as they approached the old log shelter and he told Cindi to wait while he went forward. Came a sharp gasp, followed by an anguished moan, as Bill gazed at the lifeless bodies of his friends. Horrified, the frightened hikers scrambled back up the path to seek help.

The killer didn't get far. Paul David Crews, alias Casey Horn, had assumed the role of thru-hiker and turned south on the Trail. He was soon spotted by trail maintainers and other southbounders, and the word went out. Eight days after the heinous act, National Park Service Rangers trapped Crews as he approached the middle of the pedestrian bridge that crosses the Potomac River at Harpers Ferry. The killer surrendered without a fight. He wore Clevis' boots and green backpack and carried some of his victims' personal articles. And he still packed the murder weapons, a gun and knife, both still stained with the telltale blood of Molly and Geoff.

Law enforcement agencies rolled up their sleeves and dug into Crews' past: Thirty-eight years of age . . . one of nine children from a broken home . . . most recently living under the assumed name of Casey Horn in his hometown of Lorus, South Carolina, where he worked as a farmhand. Further investigation revealed that Crews was wanted for questioning by Florida authorities in connection with the 1986 murder of a woman in that state. Crews' wife had suffered an abusive marriage and had divorced him; and he had been suicidal for the past few years. The authorities could find no record of prior convictions. A shadowy past at best!

In May 1994, after a two-week trial, Paul David Crews was found guilty of first degree murder in the deaths of Geoffrey Hood and Molly LaRue and sentenced to death by lethal injection. During the trial, a psychiatrist testified that Crews had a "schizoid personality and suffered from an organic aggressive syndrome aggravated on the day of the killings by alcohol and cocaine." Crews now languishes on "Death Row" in a Pennsylvania prison, from where he launches his dwindling appeals to delay the Commonwealth's day of reckoning.

What exactly happened at Thelma Marks Memorial Shelter in the predawn of that Thursday will probably go to the killer's grave, and he's not talking. Did Crews meet the pair in Duncannon in a roulette-type "luck of the draw" encounter and follow them to the shelter? Most likely not, for no one remembers seeing him in town. Also, he had been spotted by Karen Lutz near Boiling Springs to the south just a couple of days earlier.

Witnesses' statements during the trial seem to indicate that Crews spent the night at the shelter with Geoff and Molly and talked with them, found out that they had estimated the cost of their thru-hike at $2500 and that they were trying to overtake a fellow hiker by name of Muskratt. (Crews inserted these and other bits of information into conversations with other hikers in his attempt to pass himself off as a member of the trail community while he hiked south.)

What prompted Crews, a non-hiker as far as is known, to climb aboard a Greyhound bus, ride all night, and end up near the Appalachian Trail in

Pennsylvania? He must have had a plan or destination in mind, for his actions went beyond random impulse since he stopped at the East Berlin (Pennsylvania) Public Library and two gas stations for maps and directions to the Trail.

Schizophrenic? Yes. Drugs or alcohol involved? Probably, according to the State's psychiatrist. Would Crews have committed murder if "chance" had brought more hikers to the shelter for the night? Not likely. Guilty? You can take it to the bank!

Based on the crime scene investigation and subsequent autopsies, police speculate that Crews spent the night with Molly and Geoff and awoke in the faint light of morning twilight. He shot Geoff three times at point blank range with a revolver. According to the coroner, it took Geoff five to eight minutes to die. Crews then bound Molly's hands, raped her, and stabbed her several times. It took Molly longer—about fifteen minutes—to die.

Sometimes, it seems the frazzled cliché *Hanging's too good for that scoundrel* (or in this case, the *Commonwealth's sterile syringe*) falls short of true justice. But then, eventually the "piper" always gets paid!

July 8, 1994. I'd been dreading this stop for days, had even adjusted my schedule to avoid the possibility. No way was I going to spend the night at Thelma Marks Shelter, even if it meant reaching Duncannon in the dark! But I would risk a lunch break there, since the sun shone with optimistic radiance, hopefully bright enough to hold even the most determined "entity" at bay.

The side trail scramble down the steep slope hadn't changed. Neither had the shelter, except for the stone fire pit, which had taken another growth spurt upwards, and a picnic table that had been added off to its side—an inducement to use the shelter? No uncomfortable vibes today. Perhaps the "thing" had taken up residence elsewhere.

Relieved, I dumped my pack beside the picnic table and walked over to the shelter. The sad-sack floor hadn't changed. I looked for telltale signs of that violent morning four years ago, but the clean up had been thorough. Emboldened, I sat on the edge of the floor and let the memories tumble in. *Little Mouse, get up . . . Sleep well, Little Mouse . . . Each day is a great trip . . . .* The words, sharing space with the faint taste of cold macaroni salad, echoed inside my head. I could hear Geoff's high voice mingling with Molly's soft giggles.

I swallowed the lump in my throat and swiped a sweaty hand across the moisture that flooded my eyes. Suddenly the words came without conscious thought, unbidden, from some secret recess, piercing the silence: *You had it right, Clevis. Each day IS a great trip! And, sleep well, Little Mouse . . .*

As a rule, thru-hikers are not a picky lot. But Thelma Marks Shelter had been defiled, and hikers felt weird flopping their sleeping pads down on its tainted boards. (In 1998 I bypassed the old shelter altogether—I'd already paid my respects, been there, done that.) Only the hardiest were willing to bury their queasiness and brave the hapless shelter's spectral innards.

In September 2000, members of the Mountain Club of Maryland, who oversee this section of the Appalachian Trail, tore down the shunned shelter, dispersed forty years of ashes from the dismantled fire pit, burned the timbers, and recycled the tin roof. With the help of the Timber Framers Guild (from Becket, Massachusetts), the members had erected a new shelter a short distance away, by giving new life to timbers taken from a barn dismantled on NPS land two years earlier.

The new Cove Mountain Shelter was dedicated a month later, on October 23rd. Among the forty-odd guests attending were Molly's parents, Jim and Connie LaRue, and Geoff's mother, Glenda Hood. Guild instructor and former ATC crew leader Bob Smith delivered the dedication, of which a copy was placed in a frame joint of the new shelter. In part, it reads: "Geoff and Molly may have ended their thru-hike here, but this journey isn't ended. In the same spirit that they lived, we have built this shelter. And having finished, we continue our journey, bringing some small part of them with each of us. It is my hope that their gentle, peaceful spirits grace this place and all who pass through here."

Closure. And Amen!

(Author's note: I have written in graphic detail about the violent tragedy at Thelma Marks Memorial Shelter—perhaps more than I should. But although the crossing of our paths was brief, Geoff and Molly touched a tender spot in my heart—as they did many others. For as Bob Smith said at the shelter's dedication, ". . . we continue our journey, bringing some small part of them with each of us." I know I do.

*   *   *

As usually happens, rumors have built on rumors over the years, until some "wannabe" hikers are afraid to set foot on the Trail. Believe me, it's more dangerous to go to the local Seven-Eleven for a loaf of bread than to hike the Appalachian Trail with its bounteous adversities. In all, seven people have been murdered while hiking the Appalachian Trail, with Geoff Hood and Molly LaRue being the most recent victims.

(The 1996 deaths of Julianne "Julie" Williams and her lesbian partner, Laura "Lollie" Winans, isn't included since the incident happened *near* the Trail in the Shenandoah National Park and the pair were conducting day hikes from a stationary camp. A different "category" by ATC's accounting. Nonetheless, their attack adds to the "dark side," and I have included their account below.)

To set the record straight:

May 1974—The first recorded murder on the Appalachian Trail. Twenty-six year-old Joel Polsom, a thru-hiker from Hartsville, South Carolina, was killed in a Georgia shelter by Ralph Fox, a fugitive from Michigan. The killer turned south on the Trail and eventually caught a bus to Atlanta, where he was caught. (I was unable to find any reference to his trial or punishment.)

April 1975—Janice Balza, age 22, was killed with a hatchet at the Vandeventer Shelter in Tennessee, just north of Watauga Dam, while she ate breakfast by the fire pit. Her attacker, also a hiker and a former "tree surgeon" by name of Paul Bigley, age 51, from Tucson, Arizona, allegedly killed her for her Kelty pack, which he had taken a fancy to. He surrendered to the Carter County (Tennesse) Sheriff shortly afterwards, was tried, convicted, and subsequently died in a Nashville (Tennessee) state prison.

Janice Balzar had just graduated from the University of Wisconsin's Madison School of Nursing a month before she began her thru-hike in late February.

(In 1990, I stopped for a mid-morning break at Vandeventer Shelter. I knew of the fire pit's violent past and, on a whim, snapped a picture of it looking toward the shelter's front. In the photo, a mysterious splotch of mist is suspended at the edge of the pit. Weird!)

May 1981—In a case reminiscent of the Thelma Marks Memorial shelter murders, thru-hikers Susan Ramsey and Robert Mountford, both age 27 and from Ellsworth, Maine, were killed at the Wapiti Shelter, some twenty miles south of Pearisburg, Virginia. The killer, Randall Lee Smith, age 28, a resident of Giles County (Virginia), attacked his victims at night. He shot Robert three times in the head and then dragged Susan from the shelter, where he beat her and stabbed her over a dozen times. Smith buried his victims in shallow graves near the shelter, where they were discovered two weeks later.

Smith was caught within weeks and brought to trial in March 1982. He pleaded guilty to two (lesser) charges of second degree murder, and was sentenced to thirty years in prison. After seeking parole nine times, all of which were denied, he was released on mandatory parole on October 22, 1996. (His whereabouts at this time remain a mystery.)

Hikers immediately began to avoid the Wapiti Shelter. Eventually, the Roanoke Appalachian Trail Club built a new shelter, also called the Wapiti Shelter, a short distance away.

May 1988—Rebecca Wight, 29, from Blacksburg, Virginia, and her lesbian partner, Claudia Brenner, 31, from Ithaca, New York, were on a camping trip in Michaux State Forest when they were ambushed at their campsite by Stephen Roy Carr, a fugitive recluse who "lived" under a rock overhang in the Forest. On the morning of May 13, the second day of their vacation, the two women briefly encountered Carr twice while hiking. Frightened, that afternoon they pitched their tent in an isolated area near a stream.

Carr had stalked the hikers, and he watched from a tangle of mountain laurel as the couple set up camp. After supper, while the couple relaxed on their tent fly, which they had spread on the ground beside the stream, the killer saw his chance. From his ambush point eighty-two feet away, he fired eight bullets from his .22 caliber rifle in rapid sequence. The first shot hit Claudia in the arm. The next three slugs struck her in the face, neck, and head. Rebecca screamed for her to get down, to hide behind a nearby tree. Next, Carr turned on Rebecca, sending the next three bullets into her head and back. The eighth bullet missed.

Although Claudia was seriously wounded, Rebecca was worse. Claudia waited until she heard the killer leave and then went to aid her companion, who had lapsed to the edge of consciousness. After the initial hysteria subsided, Claudia realized that her only option was to go for help. She made Rebecca as comfortable as she could, then grabbed a map and flashlight. Propelled far beyond her normal limits by the mental picture of Rebecca lying on the ground with her life's blood oozing into the dark soil, Claudia struggled through four miles of rugged mountain wilderness, all the while terrified that the gunman was on her heels. She eventually made it to the Shippensburg Road, where two young men who happened by alerted the authorities. By the time the search party found the campsite, Rebecca had died.

The police arrested Carr ten days later. He was tried, convicted, and sentenced to life in prison, where he remains today.

*   *   *

In another bizarre case, touched on briefly in a previous paragraph, a lesbian couple was brutally murdered a half-mile from the Appalachian Trail in Virginia's Shenandoah National Park in late May 1996. Twenty-four year-old Julie Williams and her friend Lollie Winans, 26, along with their golden retriever Taj, were last seen camping in the Park on May 24th. They were discovered by Park rangers eight days later. The women had been bound, gagged, and their throats had been slit. Nothing appeared to have been stolen, and the murders had all the markings of a "hate crime." The rangers found Taj in the nearby woods, unharmed.

The FBI was called in to investigate, but the super-efficient organization, after following some 15,000 leads, failed to turn up a suspect.

Julie held a degree in geology, earned from Minnesota's Carleton College, and she planned to soon begin a research job with a Vermont firm. Lollie attended Unity College in Maine and was due to graduate that December with a degree in environmental science.

A year later, Darrell David Rice, 34, was indicted and subsequently convicted of attempting to abduct a female bicyclist in the Shenandoah National Park. (She managed to thwart his efforts to drag her into his truck, so he attempted to kill her by running her over. Authorities later found hand and leg restraints in Rice's vehicle. He entered a guilty plea and in 1998 was sentenced to 136 months—that's 11.33 years—in a Charlottesville prison, where he remains.)

While in prison, Rice began to make comments to his inmates about how he hated gays and lesbians. He even confided to his cellmate that he had killed Winans and Williams and "proved" it by revealing things known only to the authorities. The FBI began to center their case on Rice.

It took nearly six years after the slayings, but in April 2002, Rice was formally indicted on *four* counts of capital murder. (Federal law, which applies to crimes committed on National Park land, allows certain evidentiary "latitude" for hate crimes, which is lacking in conventional murder trials, so Rice was charged with two counts of capital murder for each victim.) The crime was solved at last!

So the authorities thought. The case against Rice began to unravel when the Prosecutor's forensic expert contradicted her earlier findings and stated under oath that DNA analysis of stains found on the ligatures used to bind Williams and Winans was of "male origin, excludes Rice, and most likely is that of one of the perpetrators." The stains could have been made by saliva or sweat. Additional evidence in the form of human head hairs found on glove liners and on the duct tape used to bind Winans pointed at another possibility: Serial killer Richard Evonitz, who had committed suicide in 2001 in Sarasota, Florida, as police attempted to arrest him. (The hair was "similar," but not conclusive.)

In February 2004, a Federal judge dismissed the murder charges against Rice. Still, tantalizing questions remain. How did Rice know things about the case, which he revealed to his cellmate, that hadn't been made public knowledge?

And did the forensic expert's use of "perpetrators," the plural form, indicate that two murderers might have committed the crime, of which one was Rice? The case remains open, and the families still grieve.

Need more?

How about the human skeleton found by a hiker in deep underbrush just off the Trail two miles south of Keys Gap, Virginia (Route 9), on April 22, 2001? Case pending.

And then there's the man's body that was found on May 14, 1996, stuffed inside two duffel bags and placed in a black footlocker, and left sitting in a small parking lot near the U.S. 340 bridge that crosses the Potomac River into Maryland—once the Trail's official route. (In fairness, I should explain that although the parking lot was part of the Appalachian Trail corridor in the 1980s, at the time the body was discovered the Trail had been relocated a mile or so upriver and the land transferred to the Harpers Ferry National Historical Park.)

That case was solved. Turns out it was all about Jasper Watkin's Social Security checks. Prosecutors alleged that Nancy Jean Siegel, 55, of Pikesville, Maryland, had made a career of fleecing the seventy-six year-old gentleman out of his "Uncle" handout and had knocked the old fellow in the head when he protested too loudly. She managed to continue her "career" for some time, until "Uncle" got suspicious.

*   *   *

Well, the skeletons are out of the closet and the "dark side" has been exposed to the harsh light of public scrutiny. But to put things in perspective, your odds of falling victim to violent crime on the Appalachian Trail (roughly one in fifteen million, or more) are far less than getting struck by lightning (one in three million). And if you have to drive a thousand or so miles to reach Springer Mountain, watch out! Your odds of getting killed before you even put on the pack and take that first step rises to an astounding one in forty-two thousand!

A few days ago I lay in bed and watched the local news from nearby Nashville, Tennessee. It was only Wednesday and already four homicides, seven assaults with deadly weapons, and nine robberies had happened since the previous weekend. And that didn't include two rapes, twenty-nine traffic accidents—three fatal—and a score of domestic quarrels that required police attention.

Yeah, I'll take the Trail any day, with its rattlers, stinky hikers, and the scattering of local rednecks who seem to like to party down at those high passes where the Trail crosses. Any day . . .

Chapter Twenty-eight

"Rocksylvania"

Crimminy, how long does this go on? Rocks, ga-zillions of distorted stony scales protruding from Nature's horny hide, the sharp points jabbing into the boots with each step. Tearing up the ankles, chewing up the boot soles; afraid to take my eyes off the trail for even an instant. Heck, I don't even dare to blink without stopping. Up ahead, some relief for the ankles. A pull on the nerves, though. A stretch of house-size boulders glued together in a long humpy chain through some nefarious trickery of Mother Earth. A haven for rattlers. Quid pro quo . . .

My ears pick up a faint buzzing from an unseen crevice. Another zizzing, louder, this one from the opposite side of the large boulder. Sum-a-bitch! I'm surrounded by the slithering critters! A narrow abyss, about two feet, between this snake-infested boulder and the next one. A quick glance into the shady depths and I leap across to questionable safety. How much further?

I wipe the sweat out of my eyes and push on, pounding hell out of the quartzite with my hiking stick well before I get to anything that might harbor a rattler. Gettin' pissed at this whole "Rocksylvania" deal. "Painsylvania in the ass," it should be called. Another buzzing, sounds like it's close enough to pee on—if I wanted to, which I don't—singes the stifling air. Must be close to a hundred degrees. I shudder in spite of the heat and nearly break my hiking stick as I thwack the rocks. Yeah, really gettin' pissed!

Finally, the last boulder. Back down to the blessed rock-strewn agony someone years ago diabolically designated a national scenic footpath. Ha! Old Willy Penn shoulda let the injuns keep it!

Model-T pipes up: *Quit your bitchin' and suck it up. Easy for him to say. He's only a half-ass figment superglued to my psyche. Dang'em rocks! Dang'em snakes!*

A section of the "Trail" in "Rocksylvania."

So it went off and on for well over a hundred miles, ever since I left south Pennsylvania's gentleness behind at Duncannon and climbed to the rock-clogged crest of Peters Mountain. North of the Susquehanna River, for the most part the Trail continues on top of the up-thrust layers of sharp-pointed quartzite, which define the long crests of the Blue Ridge range all the way to Delaware Water Gap. Hence, the "rocky misery" that hikers must endure—and the source of such demeaning terms as "Rocksylvania" and "Painsylvania," common derisive epithets among frustrated footsore hikers.

Thinking back now, it doesn't seem all that tough. But then, time has a way of blocking out the "bad."

Just as it dims history. And, believe me, those hardy Dutch-German pioneers who settled this area had lots more than rocks and rattlers to worry about. But first things first. Read on.

(**Warning!** I've gotten carried away with the research! More than you might ever possibly want to know: Thumbnail sketches about William Penn, his heirs, the Indian tribes with whom the whites had to deal, the Liberty Bell, the convoluted history of early Pennsylvania. Unless this kind of thing is your cup of tea . . .)

*   *   *

It began peaceful enough, even though it was "good news and bad news." After all, the name "Quaker" was synonymous with "peace," and William Penn was the top Quaker of his day. The bad news: Being a Quaker—one of the Society of Friends—in mid-1600 England's strict Anglican theocracy was a crime. Quakers were routinely incarcerated and properties confiscated. William Penn was imprisoned six times during his life.

The good news: Penn, son of an English admiral, had served as his father's naval aide in his pre-Quaker days. Through this association, young William had become a friend of the youthful Duke of York—the King's younger brother (and future King James II). Eventually this friendship would open the door for William Penn and his Quaker brethren to escape religious persecution by fleeing to the New World.

In his role of "criminal Quaker," young William soon garnered an arrest record that would have made John Dillinger take notice. At age seventeen, he got the boot from Oxford University for protesting compulsory chapel attendance and had to settle for a more tolerant French Protestant university for his education. Back in England, somewhat older and much wiser, William managed to keep his antagonistic thoughts to himself while he attended London's most prestigious law school, where he learned just enough English law to be a formidable opponent in the courts.

The "almost" barrister, working from a leveraged position, took up the cause of civil liberty and religious tolerance, and Penn's "war" began in earnest. He thumbed his short Dutch nose (he got his looks from his short-nosed Dutch mother) at the authorities and attended illegal Quaker gatherings. William Penn, Senior, the revered admiral, threw up his arms in disgust and disowned his defiant son. Young William cast himself on the mercy of his Quaker friends and survived on the crumbs of their hospitality.

In 1668, he got more than "crumbs." While staying in the Buckinghamshire home of wealthy Quaker businessman Isaac Penington, William met the man's stepdaughter, pretty Gulielma Springett. The English maiden turned the young man's life topsy-turvy, and thus began a four-year courtship. With a tender promise from Gulielma that she forever pledged her troth to his star, whether it rose high in the heavens or plunged into the murky depths of despair, Penn returned to the religious battlefield.

Emboldened, he began to attack the sacrosanct Anglican Church and even Parliament. Prison became his second home. On one occasion he became a "Guest" of the Crown for seven months in the notorious Tower of London. In general, the Quaker became a pain in the Lord Mayor of London's exalted bottom. Eventually, England's Lord Chief Justice chastised the Lord Mayor of London for falsely imprisoning Penn.

Soon after his release from the Tower in 1672, Penn and Gulielma were married. (She would bear him seven children, three of whom would live beyond infancy.)

The "war" took a different bent one day. An idea flashed into Penn's head like a brilliant lightning bolt: Why swim against the current? Why not set up a colony for Quakers in the New World! Penn went to see James' older brother, King Charles II, whose treasury owed Penn's deceased father's estate the considerable sum of 16,000 pounds in back pay. Said Penn, "Grant me a territory in the New World and I'll call it even."

Charles II viewed the request as a Godsend, a solution to the troublesome Quaker problem, even if his younger brother's friend was "one of them." But there was a problem. Nearly all the New World territory under English control had been parceled out to English nobility. There *was* one plot that lay off toward the mountains—some acreage that had been seized from the Dutch a few years earlier—but Chares I, his father, had given it to James some years back.

No problem. The King giveth; the King taketh away. So on March 4, 1681, Charles II signed a charter making William Penn "Proprietor" of a vast territory west of the Delaware River and north of Maryland. In his royal voice, the King decreed, "Let this land be hereafter known as 'Forests of Penn' in honor of your dead father who served his country so well." Nothing is free, of course, and the new Proprietor agreed to give the King two beaver pelts at the beginning of each year and a fifth of all gold and silver mined within the new territory. But all things considered, 40,000 square miles for a 16,000-pound even-steven trade wasn't a bad swap.

Thus, Pensylvania came into being.

William Penn called the new venture his "Holy Experiment"—a colony with absolute religious tolerance—and dispatched his friend William Markham to the new colony to arrange a deal with the natives to purchase southeast Pensylvania. (Although Penn was the Proprietor, he believed his grant did not override the rights of the Indians and that all land had to be properly purchased—a strange concept in the eyes of his fellow countrymen.) The new landowner kissed Gulielma farewell, quickly gathered up a shipload of Quakers, and sailed away to the New World.

When Penn stepped off the weathered deck of the *Welcome* on November 8, 1682, he found Markham waiting with the head Lenni-Lenape sachem, Tammamend, to close the land deal. The two men simply shook hands to consummate the transaction. (The sachem, Tammamend, failed to mention to Penn that the Lenni-Lenape needed the Iroquois' permission to sell land. Nonetheless, the "hand shake treaty" stood for nearly one hundred years, at which time the new republic absorbed all Penn-held lands. Voltaire described this treaty as "the one treaty with the Indians that the whites never broke.")

The Proprietor cleansed his hand with a proffered handkerchief and walked across the lush meadowland between the confluence of the Delaware and Schuylkill Rivers. He plunged his staff into the soft turf and in a loud voice proclaimed, "This shall be the site of Philadelphia, the 'City of Brotherly Love'."

As soon as Penn had set up a provisional government (with the Proprietor as governor and armed with veto power), he strode off into the wilderness to make friends with the "savages," a task at which he soon excelled.

The Proprietor of Pensylvania (as the territory became known—the additional "n" wasn't added until years later) quickly discovered two important facts about the strange dark-skinned people. First, they weren't "savages." They even had a societal pecking order and a form of government, albeit loose by

European standards. Secondly, the King's piece of paper was worthless as far as the Indians were concerned. After all, their forefathers had settled this land centuries before. But ever the diplomat when equal rights was the issue, William extended the Quaker arm of friendship and learned the dialects of the varied tribes with which he had to deal. A superb sprinter, Penn soon found that he could outdistance most braves in heated races, and his reputation grew, as did their respect for the "white father."

The Proprietor was soon negotiating for, and getting through peaceful voluntary exchanges, large tracts of land (without the aid of translators), primarily from the Lenni Lenape, whose ancestors had lived on the land long before the first white man set foot in the New World.

(The Lenni Lenape were more commonly known as "the Delaware"—a nickname associated with the large bay discovered by English explorer Samuel Argall in 1610, which he named in honor of Sir Thomas West, Third Lord de la Warr, first governor of Virginia. Governor West snubbed the honor and returned to England without ever having dipped his fingers in the waters that bear his name. The Delaware had been conquered by the Iroquois Confederation, who considered them vassals "wearing petticoats" without the right to vote in Iroquois councils or to make treaties with the Europeans.)

People persecuted for their religious beliefs flocked to the safety offered by the benignly tolerant colony with its low taxes and no conscripted army. They came in droves, war weary immigrants from Europe's bloodied fields and from Puritan New England, where Quakers were routinely flogged and pilloried in public disgrace. Came the Irish, English, Germans, Dutch, bringing with them strange dialects and customs. Came Dunkards, Huguenots, Lutherans, Mennonites, Moravians, Pietists, and Schwenkfelders, all quoting scripture from identical Bibles.

William Penn refined his political views in a document he titled "First Frame of Government," which established the framework for Pensylvania's future constitution. Happy at what he had accomplished, the Proprietor returned to England in 1684 to bolster his relationship with his old friend, the Duke of York. Four months later Charles II died, and the Duke was crowned King James II. The friendship would soon have dire consequences for Penn.

In 1688, Mary of Modena, wife of King James II, who had converted to Catholicism, produced a male heir to the throne. The news inflamed members of the "Anglican" Parliament, whom James II had thoroughly alienated by his unflinching determination to reestablish the Catholic Church in England. They pressed James to abdicate in favor of his Protestant daughter, Mary, who had married the Dutch prince, William of Orange, a grandson of Charles

I. When he refused, members of Parliament secretly invited William of Orange to "invade" England. James fled to France and his son-in-law ascended the throne as William III.

Then came a period of tribulation for William Penn, from which he never recovered. Hardly had the monarchial dust settled than Penn was (falsely) accused of treason and over the next two years was arrested three times—and quickly acquitted each time.

Meanwhile, back in his Province, matters had skewed out of control when the Three Lower Counties on the Delaware, offended by the treatment they had received from the governing body in Philadelphia, "seceded." Complaints of political unrest in the "Forests of Penn" reached the ears of William and Mary. Once again the luckless Quaker was branded a traitor by a hostile Parliament. The King stripped Penn of his governorship and gave the Governor of New York control of the domain.

For the next two years, Penn became a fugitive, hiding out in the squalid slums of London. Powerful friends interceded on Penn's behalf and finally convinced the King to allow Penn to state his case before the Privy Council. With the help of his friend John Locke, a prominent lawyer, Penn was able to clear his name, and his authority as Governor was restored, barely in time for him to rejoin his wife shortly before she died in 1694 at age 48.

Penn was crushed by her death. For two years he led a lackluster existence on the fringes of London society, a broken man. He revived somewhat when he married plain 30 year-old Hannah Callowhill, daughter of a Bristol linen draper. In 1699, he sailed again to America, this time with Hannah, who was pregnant, and their young daughter.

The Proprietor returned to find Philadelphia, now the second largest city in the New World, bustling and productive. One of Penn's first acts was to pacify the Lower Counties, still restive, by permanently separating them from the Province and giving them their own legislature. (The new territory, named Delaware, and Pennsylvania had separate legislatures, although they shared the same governor until the American Revolution.)

As a final measure of good will, Penn authored a new constitution to replace his "First Frame of Government," which established self-government and greater freedoms for the inhabitants. Worried by rumors that the Whigs sought to bring his province under Crown rule, in 1701 he hired twenty-seven year-old James Logan as Secretary of the Province and his business manager, and then he and his family packed up and returned to England. Penn would spend the remainder of his days fighting for continued independence for his Province of Pensylvania.

Then came a staggering blow. His conniving business manager in England, Philip Ford, who had embezzled large sums in his employer's absence, stole all of Penn's holdings in the New World by having his unsuspecting employer sign an innocuous piece of paper, which turned out to be a deed transferring the entire Province to Ford. The scoundrel immediately demanded Penn pay "rent" on the ill gotten holdings—an amount far beyond his ability to pay. When Ford died in 1702, his widow, Bridget, known far and wide for her cruelty, had Penn thrown into Debtor's Prison. (Talk about hard luck!) Eventually the Court declared the illegally obtained deed invalid. The old Quaker was released and his property rights restored.

But the harsh experience had taken a terrible toll, robbing the aging Quaker of his former physical vitality. William Penn never returned to the New World. Discouraged, destitute (he estimated that he had shelled out over 30,000 pounds more than he had collected in taxes to keep the Province running), Penn was weary of the whole sordid mess. He was brokering a deal to sell off his New World holdings for $60,000 when he suffered a debilitating stroke in late 1711. The deal was never finalized. For the next six years William Penn just "existed." The Proprietor of the "Forests of Penn" died on July 30, 1718.

William Penn had appointed Hannah as sole heir and "Acting Proprietor" to his estate. (The eldest son, William, from his marriage to Gulielma, contested the will but it stood.) Through James Logan, Hannah controlled the Province of Pensylvania from her home in England for fourteen years, until her death in 1726. The Proprietorship then passed to her three sons John, Thomas, and Richard, offspring of Hannah's marriage to William. But by then, the Province of Pensylvania had come of age.

The future republic's first great melting pot, Pensylvania, claimed a diverse population of 300,000—making it one of the largest colonies—and Philadelphia had become a major commercial center with nearly 18,000 residents.

On July 8, 1776, just fifty-eight years after its founder's death, the "City of Brotherly Love," basking in the light of intellectualism and stirring to the rousing cries of "liberty and justice for all," would resound with the tolling of a cracked 2080-pound bell that hung in the State House steeple. The citizenry would gather in the street to hear Colonel John Nixon read the awesome words penned on coarse hemp paper by Thomas Jefferson and affirmed by the Second Continental Congress, "We hold these truths to be self evident, that *all* men are created equal . . ."

William Penn's "Holy Experiment" would usher in the new republic.

(On November 28, 1984, President Ronald Reagan issued Proclamation 5284, granting Honorary Citizenship to William and Hannah Penn. Hannah Callowhill Penn became the first woman to be so honored. Only four other people have been awarded this esteemed honor since our nation was founded: Winston Churchill, 1963; Raoul Wallenberg, 1981; Mother Teresa, 1996; and Marquis de Lafayette, 2002.)

*   *   *

(Author's note: At the risk of straying too far from the Appalachian Trail, I feel a patriotic stirring to write a few paragraphs about the "Bell." *After all, it is a valuable part of our heritage!* Plus, it makes good fodder for a middle school report!)

The Quaker-controlled Pensylvania Assembly took seriously the admonition in Leviticus 25:10 that ". . . ye shall hallow the fiftieth year." So the officiating fathers determined that it would be most appropriate to honor their founder on the fiftieth anniversary of the "Charter of Privileges," the document that superceded Penn's "First Frame of Government" and eventually became the basis for Pennsylvania's State Constitution. The Bible-quoting Speaker of the Assembly, Isaac Norris, sent a letter to the Province's agent in London to buy a bell in the range of 2000 pounds. In his precise penmanship, Norris directed, "Let the Bell be cast by the best Workmen & examined carefully before it is Shipped with the following words well shaped in large letters round in vizt. By order of the Assembly of the Province of Pensylvania for the State House in the City of Philada 1752." The Speaker further directed that the bell have inscribed on its underneath the words from The Book of Leviticus: "Proclaim Liberty thro' all the land to all the inhabitants thereof. Levit. XXV.10."

The Province's agent, Robert Charles, placed the order with the Whitechapel Foundry. In August 1752, the *Hibernia* sailed into the Philadelphia harbor with a large bell strapped to the deck. Workmen hung the 2080-pound bell in the State House steeple the following March and tested their workmanship with a clang of the 44 ½ pound clapper against the three inch metal. To their horror, a long crack appeared.

Speaker Norris gritted his yellowed teeth and sent the cracked bell to Philadelphia foundry workers John Stow and John Pass to melt it down and give the Assembly a proper bell post haste. "The bell is too brittle," said Stow.

"That's why it cracked." Pass scratched his head and then offered, "It's an easy fix, Friend Stow. We must add more copper to soften the brittleness." After a lengthy discussion, they decided to recast the bell by adding one and a half ounces of copper per pound of bell.

When the bell went back into the belfry on March 29, 1753, the workmen again tested the bell. It didn't crack, but the pealing sounded like someone had stuffed the bell's inside with cotton. Isaac Norris pulled a few hairs out of his wig, while Stow and Pass blushed with embarrassment. "Friend Pass, I fear we added too much copper," ventured Stow.

The pair was ordered back to the foundry for another try, this time without the copper additive, for they discovered that it was the brittle nature that gave a bell its clarity. On June 11, 1753, Pass and Stow once again stood in front of the State House with Speaker Norris as workers raised the bell into the high steeple. When the clear sounds rang out, Stow and Pass puffed out their chests with rightly earned pride. But to their discomfort, the Speaker pointed an accusing finger at the foundry men and growled, "It still isn't right."

Norris sent another letter to London. "Have the Whitechapel Foundry try again." So the old bell remained in the State House belfry, a temporary fixture until a "proper" bell could replace it. When the new bell arrived from London, the Assembly members agreed that it didn't sound any better than the one already hanging in the belfry. So Norris ordered that the new Whitechapel bell be placed in the State House cupola, where it was attached to a clock to toll the hours.

Pass and Stow's State House Bell continued to serve its country well, tolling out metallic announcements of deaths and inaugurations and any other news that warranted the public's ear. On September 23, 1777, with the British Army poised on the edge of Philadelphia, officials, fearing that their bells would be melted down by the Redcoats and recast into cannons and cannonballs, took down all the bells in the city and carted them off to hiding places in other towns.

The State House Bell was hidden under the floorboards at the Zion Reformed Church in Allentown until the threat disappeared. The bell was returned the following year but could not be rehung because the State House steeple was too rotten. It lay in storage in a nearby munitions shack for seven years, until a new steeple could be built.

The State House Bell came close to becoming a puddle of molten metal. In 1799, Pensylvania moved the state capital to Lancaster but left the bell in Philadelphia. When the Commonwealth announced plans to sell the old State House to a developer who intended to raze the building and build houses, Philadelphia's citizens were furious. The city purchased the property from the Commonwealth and the bell continued to toll.

But came a day when the city council decided to reconstruct the State House steeple and replace the old bell with a new one. The city contracted with a foundry owner named John Wilbanks for a 4000-pound bell and stipulated that the old State House bell be carted away. Wilbanks failed to do so and the city sued for breach of contract. The foundry owner argued in court that the $400 hauling cost exceeded the old bell's worth. The judge decreed that Wilbanks would pay court costs, but the city would have to keep the bell, which would technically be considered "on loan" from Wilbanks.

Some residents said the first crack appeared in 1835, when the bell tolled out the news of the death of Chief Justice John Marshall, who happened to be visiting Philadelphia at the time. By 1846, when the bell rang to celebrate Washington's birthday, the fracture had grown to over two feet and further ringing was considered too risky. The bell was silenced.

Almost . . .

Taking its exalted place in history as a symbol of freedom, the Liberty Bell—as it had become known—tolled again, but only through gentle taps made by a rubber mallet. On December 31, 1926, microphones were placed around the Bell to broadcast gentle bongs as the Philadelphia mayor's wife ceremonially tapped the Bell at midnight to usher in the nation's sesquicentennial celebration for independence. And during the early 1940s, three recordings were made of a tapping of the Bell: Two were sent to radio stations for public use, and the third recording became the property of Columbia Records.

On June 6, 1944, D-Day, Philadelphia Mayor Bernard Samuel came on a coast-to-coast radio program and tapped the Liberty Bell twelve times with a rubber mallet, to signify "Independence." At the show's end, he tapped the Bell seven more times to symbolize "Liberty," and the country rejoiced at the long-awaited news of the invasion of Europe.

At 12:01 A.M. on July 4, 1976, as part of the nation's Bicentennial celebration, the Liberty Bell was moved from Independence Hall to a pavilion across the street so Americans could view the famous symbol of the freedom they enjoyed. But the Liberty Bell deserved a more fitting resting place, and on October 9, 2003, the new Liberty Bell Center in downtown Philadelphia was opened to the public.

Here, each Fourth of July, children who are descendents of the signers of the Declaration of Independence gather and symbolically tap the Liberty Bell thirteen times at exactly 2 P.M. (Eastern time) in honor of the patriots from the thirteen original colonies to whom we owe so much.

Remember Wilbank? His heirs eventually began to press the City of Philadelphia for return of the Liberty Bell, which they considered rightfully theirs. In a 1915 agreement, the family agreed to let the Bell remain "on loan" as long as it hung in Independence Hall. In 1984, another heir, James McCloskey, claimed the Bell for himself, since it had been moved to the pavilion. He wanted to display the Bell in his hometown of Baltimore, or possibly melt it down and make seven million finger rings—all cracked—and sell them for $39.95 each. His claim was denied.

No mention is made if the other heirs are satisfied with the Liberty Bell's new home, even if it violates the basic agreement.

And a parting shot: As an April Fools joke, on April 1, 1996, Taco Bell ran a full-page ad in several newspapers, including *The New York Times*, in which they claimed to have bought the Liberty Bell from the United States Government to help with the burgeoning National Debt. The company planned to rename it "The Taco Liberty Bell." The hoax backfired, leaving a lot of people with a foul taste akin to putrid refried beans in their mouths. Perhaps Taco Bell should have stuck with the talking Chihuahua . . .

*   *   *

Back to the business at hand.

Unlike their famous father, the Penn sons had no qualms about acquiring Indian lands by unscrupulous means. When John, Thomas, and Richard inherited the "Proprietorship" in 1727, they failed to inherit their father's honesty—a deficiency that ultimately led to disastrous consequences for the frontier. In 1732, James Logan summoned Thomas, the eldest Proprietor, from England to negotiate land deals with the Iroquois, who ruled the Lenni Lenape like vassals and claimed the right to conduct *all* land dealings with the whites.

Thomas, like his brothers, lived beyond his means and was deeply in debt. So when he saw an opportunity to grab off a large chunk of land from the Lenni Lenape, land that he could sell to settlers at one hundred percent profit, he leaped at the chance. Thomas enlisted the aid (innocently or otherwise— suspicions exist, though unproven) of Logan, by now one of the Province's largest land speculators, who still served the Penn family interests after thirty-six years. To assert his claim over a vast acreage in the upper Delaware and Lehigh valleys, land inhabited by the Lenni Lenape, Thomas produced a "deed" dated in 1686. The deed showed that William Penn had purchased from the Lenni Lenape all of the land west of the Delaware River and north to the Susquehanna River, "as far as a man can walk in a day and a half."

The Lenape remembered no such deed, but after a lengthy powwow the tribe agreed to honor it. After all, how far could a man walk through the tangled forests in such a short time?

Penn and Logan stacked the deck by hiring the three fastest runners in the Province, promising to reward the man who ran the farthest with five pounds sterling and five hundred acres of land. For the next two years, the runners trained while workers labored to clear a pathway through the forest that stretched beyond the Delaware River. Puzzled, the Lenape muttered among themselves at the strange ways of the white man.

On September 19, 1737, the day set for the event, the official party, which included three Lenni Lenape chiefs, looked on as the "walkers" toed a starting line drawn in the dusty street in front of the Meeting House in Wrightstown. James Logan gave a nod and the sharp report of a handgun sent the walkers *running* toward the far tree line. Immediately the Indians angrily began to protest that the men weren't walking. But Logan and the other officials turned a deaf ear.

Riders accompanied the "walkers," plying them with rum, sugar and limejuice—the first known appearance of the daiquiri on American soil—to bolster their endurance. Sol Jennings ran eighteen miles before calling it quits. He was sickly the rest of his days. James Yates made it all the way to Tobyhanna Creek, almost thirty miles, where he collapsed, blind, and died a few days later.

Twenty-seven year-old Edward Marshall continued on past the Delaware's water gap, on into the Kitttatinnny Mountains, until twelve noon on the second day, when "time" was called. Marshall had covered an astounding sixty-five miles. When Logan drew the customary right angle limits to the line of "walk," Thomas Penn had added 1200 square miles to the Penn empire. The "Walking Purchase of 1737" became known as "the day that Thomas Penn scalped the Indians."

Needless to say, the Lenape were not happy. Chief Lappawinsoe echoed the dissatisfaction in a complaint that eventually reached the King of England: ". . . the white runners should have walkt along by the River Delaware or the next Indian Path to it . . . should have walkt for a few miles and then have sat down and smokt a Pipe, and now and then have shot a Squirrel, and not have kept up the Run, Run, all day."

The King ordered an investigation, which dragged on for several years, until the principal Lenape chief, Tedyuscung, developed a strong thirst for the white man's firewater and lost interest. The investigation died a quiet death, unlike Chief Tedyuscung, who fell prey to a scheme by greedy settlers who wanted him—and all the Delawares—to leave the Wyoming Valley west of Blue Mountain, where they had been ordered to pitch their wigwams by their imperious masters, the Iroquois. Some settlers plied Tedyuscung with cheap rum, waited until he slipped into a drunken stupor, and then torched his shack. Tedyuscung woke up in the spirit world. The settlers, having tasted blood, torched the entire village, and the Delawares fled.

Logan tried to pacify the Indians by revising the property line back to the Delaware River's water gap and by setting aside a reservation of ten square miles as a hunting ground for the Lenape. But the outraged Indians, having declared the "walk" a sham, wouldn't budge. The pacifist Quaker legislature, which abhorred any form of violence, had no army and lacked the means to evict them.

But in the end the Lenni Lenape did lose. Officials bribed the Iroquois (who had conquered the Lenape and considered it the Iroquois' exclusive right to sell land to the whites) to enforce the "deed." At a meeting in Philadelphia in 1742, representatives of the Lenni Lenape tribe met with Pensylvania Governor Thomas and the Indian agent, Conrad Weiser (remember this name!), to redress their grievance. The Lenape expected the Iroquois to defend their interest. But when Chief Nutimus, who had been chosen to speak for the plaintiffs, rose to protest the "Walking Agreement," the Iroquois chief, Canasatego, silenced him with, "We conquered you. You are women, we made women of you. Give up claims to your old lands and move west. Never attempt to sell land again. Now get out."

Thus began the Lenni Lenape's long trek westward, marred by promises made and swiftly broken, which would not end until some 130 years later when they reached Oklahoma's Indian Territory.

The Lenni Lenape, stung by the violent rebuke, settled in an area west of the Lehigh Valley and shook their moccasins free of the white man's treachery. Thomas Penn and James Logan had struck a match to the fire of vengeance. It was about to blaze into a horrific conflagration!

Edward Marshall pocketed the five pounds sterling but never received his promised five hundred acres. Indians seeking revenge later slaughtered his wife and several of his children.

One hundred years later, historians examined the "deed" of 1686 and determined that the document was a forgery.

*   *   *

Enter Conrad Weiser. Born November 2, 1696, in Wurttemberg, Germany, he came to America with his Lutheran parents and settled on the New York frontier in 1709. Young Conrad lived with neighboring Mohawks for a year to learn the Iroquois language, and he became expert on the customs and tribal politics of the Six Nations—also known as the Iroquois Confederacy, which was loosely made up of Mohawks, Oneidas, Onondagas, Cayugas, Senecas, and Tuscoraras, although this last group didn't sign on until 1727.

In 1729, Weiser, now a family man of some means, left the Mohawk Valley and floated down the Susquehanna River, finally settling on a 200-acre farm in the Tulpehocken Valley (now Lebanon and Berks Counties). Within five years he had become an influential farmer, and his knowledge of Indian ways soon reached the ears of Provincial Secretary James Logan in Philadelphia. Logan appointed Weiser as the Province's Agent in Charge of Indian Affairs.

The Provincial Indian Agent quickly earned the reputation as a fair and shrewd diplomat who understood Indian customs and protocol and went out of his way to protect their interests. He developed a deep bond with the Iroquois, which would remain throughout his life. In 1737 the Iroquois named Weiser "Tarachiawagon, the Holder of the Heavens"—their highest honor—after he managed to avert war between the Iroquois and the Catawba, who were allied with Virginia. A dangerous situation, to be sure, for war between the two tribes could quickly involve white Virginia and could possibly draw Pensylvania into the conflict.

But in spite of Weiser's diplomatic band-aid, an ill wind was freshening.

Conrad Weiser had seen the handwriting on the wall a decade and a half before the fighting began. England and France had long rattled their sabers over who owned the gargantuan watersheds that drained the St. Lawrence and Mississippi Rivers. The clash of wills could be heard across the Atlantic. As early as 1741, a year before the Iroquois shamed the Lenape and drove them from their ancestral lands, Weiser wrote a letter to the Quaker legislature, in which he warned of the coming war and urged the pacifists to step down. By his thinking, and others, Pensylvania needed representatives with backboned determination who would raise a militia to defend the Province.

Naught came of the attempt, but in 1747 an influential Philadelphia newspaper owner by name of Benjamin Franklin, along with a few other concerned citizens, quietly began to form militia units without formal approval of the Quaker Assembly.

The sabers finally came out of the scabbards in 1752, when France instructed the Marquis Duquesne, governor-general of New France, to take possession of the Ohio River valley and remove any British presence. Representing the Crown, in December 1753 Virginia Governor Dinwiddie sent a twenty-one year-old militia major, George Washington, west with a letter demanding the French withdraw. The mission failed, but Washington noticed an excellent place for a fort where the Allegheny and Monongahela Rivers joined to form the Ohio River.

On Washington's recommendation, the British began to build a fort at the site, Fort Prince George; but before the walls could be raised, the French attacked. The Redcoats hightailed it back to safer ground and the French finished the fort, naming it Fort Duquesne.

The following May, Dinwiddie armed young Washington with 130 militia and sent him back to the Ohio valley with orders to kick the French out of Duquesne. En route, Washington's "army" got into a fight with fifty French soldiers and gave them a licking, killing their commander, Joseph Villier de Jumonville, in the process. However, with a superior French force hot for revenge on their heels, the young major and his men beat a hasty retreat.

On the way back to Virginia, Washington decided to call a halt and, ignoring the advice of his Mingo scouts not to stop, built a fort. The Mingo decided the white man was a fool and departed. The British flag had barely been raised above Fort Necessity when French troops arrived en masse. Washington was forced to surrender his new fort. But the French offered good terms: Commander Washington and his men would be released, but only after he signed the "terms of surrender."

Washington should have read the fine print. He unknowingly put his name to a confession for "murdering a French ambassador on a mission of peace"—to wit, Jumonville. The French government never pursued the "confession," but this incident is credited with starting the French and Indian War (although "war" wasn't officially declared until a year later, in 1756).

King George II wasn't pleased by the reports filtering in from across the water. "Sire," said the Lord Chancellor, "we must clip the wings of the French bird before it spreads its droppings throughout the New World." The king nodded his agreement, grumbling, "Incompetent rabble we have in the Colonies; else they'd take the shears to the French themselves. Very well, send Braddock."

Thus it came to pass that Major General Edward Braddock came to America in 1755 to assume command of all British forces and to put the French to rout. Armed with big plans and a small army, which included a detachment of militia commanded by Major George Washington, he led his army over South Mountain at Turners Gap, across the wide sweep of the

Great Valley, and up into the undulating hills toward Fort Duquesne at the Forks of the Ohio.

As the army slowly made its way northwestward, it toiled like a determined colony of ants, building a substantial roadway as it proceeded. The General and his men made it to within ten miles of the fort when 250 French, aided by nearly 7,000 Indian allies, attacked. Braddock had failed to heed the warnings of his own Indian scouts about the impending ambush, considering the "red man" inferior and untrustworthy. He paid dearly for his cockiness.

When the arrows stopped flying and the muskets fell silent, the British had been crushed and Braddock lay mortally wounded. Washington assumed command and wisely ordered a retreat. He had General Braddock interred beneath the roadway so that the boots and wagon wheels of the retreating army would forever hide the grave and prevent the enemy from desecrating the body.

Fort Duquesne remained as a pestilent sore in the backside of the British until the winter of 1758, when the fort was burned and abandoned by the French just before an attack by 2,000 Virginia militiamen led by twenty-five year-old *Colonel* George Washington. The British promptly built Fort Pitt on the spot.

When hostilities began, the French quickly moved to enlist the aid of the Indians. The Iroquois stood firm in their alliance with the British, while other tribes, fired up by promises of "no more Redcoats," cast their lot with the French. For the first time in centuries, the Six Nations divided their allegiance.

After General Braddock's ignominious defeat, the Lenni Lenape, a short-fused powder keg waiting for a lighted match after their rude eviction a decade earlier, sniffed the winds of war and smelled weakness in the hated white wigwams to the east. War drums echoed across the mountains as braves rushed to sharpen tomahawks and restring bows. Like angry hornets erupting from a poked nest, warriors spilled into the countryside seeking revenge. They didn't have to seek far.

The nooks and hollows that crinkled the base of Blue Mountain and gentled into the broad plains extending eastward teemed with white settlers. Prime scalps to be had; sweet vengeance waiting at the cutting edge of a tomahawk. Easier than taking wampum from a blind medicine man.

So as tomahawks began their bloody business, splitting skulls and lifting scalps with deadly indifference, a great cry went up out of the wilderness, a frantic plea for help. Frightened families abandoned homesteads and sought refuge in more densely populated areas farther east. For the only time in American history, the "frontier" moved back toward the Atlantic Ocean instead of away from it.

The cheek-turning Quaker Assembly heard the terror-stricken pleas but refused to act. After all, to the "Friends" any form of violence was considered the deadliest of sins. Much discussion filled the chambers of the State House as legislators shook their heads in wonder at what the settlers might have done to offend their red brothers. "Atone for your wrongs and make peace," they admonished. Mightily incensed at the jelly-tongued drivel that emanated from the lawmakers' mouths, the beleaguered settlers turned to another source for aid.

Benjamin Franklin was something of an enigma. By turns pamphleteer, apprentice, printer, balladeer, inventor, philosopher, politician, firefighter, family man, shopkeeper, bookseller, cartoonist, Mason, deist, part owner and publisher of the *Philadelphia Gazette,* and author of the popular *Poor Richard's Almanac,* he had caused more than a few eyebrows to raise in the Quaker-oriented Philadelphia society. Franklin had sold his share of the newspaper in 1748 (although he continued to publish *Poor Richard's Almanac* for another ten years) and put on his inventor's cap. A strange site, which caused more raised eyebrows and considerable gossip, when the citizens observed the man flying a kite during a thunderstorm on a nasty June evening in 1752!

But the man had good credentials. A member of the Pensylvania Assembly, Benjamin Franklin was known as a person who could get things done, a real "mover and shaker." And he was a *non-Quaker.* Here was a man who could yank the Quaker heads out of the sands of fanatic blindness, a man who could save the day—and their scalps!

Came rumors of French forces moving into the Lehigh Valley, taking aim at Lehigh Gap, the only break along Blue Mountain's long crest wide enough to support a major offensive against Philadelphia, which lay at the end of the natural route formed by the Delaware River. At the same time, reports circulated of daring Indian raids in force that threatened the outskirts of Reading. When news reached the Provincial capital that Indians had burned the cabins of Scotch-Irish farmers and killed several of the inhabitants—only a *two-day* ride west of Philadelphia—ripples of fear coursed through the streets of the City of Brotherly Love. Panic-stricken Philadelphians clamored for protection.

On November 15, 1755, Benjamin Franklin introduced a bill in the Assembly to raise a militia. The bill immediately ran into a Quaker logjam. For the next two weeks, the Assembly, hopelessly deadlocked, debated the issue of *Pacifism versus Defense.* Even as heated exchanges reverberated beneath the high ceiling of the State House, dirty worn farmers, mostly of German descent, accompanied by sullen hollow-eyed wives and whimpering children, began to clog the streets of Philadelphia. They arrived in droves, abandoning farms for which they had dearly paid in blood and sweat as they sought to save their families from the merciless savagery.

On the morning of November 25, four hundred wagons, accompanied by 1800 angry frustrated Germans, slowly moved through the streets of the Pensylvania capital and stopped in front of the wide ornate front gate of the Governor's Mansion. A contingent placed the scalped, charred bodies of a dozen of their own on the sidewalk between the outstretched wings of the "house of peace" that William Penn had built.

Next, the Germans moved on to the State House, where they again displayed their grisly cargo for all to see. Speaker Norris (the same Norris who later commissioned William Penn's "birthday bell") caved and Franklin's militia bill passed, with only four Quakers dissenting.

The Assembly voted 55,000 pounds for "the King's use"—their euphemism for "war." William Penn's "Holy Experiment" had been dealt a quick deathblow by Speaker Norris' gavel. The Quakers put aside their cheek-turning as religious zeal was sacrificed at the altar of rationalized necessity. But sadly, the bill arrived too late to save the missionaries at Gnadenhutten.

On the day before Franklin's militia bill passed, a Delaware war party, led by Chief Tedyuscung, incited to feverish pitch by the French, attacked the Moravian mission at Gnadenhutten (today's Leighton) as the missionaries gathered around the supper table. Eleven Moravians were slaughtered. Thirsty for more blood, marauding war parties continued to wreak havoc in the countryside, killing and plundering, dragging women and children westward to become slaves. Governor Robert Morris, suddenly faced with a crisis of Biblical proportions, called on Benjamin Franklin, the "mover and shaker," for help.

A few years before, at Franklin's persistent urging, then-Governor Thomas had given him a tacit nod to privately raise a provincial militia when hostilities between the English and French seemed likely. Thus, a substantial number of volunteers, who called themselves Franklin's Militia Association of 1747, were now ready to rush to defend Pensylvania from the savage hordes.

Fearing a French advance against Philadelphia, Governor Morris appointed Franklin, now fifty years old, as Pensylvania's *Defense* Commissioner and tasked him to organize a defense line around the city. The former newspaper owner now relinquished his pen for a sword. Franklin visited the Governor of New York, where he plied the man with wine to loosen his dour demeanor. The wine worked its miraculous wonders, and by night's end Franklin had received the loan of eighteen 18-pounders, which he ordered installed around the city.

Next, the governor appointed Franklin as commander of the Pensylvania Provincial Militia with rank of colonel. Franklin at first refused to accept the appointment—lack of experience, he insisted—but he finally acquiesced under pressure from members of the militia. Colonel Franklin was then given his marching orders: "Organize a defense line along the Blue Mountain frontier to keep the savages in their place."

Assisted by his illegitimate son, William, a professional soldier, expert strategist, and a captain in His Majesty's Army, Colonel Franklin quickly moved to establish a string of "green-wood" forts at strategic mountain crossings from the Delaware River in the north to the Susquehanna River in the south. For the most part the forts were crude log structures quickly built and surrounded by log stockades, usually manned by untrained militia whose best hope for survival was vested in the forts' only artillery—swivel guns taken from ships lying in the Philadelphia harbor. The forts were far apart and offered only rudimentary, temporary protection to the settlers. Even so, the psychological boost was immense.

Another boost, this one more pragmatic, came from Conrad Weiser, the sixty year-old Indian agent now appointed a lieutenant colonel in command of a militia battalion. He and Colonel Franklin shared responsibility for protecting the frontier forts along Blue Mountain, with Weiser's troops manning the forts along the mountain's southern portion from the Susquehanna River (Duncannon) to the Schuylkill Gap (Port Clinton). The Delaware tribe's uprising came as a harsh blow to Weiser, the man who had befriended the very people who now sought to lift his scalp.

A man of wealth and influence, Weiser had dedicated most of his life to make Pensylvania a place where Indians and whites could live in harmony, had gone the extra mile to keep the peace even after the blood-letting began. He still maintained close ties with the Iroquois. Even so, the Delawares had spoiled the soup, and his life's work now seemed for naught.

When bloody fighting erupted all along the Blue Mountain frontier, Weiser took off the gloves. No turning the other cheek for this Lutheran. His neighbors, even his family, were threatened by the butchery. With his friend and colleague Colonel Ben Franklin, Weiser urged the Board of Commissioners to recommend to Governor Morris that premiums be paid for Indian prisoners and scalps. Each male Indian prisoner above ten years of age would be valued at $150, while female Indian prisoners over the age of ten would be worth $130. Male Indian scalps lifted from heads over ten years of age could earn the scalper $130. Female scalps would be worth $50.

Governor Morris finally approved a scalp premium of $40 per Indian scalp—the equivalent of two year's pay for a militia private. Not bad money, though nearly impossible to collect for the Indians proved as elusive as dancing shadows on a flimsy back-lighted sheet.

Lieutenant Colonel Weiser and his men chased after war parties like hounds after mountain lions, and about as efficiently, more often than not reaching a gory scene just in time to bury the unlucky victims before the wolves and bears had a chance to feast. Now and then the militia got lucky and arrived in time to save the day. On a few occasions, they pursued war parties and were able to ambush the ambushers, thus freeing women and children being dragged toward hostile servitude at some distant destination. But unlike their white adversaries, the Indians had little trouble taking scalps. An estimated 600 of the grisly patches were sliced from skulls by the time the fracas ended.

And it did—twice. The first quenching of the fires of vengeance came in 1758, when a nondescript Moravian missionary, Christian Frederick Post, who accompanied British General John Forbes on the attack against Fort Duquesne, convinced the French-allied Indians to abandon their blue-coated friends. Post's extraordinary act of persuasion caused the French to flee before the first shots were fired. It also ushered in an uneasy peace to eastern Pensylvania. Bloodied and war-worn, the French finally capitulated on February 10, 1763, when they signed the Treaty of Paris, an act that ended French presence in the New World.

Barely three months later, tribes of the Great Lakes region—conspirators in a plot hatched by Ottawa Chief Pontiac to attack British-held forts and reclaim Indian ancestral lands—attacked. The melee spilled into Pensylvania, and once again war parties crossed over Blue Mountain seeking scalps.

This time the bloodshed lasted nearly two years, but the knives had dulled and the war whoops had lost their bloodcurdling timbre. The British cornered Pontiac in 1766, forcing him to give up the fight, and true "Peace" finally came to Blue Mountain. At last men could snuggle up to their robust wives and sleep like babies—or follow the wanderlust itch westward, which many did. (Though not the Germans. They were here to stay.)

But the peace would be short-lived. Paul Revere's midnight ride through the Boston countryside and the "shot heard round the world," fired at the British redcoats from Concord North Bridge, lay a scant nine years over the horizon. And the Forests of Penn—Pensylvania—would be reborn as "Pennsylvania."

Captain William Franklin continued to serve His Majesty's Army for a short time, then he began to climb the political ladder through appointments arranged by his famous father. "Billy" successively became Clerk of the Pensylvania Assembly, postmaster of Philadelphia, comptroller general of the British-American postal system, and finally the British royal governor of New Jersey, a post that he held for thirteen years.

When the American Revolution began, Governor "Billy" Franklin refused to sign an oath of allegiance to the new republic and was incarcerated as a prisoner of war. Freed after two years, he fled to British-occupied New York City, from whence he left for England. William's esteemed father, Benjamin, disowned him after he failed to sign the loyalty oath, claiming if William's England had won the war, he, Benjamin, would have had no wealth to leave his disloyal son anyway. William died in England, estranged from his father, in 1813.

Benjamin Franklin had more sense than to touch his knuckle to a key dangling at the bitter end of a kite in a thunderstorm—really! Else he would likely have been fried, and his absence from the War for Independence might have changed the course of history to favor the English. (The inventor probably had the key attached to a Leyden jar, a specially designed device engineered to gather electrical charges.) Franklin went on to greater glory. But then, any American worth his or her Fourth of July hotdogs knows the rest of the story.

Lieutenant Colonel Conrad Weiser continued at his post until the restless peace came in 1758. Weiser, then sixty-two, exchanged his uniform for a suit and returned to his business interests. He died a year later. On hearing of his death, an Iroquois lamented, "Tarachiawagon is gone. We are at a great loss and sit in darkness . . . as since his death we cannot so well understand one another." A fitting eulogy for "the Holder of the Heavens."

The Penn family continued to "rule" Pensylvania until the Revolutionary War, at which time the new nation flexed its muscle and absorbed the Proprietary into the new state of Pennsylvania.

*   *   *

A lot of history up here on rock-strewn Blue Mountain, with its copious nests of rattlers and mammoth quartzite humpbacks that seem to go on forever. The mountain's tumultuous, convulsive history seems to stretch as far as the endless rocks. But we've a bit farther to go to connect the "players" with the mountain. Else, all I've written about becomes nothing more than an eighth grade history lesson. Keep on hiking!

A half-mile north of 501 Shelter (at Pennsylvania Highway 501), just off the Appalachian Trail, a stone marker rests beside a spring from which cold, sweet water flows. The spring has been there for God only knows how long, an oasis atop the water-starved spine of Blue Mountain. Generations of Lenni

Lenape and Shawnee must have quaffed their thirst with the pure water, since the spring sat beside the ancient "Tulpehocken Trail"—a major Indian path that crossed the mountain. (Pennsylvania Highway 501 generally follows the Tulpehocken Trail up the mountainside from Bethel, two miles east.) Conrad Weiser used this trail on numerous occasions when he visited the Delaware tribes west of Blue Mountain, and assuredly he drank the spring's waters many times, as did the early settlers.

The marker was erected in 1946 by the Blue Mountain Eagle Climbing Club and the Historical Society of Berks County. It reads: "1742 Pilger Ruh (Pilgrim's Rest) named by Count Nicholas Ludwig von Zinzendorf, who with Conrad Weiser and Moravian Missionaries rested here besides this spring on their way to visit Shawnee Indians in Wyoming Valley." As usually happens, there is a "rest of the story."

Count Nicholas Ludwig von Zinzendorf arrived in Philadelphia harbor in 1741, a man on two divine missions—to unify the German Protestants of Pensylvania and to Christianize the heathens. Using his immense wealth and influence, the Count helped purchase 500 acres along the Lehigh River and there founded the town of Bethlehem, which became the center of Moravian activities in the New World.

That done, he sought out Conrad Weiser, the Provincial Indian Agent, to help him make contact with the heathens. Weiser, still smarting from the injustice done to the Delawares through the shameful "Walking Purchase," was too much occupied with business matters at the time, but he gladly drafted a letter of introduction to a Moravian missionary by name of Mack, who also spoke the Indian language.

Mack, his wife, and Count Zinzendorf traveled over Blue Mountain along the Tulpehocken Trail to Wyoming Valley, where the Shawnee had settled. As soon as the Moravians had pitched their tents beside a small stream near the Indian village, Mack assembled the chiefs and explained the purpose of Zinzendorf's visit. The Shawnee chiefs, suspecting that Zinzendorf was intent on grabbing off more of their land, resolved to assassinate the white "shaman" but to do it privately so as not to incur the wrath of their "white father" (Weiser) or the powerful English king.

The braves assigned to do the dirty deed picked a cool September evening when Zinzendorf sat alone in his tent. A small blanket covered the entrance to hold in the heat from a small fire the white "shaman" had built to ward off the chill. A large rattler, coiled in some weeds near the tent, felt the heat. It slithered inside toward the warmth and stretched across Zinzendorf's outstretched legs. The man was so deeply engrossed with his thoughts that the serpent's presence went unnoticed.

With their knives at the ready, the Shawnee braves quietly pushed aside the small curtain. In the flickering dimness, they could see the man hunched over a small table as if in a trance. The huge timber rattler lay across his legs, protecting their intended victim from harm. Big medicine; too powerful for their knives! Terrified, the braves fled.

Conrad Weiser arrived a few days after and convinced the Shawnees of Count Zinzendorf's honorable intentions. Thereafter, Zinzendorf was made welcome in the Indian camps, although his success at Christianizing the heathens was limited. The count and Weiser made several other trips across Blue Mountain to visit Indian tribes.

On their first journey together Zinzendorf must have given the spring its name—Pilger Ruh, an ideal place for "pilgrims" to rest.

A scant five hundred yards south of Pennsylvania Highway 183, smack dab on the Appalachian Trail, is the site of Fort Dietrich Snyder, one of the frontier forts "built" by Benjamin Franklin—at least that's what the faded stone marker infers. Colonel Franklin might have selected strategic locations for the Blue Mountain forts. However, Lieutenant Colonel Conrad Weiser's First Battalion actually "built" and manned the forts south of Schuylkill Gap, which included Fort Dietrich Snyder.

Fort Dietrich Snyder. All that remains is a granite marker.

Turns out that actually it was no fort at all, merely a settler's 20x40-foot log home that had two prime advantages: The site offered Dietrich Snyder, the owner, a breathtaking panorama of the surrounding Pennsylvania countryside. Secondly, the place was readily accessible, sitting astride one of the few over-mountain trails. A strategic bonanza, Snyder's place, for it could be used as an observation post to detect marauding war parties, as well as to deny the culprits an avenue of attack and escape.

Too, the house stood only two miles from Fort Northkill down the mountainside, which was more heavily defended. A warning of an impending attack could quickly be relayed. So Weiser's militiamen became houseguests of old Snyder and his wife.

No reports exist of any attacks against Fort Dietrich Snyder, although the Indians did manage to lift a couple of scalps near its closest neighbor, Fort Northkill. After the peace, the militiamen departed and life again revolved around isolated subsistence living. When Dietrich Snyder died, his wife continued to live in the old house until her death—at the purported age of 115! The property was sold to a man by name of Miller, who tore the structure down and erected a hotel one hundred yards south of the original site. As late as 1916, the hotel, then owned by Harry Nine, still stood.

The fate of the hotel, now gone, lurks somewhere in modern antiquity, interred in old inaccessible archives.

*　　*　　*

Thousands of years from now, the history of Blue Mountain and the men and women who stepped to its tune will have been dissipated by centuries of heat-choking summers and snow-packed winters, until all that remains are sketchy wonderings of what was, much like Harry Nine's hotel. Pilger Ruh, its water long given way to dust, will only be a faded question mark on ancient maps. Sadly, the mountain's stone markers will have become eroded misshapen hunks of granite that have lost their souls.

But I'd be willing to bet my hiking sticks that those darned Blue Mountain quartzite rocks will still be there!

Chapter Twenty-nine

In the Shadows of the Blue Ridge

"*W*hen *the last red man shall have perished, and the memory of my tribe shall have become a myth among the white man, these shores will swarm with the invisible dead of my tribe . . . they will throng with the returning hosts that once filled and still love this beautiful land. The white man will never be alone. Let him be just and deal kindly with my people, for the dead are not powerless. Dead, did I say? There is no death, only a change of worlds.*"

So spoke Seattle, the Duwamish chief whose name is immortalized by a thriving, bustling city where once stood bark lodges, and where success was measured by how much meat simmered in the evening cook pot. His lamentation, a poignant benediction of the red man's plight, slams against the conscience of America, shaking the Founding Fathers' concepts of justice and decency like a jackhammer run amok.

Chief Seattle's end of days did not happen, for his people have not perished. Moreover, the red man's fate is now so intertwined with the racial mixture that makes up Americana that any "perishing" will probably be a package deal. But, as a nation we have come up lacking in our dealings with our Native American brothers. The chasm between our two cultures is as deep as antiquity and stretches from Columbus' "land ho" to the reservation gambling casinos. A shame, for bridges *that span* impassable chasms allow one to journey to far horizons.

It's nigh on impossible to write a "lore and legends" book about the Appalachian Trail without including the impact of our Native Americans on the area through which the Trail passes. Indians were crisscrossing the Blue Ridge for hundreds of years before cavemen began to sketch stick animals in charcoal on Europe's cave walls. The red man's history mingles with the rushing waters of frigid mountain streams. It mixes with the early morning mist that rises from flowery dew-covered alpine meadows. Their primordial cook fires flicker like phantoms in the last fiery rays of the setting sun, which grace the high ledges where only eagles dare. Their ancient heritage can be heard in the melancholy hoot of a great horned owl . . . in the hushed scurrying of a shelter mouse. Their ancestral ghosts ride the wings of a red-tail hawk as it dives toward an unsuspecting meal.

No denying it, the grand and terrible past of the Indian is inextricably woven into the fabric of these majestic mountains that I hold so dear, to this trail that has so altered my being. Granted, the red man had more sense than to run their trails along the long crests of mountains—unless game trails led them there—for that's where the toughest traveling is. And the Appalachian Trail, with few exceptions, fails to follow the old Indian paths.

So why include a chapter about Indians in a book about the Appalachian Trail?

A fair question, simply answered. Although separated by centuries, by ethos, by purpose; yet in spite of a vast cultural void, Indians and hikers have both experienced the fragile magic of the Blue Ridge, have marveled at its gentle beauty, have respected its raw power, have shared a oneness with Nature.

Today the red man no longer roams the Blue Ridge, and the mighty crests now belong to the hikers. But as Chief Seattle said, *"There is no death, only a change of worlds."* A startling prophesy! The red man's destiny lay westward, and his noble past now lies in the shadows of the Blue Ridge.

Perhaps it is time for some "bridge building" . . .

(Author's note: During my research, I counted something in the neighborhood of 500 different Indian tribes that lived in the United States at various times. Most had specific dialects and unique customs. Several of the eastern tribes were linguistically related, members of a great language family known as the Algonquian, which included the Delaware but not their later conquerors, the Iroquois, nor their southern cousins, the Cherokee, about which I wrote in previous chapters. Only those tribes who have ties to the Blue Ridge are addressed here; otherwise, this manuscript would run into volumes!

Too, I apologize to those readers who cringe at my lack of "political correctness." I intend no disrespect in my use of terms, but "Indian, "red man," and "Injun"—"white man's" descriptives—thread the needle through which runs the tragic humiliation of the Native American, which even today continues to prick the national conscience.

I can think of no more appropriate place to start than with the Lenni Lenape, a proud people whose ignoble decline embodies the essence of Chief Seattle's lament and the downfall of the Indian nation.)

*   *   *

The "white man" called them "Delawares"; the French knew them as "Wolves." Among the Algonquian family, the Lenni Lenape tribe was (and still is) referred to as "grandfather"—a term of deference and respect that has its foundation in ancient history, for it is widely believed that the Lenape was the original tribe of all Algonquian-speaking peoples. The Lenape called themselves the "original people."

They do go back a long way, but the Lenape were not the first to cross the land bridge in the Bering Sea during some opportune epoch when Nature kindly swept the waters away and let flowers grow on the shallow ocean floor. Far from it, for by the time the Lenape crossed the narrow Bering Strait on a treacherous bridge of ice, bronze-skin natives had already spread across the North American continent. But the "original people," the Lenape, possess something no other tribe has—the oldest *written* history of a native North American tribe.

The Lenape's *Walam Olum*, or *Red Record* as it is otherwise known, was (I say *was* because the artifacts have mysteriously disappeared) a series of pictograph-etched wooden prayer sticks. Thereon was recorded the history of the Lenape people from the Creation until their forced removal to Indian Territory in Oklahoma in the early 1800s.

The *Walam Olum* has been around for untold generations and possibly represents an oral history that has survived from 14,000 to as many as 40,000 years. But its true significance was unknown to the white man until the "history book" was given to a Moravian missionary and physician, Dr. Ward, in 1820. Dr. Ward had lived among the Lenape for several years. When he saved the life of the village historian, the grateful man, who happened to be the caretaker of the ancient record, gave the painted bark and wooden prayer sticks to his savior as a show of appreciation, with the explanation, "This is our Bible."

Thus the Lenape history came in a roundabout way to the white man's world. The history is a fascinating tale of hardship and adventure, with spine tingling parallels to *The Holy Bible's* account of "the beginning," complete with Indian versions of an Adam, Eve, and a serpent, followed by a great flood!

The *Walam Olum* eventually wound up on the desk of Constantine Rafinesque, a professor of botany and natural science at Transylvania University in Lexington, Kentucky. In 1836, Dr. Rafinesque produced a written English translation of the prayer sticks, which he titled *The Red Record*.

(Author's note: Hoax or not? Much controversy surrounds the authenticity of *The Red Record*, even the existence of the *Walum Olum*. In 1976, Dr. David

McCutchen, a graduate of the University of California and the California Institute of the Arts, was hired to research the history of the Lenni-Lenape nation. McCutchen managed to locate a few fragments of the original prayer sticks and studied the translation made by Rafinesque. He then visited Linda Poolaw, Grand Chief of the Delaware Nation's Grand Council of North America in Oklahoma.

With Chief Poolaw's help, McCutchen was able to fill in the blanks and create a final translation for *The Red Record*. The Grand Council affirmed that McCutchen's translation was accurate and passed a resolution endorsing his work as a true portrayal of the Lenni-Lenape history.

On the other hand, in 1996 Dr. David Oestreicher put forth a strong argument that Rafinesque, seeking fame and recognition, which he seriously lacked, "made up" a history and translated it into the Lenape language. Charlatan or genius? There are indications that Rafinesque was unable to write even a simple sentence in the Lenape language. Yet, occasionally the man did respectable work.

Take your pick. Accurate translation of the prayer sticks or not, the Delaware say the translation is factual, and you can't get any closer to the horse's mouth than that.)

The remarkable history recorded in the *Walum Olum* goes far in explaining how and why so many of the Indian customs, manners, ceremonies, and dwellings can be so similar throughout the length and breadth of our spacious land. The last entry on the historical record was made in 1620 and reads, "Who are they?" referring to the strange men who arrived in weird-looking vessels with billowing canvas sheets.

The *Red Record* was later amended by a section known as "The Fragment," which picks up the Lenape history from the mid-1600s and ends in the 1800s with their forced removal to Oklahoma's Indian Territory. "The Fragment" ends with the poignant question: "Shall we be free and happy there?"

A "thumbnail" look at the Lenape history, according to *The Red Record:*

Long ago, the Lenni Lenape lived in a wild mountainous region in Siberia, near the present day borders of Mongolia, Russia, and China. After the Great Flood and the resettling of people, shamans began to tell of a mighty body of water "to the east." About the time of Christ's birth, a band of Lenape, some 10,000 strong, began a migration that would cover 9,000 miles and several generations. During their travels, the Lenape fought their way through lands ruled by fierce Chinese dynasties. After crossing the narrow ice-bridge over the Bering Strait, the migration split. One group traveled south and eventually populated the mesas and pueblos of the great Southwest and became the Anasazi.

The other group continued eastward until they reached a great river (the Mississippi), where they came face to face with a mighty people called the Talega—the Moundbuilders—far advanced beyond the sophistication and intellectual ability of the other tribes encountered by the Lenape. The Talega ruled their kingdom from the walled city of Cahokia (near present day East St. Louis), a cultural, commercial, and religious center that rivaled the emerging civilizations far to the south.

The Lenape petitioned the Talega chief for permission to cross the Mississippi, which was granted. But when the Moundbuilders saw how strong and many the wanderers were, they plotted to destroy the intruders, killing all those who had already crossed to the east side of the river. Thus began a cataclysmic war that raged over the lifetimes of four Lenape chiefs and ended with the ignominious defeat of the Talega, who fled south. (The Natchez are the descendants of the decimated Talega.)

The Lenape finally reached the shores of the Atlantic Ocean and settled in the general vicinity of New Jersey and Delaware. There they prospered, a thriving people who became the founding fathers (hence the reference to "grandfather") of many Algonquian-speaking tribes, including the Shawnee, Algonkin, Abenaki, Mohicans, Powhatans, Cheyenne, Cree, Blackfoot, and Arapahoe.

The Lenape were made up of three loosely associated sub-tribes, each with its own dialect and territory: The Munsee (or Minsi), translated as "people of the stony country," inhabited the hills near the headwaters of the Delaware River. The Unami, "the people down the river," occupied the region surrounded by the Delaware River, including the northern two-thirds of New Jersey and eastern Pennsylvania. William Penn's unbroken "handshake treaty," which begot the City of Brotherly Love, was done with the Unami.

The other sub-tribe, the Unalachtigo, were known as "the people near the ocean," and they dwelled on both sides of the lower Delaware River below Philadelphia, including Delaware Bay.

(As white encroachment forced the Lenape farther west, many of the Munsee crossed into Canada, where they lost most of their ties to their "elder kin," the Unami, and assumed an autonomy of their own. Today, nearly 2000 Munsee live on three reserves in Ontario and are formally recognized by the Canadian Government. The Unalachtigo were gradually absorbed by the Unami during the tribe's many removals.)

In 1524 came the first of the Swannuken—"salt water people"—in the form of Giovanni da Verrazano, an Italian navigator in the service of France. Verrazano swooped into New York harbor and attempted to grab a few natives, to what end only God and Verrazano knew.

Henry Hudson, hired by the Dutch to find a "northwest passage" to the Pacific Ocean, sailed up the Hudson River in 1609 and managed to stir up a hornet's nest with the Unami, which cost him a couple of sailors and left his arrow-pricked longboat looking like a worked-over porcupine. Hudson didn't find the "passage." But in the upper reaches of his namesake, he found something as good—a village of Mahicans loaded with furs, which they were eager to trade for trinkets. The Dutch hooted with glee over their newfound windfall and dispatched a horde of traders to the New World to grab off the easy wealth.

Thus, the land was soon flooded with Swannuken, who brought strange customs and alien ideas of land ownership, accompanied by worthless treaties and backstabbing intrigues and alliances. As if a mighty sorcerer had unleashed an invincible curse, soon came the white man's sicknesses, which refused to bow to the magical incantations and herbs of the shamans. Over the next three centuries, war, famine, and small pox would decimate the Lenni Lenape (now renamed "Delaware" by the white settlers) population of some 20,000 until, by 1910, only 2000 would remain. From Penn's first "handshake" with the Unami until their final destination in dusty Oklahoma, the Delaware would be "relocated" over twenty times, victimized by enough broken treaties to fill several archive boxes, and "dressed in petticoats" by the Iroquois—a humiliation that still rankles.

An ungrateful nation turned a blind eye when the Delawares, then removed to Kansas, joined Colonel Henry Dodge's 1835 expedition to rout the Comanches. Nor did glory come to the beleaguered tribe when eighty-seven Delaware warriors joined the American Army two years later and fought like regulars alongside their blue-hatted comrades against the Seminoles in the Florida swamps; nor when Delaware scouts accompanied the intrepid Fremont on all three of his famous expeditions. They were ignored when they aided in the capture of California and the conquest of New Mexico.

And when the shells fell on Fort Sumter, the Delaware declared for the Union. Ultimately, 170 of 200 able-bodied Delaware males of military age wore Union blue as members of the 6th and 15th Kansas Volunteer Cavalry and fought several engagements against Confederate Cherokee, Choctaw, and Chickasaw units. All to no avail. The Delaware still had to "ride into the sunset."

A final slap in the face came in 1979 when the Bureau of Indian Affairs terminated the Delaware's status as a separate tribe and tossed them into the Cherokee pot. After a lengthy legal fracas, in 1996 the decision was reversed and the Delaware Tribe of Indians has again gained federal recognition as a separate tribe. The latest census puts the population of the Delaware Tribe at around 16,000.

*   *   *

The "Iroquois" are not a single tribe of Indians, as I had always thought. Rather, it describes a confederacy of Iroquoian-speaking tribes that once shared contiguous lands in what is now upstate New York near Lake Ontario. (The Cherokee also speak the Iroquois tongue, which raises speculation that they and the New York tribes shared a common ancestry.) Fierce and warmongering, the Iroquois tribes believed in whacking first and asking questions later. And these firebrands were zingers who would as soon loose a volley of arrows over a skunk skin that no one really wanted as to steal another tribe's fair maidens— a favorite pastime.

Somewhere along the thorny path, someone decided that it might be a good idea to bury the tomahawk before they killed each other off. Emissaries bearing peace wampum brought the tribal leaders together. As flames roared from a great council fire and guttural voices rose into the heavens, *Kainerekowa*—the Great Law of Peace—was born. Each tribe pledged to lift the scalps of everyone except those of their brother tribes.

Thus, a great confederacy was joined by the Cayuga, Mohawk, Oneida, Onondaga, and Seneca. This happened sometime between 900 and 1500 A.D. A wide spread of time, but that's the best historians can come up with. Most agree, though, that the Iroquois League, or Five Nations, came into being before Europeans made contact. In 1722, to bolster their dwindling numbers, the League accepted their Virginia neighbor, the Tuscarora, into the Confederacy—but withheld voting rights—and the name was changed to the Six Nations.

The Iroquois called themselves Haudenosaunee, "people of the long house," which refers to the type of abode that prevailed among the Confederacy. The Algonkin, mortal enemies, called them Iroqu, "rattlesnakes," and the fastidious French, as they are wont to do, dressed up the name by adding "ois" to the insult. The name stuck.

The Iroquois may have been meaner than a rattler shedding its skin, but they were smarter than hoot owls. Through conquest and wise dealings with the English, who cultivated their support with bribes and perks, by 1680 the Iroquois had managed to extend their empire from southern Ontario into Ohio and south through Kentucky to the confluence of the Ohio and Mississippi Rivers. Amazingly, they controlled the vast area *in absentia* through subjugated tribes and remained for the most part in their small domain in upper New York.

When the Swannuken came, the five tribes combined boasted a strength of about 20,000—approximating the strength of the Lenape. But as happened with other tribes, by 1650 disease and war had sliced their numbers in half. The Iroquois came up with a plan to bolster their decreasing numbers. They "adopted" conquered Iroquoian-speaking tribes into their confederacy, including some 7000 Huron and a like number of Susquehannock, Erie (whom they despised and soon wiped from the face of the earth), and other "neutrals." In fact, the Iroquois adopted so many that they became a minority within their own confederacy, which in the next ten years reached a whopping strength of over 25,000.

But the Iroquois, still favoring the British, backed the wrong horse during the Revolutionary War. By the end of the conflict, less than 8,000 remained to smoke peace pipes with the new government.

A few words about the Iroquoian culture. Like the Lenape tribes, the men hunted and made war, and the women exclusively tilled the fields (from whence came nearly all the food). But the Iroquois women held considerable power. They owned all tribal property, chose the tribal sachems (male leaders), and determined kinships. When a warrior married, he moved into his wife's communal longhouse, and their children became members of her clan. Women held the power to remove a sachem for misconduct or inefficiency. Although both sexes favored tattoos, males carefully removed all facial and body hair, while the women let their hair grow long.

On the dark side, Iroquois tribes sometimes practiced ritual cannibalism and torture (as did some of the other tribes east of the Mississippi River). The Iroquois also harbored the False Face Society, a healing group that used grotesque masks to frighten away evil spirits believed to cause illnesses.

Unlike the Algonquian tribes, who lived in round or oblong wigwams covered with woven mats and smelly skins and seldom worried about fortifications, the Iroquois built villages that were usually heavily fortified and ringed with log stockades as tall as twenty feet. Inside the palisades, bark-covered communal longhouses, often two hundred feet in length, housed as many as twelve families of the same clan.

An early visitor wrote of the longhouses, "a noisy prison with four other great discomforts—cold, heat, smoke, and dogs." Villages were permanent until the fields played out—every twenty years or so—at which time the villagers moved on to better pickings.

Some historians go so far as to declare that the Iroquois were the most important native group in North American history. Arguably so. They had a sophisticated social and political system long before the Swannuken arrived to muddle the scene. The Iroquois Confederacy had a strict pecking order: The Onondaga, "keepers of the council fire," always headed the social hierarchy of tribal representation at the Grand Council with fourteen sachems, or peace chiefs. Following in order were the Cayuga (10), the Oneida (9), the Mohawk (9), and the Seneca (8). A wonderful system of checks and balances, for the Onondaga only had a small population, and their large voting bloc represented a form of compromise, crucial since all council decisions had to be unanimous.

On the other hand, since persuasion often became the hammer needed to drive the nail of decision home, a pecking order prevailed in council debates, with the Mohawk, Onondaga, and Seneca usually addressed as "elder brothers," while the Oneida, Cayuga, and Tuscarora were called "little brothers" or "nephews."

Eventually, the Iroquois found it necessary to bring non-Iroquoian tribes, such as the Delaware, Machian, and Shawnee, into the fold in order to maintain control of their empire. Politically adept, they avoided "adoption"; instead, they created a "Covenant Chain," in which they awarded tribes quasi-memberships with representation by "half-kings" who had little or no say in matters. With spiteful arrogance they made the Delaware "put on the petticoat," a slur that referred to the Lenape as a tribe of women. (A strange insult, for certain, coming from a people who gave their women such power!)

But the Iroquois *did* back the wrong horse and lost "face" with the new government! Still, in the long run they managed to avoid the long ride to Oklahoma.

I can almost feel the frustrated glares of my hiker-readers who just want to get on up the Trail and hear their aggravated, "Has he *totally lost* his marbles?"

Fair enough. I'll take the heat for straying so far from the Trail. But I thought it worth a short side trip because the Iroquois pulled the strings of their Delaware "puppets," who left their bones and tomahawks—not to mention a few hundred white bodies—scattered across the Pennsylvania and New Jersey countryside through which the Trail goes.

The Iroquois also dealt with the white men on an equal basis throughout. In spite of their shortcomings, the Iroquois' political system made them unique among North American tribes. Their political system was created without European bias; yet, it greatly influenced the political sophistication during the embryonic growth of the coming new nation. Certainly the Iroquois' elaborate system of checks and balances, social structure, and rudiments of tribal law influenced the American Articles of Confederation and the Constitution. All things considered, that's a decent legacy to leave and worth the rambling!

A final word: The Iroquois were far more than "zingers." Several enjoyed distinguished careers. Eli Parker, a Seneca chief, served as Commissioner of Indian Affairs during the Grant Administration. Educated as a lawyer, he was admitted to the bar in New York but was prohibited from practicing law there. He served on General Grant's staff during the Civil War and is believed to have written the terms of surrender that heralded Lee's capitulation at Appomattox.

Take Catherine Tekawitha, nicknamed "the Lily of the Mohawk," whom at age four lost her family to small pox and was herself disfigured and her eyesight nearly destroyed by the disease. As a young maiden she became "Christianized" by Jesuits, was forced to live in a community where debauchery was the norm, and became a living symbol of deep-seated faith. Catherine Tekawitha died in 1680. She was selected for beautification (the first step on the long road to sainthood in the Roman Catholic Church) and has now reached the final stage before saintly recognition.

And then there are the high performers. The Mohawks have long shown no fear of height, and this has placed them on an inside track when jobs are being handed out to build cloud-raking structures. In fact, Mohawks have been involved in the construction of *every* major bridge and skyscraper since architects first began to draw plans. In 1907, thirty-five Mohawk laborers were among the ninety-six killed when a bridge being built across the St. Lawrence at Quebec collapsed.

Forgiven?

*   *   *

On Schaghticoke Mountain in western Connecticut, the Appalachian Trail passes through the only Indian reservation in its entire 2174.9-mile length (2005 official mileage). The day I first crossed this forlorn strip in 1990, the mercury was threatening to blow the top off of my tiny pack thermometer, and the humidity was higher than the inside of a TV evangelist's collar. "Miserable" didn't begin to describe the state of my world. Nothing stirred, no breeze, no birds, no sounds of any kind, just an unnatural stillness—so quiet you could hear a mouse pee on cotton—except for the pounding in my ears, which came from an overstressed heart. And then I noticed the sign: Schaghticoke Indian Reservation; please stay on the trail. Or some such words. Jeez!

The sign immediately conjured up mental images from an old black and white movie about the "last of the Mohicans," something I'd seen as a child. In the flick, Mohawk warriors with their greased scalplocks hid in trees, just waiting to pounce on a few unsuspecting victims and lift some scalps! Jayzus H. Hinkledorf!

My heart did a double take and threatened to blow. I stopped in my tracks and began to search the tall trees on each side of the Trail. No Injuns! I almost passed out from relief. Shut fire-n-shinola!

Some large graybacks up ahead, just right for an ambush! I could visualize my own demise as a party of sullen, bronze-faced warriors jumped out, brandishing old flintlocks, ready to drill holes in my stinky carcass. Or would it be arrows? Did the Indians still use arrows? Damn!

I tiptoed past the rocks, throat tight like the hangman was already yanking on the noose, and nearly fainted from the let down after I'd made it past without seeing a single Injun. God-A'mighty, but it was a long trip off that mountain!

Needless to say, nothing happened. When I reached Kent, I swallowed my foolishness with a couple of frosty Sam Adams.

*   *   *

The old Pequot slowly made his way up the steep mountainside toward the rocky summit. Nearing the top, he wiped the sweat from his weathered face and forced his legs forward, anxious to see what lay beyond the other side. Briefly, he felt a twinge of guilt as the deerskin pouch tied at his waist rubbed against his leg. His home exchanged for a few paltry coins—white man's perfidy—now become his measly share of the sixty-five pounds paid for the Pequot holdings a few miles back at Dover on Ten Mile River. He and his twelve Pequot brethren had grudgingly relinquished their property to the greedy white settlers. They would find a way to take it anyway.

But because of his weakness, his wife and children now hunkered in an isolated glen beside the river, waiting for him to find another place to erect their wigwam. He reached the top, winded and gasping, and struggled to pull air into his leathery lungs. The Pequot sacrificed his eagerness and rested on a rock for a few minutes until his hammering heart subsided. Then regaining his feet, he made his way across the broad crest to a rocky ledge—and stopped short.

Far below, a shining river serpentined through a narrow tree-covered valley like a giant snake. Excited, his fatigue momentarily forgotten, the Indian made his way down the eastern slope to the rushing water. He lowered his sweat-streaked head into the numbing coolness, feeling the slight brush of hungry minnows that nibbled at his ears. Rejuvenated, he rose to his feet and walked down the bank to a deep pool. Slowly, he let a hand idle down toward the depths where a large trout rested unafraid.

Backtracking to the edge of the woods, he sniffed the air, then listened intently. No telltale odor of smoke; no banging of metal on metal that signaled the presence of white settlers. Unable to control his legs, he jogged along the bank for a few miles. No sign of the land-hungry whites! Abundant game tracks gave promise of much meat in the stew pot.

The old Indian grinned at his shimmering reflection in a shallow pool and hastened back the way he had come, already making plans to pack his meager belongings and bring his wife and family to this unsullied country.

Thus came Mauwehu, the Pequot in 1729 to the Housatonic River and a place he would call Scatacook, named after the settlement of Schaghticoke (near Albany, New York), where the remnants of several tribes had sought refuge after the brutal "King Philip's War." (More about this later.) Here Mauwehu and some Pequots had planted their roots with the Weantinocks and lived in harmony until a decade earlier—when the white governor Andros decided his settlers needed more land and "encouraged" the Indians to move on.

Mauwehu sent back word to his friends, "Come and share my good fortune. There is room for all." So they came, at first a few Peqouts, soon followed by Mohegans from the Hudson River Valley. As word spread, the Weantinock, the Potatuck, and other tribes that inhabited the upper and lower Housatonic River Valley slowly filtered in. Within ten years, Scatacook had become a thriving Indian settlement of over 600 residents.

Mauwehu laid claim to some 2100 acres of prime bottomland on the west side of the Housatonic, which included the high mountain from which he had first viewed his "paradise." The grateful inhabitants elevated Mauwehu to the honored position of tribal sachem.

In 1738, a group of eager colonials gathered around the courthouse steps at Windham (Connecticut). The event that drew the crowd on this balmy March morning: New land was up for grabs! Rumor had it that the valley along the Housatonic River was a true paradise, even if it lay a hundred miles to the west in Injun country. Fifty-three plots (shares) had been laid out on the east bank of the river.

Bidding began at fifty pounds, and the shares were gobbled up like hot gizzards in chicken dumpling stew. Thus came the new inhabitants to the beautiful place beside the rushing waters, which they incorporated the following year with the good English name of Kent.

Sachem Mauwehu had already had his fingers burned several times by encroaching white settlers and the coerced sales that inevitably followed. This time he sought to head off the coming tide by petitioning the Connecticut General Assembly for a resident missionary and schoolmaster, thereby showing his desire to have his people become "civilized Christians." The General Assembly responded by tossing the Scatacooks a cookie crumb—limited missionary support. Dissatisfied, in 1743 the Indians turned to the Moravians across the mountain in New York for their salvation.

The missionaries immediately "Christianized" the sachem by dunking him in the frigid waters of the Housatonic and blessed him with the name "Gideon Mauwee." However, the German sect ran into immediate opposition from the staid Episcopalians across the river. Consequently, the Connecticut General Assembly evicted all Moravians from the colony. (After tempers cooled, the Moravians were able to reestablish a resident mission in 1749.)

But after a few years of futile coexistence and hostility, the Moravians left Gideon Mauwee and his Scatacook to fend for themselves and returned to more peaceful climes.

Sachem Mauwee's grand strategy to join "civilization" had already failed long before the Moravians shook the Connecticut dust from their boots. Land grabbing, aided by a little rum, became commonplace, and the Scatacook watched helplessly as their fine bottomland acreage dwindled. With his people's backs against the mountain and nowhere else to turn, in 1756 Sachem Gideon Mauwee petitioned the General Assembly to appoint an overseer to protect the remaining tribal lands.

A succession of corrupt overseers followed, whose chief interest seemed to be in divesting the Scatacooks of what little they had. Disgusted, Mauwee decided it was more honorable to die than to remain and see the rape of his people. He went to meet his ancestors in 1760.

After his death, many Scatacooks left the diminished reservation and found lodgings elsewhere, aligning themselves with their northern kin, who preferred to be known by the more Anglicized spelling, "Schaghticoke." By 1774, only sixty-two Indians lived on a dismal plot by the Housatonic—mostly untenable mountain—and by 1900, only seven families with twenty-three members remained.

In 1925, the state abolished the overseer program and gave responsibility for the Schaghticoke (yes, Scatacooks were all now Schaghticokes) Reservation to the Connecticut State Park and Forest Commission. The Commission envisioned a beautiful state park on the lands inhabited by the Schaghticokes and put policies in effect deigned to encourage the Indians to abandon their holdings. Julia Coggswell Batie, who descended from one of the old cornerstone Scatacook families, wrote to the Bureau of Indian Affairs: ". . . by whose authority should the small bit of land which I and a few others call home be turned over to the Public when the state already has thousand of acres, even thousands of acres that formerly belongs (sic) to the Indians of that (Schaghticoke) reservation?" The Indians dug in and stayed.

In 1941, the "on reservation" Schaghticokes became wards of the state when the State Welfare Department took over their care. A tempting aphrodisiac, being designated as "wards." But the Indians didn't swallow it. Instead, they filed claims with the Federal Indian Claims Commission for return of lands (including the island of Manhattan!) or monetary compensation. All claims were denied. Thus began a political "cat and mouse" game that is still being played out today.

In 1981, the Schaghticoke Indian Tribe, which included *all* Connecticut members, filed for Federal recognition with the Bureau of Indian Affairs in an effort to gain sovereignty. After considerable political maneuvering, in 1991 the Schaghticoke tribe split into two factions: The "off reservation" members incorporated as the Schaghticoke Tribal Nation (STN), while the "on reservation" families retained the original title.

In July 1998, in another pressure move the STN, citing a 1790 law, the Indian Non-intercourse Act—passed by the United States Congress, which prohibited the sale of Indian lands without Congressional approval—sued several land owners in the Kent area, seeking to reclaim some 2200 acres. Among the defendants listed were (and still are) the private Kent school (1900 acres), the Connecticut Light and Power Company (148 acres), and the Appalachian Trail Conference (52 acres, which were obtained through "eminent domain" by the National Park Service. (This last section had been turned over to the ATC by the NPS, but the jurisdictional court allowed the Conference to return the property to NPS for the pending lawsuit—over STN objections—which removed the ATC as a defendant.)

It was recently revealed that the suit is being underwritten by a group of Las Vegas and foreign investors, which begs the question: Is the lawsuit all about money? Is the STN, as a sovereign nation, attempting to build Connecticut's third casino?

The Mashantucket Pequots, who evolved from a single descendant—a frail old lady who lived alone on a tiny reservation in Ledyard—into a sovereign nation managed, with the help of a few million Arab, Malaysian, and Chinese dollars, to forge a gambling empire known as Foxwoods in southeastern Connecticut. The Mohegans, too, have done okay with their Sun Casino at Uncasville, with its 6252 slots (that's almost *one* for each Marine *killed* in the assault on Iwo Jima during WWII) and 276 gaming tables, not to mention the 1256-room hotel where the lucky and not-so-lucky can rest in relatively inexpensive comfort.

Turns out Fred DeLuca, who launched the vast Subway sandwich shop chain, might want to do more than see low-cal subs sold to the Nation's hungry. DeLuca revealed that he has been the STN's principal money backer in the tribe's attempt to gain Federal recognition. The Subway's former owner, a Connecticut resident, said that he would like to see a Schaghticoke casino in Bridgeport. The STN, whose total membership rivals the number of Mohegan Sun's gaming tables, has disavowed any interest in opening a casino—for now.

On January 29, 2004, the Bureau of Indian Affairs (BIA) granted Federal recognition to the STN. The decision is being appealed by the State of Connecticut.

The Schaghticoke Indian Tribe (SIT) has split from the STN, has its own agenda, and seeks its own Federal recognition. So far, the BIA has treated the Kent Schaghticoke Indian Tribe as part of the larger STN.

Eleven determined souls continue to live in semi-squalor on the 480-acre reservation.

For now, the Appalachian Trail still crosses the small strip on Schaghticoke Mountain. A small zephyr in the gathering storm!

(Author's note: "Schaghticoke" is a corruption of the Indian word "Pisgachticok," which means "the confluence of two streams," possibly a reference to the area near Schaghticoke, New York, where a small stream runs into the Hudson River, and where the tribal remnants lived before they collectively became known as Schaghticokes. At least twenty-one different spellings of Scatacook and the later Schaghticoke exist in colonial documents.

Be that as it may, historians and the BIA agree that the Schaghticokes are a hybrid group—not a single original Scatacook to be found—made up of the Weantinocks, the Potatucks, with a smattering of Peoquots and Pequannocks thrown in. The BIA based their decision to grant Federal recognition to the

STN, hence making them Connecticut's fourth legally recognized Indian tribe, on the fact that the Weantinnocks and Potatucks were established tribes living in northeast Connecticut long before the colonials came.)

So how did a batch of mixed tribal remnants become a cohesive tribal nation?

It all goes back to an icy December 21, 1620, when William Bradford led his forty-four "Saints"—Pilgrims—and sixty-six "Strangers"—unaffiliated sects—off the deck of the *Mayflower* at Plymouth, Massachusetts. Bad timing at its worst, for half the group died from disease and malnutrition that first winter. A Wampanoag sachem, Massasoit, took pity on the miserable colony and gave them life in the form of game and maize. In the spring, he showed them how to grow the strange stalk, using decaying fish as fertilizer around the roots. The grateful survivors threw a feast for their saviors the following October, after the storehouses had been filled to the brim with the bountiful harvest (which became the basis of our national Thanksgiving Day).

As the Pilgrim colony proliferated, so did the need to expand into the interior, which drove game away and caused the Wampanoag tribe considerable woe. Massasoit managed to maintain an uneasy alliance, but when the old man died in 1661, the bonds of friendship were buried in his grave.

His son, Wamsutta, who enjoyed the status of sachem for only a year, succeeded him. Wamsutta died while sequestered by arrogant Plymouth officials, who had detained him for questioning. The stage was nearly set for brutality beyond belief.

In 1662, Massasoit's second son, Metacom, whom for some reason the whites called King Philip, became sachem. Arrogant hostility against the Wampanoag worsened. Colonists' hogs and cattle trampled Indian cornfields—a commonplace occurrence—and nothing was done. Angry Indians countered with a few well-placed arrows (and musket balls, for the Wampanong had quietly been acquiring muskets from their more friendly French neighbors to the north), which put some surreptitious meat on the table instead of the usual maize cakes.

Still, all might have been resolved peaceably with the Pilgrims, except for the Puritans with their strict authoritarian religious beliefs. The harsh Puritans detested the Indians and their heathen ways and wanted them removed from New England. In 1637, several hundred Connecticut Valley Puritans, led by Captain John Mason, surrounded a Pequot village while the warriors were on a hunting trip. They torched the village and massacred the women and children, and then gave thanks to God for the "sweet victory."

In 1675, three Wampanoag, suspected in the murder of a Christianized Harvard-educated Indian by name of John Sassamon, were hanged. With the game gone and his ancestral lands now held by enemies, humiliated and with his bronze back against a solid wall of Puritan antagonism, King Philip led the Wampanoag on the warpath.

The conflict only lasted fourteen months but quickly spread throughout Massachusetts and Connecticut as its ugly tentacles encircled other indigenous tribes. The bloodbath was horrific. Wrote one early historian, "Every eleventh family was homeless, and every eleventh soldier had sunk to his grave." For each colonist killed, three Indians died—if not from bullets, then from disease and starvation. Of some ninety Puritan towns, fifty-two were attacked and thirteen leveled.

By the time the war ended, over 600 Colonial men had perished, along with some 2,000 women and children. Twelve hundred homes had been destroyed and over 8000 head of cattle had become collateral damage. Great numbers of Indian squaws and children were forced to become house servants and field slaves, while many captured warriors were sold to slave traders in the West Indies. The total cost of the war exceeded the worth of all the personal property in New England.

Historians have argued with good cause that King Philip's War has the dubious honor of being America's bloodiest war, even exceeding per capita deaths during the Civil War. The phenomenal growth of Colonial New England came to a screeching halt and would not recover for several years.

In the end, of course, the Indians lost and the Puritans got their man. King Philip was summarily executed, quartered, and his severed head placed on a stake and paraded through Plymouth Colony. There it remained on display for two years as a grim reminder of the terrible swift retribution that awaited anyone foolhardy enough to defy the righteous sword of white justice. The ravens quickly cleansed the skull and moved on to fatter pickings. Philip's wife and son—Massasoit the Savior's grandson—were sold as slaves to the highest bidder in Bermuda.

Decimated remnants of the defeated tribes sought refuge at Schaghticoke, near Albany, New York, where they were welcomed by Governor Andros, a kindly man, who "planted a tree of welfare" to shelter the refugees.

Thus the Schaghticoke tribe, rising like a phoenix from the ashes of defeat, came to be. They went on to become staunch allies of the Colonists in the Revolutionary War, aiding in the struggle to break the shackles of the red-coated Empire by providing dozens of warriors to act as scouts and messengers.

Their numbers remain small; their future is uncertain—still hidden in the ink pen of some federal official who is tasked to review the state's appeal to overturn the BIA's decision. But hybrid or not, the Schaghticoke are here to stay.

*   *   *

If you think the aforementioned Indian tribes had it tough, read on!

The Abenaki numbered about 40,000 when they first rubbed elbows with Captain Verrazano in 1524. By the end of the American Revolution, less than 1000 remained. This proud people, who had inhabited upper New England and New Brunswick for over 10,000 years, had been nearly wiped out in a scant 200 years by no less than twenty massive epidemics spawned by small pox, measles, diphtheria, and influenza. Often there were too few survivors to bury the dead. And then there were the "wars" . . .

It might be argued that the winds of war, which would eventually usher in the hundred-year conflict between England and France, billowed in the sails of a small English frigate that followed a steadfast course toward the setting sun.

In 1497, English navigator John Cabot became excited when he heard the news that an Italian by name of Christopher Columbus had discovered a great land far to the west. According to rumor, it might even be the Spice Islands—a place reputedly overflowing with riches beyond comprehension, its air sweet with coveted spices worth a king's ransom many times over.

Cabot obtained an audience with King Henry VII and convinced the king that England should share in the fabulous wealth. The king agreed, and soon Cabot sailed away on the small frigate, Matthew, accompanied by his young son, Sebastian, and eighteen crewmen. The Matthew sailed west for fifty days and on June 24 made landfall at what is believed to be Nova Scotia's Cape Breton Island.

(Hence, John Cabot is generally credited as "discovering" mainland North America. Columbus gets credit for colliding with South America—not to be confused with his first voyage in 1492, when he bumped into a tiny nondescript island east of Cuba thought to be Plana Cays. However, Columbus' South American discovery came in 1498, a year after Cabot's journey.)

Cabot failed to find riches or spices, but his glowing reports of waters teeming with all kinds of fish quickly reached the ears of European fishermen, and soon great fleets from several nations vied for the bountiful ocean harvest on the Great Bank. Before long, rumors of a gold-laden kingdom called

"Norumbega" began to circulate among the royal courts of Europe. Norumbega supposedly rivaled the famed Seven Cities of Cibola, which kept the Spanish conquistadors busy in far off southwestern deserts. The rumor proved irresistible, and the French decided to go seeking.

They didn't find gold; instead, they found large populations of Indians with vast quantities of furs—nearly as valuable as the yellow metal. Came Samuel de Champlain and Pierre De Monts in 1604, building forts and trading furs—and planting the French flag wherever they paused (which didn't sit well with the English, who believed that Cabot's journey gave Britannia first dibs). The French thumbed their noses at the English and traded furs with all comers, which unleashed an eight-year war between the northern Micmac, on whose land the French forts were built, and the southern Abenaki, who wanted a slice of the furry pie.

The Micmac finally crushed the Abenaki and were in turn defeated by an unseen enemy—the white man's sickness. Three separate epidemics in three consecutive years (1617-1619) killed off a good seventy-five percent of the Indian population in New England and the Canadian Maritimes. War screeched to a halt, the fur trade lagged, and the French traders moved west to trade with the Hurons.

Problems, though, were just beginning for the French—and the Abenaki, who had formed a loose bond with the blue coats through the "Christianizing" efforts of the French Jesuits. Caught between a political rock and hard place, the eastern Abenaki tried to remain neutral while France and England duked it out over the next several generations.

The Iroquois Confederacy, allied with the English, was partial to Abenaki scalps; and the English, viewing the Abenaki as French allies, encouraged the Iroquois to beat their war drums. The French had their hands full with the cantankerous British and, except for a handful of Jesuits, cared less what befell the Abenaki.

The Abenaki social structure was the only thing that saved their noble bronze skins. Abenaki generally dwelled in small villages and had never ascribed to a central authority. Thus when attacked, these small groups would fade into the landscape, often crossing into Canada, and then regroup to strike again. An elusive foe, they wrote the book on modern guerrilla tactics!

But they struck out twice. The French got the boot from the British, and then the British got axed by the Revolution. Land hungry colonists of the new nation said, "The Abenaki are Canadian Indians. They have no claim to good American soil." The new states affirmed the colonial rights and grabbed off huge tracts of Abenaki land without making compensation.

But they were wrong. The Abenaki had simply faded into the background, living here and there in small bands while they waited for the cannons to fall silent. Their dispersal saved them, for unlike the Cherokee, Shawnee and Delaware, there would be no "ride into the sunset" for the Abenaki.

"Progress" has favored the Abenaki. Now they number 12,000, including the Canadian branch. Most of the Abenaki Penobscot—2000 or so—live on a reservation on Indian Island at Old Town, Maine. About 2500 Penacook, also called"Vermont" Abenaki, live in Vermont and New Hampshire, with most concentrated in the northwest corner of Vermont near Lake Champlain.

In 1978, the Federal Government awarded the Penobscot and Passamaquoddy tribes a neat chunk of change—$81.5 million as restitution for lands unlawfully obtained. The "Abenaki Nation" has asked for Federal recognition, but the decision is still pending.

*   *   *

The war chants, long since muted, have been replaced by the discordant blare of pop rock, which escapes from beneath the earphones of CD player-armed Indians. Tomahawks, now cleansed of blood wrested from resisting scalps, benignly rest in museum display cases. Teenage Native Americans, their heritage ground into the dust of squalid reservation life, have resorted to "counting coup" with a joystick attached to a video game.

And what has become of the scalps—those small swatches of mummified leather covered with a few wisps of hair that were once a token of a warrior's courage and skill? A good guess is that many, unrecognized for what they are, have been thrown out with other unwanted leavings of deceased relatives. Some are probably stashed in old forgotten trunks in cobwebbed attics or tucked away in the bottom drawers of peeling dressers. Out of sight; out of mind. Best forgotten, perhaps, these grisly reminders of a violent greed-driven past, which still grinds against the conscience of the winners and smothers the spirit of the losers.

The "players" are gone, leaving their acts blood-smeared in a grotesque mélange on history's canvas. The Trail of Tears, Wounded Knee, Custer's debacle, and myriad other incidents from those turbulent times are only vague names to most of the new generation. Just as Chief Seattle long ago prophesied, "change" has pushed the old ways into the graves of fallen warriors. The red man's past has been relegated to history tomes and eighth-grade classrooms.

Yet in the shadows of the Blue Ridge, somehow the past seems to mingle with the present, untouched by time and that catch-all we call "progress."

Chapter Thirty

Presidential Wrath

My first view of New Hampshire's awesome Franconia Ridge nearly scared the bedoozles out of me. Well, maybe not the bedoozles, but from my vantage point atop Mount Moosilauke, my heart did a double flip when I first glimpsed mighty Mount Lafayette through the misty curtains that swirled around me. Beyond the deep chasm called Franconia Notch—a couple of days further along on the long journey to Katahdin—the mountain jutted against a boiling purplish sky. *A gargantuan troll,* I thought, *waiting to swallow my carcass and spit out a couple of puny bones as a warning to others: "This is what happens to trespassers."* Thinking back, I guess it was the bedoozles after all!

Old Lafayette was kind to me the day I crossed its treeless pointed peak. I didn't get masticated, but then I didn't dally either, for dark clouds churned the heavens like some malevolent potion in a witch's cauldron. I hurried on to lower, safer ground where the blanket of red spruce made me feel like I wasn't standing vulnerable on the rooftop of the world. *Well now,* I muttered, hidden from the Almighty's eyes in the tight-knitted spruce forest, *that wasn't so bad.* And it wasn't—for the next two days.

Then I climbed Webster Cliffs, a dizzying series of ledges that rises out of Crawford Notch, and strode into the realm of the "Presidents." The heart-skipping, boulder-strewn landscape that seemed to scrape the heavens reminded me of a place where ancient titans, if they existed, would have battled for earthly dominance. All around, rippling the earth's crust, stood grand mountains bearing names of great presidents, enshrining them for time immemorial: Webster, Jackson, Clinton (Pierce), Franklin, Clay, Washington, Adams, and Madison. (On official maps, Mt. Clinton is Mt. Pierce. It was not named for Bill Clinton—he wouldn't be born until several decades later. The locals dubbed it "Clinton" for DeWitt Clinton, who promoted the Erie Canal. The New Hampshire legislature changed the name to "Pierce" in 1913 to honor the 14th president, the only one to hail from their state. Many locals still refer to the mountain by the name *they* gave it.)

A wall of monstrous barren islands rising out of a vast green ocean, this Presidential Range, which runs for some twenty-five miles. Almost all of it lies above tree line, where one *does* feel like the Creator is floating just overhead, watching every little peccadillo, ready to pounce when the sin basket gets overloaded.

(Okay, I paid enough attention in History 101 to know that Webster and Franklin, great as they were, never made the cut. Perhaps the locals who bestowed the honors hadn't taken History 101. Too, Mount Jackson wasn't named for "Old Hickory"; instead, it honors Charles Jackson, once New Hampshire's State Geologist in the 1800s.

And Mt. Clay? Undoubtedly Henry, though not a president, deserved to have one of the barren peaks as his namesake. But there are only so many mountains in the Presidential Range, and someone decided that former President Ronald Reagan needed to have his own mountain. In early 2003, the New Hampshire legislature voted to scratch Clay's name off the map and pencil in Reagan's. Reagan detractors, after being forced to throw in the towel, sniggered and remarked that the former president didn't really get all that much. The 5533-foot peak is only 150 feet higher than the ridgeline. As it turns out, the legislature jumped the gun. Federal policy requires that a person be dead at least five years before a feature can be given a commemorative name. Henry Clay gets to keep the mountain for at least another four years.)

North of Mizpah Hut, one of several "pay" facilities positioned in the Whites and operated by the Appalachian Mountain Club, the landscape rises to its zenith, a severe, exposed stretch of nearly thirteen miles that makes the skin crawl and the mind panic when the clouds begin to darken.

Skate had caught up with me the previous afternoon and we had shared a plank platform at Nauman Tentsite, adjacent to Mizpah Hut. We had also shared a horrendous thunderstorm that night. As we climbed Mt. Clinton the next morning, the weather seemed to deteriorate with each step upward toward the exposed ridge, but we decided to try for Lake of the Clouds Hut, only five miles away. Soon we came to a weatherbeaten sign that read: *STOP! The area ahead has the worst weather in America. Many have died there from exposure, even in the summer. Turn back if the weather is bad.* An ominous warning that sent a gaggle of goosies rippling up my spine.

The weather *was* BAD. Sleet-laced rain, pushed by wind gusting well over forty miles per hour, stung like B-B pellets. The fog swirled in dense swathes, so thick I could hardly read the words. I yelled, "Nice time to be letting us in on their little secret. You think we should turn back"? Skate stuck her tongue out at me like I had somehow insulted her and headed on up the trail. I followed like a dog on a short leash.

Soon came the first of a bumper crop of little white wooden crosses, which made me wonder if the unlucky hiker—whoever it was—couldn't read or had a death wish. More goosies! At last, when the faint outline of Lake of the Clouds Hut appeared through the opaque curtain, close enough that I nearly ran smack into the wall, I counted my blessings and sent up a mental smoke signal of thanks to the Almighty. No little crosses would have to be planted in the rocks for Skate and me.

On the other hand, the exhilaration that comes from struttin' on the cutting edge singed my toenails. After all, life is a daring adventure, or it is nothing at all . . . isn't it?

*   *   *

Truth be known, the mightiest of the Presidentials, Mount Washington, almost seemed anticlimactic after traipsing over Lafayette's pointed peak. But Mount Washington is by far the greater eater of the unwary and careless—a dozing tiger ready to pounce at the slightest provocation. The small white wooden crosses that sprinkle the rocky slopes crowding the narrow trail on its torturous twisting toward the mountain's stark summit attest to its vicious bent. For each cross signifies a fleshy morsel consumed by Fate to appease its cruel appetite.

Unbelievable almost, how close some of the little totems have seemed to sprout near a hut, a place of safety. Just unfathomable—almost!

I've tweaked the tiger's tail three times, each time managing to get across the windswept summit without awakening the beast. Even so, a couple of times it stirred.

Take that second time in 1994: Wednesday, August 31st, to be exact. I had been leapfrogging for several weeks with three other thru-hikers, Earth Dawg, Shirt and Tie, and Haj. As usually happens that far into a thru-hike, we'd become really close, like family, although I'd been relegated to the role of "the old guy" (at age 57!) and had somehow become a father figure for the others, crowding the clock at twice their individual ages. Such is life!

Late the previous afternoon, buffeted by near gale force winds and thickening clouds, we had reached Lake of the Clouds Hut, which clutched the high alpine ridge at the base of Mount Washington's summit like a monkey grasping the only banana in the forest. Hoping to "work-for-stay" (food and a place to sleep on the dining room floor in exchange for a couple hours of washing dishes or some similar mundane task), we immediately sought out the "Croo" chief.

The "chief" turned out to be a hefty lass with sweat beading her determined face. Getty (I'll call her) was busy directing the "Croo's" supper preparations with the finesse of a Marine drill sergeant. She glared at the interruption, with no hint of sympathy in her multitasking eyes. "Sorry, I don't need any help. The Dungeon's open though; six dollars each." (The Dungeon, as it is not-so-fondly called by hikers, is the hut's storm cellar. During a storm several years ago, wind lifted the entire roof off the hut and sailed it into oblivion.)

Earth Dawg wasn't to be put off. "Do you think there might be any food left over?" Getty shook her head. "Got a full house tonight. I wouldn't count on it." Seeing the bleak look on our faces, on a softer note she added, "You can wait over there while the paying guests eat." She stressed "paying" as she pointed to a small lounge adjacent to the dining room. "Never know if they're gonna be hungry or wimped out from hiking."

We paid our six dollars and retreated to the Dungeon. Built-in bunk platforms—enough to sleep six hikers—filled most of the tiny area, leaving barely enough floor space to dance a jig—if one wanted to do any dancing, which we didn't. One small window graced the bunk-free wall. The wind howled through a broken pane and escaped beneath a two-inch crack at the bottom of the heavy plank door. Haj stuffed his rain jacket in the broken pane, which helped some. We unrolled our sleeping bags onto the bare wood bunks and then went up to the lounge to see if Fortune would smile on us.

No such luck. The "paying guests"—seventy or more—had filled the dining room and were consuming the vittles like famished hogs rooting at a slop trough. We waited—and waited—and waited. I nudged Shirt and Tie. "Lookie there. Isn't that the Papillon Duo?" The Papillon Duo was a husband/wife thru-hiker pair who had planned to celebrate their wedding anniversary by staying at huts on their way through the White Mountains. Now there they were, slopping with more gusto that a half-dozen of the other guests combined.

At last, one by one, people dropped their forks onto soiled plates, burped, and pushed swollen bellies away from littered tables—except the Papillon Duo, who continued to stuff food down at an amazing rate (unless one happened to be a thru-hiker). Frantic, my companions said, "Model-T, go check with Getty and see if there's going to be any food left. You're older and she'll be nicer to you." Yeah, right!

I found the "Croo" chief at the sink chewing on a helper for not getting the dishwater hot enough. When I asked about any leftovers, she scoffed, "Just look at them two eat." She motioned toward the Papillon Duo. "The 'Croo'll' do good to have anything left after they get done." Getty rolled her eyes and finished the conversation with a snapped "Sorry" and stomped off to hold school on another errant croo member.

I delivered the bad news to my companions and said, "I'm going down to the Dungeon and cook supper. Free food's not gonna happen." The others nodded, and we walked outside into the inky black. Even the sun had deserted us, and none had remembered to carry a flashlight. We stumbled along the outside wall, struggling against the blustering wind, which now keened like a choir of banshees, and pushed through the cellar door.

We huddled on the small floor and cooked by candlelight, shivering as the wind assaulted the broken pane and sneaked in like a thief to rob us of what little warmth we managed to garner. As soon as I finished eating, I crawled inside my sleeping bag. The others weren't ready to settle in for the night and decided to go back up to the hut, where a ranger was supposed to give a program about the Appalachian Trail—like I needed *that* after five months of *living* the subject of his discourse. "Just close the door on the way out," I muttered through the small breathing hole I'd engineered.

Sometime later, Earth Dawg shook me awake. "Model-T, Getty said she felt sorry for us and had the 'Croo' make some butterscotch brownies. Here's yours." I couldn't see what he had for my head was covered up, but I took it on faith. "Just stick'em through the hole," I mumbled, opening my mouth to receive the precious windfall and thinking, *So the Grinch has a heart after all.*

Lake of the Clouds Hut on a good day.
Mount Washington's summit from the "back side."

The others were fast asleep when I awoke in the early dawn. The wind still howled, but not as bad. Anxious, I climbed out of the bag and opened the door to see what the morning had brought. No snow, but the rocky landscape glistened as if it had been painted with mineral oil. Ice! Just a thin covering, but dangerous nonetheless. High above, clouds blanketed the summit, over twelve hundred feet higher than Lake of the Cloud's 5000-foot elevation, and left me with an uneasy feeling in the pit of my stomach. For I vividly remembered the little white crosses that pockmarked the rock-strewn slope on the mile-long trek up to the peak, the ones I'd seen on my previous journey. *Snow up there? With this wind and ice to boot! Spells trouble with a big "T."* Then I thought of the Summit House and its cafeteria, which should be coming alive just about now. Hot coffee and donuts—hot damn! I threw on my clothes and began the climb.

It was tough going from the get-go. *Dang'em slick rocks. Dang'em fickle wind. Can't make up its mind whether it wants to grab or push. Concentrate Idiot; plant the boot . . . brace with the walking stick; take another step . . . go slow; don't rush . . . fingers numb . . . can't see for the tears; dammit all. Was that a cross? Almost close enough to touch. Damn funny, sittin' here on my skinny butt in the middle of the trail—must've slipped. Or got bowled over. Shit'n place. Chicken nasty!*

I'd just gotten back on my feet when a violent gust tossed me off the trail as if I were no more than a piece of fluff. In the blink of an eye I was sprawled on my stomach between two downslope boulders and pinned by my pack. A few feet away at eye level, a small white cross rose out of the rocks. I moved my body parts—nothing broken—and staggered to my feet, all the while staring at the grim token of another human being's demise. *Hell's bells! What if I'd been knocked unconscious, or broken a leg! How long could a body last in this subfreezing temperature, with this wind? No one could hear a cry for help. Damn, it happened so quick!*

Then came the unsettling thought: *Do these little crosses come so easily?*

By the time I reached the Summit House, Ma Nature had pummeled me good. Thinking back, I realize that I was well on the way to serious hypothermia, what with the uncontrollable shivering, fogged mind, and deep nerve-sapping numbness. I stumbled into the Summit House and hunkered down on a bench until the shivering stopped and pain began to course through my fingers and toes. Only then did I walk into the cafeteria, for I wanted to enjoy that first cup of real honest-to-God coffee.

The cafeteria wasn't open—but almost. I saw a woman setting up the serving line. Putting on my most pleasant smile (more akin to a gargoyle's scowl after being shot up with Botox), I asked, "Mam, is it possible for me to get a cup of coffee?"

"Why you poor thing. You look froze and beyond." I wondered what "beyond" entailed. "Go ahead and I'll check you out."

I filled a cup from the big commercial urn and walked toward the cash register. Unable to help myself, I took a sip—and nearly gagged on the lukewarm, bitter liquid. "Mam, could this be last night's coffee? It's terrible."

She stared at me like I'd committed a mortal sin, then slapped her forehead. "Oh my, I'm so very sorry. I guess Lottie hasn't gotten around to making a fresh batch yet. Tell you what, pour that out and when the coffee's made, you get a free cup."

I smiled my appreciation and headed for the nearest trash bin, which sat beside the kiosk that held the sugar, cream, and condiments. A small voice in my muddled head (Model-T?) whispered, *That nasty coffee wouldn't be so nasty if you doctored it some.* Great thought! I sneaked a glance at the cash register. The lady had left. I grabbed a handful of sugars and creamers, and took a seat at a table in the back of the room. Counting as I went, I ripped the tops off the little white packages and dumped in the contents: *One, two, three, . . . twenty-one. Nice!* I stirred the concoction and added a like number of creamers, again stirring with a flourish—and then chugalugged the off-white liquid. *Not bad!*

Soon the line opened and I bought two sweet rolls and got my free coffee—and made another trip to the kiosk. I had the routine down pat by this time, but common sense took over and I only added fifteen packages each of sugar and creamer, then slowly sipped the sugary mix while I ate the rolls. I had just finished when Earth Dawg and Shirt and Tie walked in. "Where's Haj?" I asked.

"Not far back," Earth Dawg said. "You already eaten?"

"In a manner of speaking." Damn, but my synapses were vibrating. "I'm outta here. See you guys at Madison Hut for lunch." Something to be said for a *sugar high.* Easiest six miles I've ever done!

On the other hand, images of small white crosses growing like strange-looking flowers among the rose-tinted rocky slopes still haunt my dreams . . .

*   *   *

The ancient Penacook (western) Abenaki called Mother Earth's awesome upheaval the *Waumbekket-Mentha,* which loosely translates as "mountains with snowy foreheads." In 1497, English explorer John Sebastian Cabot, while sailing along the New England coast in search of riches for his king, was the first *Swannuken* to spot the great mountain that crinkled the distant horizon as he stood on the salt-stained deck of his rolling ship. (Some historians argue that Giovanni da Verrazano claimed the original gander rights in 1524; but then, what are a couple of decades in the great scheme of things! Supposedly the *Waumbkklet-Mentha* rose out of the ancestral ocean some 400,000,000 years ago.)

Cabot, of course, didn't know that he was looking at the mightiest of the *Waumbekket-Mentha*, which the Penacooks reverently named *Agiocochook*, "place of the Great Spirit." (Later, the white settlers named the mountain "Sugar Loaf" or "Crystal Mountain" until they finally decided to name it after their great White Father, George Washington.) Penacooks with any sense at all never went *up there*. Even then, it was a place of death.

But Darby Field didn't have that small tidbit of Abenaki lore in his game bag—or if he did, his curiosity got the best of his good sense. From the day he had set out from his Exeter homestead near the coast to see for himself the wonders that trappers returning from the vast mountainous area to the northwest told about, he was hooked. It drove him like a burning fever, sending him canoeing up the Saco River, into the shadowy depths of an alien landscape that swelled his imagination to the bursting point.

And there was *that* mountain, the giant with the cloud-shrouded top that stood above all others, about which the Penacook whispered with awed reverence. *Agiocochook!* Even after he had returned to Exeter, the image of the mountain festered in his mind, an obsession building like a huge boil, threatening to burst his skull. *What was on top of that infernal mountain?*

Day and night it gnawed at his louse-bitten cranium like a hungry rat. Then one sunny day in July 1642, something snapped. The settler growled at his wife, "Can't stand just not knowin.' Hit keeps eatin' away at m' gizzard until tain't nothing left 'ceptin what's fit fer buzzards." With that diagnosis still dangling in the doorway, Field stuffed some jerky in his game bag, promised two Abenaki's all the rum they could drink in a day if they would go with him, and he began the journey that would carry him to the lofty peak. And into the history books.

Darby Field became the first white person to summit *Agiocochook*. When he reached the top, the farmer-turned-explorer braced against the stiff wind that swept across the mountain's broad top and tried to see through the thick blanket of swirling gray. Tired and chilled, he silently cursed his stupidity for wasting time chasing a pipe dream, what with all the work to do back at the farm. He thought, *Ain't nuthin' up here 'cept rocks n' two crazy Injuns—and a damn fool.*

Then, almost as if the mountain felt ashamed for Field's lackluster reception, Mother Earth lifted her skirt and revealed *Waumbekket-Mentha* in all its breathtaking grandeur. But the man's attention was held captive by the crystal-crusted rocks strewn all about, which sparkled in the brilliant sunshine. *By damn, gems! Valuable jewels! Th' mountaintop's covered with'em!* Field yelled, "Injuns, we's gonna be rich!" And he began to stuff his pockets and game bag with his perceived fortune.

Alas, when he returned to Exeter, Field quickly learned that his "valuable gems" were nothing more than quartz rocks sprinkled with silica. He drowned his disappointment in rum with his Abenaki companions, who had been confused as to why the crazy white man had wanted to lug several pounds of rocks down off *Agiocochook.* But all was not lost. Darby Field did get a 4000-foot mountain named after him (Mt. Field).

New Hampshire's Royal Governor John Wentworth was frustrated. True, he enjoyed governing the Royal Province, so designated by England's King Charles II nearly a century before. (Charles II wanted to lay claim to the tall white pines that covered New Hampshire's wooded slopes for masts for his navy's ships. His source had dried up when the Great Northern War between Russia and Sweden had shut down his Norway supplier.)

For sure, Wentworth's was an exalted position—a fact he proclaimed to all who would listen—for the other twelve governors in the New World merely governed "colonies." But now King George III, plagued by worries about France's burgeoning armada, urgently needed more masts and timber to upgrade his fleet. The mountain slopes still supported heavy growths of what the King demanded, mainly white pine, hemlock, and fir. The big problem—and the source of Governor Wentworth's current frustration. The massive stands of timber were west of the impenetrable White Mountains and were held captive by the lumberjacks of Connecticut, who floated the prized logs down the Connecticut River to God only knew where and sold them to God only knew who.

If only he could find a pass through the White Mountains and get the timber over to Portsmouth harbor. But that formidable barrier might as well be the Great Wall of China—although rumors of a passage did reach his exalted ears from time to time. Might it be true?

On a whim, in 1771 Governor Wentworth summoned his aide. "Spread the word far and wide that whosoever shall find a passage through the White Mountains will receive the King's blessing and the Royal Governor's reward."

It so happened that the Governor's offer had reached the ears of Timothy Nash, a Lancaster hunter of some repute. While he was tracking a moose over Cherry Mountain on the western range of the Whites, he became lost. He climbed a tree to get his bearings and in the distance glimpsed what looked like a notch in the great mountain chain toward the east. Many a night Nash had sat with other hunters around campfires and listened to tales of a hidden passage through the Whites, known only to the Indians and never seen by a white man.

Excited, Nash forgot about the moose and made his way toward the distant notch—and on to Portsmouth and the Royal Governor's mansion to claim "the King's blessing and the Royal Governor's reward."

"Not so fast," growled the excited—but somewhat skeptical—governor. "First you must bring a horse through the notch from Lancaster to Portsmouth. Then you must build a road leading east through the notch. If you can do this, I will grant you a large parcel of land at the head of the notch." As an afterthought, the wily governor added, "On the western side of the notch."

Excited, Nash returned to Lancaster and enlisted the aid of his friend, Benjamin Sawyer. The men selected a "mello" plow horse with a calm disposition and set off for Portsmouth by way of the "Notch." A good thing Nash and Sawyer picked a docile nag, for on several occasions they had to lower the poor beast over impassable boulders and cliffs with a block and tackle.

When they reached Portsmouth, the grateful governor rewarded the men with a land grant of 2,184 acres (although it is doubtful that His Honor knew about the block and tackle doings). Nash and Sawyer promptly sold the property to a group of Portsmouth businessmen before Governor Wentworth could change his mind for the tidy sum of 90 pounds (about $200). But it would take another thirteen years for a proper road to open up what would become known as the "Great Notch."

The Portsmouth businessmen merged their acquisition with a 25,000-acre land grant awarded them by Governor Wentworth and formed a township. The generous governor, before fleeing to Nova Scotia with his wife and family at the onset of the American Revolutionary War, named the township Bretton Woods after his ancestral English home, Bretton Hall. (Today, Bretton Woods is home to the Mount Washington Hotel, a plush resort complete with a 27-hole golf course and ski area. Among the four native New Hampshire families who share ownership of the property are the Bedor and Presby families, who also own the Mount Washington Cog Railway.)

The American Revolution came and went, and the Royal Province was elevated to statehood, along with its twelve other political kin that were joined in the common cause. The Great Notch languished in relative isolation for several years. In 1790 came Abel Crawford with his wife, Hannah Rosebrook (who was also his first cousin) and their growing family to Fabyans in Bretton

Woods. There, he built a crude log cabin on a large earth mound referred to as the Giants Grave. (Only two decades earlier Timothy Nash and Benjamin Sawyer had manhandled their old plowhorse across this boulder-filled landscape.)

A bear of a man, Abel Crawford stood nearly six-feet-four and had the blood of the mountains in his veins. He and Hannah didn't stay long at Fabyans—"Too crowded," he grumbled, after he smelled the smoke carried on a stiff north wind from a neighbor's cabin over a mile away.

Two years after moving to the Giants Grave, Abel and Hannah gathered up their belongings and kids and moved to Hart's Location some twelve miles east at the head of the Notch, where he planted his roots and Hannah planted roses. Abel, dressed in tan moose skin breeches, continued to wander the mountains. Before long, his prowess as hunter and guide quickly extended beyond the White Mountains, eventually earning him the venerated title, "Patriarch of the Hills." But his true joy was his young son, Ethan Allen, whose star was destined to outshine his father's.

When Abel and Hannah moved to Hart's Location, Hannah's father, Eleazer Rosebrook, moved his wife and children into the house vacated by the Crawfords. The day the Rosebrooks moved in, the snow was so deep it hid the cabin door. The temperature remained below freezing for six weeks, and the family nearly starved. If Eleazer came home with an empty game bag, which often seemed the case, the family went to bed hungry.

When the spring thaw came, Eleazer made plans for a more reliable source of sustenance. He built a fine two-story house and opened an inn for travelers passing through the Notch. Down in Hart's Location, Abel Crawford, beginning to feel the weight of his years spent roaming the mountains, also opened an inn, which he called the Mount Crawford House. In 1840, at age 79, Abel led state geologist Charles Jackson to the summit of Mount Washington on horseback and became the first person to ride to the top.

Like father; like son. When Ethan Allen's grandfather, Eleazer Rosebrook, died, the young man inherited the inn at the Giants Grave. Fully as tall as his father—possibly taller and certainly stockier—Ethan tipped the scales at 250 pounds. He liked to show off his great strength by hoisting five hundred pounds over his head and delighted his neighbors by carrying a live kicking buck around on his back. And like his father, Ethan Allen was a born mountain man, which was a fickle toss of the genetic dice for the entrepreneurial-minded innkeeper.

Almost as odd was his marriage to Lucy Howe of Guildhall, Vermont. While Ethan was gregarious, impetuous, a backslapping kind of fellow, Lucy possessed a quiet, inner strength that gave balance to their marriage. But it was inevitable that Ethan's bold nature—and eye for a quick dollar—would pull him to the summit of Mount Washington.

Going to the mountains—"green thinking"—had become fashionable. But the most sought after attraction, lofty Mount Washington, was accessible only to the hardiest. In May 1819, Ethan enlisted the aid of his aging father, and they cut a path to the mountain's summit. (Crawford Path is still in use today—the oldest, continuously maintained footpath in America.)

Ethan led groups up the mountain, including women, for several years, and sometimes had to carry an exhausted female back down the mountain on his back—a task he relished but caused good-natured Lucy to feign a small degree of jealousy. He even went so far as to build a small stone hut under the cone of Mount Washington to protect his charges from violent weather. He furnished the hut with a small stove, iron chest, a roll of sheet lead (on which visitors could scrawl their names with an iron nail), and a plentiful supply of soft moss and hemlock boughs for bedding. (A violent storm swept the hut away on the night of August 28, 1826, the same night that the ill-fated Willey family perished.)

In July 1820, Ethan guided A.N. Brackett, J.W. Weeks, and five others, all who hailed from Lancaster, New Hampshire, through much of the White Mountain range. Along the way, they began to replace the mountain names bestowed by the Abenaki with names more compatible to English ears: Madison, Adams, Jefferson, Monroe, Franklin, and Pleasant. It is probable that these men became the first whites to spend the night atop Mount Washington.

In 1821, Ethan and a neighbor set out to find an easier route to the summit after one visitor wrote about his trip to the top, calling it a ". . . villainous break-neck route. God help the poor wight who attempts that route as we did." The pair did find an easier route. But Ethan soon abandoned it in favor of his original Crawford Path, which he improved and made into a bridal path. (The abandoned path is roughly the same trail later followed by the cog railway.)

Ethan Allen Crawford's shining star eventually began to lose its luster. Unscrupulous land investors took advantage of his trusting nature, shamelessly cheating him. New, more comfortable hotels pulled visitors away from his inn. Jealous men maligned his reputation, and his bull strength faded when disease and injury beset him. And perhaps the worst blow: He was confined in the Lancaster jail for failure to make good on his debts.

Lucy stuck by him through the dark times, bolstering him with her own strength and courage. In her memoirs, *A History of the White Mountains*, she wrote about the plight of her husband: ". . . men suffer various ways in advancing civilization . . ."

In the end, Lucy's remarkable strength was not enough. After he was released from debtor's prison, Ethan sought refuge with his wife in the verdant hills of Vermont. But bad fortune continued to plague the unlucky couple and fifty-six year-old Ethan Allen, terminally ill, returned to his beloved Notch to die.

The "King of the Mountains" had been sacrificed on the altar of Progress. But the Crawford name remains alive in the deep notch beside the Saco River, which created it millions of years ago. And the Crawfords, like Darby Field, have a mountain that bears their name. (A historical slight, really, in light of how the Crawford family impacted on the history of the Whites. There's nothing spectacular about Mount Crawford, for the 3000-footer has an indiscriminate, tree-covered summit. But fittingly, it does sit athwart Ethan's old Crawford Path.)

A final tidbit about Crawford Notch—a part of its history as dark as the deepest shadows that lie in the remotest innards of the Notch. The tragedy happened near present day Willey House, barely a mile to the left down US Highway 302 from where the Appalachian Trail passes through Crawford Notch.

In the fall of 1825, Samuel Willey, Jr., moved his family from nearby Bartlett to a small house on the west edge of Hart's Location, a long narrow hamlet that still encompasses most of Crawford Notch. He immediately enlarged the house into an inn to grab some of the tourist money from the city folks who were afflicted with the "green thinking." The following June, the Willey family became worried when heavy rains triggered a massive landslide that roared into the Notch not far from their inn. Concerned, Mr. Willey had a cave-like structure built a short distance from the house, a place of safety to which the family could flee if the mountainside turned to mud and came tumbling down.

The June rains passed and a drought hit, wilting the vegetation and drying the mountain soil to an unusual depth. Then on the night of August 26, 1826, the unthinkable happened. A monster storm roared in, one of the most violent and destructive the Notch had ever witnessed, bringing torrential rains and hurricane-like winds. Ethan Allen's storm shelter near Mount Washington's summit was swept into oblivion like so much chaff. The Saco River rose twenty-four feet overnight, cutting new gorges and carrying away livestock and mighty trees in its grinding, frothing floodwaters.

In the Willey house, family members and two hired hands huddled in terrified silence as the storm raged. Finally, they decided to flee to the safety of the nearby cave. As they dashed through the storm, a great rumbling could be heard. And then the mountain convulsed.

Two days later, friends and family finally managed to thread through the tangle of twisted trees and bloated stinking animals that cluttered the Notch, at last reaching the Willey's house. It stood untouched but there was no sign of life, except for a howling dog. The huge slide had split in two, passing to each side of the house, which was somewhat protected by a large boulder. The bodies of Mr. Willey, his wife, two children, and the two hired hands were found nearby, crushed in the twisted wreckage of rocks and trees. Apparently, one side of the landslide had caught them dead on. The bodies of the Willey's other three children were never recovered.

Inside on a table, near Samuel Willey's glasses, lay the family Bible, which was opened at the 18th Psalm. Verse 7 reads, *Then the earth shook and trembled; the foundations also of the hills moved and were shaken, because He was wroth.*

A stiff price to pay for fame, but Mt. Willey, a 4000-footer soaring above the Willey House, where the old scars can still be seen, stands vigilant guard over the memory of the Willey family.

Hart's Location, the site of the Willey disaster and burial place of old Abel Crawford, still exists as New Hampshire's smallest town. Dating back to 1772 and named for Colonel John Hart of Portsmouth, the town's forty residents (2003 census—that translates into two persons per each of the town's 19.2 square mile area!) still keep a wary eye on the sky. The earthen slide that slopes up from the Willey House remains a grim, solemn reminder of man's frailty in the face of nature's fury.

*   *   *

"Mooning" the Mount Washington Cog Railway has become a frequent, albeit vulgar, tradition among the newer trompers of the Trail. (No, I didn't!)

Granted, it doesn't take much to light a fire in the fertile minds of today's environmental activists. And there's something about the black smoke belching from the little cog train's tall smokestack into the pristine air as it huffs and puffs up and down the mountainside that seems to fire up the boilers of the eco-warriors. Thus, mooning the cog train where the Appalachian Trail crosses the tracks has become a quasi-form of passive protest—and entertainment for the train's passengers. Of course, if the weather is cold enough to frostbite the butt, then the passengers have to be satisfied with a few jeers and the "finger" salute. But the cog railway does provide a means for the non-walking and non-driving set of the summit's 250,000 annual visitors to reach the top and see what all of the hullabaloo is about.

At least that was Sylvester Marsh's thinking that summer day of 1852 when he and a friend climbed to the summit of Mount Washington. The two men got trounced by a rapidly developing storm and barely made it to the summit's shelter. Marsh, then 49, had lost his considerable fortune two years earlier in the Business Panic of 1850. But he quickly amassed a new fortune by producing a breakfast cereal, which he marketed as Marsh's Caloric Dried Meal.

Obsessed by his concept of a cog railway, he retired at age 52 and began to develop his plan. By 1858, Marsh had completed a working model. He applied for a charter from the New Hampshire legislature and set up a demonstration for the lawmakers. Legend has it that the legislators were so sold on the project that one excited lawmaker offered an amendment that granted Marsh permission to extend the railway on to the moon.

"Crazy" Marsh, as some had taken to calling him, got his charter, not only to build a cog railway to the summit of Mount Washington, but to the top of Mount Lafayette as well. (That fantasy huddled in the shadows of Mount Washington's huge undertaking and never got off the ground.)

Marsh put up $5000 of his own money and went to work, laying out a route with his son, a three and a half-mile straight shot up the western slope, which as it turned out loosely followed Ethan Crawford's abandoned trail up Mount Washington. He then designed and patented the cog mechanism, which made it possible for a train to safely ascend and descend steep grades. Came the assembling of materials. Everything had to be hauled from the nearest railroad depot in Littleton, some twenty-five miles away, to a small logging camp at Twin Rivers. Then the materials had to be transported by oxen to his base camp beside the Ammonoosuc River, which he named Marshfield—a tribute to himself and Darby Field.

In 1866, the first rails were laid. The "little engine that could," Locomotive No. 1 (named "Hero") was built in Roxbury, Massachusetts. The engine, which soon came to be called "Peppersass" because it looked like an upright peppersauce bottle on wheels, was disassembled and reassembled at Marshfield. Peppersass had no fuel or water storage tanks and lacked a water pump for the boiler, so it could only go about a tenth of a mile up the track at a time.

On August 29, 1866, Marsh ordered that Peppersass make a demonstration run on the small finished section of track to stimulate public confidence in the project. A short trip, but it proved that Marsh's idea worked. Workers raced to push track to the summit while engineers added a coal car and water pump to Ol' Peppersass.

The work went fast, and on July 3, 1869, the cog engine pushed a small cart with a few distinguished passengers to the summit of Mount Washington, groaning up grades as steep as 37.4% to become the first mountain climbing cog train in the world. President Ulysses Grant and his family were among those who made the sooty trip that wondrous day. "Crazy" Marsh had done the impossible, a feat many deemed to be the greatest engineering triumph of the century.

For several years, Peppersass shared the track with other more advanced engines but was finally put out to pasture in 1878. However, the officials of Boston and Maine Railroad, who owned the Cog Railway, decided the old engine should have one final run up the mountain. On July 20, 1929, amid much fanfare, publicity, and with six governors from visiting states sitting on the V.I.P. stand, Old Peppersass pushed a small wagon with a couple of passengers up the mountain, the last in a convoy of six sister trains filled with passengers. The wheezing engine made it to the Gulf Tank, three-fourths of the way to the summit, by about 5 P.M. But the hour was growing late and officials feared that if Peppersass tried to go on to the summit, the other trains wouldn't get back to the base until after dark. Three passengers transferred from one of the other trains and joined Peppersass for its historic descent.

About a mile into the descent, a loud crack from the front of the engine suddenly punctured the train's normal creaking and groaning. A tooth had broken off of one of the gears, causing the engine to raise up, which disengaged the cog from the track. Gravity took over and, unimpeded, the train gathered speed and soon rushed downward, out of control with no way to stop. Engineer "Jack" Frost yelled, "Jump! Jump for your lives, men!"

They did, all except for Daniel Rossiter, the official photographer for the New Hampshire Publicity Bureau and the B&M Railroad. Rossiter refused to let go and managed to hang on as the train rushed across the high-trestled Jacob's Ladder. But he lost his hold on the careening car and plunged to his death at the foot of the Ladder.

Peppersass left the track after a run of nearly a half-mile, scattering parts over a wide area before it finally came to a halt. A rescue team carted off the injured and dead. Railroad workers gathered up the scattered parts and hauled the metal carcass and its pieces down to the base camp. They beat out the dents and reassembled Peppersass. Today, the old engine remains on display at the Marshfield Base Station, a metal dinosaur from bygone days.

"Crazy" Marsh, who turned out not to be crazy after all, saw little financial gain from his invention, although he claimed the railway did cure his dyspepsia. His cog railway had cost the considerable sum of $135,000, a venture that only returned eighty-eight percent to the investors. Marsh eventually sold the railway and moved to Concord, New Hampshire, where he lived out his days in quiet solitude until his death on December 30, 1884.

The cog trains continued to vomit black soot onto the mountain through the years. The railway was shut down for one year during WWI and for three years during WWII. Among its distinguished owners have been the Boston and Maine Railroad and Dartmouth College. For the most part, the cog railway has had a safe run. But on September 17, 1967, tragedy struck.

Engine #3 derailed at the Skyline Switch on its descent, about one mile below the summit. The engine rolled off a high trestle, and the uncoupled cars slid several hundred feet down the mountainside before coming to rest against a large boulder. Eight passengers were killed and seventy-two injured. Subsequent investigation revealed that the switch had not been properly set for the descending train.

The mooning still goes on. *But beware, Moonies! The cog train crews take great pleasure in tossing hot coals at bared butts should the tender exposed asses get within range!*

*   *   *

Nature has a way of tossing in a little *yang* to go with her *ying*. The most beautiful of her offspring are sometimes the most deadly. For example, take the *Amanita phalloides* ("Death Cap" to us amateur mycologists). Colorful, innocent looking; yet this little mushroom has put enough "wannabe Euell Gibbons" in the hospital to populate a good-sized city. Or consider the strikingly beautiful lion's mane jellyfish, an eight-foot diameter golden marvel with 1200 tentacles. Each tentacle can dangle more than 120 feet and is loaded with stinging venom. Another example of Nature's sneaky tricks: The Amazon's brilliantly colored poison arrow frog, which grows to the size of a man's thumbnail and whose skin contains the most powerful poison known to man. An amount the size of a grain of salt is enough to kill a grown man. Heck! You can even buy these on the web! They come in an assortment of colors, although the red and black combo reminds me of a four-legged Spider Man.

Get the picture? So it is with the starkly beautiful—and deadly—White Mountains. And with their crowning glory, Mount Washington.

Colonial Darby Field climbed it first in 1642. Ethan Allen ruled its heights for several decades in the early 1800s. On behalf of the State of New Hampshire, in 1832 a Commissioner Willey sold the gigantic mountain to Jacob Sargent of Thornton as part of a $9000 land deal. (Now that's a stretch! How did it get back into the state's hands?)

In 1852, J.S. Hall and L.M. Rosebrook scraped up $7000 and built the first summit house, a 64x 24-foot stone affair constructed from rocks blasted out of the summit's weathered quartz. The crude structure had four heavy chains to hold the flat roof on. The building was an eyesore on the majestic peak; nonetheless, Mount Washington was now ready to feather its aerie with human finery.

A year later, amazed that folks would actually pay money to sleep in the primitive accommodations offered by the unsightly facility, Samuel Spaulding dug deep into his pockets and found enough dollars to build a sister hostel, which he called the Tip Top House.

Spaulding's stone and wood building was somewhat more elaborate, and larger. With better accommodations now in place, the tourist trade began to flourish. Visitors slept in the Summit House and dined in the Tip Top House. Hoping to cash in on the sudden wealth, in 1854 entrepreneur Timothy Estus built a 40-foot high observation platform on the geographical peak. Anchored by four heavy vertical posts, the contraption had a moveable platform that could be raised and lowered by ropes and pulleys. For fifty cents each, tourists could be raised to the highest possible point on the summit to enjoy the grand view. (A neat idea, but Estus didn't do his homework. Clouds covered the mountaintop on most days and his business soon went belly up. The elevator platform was torn down the following year.)

Came the Carriage Road in the early 1860s, winding up the mountain's eastern slope from Pinkham Notch like a monstrous seven-mile serpent. Colonel Joseph Thompson, who owned the popular Glen House in Pinkham Notch, had the honor of driving the first carriage to the summit in late July 1861. The road became an overnight success, much to the Colonel's delight. He stabled as many as 125 horses at a time to provide his guests with easy transportation (for a fee) to the summit. Then on August 31, 1899, everything changed. Freelan Stanley and his wife fired up their steam-propelled "Locomobile" Stanley Steamer and chugged to the top.

Within a few years, the Colonel's horses were put out to pasture. The Mount Washington Carriage Road owners, ever with an eye toward the erratic nature of the Almighty Dollar, fired the horse pooper-scoopers and changed the name of their moneymaker to the Mount Washington Auto Road. (After the snow clears in late March, you can drive your car to the summit for $18; add $7 for each additional adult—2005 rates. You also get a CD and a bumper sticker that reads: "THIS CAR CLIMBED MT. WASHINGTON.")

Came "Crazy" Marsh's Cog Railway in 1869, delivering more tourists than the summit inns could accommodate. A new large hotel was built in 1873. Between the Tip Top House and the "new" Summit Building, patrons could dine in primitive comfort and dance to the melodic strains of an orchestra. Or if so inclined, for ten cents they could browse through the newspaper, *Among the Clouds*, printed twice daily by Henry Burt in his office at the Auto Carriage Station House right on the summit. A swell time could be had by anyone who relished the thin air among the clouds.

Then came tragedy, as if an evil dragon had swooped down and spewed its noxious breath on the helpless summit. When the sun settled behind the mountains on June 18, 1908, the "Great Fire" (cause undetermined) had turned man's puny handiwork on the summit to smoldering ruins and twisted rails. Everything, that is, except the old Tip Top House, which somehow survived unscathed.

But like the mythical Arabian phoenix rising from the ashes to regenerate itself, so the "City Among the Clouds" was reborn, this time bigger and better—although not to the extent envisioned by a couple of entrepreneurial visionaries.

In the early 1900s, a group of entrepreneurs became enamored by the hyper-optimism of a nation awash in new inventions. With imaginations—and ambitions—soaring into the ionosphere and making "Crazy" Marsh look saner than King Solomon, they had an architect draw up plans for a magnificent hotel to grace the summit. The hotel would rival the most luxurious European spas. According to the plans, the building would be three stories high, have one hundred guestrooms, and boast a dining room where four hundred diners could treat their taste buds to Epicurean delights more suited for kings' palates. Afterwards, overstuffed revelers could promenade around a great rotunda and marvel at the mighty mountain's apex, which would extend up through the floor of the grand lobby and allow guests to climb to the summit without having to leave the comfort of their metal and glass cage.

Of course, the Mount Washington Cog Railway couldn't begin to transport the large numbers of tourists that the hotel would attract. Railroad magnate Charles Mellen, president of the influential New York, New Haven, and Hartford Railroad, along with his financier J.P. Morgan, was ready to solve that tiny problem. He would build a super transit line to replace Sylvester

Marsh's outdated creation. But his would not be dependent on a slow acting cog contraption; instead, he would build an electric trolley line powered by overhead wires, with a comfortable grade never exceeding six percent in its *nineteen-mile* run to the summit. No vulgar black smoke; no creaking, groaning cars, no runaway trains. Mellen told Morgan to keep his ink pen and checkbook handy and set out to gain control of the Boston and Maine Railroad, which owned the Cog Railway.

Since the majority of the western slope was owned by timber companies that depended on the Boston and Maine to haul their logs to market, they had no desire to butt heads with the railroad baron. Thus, Mellen had free rein to run his trolley anywhere on the western slope he desired. The cornerstone had been set.

Although surveying of the right of way began on July 4, 1911, the project soon became bogged down in much larger problems that had descended on Mr. Mellen. Even before anti-trust forces fed the paperwork into the Federal gristmill that would soon wrest control of the Boston and Maine Railroad from Mellen's New York, New Haven, and Hartford Railroad, the ink had barely dried on President Taft's signature, which signed the Weeks Act into law. This Act authorized the National Forest Service, in conjunction with parent states, to purchase large tracts of land to establish national forests.

The timber barons in the White Mountains saw the handwriting on the wall and sold much of their holdings, including Mount Washington's western slope and the trolley's proposed right of way, to Uncle Sam. The entire project, including the grandiose hotel, was quietly abandoned.

J.P. Morgan died in 1913, and Charles Mellen resigned soon after. But the Mount Washington Cog Railway continued to haul passengers up the west slope, one protesting cog tooth at a time.

Came the Mount Washington Observatory in 1932, when four determined men came to the summit to record weather conditions—and stayed. A good thing they did. Otherwise, when the wind roared across the ice-covered summit on April 12, 1934, there would have been no anemometer anchored on the roof of the old Auto Road Stage Building to record the extreme violence of Nature that day.

Salvatore Pagliuca, Alex McKenzie, Wendell Stephenson, Robert Stone had made a home for the fledgling Mount Washington Observatory in the Stage Building, had even managed to survive two winters in the harsh isolation that came with wintering on the mountaintop. So for the tight-knit crew, it was like losing a family member when Robert had to be taken down the mountain on a toboggan to let the doc have a look at the hip he had bruised while skiing a couple of days before. But his fellow teammates weren't worried. A huge high pressure area had settled over eastern Canada and the northern Atlantic, bringing unusually mild, sunny weather to the White Mountains. The only fly in the soup: A weak storm system had developed over the western Great Lakes, but the high had put a brake on the storm's eastward movement. Not to worry.

Then an odd thing happened. The blocking high pressure area became stronger, forcing a large low in the Carolinas to move north, where it quickly combined with the other low over the Great Lakes. This caused a very narrow pressure gradient to form, and this spelled trouble. For the more narrow the pressure gradient becomes between opposing high and low pressure systems, the quicker the air is forced from the high to the low.

On the afternoon of Wednesday, April 11th, clear skies gave way to thickening clouds and the temperature began to drop. By evening, rime ice a foot thick covered the summit. The crew's feline members huddled behind the wood stove. Oompah and her five kittens inched closer as the inside temperature dropped. Ammonuisance, a feline visiting from Lake of the Clouds Hut, meowed his displeasure while shy Elmer and tailless Manx snuggled together to stay warm.

Stephenson checked the wind gauge: 136 mph. The crew had experienced worse; he saw no need for the entire staff to stand an all night vigil. Since Pagliuca was responsible for taking the morning readings and McKenzie worked the radio during the day, Stephenson volunteered to stay up and keep the wood stove burning.

Around four o'clock he roused from a short nap and checked the wind recorder. It showed a reading of 105 mph, but the wind's ferocious roar indicated otherwise. "Gotta be ice built up on the anemometer," he grumbled. He suited up, grabbed a wooden club, and opened the door. The intense force of the wind knocked him back inside. He battled his way outside and onto the ladder. With the wind at his back, he climbed up until he could reach the anemometer and clubbed the ice away. The wind snatched the club out of his hand and it sailed off into the void.

Back inside, Stephenson saw that the wind speed was over 150 mph. He awoke the others, and they went to "general quarters," with each monitoring his assigned instruments. As the morning wore on, it became evident that a meteorological event of Biblical proportions was taking place. Several times the wind reached 220 mph. At 1 PM, came a gust of 229 mph. Then at 1:21 PM, the anemometer spun at its fastest velocity, recording a phenomenal speed of 231 mph! (No anemometer has since spun as fast!)

Nature's violence continued through the afternoon, and then it slowly diminished as the storm moved off to the east. Shocked, Pagliuca wrote in the Observatory logbook: "'Will they believe it?' was our first thought. I felt then the full responsibility of that startling measurement. Was my timing correct? Was the method OK? Was the calibration curve right? Was the stopwatch accurate?"

(Afterwards, the anemometer was subjected to several tests by the National Weather Bureau. The historic measurement of 231 mph was confirmed as valid. The record was challenged by Super-typhoon Paka, which ravaged the island of Guam on December 16, 1997. Andersen Air Force Base reported a wind gust of 236 mph, but subsequent investigation by the National Weather Service determined that the velocity could not be substantiated. Mount Washington's record still stands to this day—the highest natural surface wind velocity ever officially recorded by means of an anemometer anywhere in the world. The stuff of legends!)

Today, Mount Washington has a modern summit house. Not quite the grandiose building dreamed of by Mellen and associates, but the Sherman Adams Summit Building is impressive—and it does have a cafeteria. The old Tip Top building still reposes just below the craggy tip, albeit with a total body transplant and a face lift. For a while after the Great Fire of 1908, it was the only structure on the summit. Workers quickly renovated it, and for a time the building provided the only accommodations and meals for visitors.

Shortly after the new Summit Building was completed, the Tip Top house burned, leaving a blackened rocky hulk. However, like a rotting potato, the eyesore grated on the tourists' nerves and offended the senses until officials, deciding it was easier to restore the facility rather than tear it down, made it into an annex for the Summit House. Progress finally put an end to its usefulness, and the Tip Top was abandoned in 1968. But the old building refused to die an ignoble death. In 1987, the building was once again restored and designated a State Historic Site. It now enjoys the venerated status as the oldest standing hostelry in the world.

A new Stage Office was built in 1976. It sits beside three large paved parking lots to handle the fleet of vehicles that are driven to the summit. Most often a cog train idles beside the Summit Building's platform, hissing and blowing black nastiness out of the tall narrow smokestack as it disgorges eager sightseers into the thick chilly fog that seems to plague the mountaintop.

And hikers still meander up the steep mountainside with its sprinkling of little white wooden crosses. Determined, they push up to the broad summit, then on up to the small rocky crag that claims the honor as the highest point in New England, where once excited visitors paid fifty cents to be hoisted by rope on a shaky moving platform confined by four wobbly poles, as much for the excitement as for the chancy view. With chests heaving, the peak baggers suck rarefied air into their lungs and marvel that they were able to do this wondrous thing.

*   *   *

Records reveal that 135 fatalities have occurred on and around Mount Washington since the first recorded death in 1849. Apples and oranges, true, but this number rivals the 170-odd fatalities that have occurred on Mt. Everest since Sir Edmund Hillary and his Sherpa companion, Tenzing Norgay, became the first humans to stand on the 29,035-foot summit in May 1953. Many of the bodies still lie frozen on Everest's inaccessible slopes, harsh reminders that *It can't happen to me* really *can*.

No bodies litter the barren heights of the Whites, though. Instead, these victims got the little white crosses—at least a few did. Most did not.

Tickling the math synapses for a breakdown of the 135 fatalities shows that twenty-nine died from hypothermia; six by drowning; five from falling ice; eleven from avalanches; forty from accidental falls; seventeen from natural causes; and two cases where the victims just disappeared, never to be seen again. Then you have the "others": Ten died in airplane crashes; eight in the tragic accident on the cog railway; one when Old Peppersass ran awry; one when a buggy overturned on the Carriage Road; one from an automobile crash; and four from sliding down the cog railway on slideboards.

Undoubtedly, more fatalities occurred earlier than 1849, when the record keeping began. And of course, gobs of near misses, many unreported, have happened.

Strangely, no one has been killed by lightning in the Whites.

The Willey family didn't get their names recorded on the "fatality" list. Nor did Nancy Barton (for whom Nancy Brook, Nancy Pond, and Nancy Cascades in Crawford Notch are named). Nancy was a servant girl who worked for Colonel Joseph Whipple of Jefferson, New Hampshire. She had the misfortune to lose her heart to a strapping fellow by name of Jim Swindel, who also worked for the Colonel. In a moment of love-induced weakness, Nancy entrusted her betrothed with her small life savings, to be used for their wedding. A pittance, but it served to seal the binding of two hearts.

Or so she thought. When the Colonel and Jim inexplicably left for far off Portsmouth on a wintry day in December 1778 without so much as a howdy-do or goodbye, the poor girl became hysterical. Indications are that Colonel Whipple planned to recruit Jim to serve in the Continental Army, as the American Revolution was in full swing, and Jim feared that Nancy would try to talk him out of joining. Whatever the reason, the distraught girl pursued the men on foot through snow and a freezing wind. After twenty miles, she came on the still-warm embers of their last campfire. Heartened, Nancy continued the chase until she became exhausted and incoherent. The poor girl slipped and fell into the brook that today bears her name. A search party found her nearby, sitting with her head in her hands, frozen solid. Her walking stick lay beside the brook.

Wild with grief, Jim had to be carted off to an insane asylum, where he died soon thereafter, probably from suicide. And Nancy Barton's cries for her lover can occasionally be heard near the brook—so they say.

Some victims refuse to stay buried. At least that seems to be the case of sixteen year-old Betsy Roberts of Newton, Massachusetts. Betsy, along with her parents and two older brothers, had come to the Whites to vacation and do some hiking. Bad timing, for Tropical Storm Doria came scooting up the coast, dumping lots of rain and blowing over garbage cans and toppling a few shallow-rooted trees. By Saturday, August 28, 1971, Doria had begun to churn the waters off New Hampshire.

Betsy and her family knew that a storm threatened to throw a damper on the hike they had planned for that day. But they had hiked in foul weather before, and the temperature didn't spell hypothermia. Anyway, they planned to keep to the lower elevations, mainly hike the Dry River Trail and part of the Isolation Trail that led up toward Mt. Washington.

Tropical Storm Doria didn't carry much of a punch. But in the western quadrant, over in the Whites, rain fell from the angry clouds with a fury that made the old timers in Hart's Location sneak worried glances up the steep sides of the Notch and speak in hushed tones about "other times." Not far away, the Roberts (less the mother, who had decided to stay in camp) were making their way alongside the Dry River, with Betsy in the rear. The picturesque river had quickly become a swollen, angry beast threatening to break its bonds.

Suddenly a scream pierced the roar of the torrent. Horrified, Mr. Roberts and his sons watched as Betsy swept past, clawing at the muddy water, screaming for help, her long blond hair leading her pale, stricken face downstream. And then she was gone.

The men ran downstream, panicked, frantically searching, calling out "Betsy; Betsy," until they became hoarse. Desperate, Mr. Roberts and the younger son struck out for Mizpah Hut, a couple of miles away, to seek help. The older son remained at the river and continued to look for his sister. A search party was quickly organized and left for the accident site. They found the older son exhausted and injured from falls, but there was no sign of Betsy.

Doria slowly moved up the coast, taking her watery baggage with her. The rain ceased and the water began to recede. Late that night the rescue party found Betsy's crumpled body downstream, trapped in a tangle of tree limbs not far from where she had fallen. The men carried her body back to Mizpah Hut and placed it in the hut's basement until it could be removed to Hart's Location the next day.

One evening a few weeks after Betsy died, a young girl walked through the hut's open doorway and asked if anyone had seen her mother. Staring vacantly into the dimly lit room, she ignored the astonished looks of the "croo" and slowly turned and walked back outside, disappearing in the soft gloom. The girl had long flaxen hair and pallid skin that looked as if it were beginning to decompose. Her dress, torn and dripping water, reeked of rotting leaves. A "croo" member who had been at the hut the night the search party had brought Betsy's body insisted she was a dead ringer for the drowned girl.

On several occasions since Betsy's tragic accident, various "croo" members at Mizpah Hut have told of encounters with the young girl. She seems to appear out of nowhere and has been seen in the hut's basement and upstairs where the guests congregate. In a sobbing, hollow voice, the girl asks if anyone has seen her mother, then she gazes at something unseen before mysteriously disappearing. A strange thing, but she only appears—when she does—on August 28th. Strange indeed!

In 1990, I happened to wind up at Nauman Tentsite, adjacent to Mizpah Hut, on the afternoon of August 28th with Skate and some other thru-hikers. We shared supper with the tentsite caretaker, Mark Lucas. While we ate, Mark related the "Betsy" legend to us. (*Walkin* . . . pp 498-501) An intense thunderstorm rolled in during the night, and by morning the weather had deteriorated. With a nasty five-mile walk on the exposed ridge to Lake of the Clouds Hut staring me in the face, I forgot about Betsy.

But later the thought tugged at my mind: Did Betsy show up at the Hut that night while I lay in my tent, cringing at the thunder boomers that seemed to hang just above my head? And does she still roam the Hut, looking for her mother?

Are there other wraiths that wander the isolated slopes of the Whites, each seeking release from—something? A scary thought that makes one jump when a twig snaps or a rock clinks in the darkness beyond the reassuring glow of the flashlight. Several reliable witnesses might have thought so when they encountered John Keenan over ninety years ago.

In September 1912, John Keenan carefully placed his new high school graduation certificate in the small bag with his few belongings, kissed his ma goodbye, and walked away from his Charlestown, Massachusetts, home as he headed north to make his fortune. Mr. Mellen's Mount Washington trolley project seemed as good a place to begin as any, so John signed on with the survey crew. Mr. H.S. Jewell, who supervised the twenty-one man crew, had some reservations about the slight youth wearing a white and pink striped shirt and street shoes, but the boy seemed earnest. He would do as the "gofer" at base camp. Mr. Jewell decided to give him a chance.

The life of a survey crew revolved around the philosophy, "Work hard; play hard." The crew soon discovered that their newest member was more suited for the life of a store clerk or a schoolteacher. The young man seemed afraid of his own shadow, not to mention the wild animals, dark nights, and the rough and tumble antics that prevailed in the off-hours. But Keenan was determined to hang on, despite the constant teasing.

Then came the day a week later that the supervisor needed a back-flag man, the person who holds the flagged pole at the "back" point so that the transit reader can get a bearing to the next point in the survey. "Keenan, you just follow them other fellers up th' mountain," Jewell said. "And do what they tell you."

The transit crew happened to be working on the south side of Mount Washington near the summit cone that day. Overcast skies spread an ominous pall over the mountainside. The wind gusted above fifty miles an hour which, combined with the forty-degree temperature, numbed fingers and ears and threatened hypothermia weather. From where the topmost crewmembers stood, they could see the spot where William Ormsbee had died from hypothermia only twelve years earlier, on June 30, 1900. Beyond, just below the base of Mount Monroe, on a small plain called Bigelow Lawn, they could see where Father William Curtis had died that same tragic day, also from hypothermia. A little further down from the cone was the place hypothermia had claimed Harry Hunter in 1874.

But the surveyors were hardy men used to weather extremes, and this was a normal September day for Mount Washington. The transit crew chief got in Keenan's face and growled, "This kind of weather can turn on you quicker'n you can say Jack Sprat. Clouds can pour in like spoiled milk and hide everything. That happens, you stay put an' we'll come get you. Understood?" Young Keenan nodded "yes," and the crew went to work.

Around midmorning, as predicted the clouds suddenly rolled in, forming an opaque blanket over the mountain. Keenan, holding the back flag about a hundred feet away on the downslope, sunk into the soupy mix. The crew waited half an hour for the cloud to lift, but it grew thicker. Finally the chief yelled into the wind, "Keenan, get your lazy arse up here. Just walk toward my voice." No reply. The entire crew yelled as loud as they could, but the only sound was the howling wind. One member stumbled through the fog to the place where Keenan had last been seen, but the boy had disappeared.

Came more shouts, then guns were fired, but still no Keenan. Now desperate, the chief climbed to the summit where a phone had been wired directly to base camp. He shouted into the mouthpiece, "Mr. Jewell, that new fellow you sent up here. We lost him." Jewell yelled back, "Well, stay up there until you find him," and slammed the receiver down.

The transit crew searched until nightfall without finding any trace. The large bell on the summit rang all night, while the whistle at the base station steam plant pierced the inky darkness every few minutes. Mr. Jewell sent a telegram to the Boston and Maine headquarters in Boston, alerting them to the crisis. The reply came back: "Spare no expense. Find the boy." Word spread throughout the area and search parties combed the cloud-besieged heights, but to no avail. Young John Keenan had vanished into thin air.

Two days after the mysterious disappearance, Warden Briggs happened to be near Pinkham Notch on an inspection tour of some skidder trails left from logging operations. A young man wearing city shoes and dressed in a white and pink striped shirt approached him and asked for a piece of spearmint gum. The stranger then asked what day it was. Briggs told him that it was Friday, and the man said that he'd been working with a survey team two days ago and had gotten lost, and that he was looking for the Keenan farm.

Briggs had heard of the missing man but dismissed the stranger's story as poppycock, the ramblings of a dimwit. After all, who would work on the heights of Mount Washington in clothing more suited for an afternoon tea? Besides, Briggs knew that no family by name of Keenan lived in the area. He told the stranger that he didn't have any gum and left.

A few hours later, the young man was spotted on the Pinkham Notch road not far from the Glen House by the Honorable George Turner and Dr. Gile, state officials who were on their way to inspect roads in the country west of Crawford Notch. The man looked "strange" (their words) and even more weird was the way he stood there pointing up at the distant summit of Mount Washington. Turner and Gile waved at the man and continued on.

An hour later, Howard Lightfoot, a chauffeur who had been hired to transport the officials' luggage to Fabyans (where they planned to spend the night), was flagged down by the same young man in the vicinity where he had been seen by Turner and Gile. Since it was cold and raining hard, Lightfoot gave the man a ride. After a couple of miles, as they approached an old lumber camp near Darby Field, the man said, "I think this will do. Yes, here's where I need to get out." Before the man stepped out into the driving rain, he asked if Lightfoot knew where the Keenan farm was, and how far it was to Charlestown. "Nope, don't know of any Keenans hereabouts," replied Lightfoot. "An' Charlestown is about 150 miles away, on th' other side of th' mountain." The man seemed unperturbed, almost as if he were in a trance. Nodding, the stranger walked away into the rain.

News that the missing man had been spotted near the Glen House sent search parties rushing to the area. John Keenan's parents, filled with renewed hope, came from Charlestown. But as before, the massive effort turned up nothing. The search was soon disbanded and the grieving parents went home.

A week later strange noises, as if someone were shouting or crying out for help, interrupted the nightly peace near the Glen House. A search party went out at first light, found nothing, and disbanded by nightfall.

Over the next several weeks, reports filtered in from individuals as far away as Woodstock, one hundred miles distant, who claimed to have seen or had contact with a young distraught man dressed in a pink and white dress shirt. All of these "sightings" were investigated, and all turned out to be crank calls or mistaken identity.

To this day, John Keenan's disappearance remains a perplexing mystery. His remains are hidden in the depths of a dark puzzle. Keenan's encounters with Warden Briggs, and subsequently with Turner, Gile, and their chauffeur, Howard Lightfoot, are equally puzzling. A young man in shock, too overcome by cold and exhaustion to think rationally, or an apparition trapped in a time warp beyond our comprehension? Flip a coin . . .

Or could he have become "The Presence"?

Wintertime conditions on Mount Washington's summit are almost unimaginable: Yard-thick rime ice covers everything exposed; twenty-foot snowdrifts bury whole buildings; wind chill temperatures frequently sink to minus120 degrees Fahrenheit, crushed downward by 100-plus mile per hour winds and eye-boggling negative fifty degree temperatures. Except for an occasional hiker with a death wish who's willing to duke it out with Ma Nature in order to bag the mountain's wintertime peak, only the bold and the brave can be found *up there*.

I refer to the small crews who keep the weather observatory and the WMTW TV station up and running—those professional, learned men who stoically accept whatever the mountain cares to dish out and, regardless of the hardships, do their jobs day in and day out. And that includes dealing with "The Presence," even though that task wasn't listed in their various job descriptions.

"The Presence" showed up several years ago. However, no one can really recall the first time "it" made itself known. Old timers swear the thing is alive—but not physical. Nor does it fit the traditional definition of a ghost. (Explain that one!) But it is there nonetheless, hiding things, tossing clothing about, making odd noises in empty spaces, occasionally showing a malevolent streak. Some folks even lay the faulty switch that caused the tragic Cog Railway accident in 1967 to the nimble otherworldly fingers of "The Presence."

Shortly after the accident, railway worker John Davis, who lived at the Tip Top House, began to notice strange, unexplained happenings. A locked safe would be found open with its contents in place. Chairs and tables would somehow rearrange themselves overnight. On several occasions money would vanish, only to be found in a different place. No matter how closely Davis watched, the antics continued. The company eventually summoned the state police, who drove to the summit and searched every cranny of the Tip Top House, even brought in the canine troopers and remained on watch overnight. Finding nothing, the police took their dogs and left.

Apparently "The Presence" was endowed with a good set of muscles or had the remarkable gift of mind over matter. On a stormy evening not long after the police had departed, the weather observatory staff got a visit. Came a loud pounding on the door, which startled the men. A knock at this time of night in such violent weather could only mean one thing: Someone needed help!

Staff member Peter Zwirken was first to reach the door. He yanked it open—and stared at the empty space. The men pushed through the doorway, out into the hurricane force wind and stinging sleet. Nothing. Then Peter saw a heavy bronze plaque lying on the doorstep and recognized it as the one that had been affixed to a memorial a mile away, to mark the demise of a climber. The plaque had been ripped from its base!

Others have had weird experiences, which they attribute to "The Presence." Jon Lingel, who worked at the Yankee Building's TV station, had several "close encounters." The one that sent him packing his bags, swearing never to sleep in the building again, happened one night as he manned the station by himself.

Lingel awoke in the middle of the night to the echo of footsteps outside his open bedroom door. Wondering who might have entered the building at such a late hour, he got up and checked the corridor. It was empty. Lingel went back to bed but he soon heard the footsteps again, this time closer and accompanied by heavy breathing. Frightened, he got up and locked the door, and lay there with his heart thumping like a jackhammer. Then came laughter, music, and the sound of tinkling glasses from downstairs, as if a party was in full swing. He mustered up enough courage to unlock the door and ease down the steps. The large area was dark and vacant. Lingel ran up to his room, threw a few essentials in a bag, and abandoned ship.

Writer Austin Stevens from *Yankee Magazine* went to the summit to *expose* the so-called ghost stories. He came back down convinced that the wintertime crews experienced a "curious, watchful, and malevolent force." Photographer Mike Micucci claimed that the day after he began his work on the summit, he was pushed while standing on a precipitation platform—and he was the only person on the platform at the time.

And "The Presence" is still on the move. In January 2004, a staffer at the weather observatory, Jeff de Rosa, reported that as the men were eating supper, they heard the tower door blow open and then shut itself. Okay, so blame it on the wind, which pummeled the summit at over a hundred miles per hour. But when the "wind" turned on the TV thirty seconds later and began to watch the evening news, De Rosa and the other staffers began to trot out the old "The Presence" theories. Good grist for the mind mill on an otherwise boring evening atop Mount Washington!

Long time television weatherman Marty Engstrom won't even talk about some of the things that have happened to him over the years. He will give you a hint, though, as he paraphrases in a gravelly voice from the Holy Writ: "It tells you that there are such things and it tells you not to mess around with them." Sage advice!

Hauntings, apparitions that defy the trappings of the coffin, wraiths that wander the high ridges like fleeting shadows—are they actual encounters from a gap between dimensions or hallucinations from overactive minds? But then, these are questions that can only be answered on the other side of the tomb . . .

*   *   *

In 1998, my eldest son, Kelly, joined me at Franconia Notch for the hike across Franconia Ridge and through the Presidentials. We spent a rainy blustery night at the Dungeon, along with nine other hikers and two wet dogs. One of the dogs had been "skunked" in the recent past. The Dungeon was not a place to linger, so Kelly and I left at first light.

No ice this time, but the temperature hovered near the forty-degree mark and the wind tipped the gauge at the Summit House at seventy-five miles per hour, gusting into the eighties at times. A normal August day on Mount Washington.

As we struggled against the wind on the hike toward the summit, the small white crosses shuddered, as if the souls they represented might be straining to take flight to more gentle climes. And thankfully, we didn't become appetizers for Fate's insatiable appetite that day.

But the crosses remain as solemn grim reminders of the life and death power of "Presidential wrath."

Chapter Thirty-one

"Seen worse"

I hadn't been in Maine even an hour when it grabbed me by the balls. The rascal sucker punched me in the solar plexus and dumped me on my scrawny thru-hiker butt.

Sprawled upside down on my back in a jumble of boulders that tumbled straight down into Carlo Col didn't exactly fit the bill of a friendly greeting. The backpack kept me glued to the crevasse, and I probably did a crazy charade of a flipped turtle as I squirmed and tried to get right side up.

Model-T, who had been blessedly silent since I left Gorham, New Hampshire the day before, immediately piped up. *Jayzus, J.R. What did you do, piss on the Pope's shoes? Show a little respect to this rocky beast, for crying out loud. You're playing with the big guys now.* He had a point.

This *was* "big guy" country, where intimidating granite giants thrust up into cobalt skies, seeming to play tag with soaring raptors, even tickling the long skinny contrails of passing jetliners. The gargantuan landscape of mammoth peaks overwhelms the senses and captures the mind, not to mention spawning a bad case of stomach flutters. Comes a rushing sensation that you're going to pee in your shorts as you catch the faint trace of a path on a *really* high slope and suddenly realize *Oh my God! That's the Trail up there!*

This was definitely the Big League! And I hadn't even gotten to that terror trap called Mahoosuc Notch! Yeah, when I got my first glimpse of what was to come, I felt like I was gonna pee—or upchuck my oatmeal, whichever grabbed me first.

I finally managed to extricate myself from the trap and went on, somewhat humiliated, but with *respect* now mixed with the stinking sweat-fear that oozed from nasty pores in bad need of a bath.

Mahoosuc Notch! A mile-long gorge filled with house-size boulders, remnants of high cliffs that once lined the deep ravine but, like the walls of Jericho, came tumbling down—no horns this time, just a few million years of freeze and thaw. As I stood on the brink of the tangled maze, the urge to flee or pee hit me hard. *Sumabitch! What malicious sadist dreamed this up!* The Alter Ego growled, *Ed Garvey came through here yesterday and he didn't look any worse for the wear.*

I asked Ed about Mahoosuc Notch. "Seen worse," came his gruff reply.

True. I'd met the venerated hiker, now traveling south after doing a "flipflop" from Katahdin, coming toward me on a high saddle between the Goose Eye peaks. We paused to chat and I asked him about the Notch. Ed had shrugged his shoulders and muttered, "Seen worse."

Standing here now, looking at the monstrosity's angry maw, I wondered if "worse" lay somewhere between me and Katahdin and wished I had pinned Ed down about the specifics. *Oh Momma!* I garnered all the *Respect* I could and charged in—butt first.

Two hours later, I emerged from the other end. Adrenaline coursed through my veins, shunting the blood aside as if it were air. I'd been contorted and squeezed by impossible crevices barely large enough to wiggle through, even by pushing or pulling the backpack—hiker's choice. Up, over, around, under the jumble . . . was that yellowish off-color down in the deep rocks—ice? I'd become a two-legged needle threading through a rock-packed nightmare.

Then suddenly I crawled past the last boulder to—FREEDOM! A few bruises and scrapes showed through sweat-streaked dirt—my badge of passage. Otherwise, I floated on Cloud Nine, bolstered by the adrenaline high, for I had conquered the beast and he was mine! Ecstatic, I whooped and bellowed out a couple of "ooogas," which bounced off the boulders like a horny elephant's trumpeting. *Dang, Model-T, whoever put the trail through here sure knew what thru-hikers want!* His response could have used some *"respect."*

But I ignored my conjoined thorn in the ass. This was Maine, the last state on the long journey north, and thoughts of Katahdin crowded my mind. Hell, for northbounders, Maine *was* Katahdin! Take the thru-hiker lingo: "When you gonna get to Maine?" Or, "No rain, no pain, no Maine." And, "You're gonna be buzzard bait by the time you get to Maine." What they really mean is "Katahdin." Got the picture?

After nearly six months, I could almost see light at the far end of the long green tunnel. But by damn! Those mountains still between me and the big "K," those big sumabitchin' Maine mountains, still to be climbed! Where was Ed's *"seen worse"*?

A few minutes after crawling out of the Notch, I found out. Or so I thought.

The climb up Mahoosuc Arm began easily enough. The mile and a half climb soon turned into a steep no-holds-barred rock scramble that seemed to go right up to Saint Pete's Golden Gate. As I neared the top, a nor'easter roared in, quickly becoming a cat-o'-nine tails, a scourge of driving sleet that numbed my mind and seduced my body with a deadly hypothermic elixir. I can remember nothing about the mile-long battle from Mahoosuc Arm's top to Speck Pond Shelter. What remains are muddled snatches of memory after I reached the shelter, the violent shivering as I maneuvered into my sleeping bag and tried to pull the zipper up with my teeth. Shittin' fingers wouldn't work, and the zipper refused to cooperate. (*Walkin'. . .* pp517-519)

Later, after rational thought returned, I sipped hot chocolate and pondered Ed's short reply. The two words played over and over like a scratched record: "Seen worse" . . . "Seen worse" . . . Seen worse" . . . *Oh Momma!*

The rocky maze called Mahoosuc Notch wasn't Ed Garvery's "worse."
I couldn't imagine anything "more worse"!

Harsh, unforgiving country, this untamed part of the globe. And after three thru-hikes, I still don't have a clue as to where Ed Garvey's cryptic *"seen worse"* is. Too many possibilities. In 1990, the day after Mahoosuc Notch, hurricane force winds splatted me against the rocks on Old Speck's summit. In 1994, Bald Pate Mountain's steep south slope treated me to a belly slide for fifty feet or so—no charge. Saddleback Mountain got into the act that same year, playing "hide and seek" with the Trail when thick fog rolled in, leaving me stalled for a lifetime in a white opaque void where dimensions ceased to exist. Bigelow Mountain became a major player in 1998, when fierce winds tried to topple me off the mountain and into Flagstaff Lake a couple of thousand feet below.

It became standard fare on each trip to get bloodied by the Mahoosucs, mauled by the Chairbacks, dunked in the icy, slick-bottomed fords of bridgeless streams, and masticated by mighty Katahdin. Switchbacks and bridges evidently aren't terms the Mainers have come to grips with.

But what the heck! Each time, Maine's rugged beauty has grabbed my soul and made me want to shout and dance like a holy-roller when I have planted my boots on the summit of a towering granite mastodon. By damn, but those are some mountains!

But had I seen Ed Garvey's *worse?*

Even today, it's still a big question mark. However, I've learned a few things about "worse." It's a relative term. One person's "worse" can be another's trip to the stars. It always commands respect and usually demands a price—in blood, pain, exhaustion, sacrifice, or more often, a liberal sprinkling of each. But when you conquer "worse," the rewards can be soul filling, as nothing else can.

In retrospect, maybe I did see Ed's *worse* and just didn't recognize it. After all, Maine is filled with'em. And arguably, Katahdin tops the list!

Even the bronze-skinned natives shunned it.

$$* \quad * \quad *$$

The eastern Abenaki who called themselves the Penawapskewi, or "dawn dwellers," had great respect for *Kette-Adene*, the name they gave the majestic "greatest mountain" that rose up out of the endless forest like a giant turtle. They declared the mountain sacred and relegated its heights to Pamola—a malevolent god in the form of a man-eagle with a moose head, whose giant wings thrashed the atmosphere and ushered in huge storms atop the mountain.

The white settlers came and quickly corrupted the strange Indian words into more familiar sounds. "Penawapskewi" became "Penobscot," and they called *Kette-Adene,* "Ktaadn." As for the storm god, Pamola, the settlers scoffed at the Indians' superstition and began to explore Ktaadn's lower ranges, while the Penobscots stoically waited for the wrath of Pamola to descend on the unbelieving, sacrilegious heads of the intruders.

Then on August 14, 1804, Charles Turner, a surveyor from Scituate, Massachusetts, picked a calm day and scaled the boulder-strewn slopes to become the first man, red or white (as far as is known), to stand on the sacred summit. The Penobscots scratched their heads and muttered that Pamola must have been elsewhere churning up storms; otherwise, Turner would have become buzzard bait.

Others followed, including a few intrepid botanists who were curious about the reports Turner circulated when he returned to civilized parts about the strange and wonderful alpine vegetation on the upper reaches of Ktaadn— see for yourself, thank you. In 1819 and '20, the Maine Boundary Commission, wary of their northern neighbor's groping tentacles, had the mountain surveyed and put out the word: *Hands off. It's ours!*

Dr. Charles Thomas Jackson, Ralph Waldo Emerson's brother-in-law and Maine's State Geologist (who also made his mark on New Hampshire's White Mountains and for whom Mt. Jackson in the Presidential Range is named), climbed Ktaadn in 1837. He took some measurements and declared, "Ktaadn is over a mile high; 5300 feet to be exact." There it remained until more reliable instruments lowered its summit to 5267 feet several years later.

In 1846, Henry David Thoreau declared a holiday from his transcendental meditations at Walden Pond and came to the mountain. And Ktaadn has not been the same since!

Nathaniel Hawthorne's September 1, 1842 journal entry reads, "Mr. Thorow (sic) dined with us yesterday. He is a singular character—a young man with much of wild original nature still remaining in him; and so far as he is sophisticated, it is in a way and method of his own. He is as ugly as sin, long-nosed, queer-mouthed, and with uncouth and somewhat rustic, although courteous manners, corresponding very well with such an exterior. But his ugliness is of an honest and agreeable fashion, and becomes him much better than beauty."

Such was the description of the genteel Harvard-educated "dreamer" who came to Ktaadn in 1846 to pit his strength against Pamola's vengeful wrath.

Thoreau traveled inland from Bangor, Maine, where he had joined up with two companions. Along the way, they happened upon an old Penobscot by name of Louis Neptune, who had accompanied Charles Jackson to Ktaadn nine years earlier. Thoreau asked Neptune if he thought Pamola would let them climb to the summit. Replied the old Indian, "You must plant a bottle of rum on the top to appease Pamola. I have planted a good many, and when I looked later, each time they were gone."

When Thoreau and his friends reached "Uncle" George McCauslin's homestead (the first settler at East Millinocket), they learned that he was familiar with the backcountry around Ktaadn and talked him into joining their expedition. His knowledge and wood lore skills made a deep impression on Thoreau, as evidenced in his later writings.

In early September, Thoreau and company paddled up the Penobscot and made camp at the mouth of the Aboljacknagesic (Abol) Stream. The next morning, they, in Thoreau's words, ". . . mounted our packs and a good blanketful of trout, ready dressed, and swung up such baggage and provision as we wished to leave behind upon the tops of saplings to be out of the reach of bears . . ." Then the men set out for the summit by way of Abol Slide. The massive landslide had tumbled down from the upper slopes in 1816; although steep and tricky, it happened to be the shortest way to the top. The others, not so afflicted with eagerness as Thoreau, soon gave up the quest and decided to dawdle on the side of the mountain and gorge themselves with blueberries and mountain-cranberries while Thoreau otherwise indulged himself.

As he reached the broad tableland, dense clouds rolled in, bellowing in and out—a "cloud factory," as Thoreau described it—tantalizing him with brief glimpses of "almost views," until at last the thickness smothered everything. Thoreau waited in vain, stoically tolerating the fierce wind and bone-chilling dampness. Finally, consumed with anxiety that he and his companions might become stranded in darkness, he threw in the towel and retreated down the mountain to where the other men idled in bright sunshine and licked their blue-stained fingers.

In retrospect, one wonders if Thoreau failed to heed Louis Neptune's advice and neglected to appease Pamola with a bottle of rum. For in spite of McCauslin's help, the mountain spirit won, hands down.

Ktaadn etched deep scars on Thoreau's psyche. He made two more trips to the Maine woods, but never again did he wrestle with the irascible storm god. Instead, the transcendentalist retreated to the more familiar haven of pen and paper and spent fifteen years authoring and refining a manuscript, *The Maine Woods*, in which he wrote of Ktaadn in gripping terms. The manuscript told of a mountain covered with a vast aggregation of loose rocks, as if it had rained the rocks and they had rested where they had fallen. Vivid descriptions flowed through the pages: . . . raw materials of a planet dropped from an unseen quarry . . . tops of mountains among the unfinished parts of the globe . . . a place where only daring and insolent men go. And his admission of defeat: "Pomola (sic) is always angry with those who climb to the summit of Ktaadn."

Thoreau's words captivated the soul of a nation and immortalized the mountain—and its rum-swilling protector—and forever entwined Thoreau's name with Ktaadn.

(After his failed attempt to conquer Ktaadn, Henry David Thoreau returned to Walden Pond and listened to the bullfrogs croak as he mulled over what the experience had meant. A year later, he moved in with the Emerson family and tutored the children while Ralph Waldo lectured in England. A few months later, restless, with a torrent of words threatening to burst through the dam of his mind, he moved into his parents' home at Concord, Massachusetts, and began to write. Came *Walden* in 1854; and along with that work came three essays: *Ktaadn, Chesancook,* and *Allegash and East Branch*, which were eventually combined into a single book, *The Maine Woods*—although it wasn't published until 1864, two years after his death.

While counting tree rings in December 1860, Thoreau contracted severe bronchitis, which aggravated his tubercular lungs. He suffered severe bouts of the disease over the next two years but was unable to regain his health. The great transcendentalist, naturalist, and strong vocal advocate for things "forever wild," died at his parents' home in Concord, Massachusetts, on May 6, 1862 at age forty-four.

Thoreau lies in the family plot on Author's Ridge in Concord's Sleepy Hollow Cemetery, near the graves of his friends Nathaniel Hawthorne, Ralph Waldo Emerson, and Louisa May Alcott.

The shallow spring on Katahdin's Tableland, which bears his name, still gives forth good water to ease the thirst of tired climbers. Likewise, the lingering, haunting words written by the great man nearly 160 years ago continue to ease another kind of thirst, which often comes to seeking minds.)

*   *   *

Come a few men and women to every generation who climb out of the rut, scratch their heads, and ponder the fate of the human race. Most of these chosen ones do something about their ponderings. Percival Proctor Baxter was of that ilk.

Percy was born in 1876 in bustling Portsmouth, Maine, the youngest of eight children, of which six were sons. His father, James, an influential man— six times mayor of Portland, creator of Portland's modern park system, and the state's foremost historian—made his fortune in the canning business.

Percy and his father bonded like chewing gum on a boot sole—far closer than the other sons. As soon as the lad learned to handle a fishing rod, he and his father were off on excursions into the great Maine woods, where they hooked lunker trout, and young Percy's innards got hooked by a different kind of bait. As he grew, so did his unshakable love for the Great Outdoors.

In 1903, at age twenty-six, Percy had already picked the spot on the family home's living room wall to hang his law degree from Harvard. Looking beyond his approaching graduation, he had begun to contemplate a future role in Maine's political machine. While home on vacation, Percy accompanied his father on a fishing trip to the remote wilds west of Millinocket. On the way, he caught his first glimpse of Mount Katahdin, massive and mysterious, its top shrouded in clouds, and he felt a stirring inside that excited him more than any fish he had ever landed.

Even as he cast his rod into the placid waters of Kidney Pond, the words of Thoreau, who had long since gone to the grave, echoed in the hollow recesses of his mind . . . only the daring and insolent go there. Percy's eyes strayed up to the mountain, again and again at the grand uplift of granite that filled the sky. Backcast, retrieve . . . tops of mountains are the unfinished parts of the globe . . . backcast . . . perfect fly cast, landed right beside the rock . . . daring and insolent . . . Wham!

Long after he returned to Portsmouth, the image of Katahdin continued to haunt his days.

Came three terms in Maine's House of Representatives, followed by two terms in the State Senate, and suddenly it was 1920. Percival Proctor Baxter placed his hand on the family Bible and solemnly swore to uphold the laws of the great State of Maine. By so doing, he became Maine's fifty-third governor.

The new governor took his oath seriously, and after the political pot had settled down to a slow simmer, he broached the subject of Katahdin. His strong, vibrant voice echoed in the statehouse chambers: *We must obtain this precious treasure for our people and their children, and their children's children, in perpetuity! A place that will forever be wild; a place where our citizens can come and gaze on Almighty God's masterpiece, where they can absorb Nature and experience its joys!* His pleas sounded grand, but they rattled against the statehouse windows like old skeleton bones in a washtub—and were about as effective.

Deciding that his words needed flesh, on a fine morning that summer he gathered his political brood under his wing and led the way up Mount Pamola, traversed the Knife Edge, and planted his feet on the high summit of Mount

Katahdin. (Chancy, for the new governor carried nary a single drop of rum for Pamola!) Overjoyed at what he beheld, Baxter swept his arms in a wide arc that encompassed a mind-gripping view of earthly infinity, an endless green carpet sprinkled with shimmering ponds.

As he stood there, the words of *Bangor Courier* reporter J.K. Laski, which he had used to describe the vast panorama after his visit to the mountain sixty-odd years earlier, rushed in like a whirlwind: ". . . a mirror broken into a thousand fragments, and wildly scattered over the grass, reflecting the full blaze of the sun." (Thoreau has frequently been given credit for this phrase. He was captivated by the stunning view when he broke out of the clouds on his way down off the mountain, and he may have played the words in his mind; but Laski put them on paper.)

Passionately, Governor Baxter pleaded his case to his comrades. "Katahdin must be preserved. It must be wrested from the timber barons who hold the deeds of ownership, who will in time denude the countryside and leave a lasting scar on the land and our state. Beautiful wild Katahdin must belong to the people of Maine!" And in his heart, the new governor, the first of his predecessors to climb Mount Katahdin, dedicated himself to this mammoth cause.

His followers retreated from the mountain, impressed but divided. Baxter's eloquent call to arms sounded over and over; yet each time, again and again, the pleas fell on apathetic ears. And nothing was done. But the governor would not be turned aside.

Governor Baxter was not without substantial means. His father had left the family wealth to his favored son. At the end of his term in 1925, he left the political arena and embarked on a mission that would span the next thirty-one years.

In 1930, he *bought* Mount Katahdin, along with six thousand acres that surrounded the mountain, and the following year donated the land to the state. His proviso: ". . . shall forever be used as a public park . . . forever left in the natural wild state . . . forever kept as a sanctuary for wild beasts and birds . . . no roads or ways for motor vehicles shall hereafter ever be constructed thereon or therein."

With deed in hand, in 1933 the Maine legislature created Baxter State Park and named Katahdin's highest peak after their gift giver. In the coming years, Percival Baxter continued to battle near-sighted politicians, obstinate landowners, haughty timber barons, sportsmen who were worried about the loss of hunting grounds, and the Federal Government, who had its greedy eye on the area as a possible national park. Baxter slugged it out in the trenches, sometimes retreating when discretion dictated, often renewing the assault from the flank or rear, but always attacking.

In 1962, Baxter presented his twenty-eighth deed to the people of Maine (bringing his total gift to 202,018 acres), along with a check for seven million dollars in trust to protect and maintain his gift in perpetuity. Victory declared!

Percival Proctor Baxter died in Portland, Maine, on June 12, 1969. According to his wish, his ashes were scattered throughout Baxter State Park. He left a grand legacy, not only to the people of Maine, but for all comers who seek to walk in a place "forever wild."

A shame that a man with a heart as big as the mountain that had captured his so many years ago doesn't have a monument to match his generosity. Bangorians brag about their huge statue of Paul Bunyan. Portland residents bask in the shadow of the large monument to their homespun boy, Sean Aloysius O'Fearna—aka movie director John Ford. And Brunswick has immortalized Maine's Brewer-born native son Joshua Chamberlain, who saved George Meade's hide at Gettysburg and later became Maine's twenty-eighth governor, with a large bronze likeness. Percival Baxter got short shrift.

But on reflection, perhaps Maine's generous benefactor has the greatest monument of all—Katahdin! For it stands as an eternal memorial, the lasting evidence of Baxter's indomitable will and ceaseless dedication to the fulfillment of a dream. And on a higher level, the Park that bears his name exemplifies altruism in its purest form—man's unselfish humanity to his fellow man.

On a simple bronze plaque set into a large rock beside Katahdin Stream, which tumbles down from the heights where once Pamola ruled and humans feared to walk, words are etched in bronze, words combined in a way that would have made Henry David Thoreau jealous, Percy Baxter's terse words, which reaffirm his legacy with gripping clarity:

"Man is born to die. His works are short-lived. Buildings crumble, monuments decay, and wealth vanishes, but Katahdin in all its glory forever shall remain the mountain of the people of Maine."

Amen!

Today, Baxter State Park remains "forever wild" under the wise leadership of another great man, "Buzz" Caverly, whose love for the land can be seen in his smile, his voice, his works. Another 1000 acres—and a few carefully planned roads—have been added to the Park's area, bringing the total acreage to 204,733 acres. Over the years, zealous hikers (many of them thru-hikers who have carried a small pebble from the Appalachian Trail's southern terminus on Springer Mountain) have added a thirteen-foot rock cairn to Baxter Peak's 5267-foot height to make the mountain exactly one mile high. The tiny pebbles carried by the thru-hikers and placed with great reverence on the cairn are easily identified—Springer Mountain pebbles are hog-lot white, in contrast with the pink-tinted granite atop Mount Katahdin.

Thanks to Percival Baxter's far-sighted vision, no cog railway scars the slopes of Katahdin. No cog engine huffs up toward the Tableland, spewing dense soot into the pristine Maine air. And no "Presence" wanders around on Katahdin's summit—no buildings are there for the "Presence" to set up housekeeping in. Besides, jealous Pamola would quickly swoop in and send it—whatever "it" is—scurrying down the mountainside.

Like his big brother down New Hampshire way, Katahdin is both beautiful and deadly. According to official Baxter State Park records, twenty-two people have died on Katahdin's slopes since 1926. Katahdin's numbers are intertwined with the Park's overall total of forty-eight fatalities. (This figure is somewhat questionable but is in the ballpark.) Plus, chalk up seven more victims from the crash of a military C-54 cargo plane on nearby Fort Mountain on June 20, 1944. And then there are the six ancient, marred graves within the Park's boundary that hold (presumed) drowning victims from the late 1800s.

As with Mount Washington, there have been numerous near misses— "almost" tragedies—only averted through the hangdog, superhuman efforts of Buzz Caverly's rangers. Comes the report of a hiker in trouble, and the rescue team rolls out, armed with tent, blankets, hot toddy makings, stretchers, flashlights, rope, and a pack filled with indomitable will. The calls for help can come at any time, day and night.

Often the first indication of trouble happens when a haggard hiker staggers into a ranger station after dark, spent and near hysteria, babbling in a surreal voice. Example: "That old lady has to be eighty if she's a day. She just ran out of steam; left her laying up on there on the Tableland near Thoreau Spring; gasping like a fish outta water and groaning like she's having a baby, for chrissake. Damn, but I hated to leave her; rainin' up there, you know; covered her up as best I could an' come to get help.

How about this one? "Hell, the old geezer already had one foot in the grave, never shoulda tried to climb the mountain in the first place. He's up in them rocks near the Gateway on the Hunt Trail. I almost broke my neck coming down in the dark. Hell, he may already be dead, poor old bastard." And so it goes.

All kinds of scenarios, and the Park rangers have heard it all! In 2004, they responded to thirty-three calls for help, most involving torturous, backbreaking, stretcher-lugging descents. Last year's tally also included two "recovery" operations. A hiker died when he was crushed by a falling rock on the Cathedral Trail; the other died of a heart attack at Kidney Pond. But then, considering that around *fifty thousand* people climb Mount Katahdin each year, on balance it could be a lot worse! The fact that it isn't speaks loads for Buzz Caverly and his rangers!

* * *

Each year, on a couple of very rare days in the spring and summer, the hills of Canada block the rising sun from touching Maine's 1748-foot Mars Hill, which usually receives the celestial ball's first greeting on North American soil at this time of year. And then a small miracle happens. Katahdin steps up and takes the first sweet drink from the great orb's golden well.

And on such fair mornings, as the sun begins its eternal dance across the dew-speckled pink granite of Baxter Peak, one can almost see Percy Baxter standing on the topmost rock, his mouth fixed with a contented smile as he faces east and spreads his arms in a benevolent blessing to the people far below. Nearby, old Louis Neptune hoists a bottle of rum toward the dazzling brightness, then searches the sky for the wrathful god-bird. Quickly he takes a long pull at the fiery liquid, then replaces the cap and hides the bottle beneath a rock.

From his lair on a neighboring peak, ever-vigilant Pamola watches the transgression with little interest—a small peccadillo pricking at the ancient circle that binds gods, mountains, and mortals. Certainly not worth a fly-over on this tranquil morning. Another time, perhaps.

* * *

"Seen worse," he said. Well, forget Katahdin. It's not my *seen worse.* But Ed, I'm still looking . . .

Epilogue

F ifty years zipped past at warp speed. Drive-in theaters gave way to TV "Movietime" and teens relinquished '59 Chevy back seat trysts for more comfortable living room couches. Fifty thousand body bags—filled— trickled out of the steamy disease-riddled jungles of southeast Asia, into flower-scented funeral parlors all across the country. America wept at the awful waste and rent her star-spangled conscience in two. Came space travel and men on the moon. Not satisfied, space brokers cast their eyes to Mars and beyond.

Convenience stores sprouted like mushrooms at every conceivable location where two or more vehicles could gather in the name of "Almighty Gas." Overnight, brash eighteen-wheelers became kings of the interstate highways, while abandoned railroads metamorphosed into hiking and biking trails. Vocabularies sported words such as "Velcro," "Gortex," global warming, emissions trading, world wide web, along with the scary prophetic signs of the early '70s: "Sorry, pumps closed—no gas." Forward looking conservancy groups spat with developers, lawsuits were won and lost, and lawyers began to join America's *nouveau riche.*

Oppressed people seeking "more" toppled the Berlin Wall and then broke the back of America's great adversary, the Soviet Union. The drug culture flourished, while churches struggled to keep the pews filled. And instant gratification, in the guise of a small plastic card—or more often, several—held sway over America's masses.

Earl Shaffer held to a simpler lifestyle. Some folks might have called him an eccentric recluse, but nothing could be further from the truth. He just didn't need all that foofaraw. Never married, no family responsibilities, no electricity in his humble abode and no water bill, no "plastic" in his hip pocket— he came and went as he pleased. Never far from the mountains and his beloved Trail, in body or mind, he wrote poetry—words that stuck like glue to the soul and made the Trail come vibrantly alive in the mind.

Sometimes the "Crazy One" would show up at a hiker campfire to share some talk and play a few songs on his old scarred guitar. Nothing pretentious about this man. What you saw was what you got. The real item!

In 1965, the Crazy One got restless. He dusted off his old rucksack, pulled on the moccasin boots, and headed for Katahdin, this time walking south. Ninety-nine days later, the forty-six year-old southbounder touched the marker on Springer Mountain and became the first person to thru-hike the Appalachian Trail in both directions.

His restless urge now satiated, Earl went back to his small Pennsylvania farm, where he worked in his garden, played with his animals, and helped found the Susquehanna Appalachian Trail Club and the Pennsylvania Keystone Trails Association. And for five years, Earl shared his poetry-writing time with the Appalachian Trail Conference, as their Corresponding Secretary.

Others sought out the Trail to emulate the Crazy One's feat. Gene Espy had already walked the long pathway to Maine in 1951, becoming the Trail's second reported thru-hiker. Chester Dziengielewski (pronounce that one!) became the Trail's first southbounder that same year. Like Dr. Seuss's "north and south going zaxes," Chester and Gene collided head on in Pennsylvania. Unlike the zaxes though, the hikers exchanged hellos and let each other pass.

Within a decade, a half dozen hikers had conquered the Trail. The odor from Gene Espy's boots had barely dissipated from the long brown path when, in 1952, forty-four year-old Mildred Norman Ryder, seeking a higher level of inner peace, stepped up to the challenge. In company with Dick Lamb, a steadfast friend, "Peace Pilgrim," as she later became known, took honors as the first woman to hike the entire length of the Appalachian Trail in a single season, and the first "flop-flopper"—someone who hikes part of the distance, then jumps to the other end and comes back to the finish point. Mildred carried only a pair of slacks, one shirt and sweater, a blanket, and two plastic sheets, which she sometimes filled with leaves. (Ray Jardine, the modern day "ultra-light" guru, would have been mightily impressed!)

Over the next twenty-eight years, Peace Pilgrim would walk over 43,000 miles, cross the country seven times, and wear out twenty-nine pairs of children's sneakers—that's over 1500 miles per pair! As she walked, she spread her simple message: Overcome good with evil; hatred with love; falsehood with truth. The five-foot, two-inch lady usually traveled penniless, no organizational support, and, like Earl Shaffer, never carried a stove. She usually ate two cups of uncooked oatmeal soaked in water and flavored with brown sugar, morning and night. For noon, it was two cups of double strength dried milk embellished with whatever nuts and berries she had gathered on the morning's walk.

Her diet seems pretty skimpy when compared to today's calorie-packed meals cooked over "Pocket Rockets" and MSR "Whisper Lights"! No question but that the Crazy One's 1948 hike greatly influenced Mildred's choice of gear and diet. (She and Earl corresponded regularly during and after her hike.)

Came Grandma Emma Gatewood in 1955, scooting along in her "Keds," and like her predecessor, lugging a hand-sewn denim duffle bag filled with hope and little more—to claim her place in hiker archives as the first woman to *continuously* thru-hike the Trail in a single season—no flip-flop. And she did it alone! (Before her walking days ended, "Grandma" would become the first *person* to hike the Trail *three* times!)

As word spread about the magical path that stretched along the backbone of eastern America, they came, first by the teens, then by the hundreds, to make the pilgrimage from Georgia to Katahdin's sacred peak. By 1990, over 2,000 hikers had laid claim to the coveted title, "2000 Miler." (Now the tally is in the vicinity of 8000!)

The sands slipped silently through the hourglass of time, and suddenly the calendar page flipped over to 1998. Down Washington way, President William Jefferson Clinton faced impeachment charges over his hanky-panky with a young rosy-cheeked intern. The Denver Broncos had trounced the Green Bay Packers in Super Bowl XXXII, while St. Louis Cardinals' slugger, Mark McGwire was beginning what he hoped would be a run for the baseball Hall of Fame by sending the first of seventy home runs—a season record breaker—into the stands. Senator John Glenn had begun to toughen up his muscles for his second return to space on the shuttle Discovery, which was due to rise into the heavens on October 29th. And that year Earl Victor Shaffer quietly celebrated his seventy-ninth birthday.

Earl celebrated by once again launching the "Lone Expedition." When asked "why," the almost-octogenarian explained, "I couldn't stay home. I couldn't pass up the chance to celebrate this anniversary on the Trail itself—or at least try to."

On May 2, Earl Shaffer gave his cat and goat a final pat, cast a lingering look at his rustic cabin, and hefted his old rucksack. Two carloads of relatives hauled him down to Springer Mountain. (The southern terminus atop Mount Oglethorpe and the old trail had long since been abandoned.) This time there was press aplenty, and the world watched in awe as the aged man in the blue checkered flannel shirt and his trademark pith helmet made his way north.

This journey seemed harder than Earl remembered. Like his waistline, the Trail had grown since 1948—nearly one hundred ten miles. Too, much of the

Trail had been relocated off of roads, up to the humpbacked spine of the Blue Ridge where the going was tough. Really tough! Came a few falls . . . a cracked rib . . . sprained ankle . . . scrapes and bruises. No picnic this hike; but then, neither had the others been. More shelters now . . . more places to buy food along the trail . . . lots of young faces looking expectantly at the Crazy One, their role model, the founding father of the thru-hike. A weighty responsibility to "measure up." But those gosh-awful climbs . . .

The author hams it up with Earl Shaffer and Ed Garvey during Trail Days (May 1999) in Damascus, Virginia. Earl had finished his third "Lone Expedition" the previous fall. Ed died in September 1999.

In Maine, Earl teamed up with another thru-hiker, David Donaldson, aka "Spirit of '48." Beseiged days on end by weather that had turned vicious, Earl felt the first defeating twinges as "quitting" began its siren song.

At Spaulding Mountain Leanto, things came to a head when Earl awoke to another day of chilling cold, wind, and rain. He said to his new friend, "Dave, I can't. I can't. I'll wait here until the weather clears, then head for home." But even as the words came from his grim, shivering mouth, he began to pull on his wet, cold boots and get his pack ready. Earl he knew he had to go on.

David listened as Earl muttered to himself, "You've known all along that this is your last hike. Isn't that why you couldn't stay at home? Make the most of it. The cracked rib is healed, the twisted knee is better, the black eye and bruises are gone. The stress and strain, the rocks and roots and deep mudholes, the logs and bogs, the sheer rock climbs, and cold rivers to wade are part of the package, so carry on." Without another word, he hoisted his rucksack and stepped out into the dismal morning.

At the Kennebec River, "Buzz" Caverly sent word that Katahdin was being stubborn; that the mountain had been closed because of dangerous icing. It was climbable *now* but probably wouldn't be by the time Earl reached the Park.

Decision time. Earl and David decided to heed Buzz's advice and shuttled up to Baxter State Park. Pamola stayed on his nest, and the weather cooperated. Earl and several thru-hikers who had been holed up at Katahdin Stream Campground climbed the mountain, and then Earl and David hiked back through the Park from Abol Bridge to the mountain's base—just in case the Park might be closed by the time they returned.

The pair then traveled back to the Kennebec to resume their journey north, battling Maine's October nastiness, described as "rocks, roots, seldom sunshine, frosted fingers, fog, and rain"—in all, a grueling, tormenting test of man's will in the face of extreme adversity.

One hundred and fifty miles to go!

In late October, 173 days and 2168 miles after leaving Springer Mountain, the Crazy One, chilled to the bone and emaciated by the grueling hike, walked across the steel bridge that spans the Penobscot River, to Abol Store. When he touched the doorknob, his final few inches, Earl Victor Shaffer became the oldest person to complete a thru-hike of the Appalachian Trail. The "Lone Expedition" was finished!

*   *   *

Earl's record stood for six years. In 2004, Lee Barry (aka "The Easy One") from Shelby, North Carolina, completed his thru-hike at age eighty-one. Between 1990 and 2004, the thru-hiker finish rate of ten percent each year—give or take a couple of points, depending on weather and the eclectic mixture of will and means—had doubled to the vicinity of twenty percent, possibly because of ultra-light gear and more dependence on town amenities, including motels. The Trail had grown another fourteen miles and had been joined with the International Appalachian Trail, which extends north from Katahdin to Quebec's Cape Gaspe.

The tall monument on top of Mount Oglethorpe, Earl's only companion that morning in early 1948, had fallen prey to vandals and the elements. County officials hauled it off the mountain in the late nineties and turned its restoration over to the skilled hands of master sculptor Eino. Sprouting a new facelift, the monument now stands in front of the Old Jail on Main Street in downtown Jasper, Georgia.

With his health steadily failing, Earl returned to his rustic cabin (now furnished with electricity), rolled up his flannel sleeves, and went to work compiling a book about the third "Lone Expedition." *the Appalachian Trail: calling Me Back to the Hills* is a masterful creation. Embellished by photographer Bart Smith's gripping photos, Earl's book, his legacy, reveals the beauty of the Trail and the inner passion that besets thru-hikers. The book is also a grand tribute to Earl, to his love for the Trail, to what he stood for.

At age 83, Earl succumbed to cancer in Lebanon, Pennsylvania, on May 5, 2002. He died in the arms of his friend David Donaldson, "Spirit of '48," his hiking companion who had stood by him, had suffered with him during those darkest spirit-sapping days in Maine. After all, that's what true friends do.

Alas! A remarkable American, a living legend who had inspired and excited minds, had breathed life into a fledgling pathway and nurtured it into a national treasure was gone. There would be no more "Lone Expeditions."

An era had ended.

Appendix: Research Sources

Prologue

Walking With Spring by Earl V. Shaffer, published by the Appalachian Trail Conference; 1983

"Brainy History" (web site: brainyhistory.com/events/1948/April_4_1948_109080.html)

"Spring Battles to Remember"; web article from ESPN, Page 2 (web site: sports.espn.go.com/espn/page2/story?'list/050222/springbattles)

"Oglethorpe, Mount, Georgia"; web article from AllRef.com (web site: reference.allrefer.com/gazetteer/0/000835-oglethorpe-mount.html)

"Oglethorpe Monument"; web article from Pickens County Chamber of Commerce: Visitor Information (web site: pickenschamber.com/visitor.html)

"About Earl Shaffer" from "The Earl Shaffer Web Page" (web site: earlshaffer.com/aboutearl.html)

"Earl Shaffer Article" by David Corriveau, Staff Writer for *Valley News*, September 17, 1998 (abbreviated version found on web site: fred.net/kathy/at/earlsart.html)

Chapter One

Springboard to Adventure

Walking the Appalachian Trail by Larry Luxenberg: Stackpole Books, Mechanicsburg, PA; 1994

Appalachian Trail Thru-hikers' Companion, 1996; Appalachian Trail Conference, Harpers Ferry, WV; 1996

"The Story Behind Springer" by Victoria Logue; 1990 (web site: planetanimals.com/logue/springer.html)

Chapter Two

Counting Coup

Walking With Spring by Earl V. Shaffer; Appalachian Trail Conference, Harpers Ferry, WV; 1983

Appalachian Trail Thru-hikers' Companion, 1996

Walking the Appalachian Trail by Larry Luxenberg

"Amicalola Falls State Park" (web site: ngeorgia.com/parks/amicalola.html)

Chapter Three

Camp Frank D. Merrill

Personal visit to Camp Merrill

Chapter Four

Woody Gap—An Escape Hatch

Hiking the Appalachian Trail, Volume One; Rodale Press, Inc., Emmaus. PA; 1975

The Appalachian Trail by Ronald M. Fisher; National Geographic Society; 1972;

"Ranger Woody: He Knew Georgia's Deer Personally"; Article by Paul Jones; *The Atlanta Constitution*; Atlanta, GA; October 29, 1975 (web site: homepages.rootweb.com/%74woodygap/arthur1.htm)

"Arthur Woody: A North Georgia Notable" (web site: ngeorgia.com/people/woody.html)

Chapter Five

Ta-lo-Ne-Ga

Gold Fever, America's First Gold Rush by Ray C. Rensi and H. David Williams; Georgia Humanities Council, Atlanta, GA 30322; 1988

A People's History of the United States by Howard Zinn; New York: Harper and Row; 1980

Trail of Tears by John Ehle; Doubleday, New York City, NY; 1988

The Gold of Dahlonega by Lou Hartman; Hexagon Company, Asheville, NC; 1976

"Archives of Lumpkin County" (web site: roadsidegeorgia.com/county/lumpkin.html)

"Historic Dahlonega, Georgia" (web site: dahlonega.org/history/historic.html)

"North Georgia's Gold Rush" (web site: ngeorgia.com/history/goldrush.html)

"Archives of White County" (web site: roadsidegeorgia.com/county/white.html)

Chapter Six

Much Ado About Hamburgers

A North Georgia Journal of History, Volume III by Olin Jackson; Legacy Communications, Inc., Roswell, GA

Interview with Kari Morris at Turners Corner Café on April 9, 2000

Chapter Seven

The Fine Art of Yogi-ing

Walkin' on the Happy Side of Misery by J.R. "Model-T" Tate; Xlibris Corp., Philadelphia, PA; 2001

Chapter Eight

Land of the Noonday Sun

"William Bartram" (web site: mounet.com/~jdye/bartram.html)

Cherokee and Nikwasi (web site: genealogy/forum.com/gfael/resource/NA/gfe/ma3.html)

The Appalachian Trail by Ronald M. Fisher

Footsteps of the Cherokees by Vicki Rozema; John Blair Publisher, Winston Salem, NC; 1995

Foxfire 4, edited by Eliot Wigginton; Anchor Press/Doubleday, Garden City, NY; 1977

Walking the Appalachian Trail by Larry Luxenberg

"Rufus Morgan, Moses of the Mountain" (web site: dnet.net/iparker/StFrancis/RevMorgan.html)

Chapter Nine

Snowbirds

Footsteps of the Cherokee by Vicki Rozeman

Chapter Ten

Drillzibblers, Woggletobblers, and Slumgullionholes

Foxfire 10, edited by Eliot Wiggington; Anchor Press/Doubleday, Garden City, NY; 1993

Chapter Eleven

A Matter of Altitude, Aptitude, and Attitude

Footsteps of the Cherokee by Vicki Rozeman

More Tales of Tennessee by Louise Littleton Davis; Pelham Publishing Co., Gretna, LA; 1978; pp.37

Tsa'li selection from "I Love Graham County, A Guide to the Area and its Attractions"; published by *The Graham Star*, Robbinsville, NC, 28771 (web site: main,nc.us/graham/cherokee.html)

"Tsali: A Cherokee Hero" from *Blood of a Warrior* by Bruce Redhawk; 2003 (web site: http://members.tripod.com/blackrose77sc/tsali/)

Strangers in High Places by Michael Frome; Doubleday and Company, Inc., Garden City, NY; 1996

Amazing Tennessee by T. Jensen Lacey; Rutledge Hill Press, Nashville, TN; 2000

"All Taxa Biodiversity Inventory" (web site: dia.org/atbi/species/animals/vertebrates/mammals/suidae/Sus_scrofa.html)

"Examining Boar Control Efforts" by Robert D. Keller, Gary Litchford, James C. Brinson, Andrew M. Carroll, Jason M. Houck, H. Ford Mauney, and M. Taylor McDonald; The University of Tennessee at Chattanooga GIS Research Laboratory (undated) (web site: esri.com/news/arcuser/0103/hogs.html)

"Great Smoky Mountain National Park Information Page" (web site: great.smoky.mountains.national-park.com/info.htm#bear)

"Wildlife in Cades Cove" (web site: cadescove.net/wildlife_cades_cove.html)

Chapter Twelve

Hot Springs

The German Invasion of North Carolina by Jacqueline B. Painter; Biltmore Press, Asheville, NC; 1992

"The Colorful History of Hot Springs, North Carolina" (web site: hotspringsspa-nc.com/history.html)

Selection: "Vaterland During the War" (web site: ocean-liners.com/ships/vat.asp)

"Commodore Ruser" (web site: groups.msn.com/theultimateimperator/voyagehistory.msnw)

Personal interview of Vicki Rathbone at Hot Springs Spa on April 1, 2000

Western North Carolina: a History from 1730 to 1913 by John Preston Arthur: The Overmountain Press, Johnson City, TN; 1914

"Hot Springs Spa" (web site: hotspringsspa-nc.com/spa/spa.html)

Telephone interview with Cathy Hubert re: update of Hot Springs information on December 18, 2003

"Terror of the Mountains: Col. George Kirk, USA" by Derrick Shipman (web site: goecities.com/jdsreb/terrorinthemountains.htm)

Guide to the Appalachian Trail in Tennessee and North Carolina, Seventh Edition; Appalachian Trail Conference; Harpers Ferry, WV; 1983

Chapter Thirteen

Shelton Graves

Off the Laurel by Earl W. Fletcher, Jr. (self published, 2001); 360 Marcella Dr., Mosheim, TN 37818

Memoirs of William Wood Holden by W.W. Holden; The Sherman Printery, Durham, NC; 1911

"3d NC Mounted Infantry, US" (web site: nctroops.com/3usmnt.htm)

"Terror in the Mountains: Col. George Kirk, USA" by Derrick Shipman (web site: same as above)

Mountain Rebels: East Tennessee Confederates and the Civil War, 1860-1870 by W. Todd Groce; Knoxville: University of Tennessee Press; 1999

Western North Carolina: a History from 1730 to 1913 by John Preston Arthur

The Civil War: a Pictorial Profile by John S. Blay; Bonanza Books, NY; 1959

"The Shelton Laurel Massacre, Madison County, NC, Winter of 1863" by Col. William R Shelton, Jr. (web site: members.tripod.com/~verlee/sheltonlaurel.htm)

Western North Carolina: a History from 1730 to 1913 by John Preston Arthur

Telephone interview with Earl W. Fletcher, Jr. (descendant of Millard Filmore Haire) on December 17, 2003

Chapter Fourteen

The Hermit of Big Bald

"Outdoors with Bob Caldwell" (web site: wlos.com/news/outdoors/hermit_cave.html) "Hermit Cave" (aired 12/08/2000)

"North Carolina's Appalachian Trail" (web site: ibiblio.org/kelly/vnc/at/)

Guide to the Appalachian Trail in Tennessee and North Carolina, Seventh Edition, Appalachian Trail Conference

"Longstreet Guide to the North Carolina Mountains" by Lynda McDaniel (web site: sherpaguides.com/north_carolina/mountains/long_trails/suggested_day_hikes. html)

"America's Roof" (web site: americasroof.com/highest/nc.shtml)

"Peregrine Falcons" by Regency Square Area Society (web site: regencybrighton.com/birds/?content=info)

"Zebulon Baird Vance", State Library of North Carolina; North Carolina Encyclopedia (web site: statelibrary.dcr.state.nc.us/nc/bio/public/vance.htm)

The Hermit of Bald Mountain by John Biggs Alderman; *Papers of John Biggs Alderman; Archives of Appalachia*; East Tennessee State University, Johnson City, TN, 37614

Guide to the Appalachian Trail in Tennessee and North Carolina, Seventh Edition, Appalachian Trail Conference

Chapter Fifteen

The Hanging

There's a Skeleton In a Trainyard In East Tennessee by Joan Vannorsdall Schroeder; Leisure Publishing Company;, Johnson City, TN; 2000

"The Hanging of Mary the Elephant" by Hilda Padgett (web site: rootsweb.com/~tnunicoi/mary.htm)

"1916 Elephant Hanging Still Haunts Town" by Angela K. Brown, Staff Writer;
The Oak Ridger (web site: oakridger.com/stories/110899/stt_1108990033.html)

Erwin, Tennessee Historical Events, "The Hanging of 'Murderous Mary'";
Compliments of the Antique Mall and the Unicoi (web site: pe.net/
~rksnow/tncountyerwinhev.htm)

"Murderous Mary" from The Storyteller's Cabin by Craig Dominey (web site:
themoonlitroad.com/members/archives/mary/intro_mary.html)

The Day They Hung the Elephant by Charles Edwin Price; The Overmountain
Press; Johnson City, TN; 1992

Wikipedia, The Free Encyclopedia: "Erwin, Tennessee" (web site: en2.wikipedia .org/
wiki/Erwin,_Tennessee)

"The O'Leary Legend" (web site: chicagohs.org/fire/oleary/)

"1916 World Events" (web site: museum.tv/archives/etv/c/html/c/cronkitewal/
csame.htm; also web site: infoplease.com/year/1916.htm)

"United States Naval Ships" (web site: history.navy.mil/photos/sh-usn/usnsh-
p/bb38.htm)

"1916 Events" (web site: din_timelines.com/1916_timeline.shtml)

"The Irish War for Independence" (Easter Monday Uprising) (web site:
home.fiac. net/marshaw/1916.htm)

"The Reader's Companion to American History" (Model-T Fords) (web site:
college.hmco.com/history/readerscomp/rcah/html/ah_032200_fordhenry.htm)

"BBC Wild Facts—Asian Elephant" (web site: bbc.co.uk/nature/wildfacts/
facilities/178.shtml)

"The Elephant Sanctuary" (web site: elephants.com/sanctdescription.htm)

Chapter Sixteen

In Memorium

John Wasilik

"Side Trails in the Nantahalas" (web site: maconweb.com/nhc/sides.html#John)

"Standing Indian Basin" (GORP) (web site: gorp.away.com/gorp/resource/
us_national_forest/nc/nc_stand.htm)

"The Ancient Bristlecone Pine" by Dr. Edmund Schulman (web site: sonic.net/
bristlecone/home.html)

"Poplar Park" (web site: ci.bedford.va.us/poplar.shtml)

"Yellow Poplar or Tulip Tree", Virginia Dept. of Forestry (web site: vdof.org/
mgt/trees/poplar-yellow.shtml)

"Virginia and National Big Tree Champion" (web site: fw.edu/4ᵗʰ/bigtree/
index.htm)

"What You Need to Know About Forestry" by Steve Nix; (web site:
forestry.about.com/library/tree/bltulip.htm)

"The Herbs, Roots, and Bark Library" by Magia D'LaLuna (web site:
magialuna.net/p.html

"Oldest Tulip Poplar" (web site: kdla.ky.gov/resources/KYTree.htm)

"Tree Hunt" by g&l Publishers (web site: daily-tangents.com/TreeHunt/SP-litu/)

Telephone interview on March 8, 2004, with Bill Lea, Resource Specialist,
National Forests in North Carolina

The Franklin Press; Franklin, NC; Thursday, June 6, 1968 issue; Thursday,
September 4, 1969 issue

Wade Sutton

"Fighting Forest Fires is a Dangerous Profession" by Marshall McClung; Graham
County, NC; 1994 (web site: main.nc.us/graham/mcclung/
Forest%20Fires.html)

"FEMA Forest Fire Fatalities Report. 1997 (web site: wildfirelessons.net/Library/
Incident_Reviews/Fatalities/FEMA_USFA_Report1997_ Fatalities.doc)

"Historical Wildland Firefighter Fatalities" by National Wildfire Coordinating
Group; March 1997 (web site: nwcg.gov/pms/docs/fat_pdf.pdf)

Interview with R.Q Canby at Bryson City, NC, on April 21, 2003

Smoky Mountain Times; Bryson City, NC, December 12, 1968 issue

The Cemeteries of Swain County, NC by the Swain County Genealogical and
Historical Society, PO Box 267, Bryson City, NC 28713

Rex Pulford

"In Flanders Fields the Poppies Grow"; poem by John McCrae (1878-1918)
(web site: lib.byu.edu/~english/WW1/over/over.html)

Telephone interview with Dorothy Hansen on January 19, 2004

"Primitive Paradise": excerpt from *Maiden Effort* by Lu Murphy; 1956

Rex Pulford's 1983 Appalachian Trail Journal

Little Ottie

"Ghost in Our Mountains" by Rosemary Dunne, from her article published
in the November/December 1994 issue of *Blue Ridge Country Magazine*
(web site: members.aol.com/achmuseum/muse/musefall-1998.html)

Telephone interview with Rosemary Dunne on 19 January 2004

Little Lost Boy in Mountains of Virginia by J.B. Huffman; Buena Vista, Virginia; 1925 (Reprinted in *In and Around Rockbridge,* Rockbridge Area Genealogical Society Newsletter Vol 10, No. 2 (Spring 2003); Rockbridge Baths, VA 24473

"Who Are the German Baptist Brethren?" from *The Roanoke Times;* copyright 1998 (web site: garstfamily.com/ogbb/gbb.html)

"Dunkards", from "The 1911 Edition Encyclopedia" (web site: 43.1911 encyclopedia.org/G/GE/German_Baptist_Brethren.htm)

The Story of a Kansas Pioneer by Melissa Genett Anderson; Manufacturing Printers Co., Mt. Vernon, Ohio; 1924

"Kimmel Cemetery" from Union County (Illinois) Home Page (web site: iltrails.org/union/dextercems.htm)

"Clifton Webb" (web site: members.aol.com/Rdkone/CliftonWebb.html)

"Dr. James Naismith" (web site: hoopball.com/halloffamers/Naismith.htm)

"Thomas Edison" (web site: en.wikipedia.org/wiki/1891)

"What Happened All Those Years Ago" (web site: andibradley.com/whatya/nov09.htm)

Appalachian Trailway News", November-December 1995 ("In Search of Little Ottie Cline Powell"); *September-October 1996* ("Ottie Powell Memorial Completed")

Chapter Seventeen

Uncle Nick

Nick, the Hermit" by Adam M. Daugherty; Bakers Gap, Tennessee; 1926

Chapter Eighteen

Mock's Mill

"Mock Family Historian 'Working Chart '#19b" by Barbara Eichel Dittig (web site: *home.kc.rr.com/kenneal/mock/19b.html*)

"Henry A. Mock, Jr." by Elizabeth Gilchrist; June 1998 (web site: gendex.com/users/bobspu/spurgeon/d0015/g/0000056.html)

"Damascus—A History" by John Reese (web site: appletreebnb.com/history.htm)

A History of Damascus by Louise Fortune Hall, an excerpt (web site: damascus.org/about.html)

"Chronology" from *The Life and Legend of an American Pioneer* by John
   Mack Faragher, 1992 (web site: lucidcafe.com/library/95nov/boone.html)
John Imboden" by Eric and Susan Wittengberg (web site: gng.org/jimboden.html)
Appalachian Trail Thru-Hikers' Companion, Appalachian Trail conference

Chapter Nineteen

Sarver Hollow

"The Mountain That Moved", from *Geologic Wonders of the George Washington
   and Jefferson National Forests*, USGS Publication, 2000
*Birth of the Mountains—The Geologic Story of the Southern Appalachian
   Mountains* by Sanndra H.B. Clark, USGS Publication
"Sarver Hollow Dedication" by Stephanie Kent, from *RATC Trail Blazer,
   Winter 2002*
"Nationmaster Encyclopedia: Appalachian Mountains—Geology" (web site:
   Nationmaster.com/encyclopedia/Appalachian-Mountains)
"The Appalachian Mountains" by Michellle Melikian (Westfield State College,
   Westfield, MA, undated (web site: physci.wsc.ma.edu/young/hgeol/
   geoinfo/timeline/appalachians/appalachian.html)
"California Untold Stories—Gold Rush" by Oakland Museum of California
   (web site: museumca.org/goldrush/
"The Trail of Tears" from *About North Georgia* by Goldenlink (web site:
   ngeorgia.com/history/nghisttt.html)
Sarver Family Genealogy, GENFORUM, Genealogy.com (web site:
   genforum.genealogy.com/sarver/messages.html)
Craig County Archives: "A Biographical Narrative of John Reynolds" (web
   site: searches.rootsweb.com/cgi-bin/search)
A History of Middle New River Settlements and Contiguous Territory by David
   E. Johnston; Standard Printing and Publishing, Huntington, WV; 1906
"The History of the 22nd Virginia" from The Official Website of the 22nd
   Virginia Vol. Inf. (web site: homepagez.com/22ndvirginia)
Point Lookout, Md., Prison Camp Records from William L. Clements Library;
   The University of Michigan; *Schoff Civil War Collections*
"The Battle of Ft. Sumter" from Shotgun's "Home of the American Civil
   War: (web site: civilwarhome.com/ftsumter.htm)
"Events of 1853" from WIKIPEDIA, The Free Encyclopedia (web site:
   en.wikipedia.org/wiki/1853)

Personal interviews with Bob Ross and Clarence Givens on March 25, 2004, at Blacksburg, VA

Telephone interview with Bob Ross on August 25, 2004

Telephone interview with Clarence Givens on August 29, 2004 and subsequent email correspondence

Chapter Twenty

To Hell and Back

"To Hell and Back" by Audie Leon Murphy; MSF Books, 60 West 66th St., NewYork City, NY 10023; 1949

Dog Face Soldiers: The Story of B Company, 15th Regiment, 3rd Infantry Division: From Fedala to Salzburg: Audie Murphy and His Brothers in Arms by Daniel R. Champagne; Merrian Press, Bennington, VT; 2003

Audie Murphy, American Soldier by Harold B. Simpson; Hill Jr. College Press, Hillsboro, TX; 1975

The Films and Career of Audie Murphy by Sue Gossett; Empire Publishing, Madison, NC; 1996

"Audie Murphy Memorial Web Site", web author Richard L. Rogers (web site: audiemurphy.com)

"From WWII Hero to Hollywood Movie Star" by Dr. Ivan M. Tribe, from *Knight Templar Magazine*, Oct 1998

"Audie Murphy: Army Legend" by John Silva (web site: grunts.net/audiemurphy.html)

"Murphy, Audie" from The Handbook of Texas Online (web site: tsha.utexas.edu/handbook/online/articles/view/MM/fmul13.html)

"Veterans for Peace" by Rick Anderson; reprinted from the *Seattle Weekly* (web site: seattleweekly.com/features/0315/news-anderson.php)

Joe Hooper article reprinted from the *Joliet Herald-News*, Joliet. IL; January 22, 1986 issue (web site: dtman.com/archives2.htm)

"Just a Little Walk in the Woods" from *Delta Raider Newsletter*, Issue # 20, December 1989; reprinted from the *Seattle Times* (web site: blackied 2501.com/stories/hooper_2.htm)

"Joe Hooper's Medal of Honor Citation" (web site: mishalov.com/Hooper.html)

"Kentucky Derby Statistics" (web site: Kentuckyderby.com/2003/derby_history/derby_statistics/1976_2002.html)

Chapter Twenty-one

Mosby's Confederacy

The Memoirs of Colonel John S. Mosby by John S. Mosby; edited by Charles Wells; Little, Brown, and Company, Boston, MA; 1917

Archives of the John Singleton Mosby Museum, Warrenton, VA, 20188

"John Singleton Mosby" from Shotgun's "Home of the American Civil War, Civil War Biographies" (web site: civilwarhome.com/mosbybio.htm)

"John Singleton Mosby" from Wikipedia, the free encyclopedia (web site: en.wikipedia.org/wiki/John_Singleton_Mosby)

"John S. Mosby: Gray Ghost" from CJ's Civil War Home Page (web site: members.tripod.com/~beag27/jmodby.html)

"Biography of John Singleton Mosby" from Mosby's Rangers.com (web site: mosbysrangers.com/bio/)

"Mosby's Rangers" from Fauquier Heritage & Preservation Foundation, Fauquier County, VA (web site: fhs.org/Dig/page21.htm)

"Loudoun County Burning Raid" from "The History of Loudoun County, Virginia" (web site: waterfordva-wca.org/history/loudoun-cw-mosby.htm)

"History of Military Units at the University of Virginia", researched by 2LT Brendan Dignan, 2001 (web site: virginia.edu/arotc/Overview/history.htm)

"The Real Casey Jones Story" from the Water Valley Casey Jones Railroad Museum (web site: watervalley.net/users/caseyjones/casey.htm)

Chapter Twenty-two

The Legacy of "The Hole"

A Walker's Guide to Harpers Ferry, West Virginia by Dave Gilbert; Harpers Ferry Historical Association, P.O. Box 197, Harpers Ferry, West Virginia 25425; 1983

"John Brown" (web site: civilwarhome.com/johnbrown.htm)

"The John Brown Farm" (web site: www2.plallsburg.edu/johnbrown/farmtext.htm)

"Say, Brother, Who Wrote This Melody?" by Robert W. Allen (website: johnbrownsbody.net/SayBrother.htm)

"Various Versions of the John Brown Song" (web site: johnbrownsbody.net/JBBSong.htm)

"John Brown and His Family" (web site: jefferson.village.virginia.edu/jbrown/family.html)

"Harpers Ferry National Historical Park" (web site: nps.gov/hafe.htm)

"John Brown's Holy War" from "The American Experience" (web site: pbs.org/ wgbh/amex/brown/sfeature/fort.html)

"Bleeding Kansas: Prelude to Civil War" (web site: civilwaralbum.com/misc/ kansas_bld1.htm)

"John Brown Biography Page" (web site: johnbrown.org)

"Thomas, Sixth Lord Fairfax, Baron of Cameron" (web site: behelp.com/ route50/people/6thlordfairfax.htm)

"The Fairfax Grant" (web site: hottelkeller.org/northernneckproprietary.htm)

"In the Harpers Ferry Region" by Jean Stephenson, from the *PATC Archives* (web site: patc.net/history/archive/harpfery.html)

"Harpers Ferry: The Journal Online" (web site: wvweb.com/cities/harpers_ferry/)

"The Battle Hymn of the Republic" (web site: allmusic.com/cg/amg.dll? p=amg&sql+42:225098-T1)

"Julia Ward Howe's Account of the Writing of the 'Battle Hymn of the Republic". Extract from: Julia Ward Howe's "Reminisces, 1819-1899" (web site: johnbrownsbody.net/JWHSong.htm)

"Chaplain Charles Cardwell McCabe, 122nd Ohio: The Man Who Made Howe's 'Battle Hymn' Famous" (web site: johnbrownsbody.net/ CCMcCabe.htm)

"The Cambridge History of English and American Literature, Volume XXVI: Patriotic Songs and Hymns" (web site: bartleby.com/228/ 0305.htm)

"Battle Hymn of the Republic" (web site: amcivilwarmonth.homestead.com/ bhofrepublic.html)

"More on William Steffe" (web site: folkarchive.de/battle.html)

Chapter Twenty-three

John Brown's Fort

"John Brown's Fort" by Clarence S. Gee, from West Virginia History, Volume Nineteen, Number Two (web site: wvculture.org/history/jb6.html)

"John Brown's Ghost" from "Ghosts of the Prairie" (web site: prairieghost.com/ ferry.html)

"Dangerfield Newby" (web site: wesclark.com/jw/newby.html)

"Ghost Stories of Harpers Ferry" by Shirley Dougherty (web site: harpersferry wv.net/ghosts_stories_of_harpers_ferry__htm)

Chapter Twenty-four

The Gaps of South Mountain

Civil War Curiosities by Webb Garrison; Rutledge Hill Press, 211 Seventh Avenue North, Nashville, Tennessee 37219; 1994

"Gathland State Park History" (web site: dnr.state.md.us/publiclands/western/gathland.html)

"History of the Antietam Fire Company" (web site: antietamfirecompany.org/lhistory.htm)

"Gathland State Park" from The Friends of South Mountain Battlefield (web site: fsmsb.org/gsp.html)

"Biographical Note" from "George Alfred Townsend Collection", University of Delaware Library, Special Collections Department (web site: lib.udel.edu/ud/spec/findaids/townsend.htm)

"The Civil War Correspondents Memorial Arch" (web site: civilwarhome.com/Gathland.htm)

"Gapland: A Ghost on the Trail" by Orville Crowder, from the *PATC Archives, The Potomac Appalachian Trail Club: History* (web site: patc.net/history/archive/gapghost.html)

"Fallen Journalists Honored at Gathland State Park" by Angela Pfeiffer, Staff Writer, "Gazette.net" (web site: gazette.net/200340/brunswick/news/180915-1.html)

"The Truth About the War Memorial to Fallen Journalists" by Timothy J. Reese (web site: hnn.us/articles/1711.html)

"The Battle of South Mountain" from "Civil War Crossroads" (web site: civilwarsites.com/html/southmountain.asp)

"The Battle of Boonsboro Gap or South Mountain" by Judge George D. Grattan, Harrisonburg, Va., Captain and A.A.G. Staff of General Colquitt (web site civilwarhome.com/boonsborogap.htm)

"Special Orders No. 191" from the "History of the 27th Volunteer Infantry Regiment" (web site: geocities.com/pentagon/barracks/3627/lostorder.html)

"Lee's Special Order 191" (web site: nps.gov/anti/ordr_191.html)

"Frequently Asserted Claims Concerning Geo. B. McClellan" (web site: georgebmcclellan.org/faq2.html)

"Forcing Fox's Gap and Turner's Gap" by Jacob D. Cox, Major General, U.S.V., from "Battles and Leaders of the Civil War" (web site: civilwarhome.com/foxsgap.htm)

"The Battle of South Mountain: Fox's Gap—Wise's Well" (also Fox's Gap and Turner's Gap) from The Central Maryland Heritage League Land Trust (web site: cmhl.org/wise.html)

"Lost Legion—The Phillip's Legion Infantry Battalion at Fox's Gap, Maryland, Sept. 14th, 1862" by Kurt D. Graham (web site: angelfire.com/ga2/PhillipsLegion/lostlegion.html)

"23d North Carolina Regiment at the Battle of South Mountain" (web site: spaceportusa.net/doorgunner/23nc01.htm)

"Brave and Accomplished" by Paul R. Martin III, from the Official Web Site of Silent Sentinel Studio "Honoring Those Who Served" (web site: paulmartinart.com/GenSamuelGarland.html); also "Remember Reno" at paulmartinart.com/GenJesseReno.html)

"Crampton's Gap Battlefield" (web site: earthlink.net/~tjreesecg/id9.html

"Hayes of the Twenty-third: A Civil War Chronology" from the Archives of the Twenty-Third Ohio Volunteer Infantry (web site: rbhayes.org/ov.htm)

"A Gap in Time: The Wise Farmstead/Fox Gap Archaeological Project" (web site: iuparchaeology.iup.edu/FoxGap/background_data.htm)

"John Adolphus Dahlgren, Commander South Blockading Squadron" (web site: member.aol.com/WaltESmith/dahlgren.htm)

"The Dahlgren Family" from The Central Maryland Heritage League Land Trust (web site: cmhl.org/dahlgren.html); also see "Dahlgren Chapel"

"Stepping Back in Time Along the Appalachian Trail" by Brian Hayek (adapted from "Stepping Back in Time: A Hike Through History on the Crest of Maryland's South Mountain", *Appalachian Trailway News, March/April 1995* (web site: crm.cr.nps.gov/archive/20-1/20-1-14.pdf)

"A History of the Old South Mountain Inn" (web site: oldsouthmountaininn.com/)

"A Civil War Spy: Miss Elizabeth Van Lew" from *Richmond: The Story of a City* by Virginius Dabney; University of Virginia Press, Charlottesville, Virginia; 1990

"The Story Behind the Name!" (web site: geocities.com/brett4733/barname.html)

"eHistory: Hugh S. Kilpatrick (Kilcavalry)" (web site: ehistory.com/world/peopleview.Cfm?PID=338)

"In River Time: The Way of the James: Pausing for War" (web site: vcu.edu/engweb/Rivertime/chp13.htm)

Central Maryland Heritage League Flyer depicting "Dahlgren Chapel" by P. Buckley Moss (web site: cenmd.com/psa/CMHLflyer.pdf)

"Maryland Campaign: September 1862" from Houghton Mifflin's "Civil War Battlefield Guide" (web site: college.hmco.com/history/readerscomp/civwar/html/cw_003001_harpersferry.htm)

"Lee Invades the North: Stonewall's Brilliant Victory: The Siege and Capture of Harpers Ferry" (web site: nps.gov/hafe/jackson.htm)
"Traveller, Robert E. Lee's War Horse" (web site: equinenet.org/heroes/traveller.html)
Gettysburg: Day Three by Jeffry D. Wert; Simon and Schuster, NY, NY; 2001

Chapter Twenty-five

A Case of One-Upmanship

"The Washington Monument" from "Your Guide to U.S./Canadian Parks by Darren Smith (web site: usparks.about.com/cs/natlparkbasics/a/washingtonmon.htm)
"History of the Washington Monument and Mount Vernon and Washington Places" (web site: wam.umd.edu/~jlehnert/history.htm)
"Patriotic Sites in Maryland" from "Maryland Welcome" (web site: mdisfun.org/PressReleases/25.asp)
"Washington County, Maryland Fun Facts" (web site: members.aol.com/dankmd/da00005.htm)
"Washington Monument State Park: Hawk Count" (web site: hawkcount.org/month_summary.php?rsite=279)
"Washington Monument" (web site: nps.gov/wamo/memorial/8399.htm
"The National Road" (web site: nps.gov/fone/natlroad.htm)
"The Road That Built the Nation" (web site: nationalroadpa.org/)

Chapter Twenty-six

To Perdition and Back

"Camp Michaux" Web site by Lee Schaeffer: (beulahpresby.org/webmaster/michaux.htm), which includes the following links:to: *The History of Camp Michaux* by M.S. Reifsnyder; The Carroll Record Company, Inc., Taneytown, MD; April 1955
"The Pine Grove Prisoner of War Camp" by Patrick L. Metcalf; from *Cumberland County History, Winter 2000, Volume 17 Number 2*
"The History of Pine Grove Furnace" from Department of Conservation and Natural Resources Archives, Commonwealth of Pennsylvania
"A Short History of Camp Michaux", taken from Pine Grove Furnace Park Archives
"Recollections, Historical and Otherwise, Relating to Old Pine Grove Furnace" by Horace Andrew Keffer; From the *PATC Archives* (web site: patc.net/history/archive/pine_grv.html)

"Caledonia State Park", from Archives of Department of Conservation and Natural Resources, Commonwealth of Pennsylvania (web site: dcnr.state.pa.us/stateparks/parks/caledonia.aspx)

"The Iron Furnaces of Franklin County Pennsylvania: Caledonia Furnace" by Raymond A Washlaski; from *Virtual Museum of Pennsylvania Iron Furnaces & Iron Works: A Publication of the 19th Century Society of Pennsylvania* (web site: paironworks.rootsweb.com/fracaledonia.html)

"Pennsylvania's Environmental Heritage: Dr. Joseph Trimble Rothrock" from *The Legacy of Penn's Woods: A History of the Pennsylvania Bureau of Forestry* by Lester A. DeCoster, 1955 (web site: dep.state.pa.us/dep/PA_Env-Her/rothrock_bio.htm)

"A Century of Conservation: The Story of Pennsylvania's State Parks" by Dan Culpepper; from *Pennsylvania Heritage Magazine* (web site: dep.state.pa.us/dep/PA_Env-Her/stateparks/state_parks.htm)

"Andre¢ Michaux: A Biography", compiled by Charlie Williams; Public Library of Charlotte and Mecklenburg County; October 1999 (web site: michaux.org/michaux.htm)

"Pennsylvania CCC Archive: General History" (web site: dcnr.state.pa.us/stateparks/ccc/history.aspx)

Thaddeus Stevens: Nineteenth-Century Egalitarian by Hans L. Trefousse; Chapel Hill: University of North Carolina Press; 1997

"The American Civil War: Thaddeus Stevens"; Web site prepared by Douglas Harper; 2002 (web site etymonline.com/cw/stevens.htm)

"Past Anti-Masons: Thaddeus Stevens" by C. Clark Julius, MPS; from 1986 edition of *Philalethes Magazine* (web site: masonicinfo.com/thaddeus.htm)

Chapter Twenty-seven

The Dark Side

"Facts About Appalachian Trail Crime" from the Appalachian Trail Conservancy web page (web site: appalachiantrail.org/hike/plan/crime.html)

"Death on the Trail: Appalachian Hikers Crossed Paths With Many Friends—and a Murderer" by Earl Swift, Staff Writer; from *The Virginia Pilot*, Sunday, June 2, 1991 (web site: hamptonroads.com/plotonline/archives/free/trail5.html)

"Trail's End: Killings Spoil Serenity" from *The Virginia Pilot*, Monday, September 24, 1990 (web site: hamptonroads.com/pilotonline/archives/free/trail1.html)

"Precendential in the United States Court of Appeals for the Third Circuit (No. 99-9908: Paul D. Crews, Appellant" (web site: ca3.uscourts.gov/opinarch/999008p.pdf)

"A Formula for Old Time Construction" by Martin Johnson; from *The Register*; Fall 2000; Vol. 24, No. 3 (web site: appalachiantrail.org/about/pubs/register/archives/RGfall00.pdf)

"Cove Mountain Shelter Dedication"; from *The Register*; Summer 2001; Vol. 24, No.6 (web site: appalachiantrail.org/about/pubs/register/archive/Rgsumm01.pdf)

"Rites Set for Victim of Slaying" from *Green Bay Sentinel*; undated (web site: homepages.rootsweb.com/~balzarm/d0001/g0000137.html)

"Out of the Ashes" by Martin Sussman; from *Appalachian Trailway News*, May—June 2001

"Trail Hikers' Killer Denied Parole for 8th Time" by Kathy Loan, Staff Writer; *Roanoke Times*, August 13, 1994 (web site: fred.net/kathy/at/parole.html)

Eight Bullets: One Woman's Story of Surviving Anti-Gay Violence by Claudia Brenner with Hannah Ashley; Firebrand books, Ithaca, NY; 1995

"Brenner Talks About Her Ordeal" from *Out in the Mountains*; January 1989 (web site: mountainpridemedia.org/oitm/1989/01jan1989/)

"Death Penalty Sought in 1996 Park Murders" by Jen McCaffrey, *Roanoke Times*; January 31, 2003 (web site: aldha.org/arrest02.htm)

"Prosecutors Request Delay in Trial of Rice" by Carlos Santos, Staff Writer; *Richmond Times-Dispatch*, October 28, 2003 (web site: truthinjustice.org/Darrell-Rice.htm)

"Human Skeleton Found by Appalachian Trail Hiker" from *leesburg 2'day.com*; January 25, 2005 (web site: leesburg2day.com/current.cfm?catid=6&newsid =3336)

"Old Trail Mystery Partially Solved" from *Appalachian Trailway News*, June—July 2003

"Maryland Woman Indicted in Murder of Man Left on Former Trail Lands" from *Appalachian Trailway News*, January—February 2004

"Heterosexual AIDS Risk Versus Being Struck by Lightning" (web site: righto.com/theories/lightning.html)

Chapter Twenty-eight

"Rocksylvania"

"William Penn, Americas First Great Champion for Liberty and Peace" by Jim Powell; article from *The Freeman* (web site: quaker.org/wmpenn.html)

"William Penn founder of Pennsylvania", an excerpt from *Our Country: A Household History for All Readers, Vol 1* by Benson J. Lossing; publisher:

Henry J. Johnson, NY, NY, 1877 (no known copyright) (web site: publicbookshelf.com/public_html/Our_Country_Vol_1/ williampe_ja.html)

"Biography of William Penn" adapted from *We the People, Volume I: Laying the Foundation* by James F. Gauss, Ph.D.; Copyright 2002/2003 (web site: thepatriotscorner.homestead.colliam_Penn_Biog.html)

"Penn and the Indians" from "William Penn: Visionary Proprietor by Tuomi J. Forrest (web site: xroads.virginia.edu/!CAP/PENN/pnind.html)

"William Penn and the native inhabitants (Lenape) of what would become Pennsylvania", a web article by Lee Stultzman (web site: quakers-swfl.org/ penn-natives.html)

"Proclamation 5284—Honorary United States Citizenship for William and Hannah Penn: November 28, 1984" by the President of the United States; Filed with the Office of the Federal Register, 11:28a.m., November 29, 1984 (web site: reagan.utexas.edu/resource/speeches/1984/112884a.htm)

"Pennsylvania's Great Walking Purchase" from BBC Homepage (web site: bbc.co.uk/dna/h2g2/A219070)

"The Walking Purchase", web article from the Delaware Tribe of Indians homepage (web site: delawaretribeofindians.nsn.us/walking_purchase.html)

"The Walking Purchase August 25, 1737" from Pennsylvania State Archives, "DOC Heritage" (web site: docheritage.state.pa.us/documents/ walkingpurchase.asp)

"Liberty Bell Facts", "Liberty Bell Timeline", and "Liberty Bell Triviata" from ushistory.org (web site: ushistory,org/libertybell/facts.html)

"An abstract of the life of James Logan", from Gwynedd (Pennsylvania Friends Meeting web page; article abstracted from *James Logan and the Culture of Provincial Pennsylvania* by Frederick B. Tolles; 1957 (web site: gwyneddfriends.org/JamesLogan.html)

"A Brief History of the French & Indian War", web article from *The Philadelphia Print shop, Ltd.* (web site: philaprintshop.com/frchintx.html)

"French and Indian War", excerpt from *History of Berks County* by Morton Montgomery, 1909 (web site: horseshoe.cc/pennadutch/history/american/ frenchin.htm)

"The French and Indian War" article excerpted from *The Pennsylvania Dutch* by Frederick Klees; Macmillan Company, 1961

"Biography of Conrad Weiser" from Berks Web web page (web site: berksweb.com/weisertext.html)

"Conrad Weiser" from Pennsylvania State Archives (web stie: phmc.state.pa.us/ ppet/weiser/)

"Conrad Weiser, Peacemaker of Colonial Pennsylvania" by Frederick S. Weiser from The Historical Society of Berks County archives (web site: berkshistory.org/peacemaker_1960.html)

"Colonel Benjamin Franklin" by Willard Sterne Randall from *MHQ: Quarterly Journal of Military History, Winter 2001*

The Autobiography of Benjamin Franklin by Benjamin Franklin, translated from the French and reprinted by J. Parsons; London, 1793

William Franklin" web article from Wikipedia (web site: en.wikipedia.org/wiki/William_Franklin)

"How Did Benjamin Franklin's Kite Experiment Work" from The Bakken Library and Museum (web site: thebakken.org/electricity/franklin-kite.html)

"Battle of Concord: A Brief History" from web article, Worcester Polytechnic Institute (WPI) Military Science Dept. (web site: wpi.edu/Academics/Depts/MilSci/BTSI/Lexcon/)

"Count Nicholas Ludwig von Zinzendorf", web article by Rev. John Jackman (web site: zinzendorf.com/countz.htm)

History of the Lackawanna Valley by H. Hollister, M.D.; C.A. Alvord, NY, NY; 1869

Report of the Commission to Locate the Site of the Frontier Forts of Pennsylvania, Volume One (web site: rootsweb.com/%7Eusgenweb/pa/1pa/1picts/frontierforts/ff6.html)

Frontier forts of Pennsylvania, Vol. 1 by Thomas Lynch Montgomery, 1916

"Family of Hans Peter Sumi, Sr. Born 1675" (web site: rci.rutgers.edu/~deis/summy.html)

"Chief Pontiac" from Enchanted Learning (web site: enchantedlearning.com/explorers/page/p/pontiac.shtml)

BMECC "Winter Scenes" by Barry Baskins (web site: bmecc.org/images/Winter_PilgerRuh_01.jpg)

Chapter Twenty-nine

In the Shadows of the Blue Ridge

The World of the American Indian, Published by The National Geographic Society; Jules B. Billard, editor; 1974

"Delaware History" by Lee Sultzman (web site: tolatsga.org/dela.html)

"Iroquois History" by Lee Sultzman (web site: tolatsga.org/iro.html)

"Iroquois Indians"; web article by Ohio History Central (web site: ohiohistorycentral.org/ohc/history/h_indian/tribes/iroquois.shtml)

"Algonquian Indians"; web article by Ohio History Central (web site: ohiocentralhistory.org/ohc/history/h_indian/tribes/algonqui.shtml)

"Looking Back: The Lenni-Lenape and the 'Red Record'" by Julia White (web site: meyna.com/lenape.html)

"*The Walum Olam: Its Origin and Authenticity*" from *The Lenape and Their Legends* by Daniel G. Branton; 1884 (web site: abob.libs.uga.edu/bobk/walamc.html)

"Delaware Indians"; web article by Ohio History Central (web site: ohiohistorycentral.org/ohc/history/h_indian/tribes/delaware.shtml)

"Delaware Indian History; web article by Native American Genealogy (web site: accessgenealogy.com/native/tribes/delaware/delawarehist.htm)

"Delaware Indian Tribe; web article by Kansas Genealogy (web site: kansasgenealogy.com/indians/delaware_indian_tribe.htm)

"Schaghticoke Indian Tribe"; web article by the Schaghticoke Indian Tribe (web site: schaghticoketribe.com/pages/463223/)

"Mattabesic History"; web article by Lee Sultzman (web site: clickshovel.com/matta.html)

"Shag's Receive Federal Recognition" from *The Day*; news article dtd 1/30/2004 by staff writer Eileen McNamara (web site: connecticutalliance.org/docs/20040130STNReceive.pdf)

"The Trail and the Schaghticoke Reservation" from the Appalachian Trail Conference archives (web site: appalachiantrail.org/protect/issues/schaghticoke.html)

"With Apologies to the Schaghticokes" by Dr. Paul Loatman (web site: mechanicsville.com/history/articles/schaghticokes.htm)

"The History of Molly Fisher Rock"; web article by Carol A. Hanny (web site: members.skyweb.net/~channy/Mfpage.html)

"King Philip's War"; web article reprinted from discontinued Medfield, MA community web page (web site: members.aol.com/netpotato/king_philips_war.htm)

"King Philip's War: 1675-76" web article from U-S-history.com (web site: u-s-history.com/pages/h578.html)

"Sandwich Shop Chain Founder Says He Will Push for Bridgeport Casino" from *The Boston Globe* dtd 2/13/2004 (web site: boston.com/news/local/connecticut/articles/2004/02/13/)

"*Hitting the Jackpot: Inside Story of the Richest Indian Tribe in History*" by Brett D. Fromson; Atlantic Monthly Press, NY, NY 10003; 2003

"Who Were the Abenaki Indians?"; web article by Page Wise, Inc. (web site: scsc.essortment.com/abenakinewengl_mru.htm)

"Abenaki History" by Lee Sultzman (web site: tolatsga.org/aben.html)

Chapter Thirty

Presidential Wrath

"The Columbus Landfall Homepage" by Keith A. Pickering (web site: www1.minn.net/~keithp/cclandfl.htm)

"Hiking the White Mountains" by Bob Taylor (web site: members.tripod.com/~wmnfhiker/index.html)

"Timothy Nash & Benjamin Sawyer: Footnotes With a Twist" by W. Douglas Roy; from *Heart of New Hampshire Magazine* (web site: heartofnh.com/LegendsLore/Nash_Sawyer.html)

"Mount Washington Hotel Time Line" (web site: mtwashington.com/hotelinformation/index.cfm?edit_id=38)

"The Knowledge Network: Our NH Teacher's Guide: Mt. Washington (web site: nhptv.org/kn/itv/ournh/ournhtg11.htm)

"Trail of Years" from *AMC Outdoors* (web site: outdoors.org/publications/outdoors/2000/2000-crawford-crawfords.cfm)

History of Coos County, New Hampshire by George Drew Merrill; Syracuse, NY: W.A. Fergusson & Company; 1888

"The History of Crawford Notch" from *AMC Outdoors* (web site: outdoors/pdf/upload/Highland-Center-Press-Kit-History-of-Crawford-Notch.pdf)

"History of Research of Glaciation in the White Mountains, New Hampshire (U.S.A.)" by Woodrow B. Thompson (web site: erudit.org/revue/gpg/1999/v53/n1/004879ar.html)

"Hart's Location, NH" (web site: nhes.state.nh.us/elmi/htmlprofiles/harts location.html)

"The Willey Slide" from "The Weather Notebook" (web site: weathernotebook.org/transcripts/2000/03/01.html)

"Crawford Notch State Park: The Story of the Willey Family" (web site: nhstate parks.org/ParksPages/CrawfordNotch/CrawfordNotchWlyHse.html)

"History of Crawford Notch State Park" (web site: nhstateparks.org/ParksPages/CrawfordNotch/CrawfordNotchHist.html)

"Crawford Family of Grafton County, New Hampshire Genealogy Page" by R.W. Trask, 1998 (web site: dpsinfo.com/tree/crawford/)

"High on a Wing #03" by Jim Mick (web site: ridingiswonderful.com/highonawing_sample.html)

"The Summit of Mt. Washington: from MOUNTWASHINGTON.COM (web site: mountwashington.com/summit/)

"Presidential Range"; web article from infoplease (web site: infoplease.com/cc6/us/A0840074.html)

Not Without Peril: 150 Years of Misadventure on the Presidential Range of New Hampshire by Nicholas Howe; published by Appalachian Mountain Club; 2001

"Mt. Washington Cog Railway" (web site: mountwashington.com/cog/)

"History of the Mount Washington Cog Railway" (web site: thecog.com/cog-history.php)

"Mount Washington Cog Railway" by The American Society of Mechanical Engineers and The American Society of Civil Engineers; June 26, 1976 (web site: asme.org/history/brochures/h018.pdf)

"Last Run of Old Peppersass, July 29, 1929"; web article by The Mount Washington Cog Railway (web site: cog-railway.com/lastrun.htm)

"Surviving Mount Washington" from Mount Washington Observatory web page (web site: mountwashington.org/visitor/surviving.html)

"Sylvester Marsh" from Stan Klos web page (web site: famousamericans.net/sylvestermarsh/)

A Tour Among the Mountains: Mount Washington and Surroundings by Frank H. Burt; published by Office of *Among the Clouds*, Mount Washington, NH and copyrighted by Henry M. Burt, 1879

"Mount Washington State Park: Tip Top House" (web site: nhparks.state.nh.us/ParksPages/MtWash/MtWashTipTop.html)

"The Story of the World Record Wind From Mt. Washington Observatory" (web site: mountwashington.org/bigwind/)

"Super Typhoon Paka; (1997): Surface Winds Over Guam" (web site: aoml.noaa.gov/hrd/project98/sh_proj1.html)

"Abstract: A New England Tropical Cyclone Climatology 1938-2000, Direct Hits and Near Misses . . . Update; web article by Marc P. Mailhot, EMA Storm Coordination Center, Westbrook, ME (web site: home.maine.rr.com/mailhot/netrop.html)

"At the Mountain of Madness", Excerpt from "Out Past The Campfire Light: Hauntings, Horrors & Unsolved Mysteries of the Great Outdoors" by Troy Taylor; copyright 2004 (from web page, "Haunted America Update") (web site: paranormalnews.com/eyefriendly.asp?articleID=959)

Chapter Thirty-one

"Seen worse"

The Appalachian Trail by Ronald M. Fisher; published by National Geographic Society; 1972

Walking the Appalachian Trail by Larry Luxenberg; Stackpole Books, Mechanicsburg, PA, 17055; 1994

The Maine Woods by Henry David Thoreau; republished by Princeton University Press; 1983

The Baxters of Maine: Downeast Visionaries by Neil Rolde; Tilbury House, Gardiner, Me. 04345; 1997

Encyclopedia of North American Indians: Abenaki; Houghton Mifflin (web site: college.hmco.com/history/readerscomp/naind/html/na_000200_abenaki.htm)

Web article: "Ktaadn (Mt. Katahdin, Maine)" from "Thoreau Country: Location Note" (web site: homepage.mac.com/sfe/henry/country_not_esta/katahdin.html)

Web article: "Katahdin, Mount" (web site: maine.com/users/publius/almanac/encycweb/htm/Katahdinmt.htm)

Web article: "Mr. Thoreau" from "Hawthorne's Journal" (web site: eldritchpress.org/nh/nhhdt1.html)

Web article: "About the Author" from Chapter.indigo (web site: chapters.indigo.ca/item.asp?Item=9780140170136&Catalog=Books&Ntt=0140170138&N=35&Lang=en&Section=books&zxac=1)

Web article: "Thoreau, the Man" (web site: walden.org/imstitute/thoreau/overview/thoreau_the_man.htm)

Web article: "Henry David Thoreau" from "American Transcendentalism Web" (web site: vcu.edu/engweb/transcendentalism/authors/thoreau/hawthorn eonhdt.html)

Web article from MaineToday.com: "Percival Baxter, despite his philanthropy, is a mystery" by Deirdre Fleming; July 20, 2003 (web site: outdoors.mainetoday.com/camping/030720baxter2.shtml)

Web article: "Percival Proctor Baxter, Cornelius Amory Pugsley Gold Medal Award, 1948" (web site: rpts.tamu.edu/pugsley/Baxter.htm)

Web article: "Baxter State Park: A Brief History" (web site: katahdinoutdoors.com/bsp/history.html)

Web article: Baxter State Park: Fatalities" (web site: katahdinoutdoors.com/bsp/fatalities.html)

"Unprepared Katahdin Hikers Burden Baxter Park Staff" by Phyllis Austin from *Maine Environmental News, 10/25/04* (found on web site: meepi.org/files04/pa102504.html)

Web article: "Katahdin, Maine" from Peakbagger.com (web site: peakbagger.com/peak.aspx?pid=6820)

Epilogue

the Appalachian Trail: calling Me Back to the Hills by Earl Victor Shaffer; photography by Bart Smith; Westcliffe Publishers, Englewood, CO; 2001

"About Earl Shaffer" from "The Earl Shaffer Web Page" (web site: earlshaffer.com/aboutearl.html)

"Peace Pilgrim's 1952 Appalachian Trail Journey", web article by Bruce Nichols (web site: peacepilgrim.org/ap_trail.htm)

"Oglethorpe Monument"; web article from Pickens County, Georgia, Chamber of Commerce web page (web site: pickenschamber.com/visitor.html)

"CNN Year in Review" (web site: cnn.com/SPECIALS/1998/year.review/)

"Lee Barry at 81 Becomes Oldest A.T. Thru-hiker; web article from Americasroof News (web site: americasroof.com/wp/?p=198)

Printed in the United States
63782LVS00003BA/12

9 781599 263779